# A SUPPLEMENT TO

# *A GUIDE TO MANUSCRIPTS RELATING TO THE AMERICAN INDIAN*

MEMOIRS OF THE

AMERICAN PHILOSOPHICAL SOCIETY

*Held at Philadelphia*

*For Promoting Useful Knowledge*

VOLUME 65 S

# A SUPPLEMENT TO *A GUIDE TO MANUSCRIPTS RELATING TO THE AMERICAN INDIAN IN THE LIBRARY OF THE AMERICAN PHILOSOPHICAL SOCIETY*

*Compiled by*

DAYTHAL KENDALL

THE AMERICAN PHILOSOPHICAL SOCIETY

INDEPENDENCE SQUARE

PHILADELPHIA

1982

Library of Congress Catalog Card Number: 65-23435
International Standard Book Number: 0-87169-650-9
International Standard Serial Numbers: 0065-9738

Publication of this volume has been subsidized in part by a grant from the Phillips Library Fund.

# FOREWORD

This volume is a supplement to *A Guide to Manuscripts Relating to the American Indian in the Library of the American Philosophical Society,* compiled by John F. Freeman with the assistance of Murphy D. Smith and published by the Society in 1966. It is the latest evidence of the Society's continuing interest in the languages and history of the North American Indians. The history of that interest from the time of Thomas Jefferson (president of the Society as well as of the United States) and Peter S. Du Ponceau is told by Dr. Freeman in the introduction to his *Guide;* and in his foreword to the book Dr. Richard Harrison Shryock, librarian of the Society, gives an account of the Library's current activity in research in American Indian linguistics and ethnohistory. The principal support the Society gives these activities nowadays is through the Henry Phillips, Jr., Library Fund. Each year the Library makes fifteen or twenty small grants to assist students and mature scholars in studying and recording the languages and history of the Indians. In return recipients of the grants are requested to deposit in the Library copies of their publications, reports, and field notes. In only a dozen years since the publication of Freeman's *Guide,* substantial additions to the collection, principally from Phillips Fund grantees, reached the point where a revision or supplement to the Freeman *Guide* was desirable and even necessary.

For this purpose the Library was fortunate to obtain the services of Dr. Daythal L. Kendall, then a graduate student in the University of Pennsylvania, whose own research on the language of the Takelma Indians eminently qualified him for the undertaking. As he states in his introduction, Dr. Kendall has not only followed the format of the predecessor volume, but has introduced into his own text cross references to Freeman's *Guide.* The Supplement therefore is closely linked with its parent volume, and for that reason copies of the Freeman *Guide* and the Kendall Supplement have been given consecutive numbers (65 and 65 S) in the Society's *Memoirs* series. From the "rich and numerous sources" assembled in the Library and for which a key has thus been provided for the scholarly researcher, we flatter ourselves— I am quoting from Du Ponceau in 1819—"that much light will be thrown on the character and affinities of the aboriginal languages of this part of the American continent."

During the period when Dr. Kendall was preparing this Supplement, the members of the Phillips Committee were C. F. Voegelin of Indiana University, Anthony F. C. Wallace of the University of Pennsylvania, William N. Fenton of the State University of New York, and Eric P. Hamp of the University of Chicago. All took a keen interest in the progress of the work; and, with the Committee on Library, all rejoice in its swift completion. I want also to record here that valuable assistance of several kinds was given to Dr. Kendall in preparing this work by Murphy D. Smith, associate librarian, Hildegard G. Stephans, assistant librarian and cataloger, J. Stephen Catlett, manuscripts librarian, and Roy E. Goodman, reference librarian.

Whitfield J. Bell, Jr.
Librarian

January 17, 1980

# CONTENTS

PAGE

Foreword v
Introduction 1

**Part V. Collections**

Manuscripts (4001-4023*a*) . . . . . 6
Microfilms (4024-4047) . . . . . . 12
Recordings (4047*a*-4098) . . . . . 16

**Part VI. Languages, Tribes, and Areas**

Abipon (4099) . . . . . . . . . . . . 26
Achumawi (4100-4102) . . . . . . 26
Ahtena (4103-4106*a*) . . . . . . . . 26
Alaska (4107-4107*a*) . . . . . . . . 27
Algonquian (4108-4109*d*) . . . . . 27
Archeology (4110) . . . . . . . . . 27
Athapascan (4111-4116) . . . . . . 27
Atsugewi (4117-4118) . . . . . . . 28
Aymara (4119-4121) . . . . . . . . 28
Bibliography (4122-4130) . . . . . 29
Blackfoot (4130*a*) . . . . . . . . . 29
California (4131-4142) . . . . . . . 29
Campa (4143) . . . . . . . . . . . . 31
Canada (4143*a*-4148) . . . . . . . . 31
Catawba (4148*a*-4149) . . . . . . . 31
Central America (4149*a*-4159*b*) . 31
Chatino (4160) . . . . . . . . . . . 33
Cherokee (4161-4171) . . . . . . . 33
Cheyenne (4171*a*-4173) . . . . . . 34
Chinook Jargon (4174) . . . . . . . 34
Chiricahua (4175-4177) . . . . . . 34
Chiwere (4177*a*-4179) . . . . . . . 34
Choctaw (4179*a*-4182) . . . . . . . 35
Cholon (4183) . . . . . . . . . . . . 35
Columbian (4184-4185*a*) . . . . . 35
Conibo (4186) . . . . . . . . . . . . 36
Cree (4187-4194) . . . . . . . . . . 36
Dakota (4194*a*-4210) . . . . . . . . 37
Delaware (4211-4231) . . . . . . . 38

PAGE

Dhegiha (4231*a*-4232) . . . . . . . 40
Diegueño (4233-4234) . . . . . . . 41
Dogrib (4234*a*-4238) . . . . . . . . 41
Eastern North America (4238*a*-4247) . . . . . . . . . . . 41
Eskimo (4248-4256) . . . . . . . . 42
Fox (4256*a*-4258) . . . . . . . . . . 43
Galice (4259) . . . . . . . . . . . . 44
General (4260-4341) . . . . . . . . 44
Haida (4341*a*-4342) . . . . . . . . 52
Hidatsa (4343-4344) . . . . . . . . 52
Hopi (4345-4364) . . . . . . . . . . 53
Houma (4364*a*-4365) . . . . . . . . 55
Huave (4366) . . . . . . . . . . . . 55
Huichol (4367-4368) . . . . . . . . 55
Hupa (4369) . . . . . . . . . . . . . 56
Indiana (4370) . . . . . . . . . . . . 56
Iroquois (4371-4425) . . . . . . . . 56
Jicarilla (4426-4433) . . . . . . . . 60
Jivaro (4434) . . . . . . . . . . . . 61
Keres (4436-4470) . . . . . . . . . 61
Kokama (4471) . . . . . . . . . . . 63
Kwakiutl (4472) . . . . . . . . . . . 64
Lipan (4473-4475) . . . . . . . . . 64
Locono (4476) . . . . . . . . . . . . 64
Loucheux (4477) . . . . . . . . . . 64
Maine (4478) . . . . . . . . . . . . 64
Malecite (4479-4480) . . . . . . . . 64
Mam (4481-4483) . . . . . . . . . . 64
Mandan (4484-4486) . . . . . . . . 65
Maratin (4487) . . . . . . . . . . . 65
Massachusett (4488-4494) . . . . . 65
Matlatzinca (4495-4496) . . . . . . 66
Maya (4497-4498) . . . . . . . . . . 66
Mayan (4498*a*-4500) . . . . . . . . 66
Mazatec (4501) . . . . . . . . . . . 67
Mescalero (4502-4504) . . . . . . . 67
Mexico (4504*a*-4526) . . . . . . . . 67
Micmac (4527-4528) . . . . . . . . 69
Mixtec (4529) . . . . . . . . . . . . 70
Mohawk (4530-4538) . . . . . . . . 70
Mohegan Tribes (4539-4541) . . . 71

| | PAGE |
|---|---|
| Mountain Tequistlateco (4542-4546) | 71 |
| Muskogee (4546*a*-4551) | 71 |
| Na-Dene (4552) | 72 |
| Nahua (4553-4557) | 72 |
| Nanticoke (4558-4559) | 73 |
| Navajo (4560-4582) | 73 |
| Nootka (4583-4586) | 75 |
| North America (4586*a*-4593) | 75 |
| Northeast (4594-4598*a*) | 77 |
| Northwest Coast (4599-4602*a*) | 78 |
| Ojibwa (4602*b*-4610) | 78 |
| Okanagan (4611-4612) | 80 |
| Oklahoma (4612*a*-4616*a*) | 80 |
| Otomi (4617-4622) | 80 |
| Papago (4622*a*-4641*a*) | 81 |
| Passamaquoddy (4642-4645) | 82 |
| Patagonian (4646) | 83 |
| Pawnee (4647-4649) | 83 |
| Pennsylvania (4650-4655) | 83 |
| Penobscot (4656-4665) | 84 |
| Penutian (4666) | 85 |
| Pima (4667) | 85 |
| Pima Bajo (4668-4682) | 85 |
| Plains (4682*a*-4683*b*) | 86 |
| Pocomam (4684-4687) | 87 |
| Powhatan Tribes (4687*a*-4688*d*) | 87 |
| Quechua (4689-4692) | 88 |
| Quiché (4693-4693*a*) | 88 |
| Quileute (4694-4698) | 88 |
| River Yuman (4698*a*-4699) | 89 |
| Sahaptin (4700-4701*a*) | 89 |
| Salinan (4702) | 90 |
| San Carlos (4703-4704) | 90 |
| Sarsi (4705-4708*a*) | 90 |
| Seneca (4709-4732) | 90 |
| Shawnee (4732*a*-4734*b*) | 92 |
| Shuswap (4735) | 93 |
| Siouan (4736-4737) | 93 |
| South America (4738-4762) | 93 |

| | PAGE |
|---|---|
| Southeast (4763-4763*a*) | 95 |
| Southern Paiute (4764-4766*a*) | 95 |
| Southwest (4767-4800) | 96 |
| Spokane (4801) | 98 |
| Takelma (4802-4803) | 98 |
| Talamanca (4804) | 99 |
| Tennessee (4805) | 99 |
| Tepecano (4806-4812) | 99 |
| Tepehuan (4813-4833) | 99 |
| Tewa (4834-4839) | 101 |
| Tillamook (4841) | 102 |
| Tiwa (4842-4848) | 102 |
| Tlingit (4849-4851) | 103 |
| Totonac (4852) | 103 |
| Tsimshian (4853-4855) | 103 |
| Tualatin (4856-4858) | 103 |
| Tupi (4859) | 104 |
| Tuscarora (4860-4864*a*) | 104 |
| United States (4865-4865*b*) | 104 |
| Upland Yuman (4866-4868) | 105 |
| Uru (4869) | 105 |
| Uto-Aztecan (4869*a*-4889) | 105 |
| Virginia (4890) | 107 |
| Wasco (4891-4894) | 107 |
| West Indies (4896) | 107 |
| Wichita (4897-4900*a*) | 107 |
| Winnebago (4901-4904*a*) | 108 |
| Wintun (4905) | 108 |
| Wishram (4906-4909) | 108 |
| Wyandot (4910-4911) | 109 |
| Xinca (4912-4915) | 109 |
| Yana (4916-4917) | 109 |
| Yaqui (4918-4920) | 109 |
| Yuchi (4922-4925) | 110 |
| Yuki (4926) | 110 |
| Yuman (4927) | 110 |
| Yurok (4928) | 110 |
| Zapotec (4929-4931) | 110 |
| Zuni (4931*a*-4935) | 111 |
| **Part VII. Bibliography** | 112 |
| **Part VIII. Index** | 113 |

# INTRODUCTION

## PREPARATION OF THE SUPPLEMENT

Continued acquisitions of materials relating to Native American languages and cultures have made an update of the Freeman and Smith *Guide*[1] desirable. The Library Committee proposed that this update be in the form of a supplement, and funding was made available through the American Philosophical Society Library programs, which are generously supported by the Andrew W. Mellon Foundation.

The bulk of the work on the *Supplement*, including much of the indexing, was done from 1976 through early 1978. During late 1978 and into 1979, the most recent acquisitions were added to the material already compiled. This volume is therefore current through mid-1979.

In addition, during the 1978-1979 period, the compiler was able to sort and identify photographs in the Frank G. Speck collection. Although these photographs are included in the *Guide*, they have been given more detailed coverage in the *Supplement*.

The recording collection has grown considerably and now numbers several hundred reels. For many recordings it was, unfortunately, not practical to describe the contents in detail; many reels given to the Library by scholars carry no information other than the language, and their number is far too great even to sample each reel. Therefore the researcher interested in the language, culture, history, and other topics regarding any group should check the appropriate recordings himself, since information on a variety of topics is often included among the materials obtained in the field.

Since the materials under consideration pertain mainly to Native American languages, the basis of classification in this volume is linguistic. Most dialects, tribes, and various other divisions are classified and entered under the primary language name as given in Voegelin and Voegelin,[2] but there are some exceptions.

[1] John F. Freeman, comp., Murphy D. Smith, ed., *A Guide to Manuscripts Relating to the American Indian in the Library of the American Philosophical Society*, Mem. Amer. Philos. Soc. **65** (Philadelphia, 1966).

[2] C. F. Voegelin and F. M. Voegelin, *Classification and Index of the World's Languages* (New York, Oxford, and Amsterdam, 1977).

Items included in the *Supplement* have been identified and labeled as specifically as was practical from information readily available. Time limitations and the bulk of the materials did not permit extensive research with regard to individual items. In addition, the *Supplement,* like the Freeman and Smith *Guide,* is intended as a research tool; it does not attempt to do the researcher's work for him.

Additions, corrections, and comments regarding entries both in the *Guide* and in this *Supplement* will be welcomed from both the user and the donor of any item. These contributions toward a better *Guide* should include the entry number and page reference and should be sent to:

Manuscripts Librarian
American Philosophical Society Library
105 South 5th St.
Philadelphia, Pa. 19106

Such notes will be kept on file for incorporation into the next edition.

The compiler gratefully acknowledges the financial support of the Andrew W. Mellon Foundation, which made the preparation of this volume possible.

Also, I would like to express my appreciation to members of the Library staff and the Publications staff who have assisted in various ways and to my wife, Carolyn O. Kendall, who assisted in the preparation of the index and who functioned as consultant and critic.

## FORMAT OF THE SUPPLEMENT

The *Supplement* is in the same basic format as the Freeman and Smith *Guide.* There are four major divisions (numbered V through VIII in the *Supplement* corresponding to sections I through IV, respectively, in the *Guide*):

V. Collections (including manuscripts, microfilms, and recordings)
VI. Languages, Tribes, and Areas
VII. Bibliography
VIII. Index

To facilitate retrieval, entries under *Collections* include the information necessary to locate items: call numbers for manuscripts, film numbers for microfilms, and recording numbers for recordings.

Since the *Guide* includes almost 4000 entries, numbering of entries in the *Supplement* begins with 4001. Thus, any cross-reference to a number less than 4000 indicates an entry in the *Guide,* while 4000-numbers are found in the *Supplement.*

More than two hundred entries were added after the compiling and indexing were nearly complete; these entry numbers include a lower case letter at the end, for example, 4020*a.* Such entries are not subsections of others, but are entirely separate entities which follow in the alphabetical sequence.

Within the entries of the *Supplement, includes* and *re* are used extensively. In general, these may be interpreted as follows:

*Includes* indicates divisions by topic (e.g., food, dance, body parts, phonology), by type of materials (e.g., typed manuscript, photographs, maps), etc.

*Re* indicates topics addressed, usually without clear divisions devoted to each.

## HOW TO USE THE SUPPLEMENT

The key to the successful use of this volume is the index. The indexing is thorough, and there are numerous cross-references within the index.

The index is arranged alphabetically letter by letter, ignoring spaces, with comma preceding *a.* The location of each item is given by entry number.

An entry in Part VI, *Languages . . . ,* usually includes a reference to an item in Part V, *Collections,* of which the entry is a part. For example, the researcher may find, at the lower right of an entry:

[4020*b*(9)]

where 4020*b* is an entry in the *Manuscripts* section of *Collections.* The entry 4020*b* is the *Frank G. Speck Collection of Photographs,* and (9) indicates the box number within that collection.

One may also find:

[30(Pn1.1)]

indicating that the item is part of a collection noted in the *Guide* (numbers less than 4000). Entry number 30 is the *Franz Boas Collection of American Indian Linguistics,* and (Pn1.1) is a specific item within that collection.

The researcher who is interested in a specific tribe, group, or language should look in the index under the language name, not just in the *Languages. . .* section. References to a particular tribe or language frequently occur as secondary items in entries devoted to other tribes or languages and in general entries which cover a number of tribes or languages on some particular topic. The index notes such occurrences.

If the researcher is concerned with a particular geographic area, he should check the index not only for that area, but also for languages presently or formerly spoken in the area.

In the index under specific languages, the researcher may find subheadings such as *cognates, comparative vocabulary,* and *historical linguistics,* which, strictly speaking, are not applicable to a single language, but which imply two or more languages. However, these terms were deemed the appropriate ones to alert the researcher to the existence of such materials.

With the personal names of Native Americans, a tribe or language identification is usually given. When linguistic data are involved, the identification indicates the language in which that person functioned as an informant, not necessarily his native language.

In addition to very specific index entries for names of individuals, tribes, languages, language families, and such subjects, considerable effort was devoted to including general topics of frequent interest to researchers in linguistics, anthropology, history, and various other fields, for example:

archaeology
artifacts
baskets
bibliography
body parts
ceremonies
chiefs
dwellings
ethnography
fauna
flora
history
Indian-White relations
informants
kinship
morphology
music
people
phonology
pictures
recordings
religion
songs
syntax
texts
vocabulary

Other general topics include geographical areas, such as continents and countries. Since *Native American* applies to all the material, very little is indexed under this topic.

Throughout the index, entry numbers marked with an asterisk (*) indicate that the entry includes pictures. In the index, *Pictures* has been divided into several separate entries for ease of reading.

In using the index, the researcher will encounter entries such as the following:

Mason, John Alden, . . . ; **author** . . . ; **collector** . . . ; **compiler** . . . ; **corres. with**: Bernard W. Aginsky, 4295*a;* Ethel G. Aginsky, 4295*a;*. . . ; John Witthoft, 4171; **donor** . . .

where the boldface **author, collector, compiler, corres. with,** and **donor** are subheadings and the individuals named in roman type are further divisions within a subheading. This format should increase the readability of the index.

## ABBREVIATIONS USED

| | |
|---|---|
| A. | — Autograph |
| c.c. | — carbon copy |
| coll. | — collector |
| comp. | — compiler |
| D. (with language) | — Dialect |
| D. | — Document |
| ditto | — spirit master reproduction |
| L. | — Letter |
| L. (after a number) | — Leaves |
| N.W.T. | — North West Territories |
| p. or pp. (after a number) | — page or pages |
| pc. or pcs. | — piece or pieces |
| S. | — Signed |
| T. | — Typed |

# PART V

# COLLECTIONS

## MANUSCRIPTS

4001. BARBEAU, CHARLES MARIUS. Cayuga: an Iroquoian dialect; 1964. A.D.S. 82 pp.

Vocabulary includes: body parts; terms for people by age, function, etc.; foods; flora; fauna; kinship terms; other nouns; verbs; adjectives; pronouns; numerals; other expressions. Also includes some verb paradigms and noun paradigms with possessive person markers. Informants: Mr. and Mrs. Cuthbert Davey.

Donor, author, Oct. 1964.

[Call No. 497.2:B235c]

4002. BARBEAU, CHARLES MARIUS, comp. Raven-Clan outlaws on the North Pacific coast; n.d. T.D. 447 pp. c.c.

Includes: Tsimshian myths in translation; a few Haida myths in translation.

Donor, compiler, Apr. 1963.

[Call No. 970.6:B23r]

4003. BARTON, BENJAMIN SMITH. Papers; 1788-1815. D. *ca.* 5000L.

Includes: correspondence regarding American Indians, medicine, botany, and other topics; sketches. Table of contents available.

[Call No. B:B284.d]

4003*a*. BELL, ROBERT. Papers; 1880-1908. A.L.S. 77 items.

Correspondence from Franz Boas, Elliot Coues, William Isbister, J. M. LeMoine, James C. Pilling, and E.F.S.J. Petitot regarding Canada, geography, geology, geological survey of Canada, Indians of North America, and paleontology.

[Call No. B:B421]

4003*b*. BOAS, FRANZ, coll. Field notebooks and physical anthropological data; 1889-1897, n.d. T. and A.D. *ca.* 3000 pp., 10 notebooks.

Includes: anthropometric measurements from various Native American groups; language materials from the Northwest Coast and Mexico; typescripts of papers; diary of a field trip to Baffin Island, N.W.T., Canada; Boas's genealogical data.

Donor, Northwestern University Library.

[Call No. B:B61.5]

4004. BOWERS, STEPHEN. Papers; 1862-1916. D. *ca.* 150 items.

Correspondence pertaining to geology, religion, archeology, ethnography, paleontology, California languages, etc.

[Call No. B:B672]

4005. CARRINGTON, HENRY BEEBEE. Notes on the Six Nations of New York, successors of the Five Nations of the Iroquois Confederacy, as of Jan. 1, 1890. D. 1 v. of 251 pp.

Taken for the eleventh Census of the U.S., 22nd Division. Lists chiefs, crops, population, diseases, houses, other property, and values.

Donor, William N. Fenton, Sept. 15, 1971.

[Call No. 970.4:C23]

4006. CORNPLANTER, EDWARD. The code of Handsome Lake; Nov. 10, 1933. Photocopy of A.D. 102 pp.

From a manuscript by Edward Cornplanter. Copy is from a document in possession of Edna (Mrs. Nick) Bailey, Tonawanda Reservation. In the hand of and signed by Jesse J. Cornplanter. In Seneca.

Donor, Elizabeth Tooker, Sept. 1968.

[Call No. 970.6:H19.c]

4006*a*. DIEHL, H. C., comp. Hopi language materials; 1955-1959. Photocopy of D. 600 pp.

Contents and transcripts of Hopi recordings in No. 4349*a*. **Restricted research use only**: may not be reproduced until 1986.

Donor, Department of Anthropology, Northern Arizona University, through P. David Seaman, May 1976.

[Call No. 497.3:D57]

4007. ENOS, SUZIE, comp. Papago stories narrated by Jose Ventura; n.d. Photocopy of T.D. 31 pp.

Papago texts with indication of syntactic function of elements in sentences, other grammatical notes, and English translations.

Donor, Dean Saxton, 1968.

[Call No. 497:P21]

4008. Fort William Henry, copy of a journal kept during the siege of; Aug. 2-10, 1757. A.D. 1 bound v. of 8L. of which 6L. are used.

Re: the participation of Indians in the siege; atrocities committed by the Indians; failure of the French to attempt any control; receipt of plunder by the French from the Indians.

[Call No. 973.2:F77]

4009. GARVIN, PAUL L., comp. Wichita paradigms; 1962. Ditto of T.D. 544 pp.

Includes: verb paradigms; a few noun paradigms with possessive person markers.

Donor, compiler, 1962.

[Call No. 497.3:G19]

4010. GILLESPIE, JOHN DOUGLAS. Miscellaneous items pertaining to the American Indian; 1947–*ca.* 1961. D. and printed items. *ca.* 350 manuscripts, *ca.* 75 photographs, *ca.* 75 newspaper clippings, and *ca.* 70 printed items.

Primarily regarding Cherokee (North Carolina and Oklahoma) ethnography, folklore, linguistics, archeology, history, music, etc. Also contains material on: Apache, Calusa, Chippewa, Choctaw, Delaware, Eskimo, Fox, Iroquois, Karankawa, Kuchin, Louchens, Mattaponi, Muskogee, Navajo, Onondaga, Pueblo, Sauk, Seminole, Seneca, Shawnee, Sioux, Slave, Timucua, Tuscarora, Tutelo, and Wyandot.

[Call No. 497.3:G41]

4011. GROSSMAN, JULIAN A. One lying across: Lewis Henry Morgan. The birth of American ethnology; 1965. T.D. 29 pp., ill.

Re: Morgan's interest in and study of the Iroquois. Some details of development of Morgan's interest.

Donor, author, 1966.

[Call No. B:M823g]

4012. HOIJER, HARRY. Collection of American Indian linguistic materials; 1930-1934, 1956, n.d. 40 notebooks, *ca.* 2500L., *ca.* 1400 slips, 4 reels of tape.

Includes: Carrier, comparative Athapascan, Chiricahua, Galice, Jicarilla, Lipan, Loucheux (Kuchin), Mescalero, Navajo, Sarsi, and San Carlos. In addition to Hoijer's own materials, includes materials from Berard Haile, Diamond Jenness, and Edward Sapir.

Donor, Mrs. H. Hoijer, Sept. 1976.

[Call No. 497.3:H68]

4012*a*. JONES, WILLIAM. Ethnographic and linguistic field notes on the Ojibwa Indians; n.d. *ca.* 250 pp., 42 photographs.

Re: government, mythology, festivals, customs, games, etc. Also includes: comments on the language; vocabulary, some items with English glosses; lists of bands and locations; photographs of people, activities, dwellings, canoes, etc.

Donor, Ruth Landes, Dec. 1977.

[Call No. 497.3:J71]

4013. KENDALL, DAYTHAL L. A syntactic analysis of Takelma texts; 1977. Photocopy of T.D. 147 pp.

Re: decoding and generation of sentences (both simple and complex) and of texts; morphology. Doctoral dissertation in linguistics, University of Pennsylvania.

Donor, author, May 1977.

[Call No. 497.3:K34]

4014. KIDDER, ALFRED V. Correspondence with Neil Judd; 1920-1962. A.L.S., T.L. and L.S., printed D. 88 pp.

Re: archeological work in the Southwest at Pueblo Bonito, Chaco Canyon, etc.; *kivas;* the Alfred Vincent Kidder Award.

Donor, Neil M. Judd, Jan. 1965.

[Call No. B:K53]

4015. KURATH, GERTRUDE. Senshare Ceremony; 1964. D. 9 pp. analysis and 13 pp. sheet music.

From tapes made by Antonio Garcia, Juanito Trujillo, and Peter Garcia at San Juan Pueblo, New Mexico. **Restricted.**

*Cf.* Nos. 4059, 4834-4835, 4839.
Donor, author.

[Call No. 970.6:K96s]

4016. Letters of Onondaga Indians; 1850-1855. L. 32 pcs.

Re: travel by Indians; land; education; difficulties on the reservation. Includes letters to Ebenezer Meriam from Thomas La Fort, David Hill, L. A. Hill, and Jameson L. Thomas.

[Call No. 970.3:On1]

4016*a*. LIBRARY OF THE AMERICAN PHILOSOPHICAL SOCIETY: Print Collection; eighteenth-twentieth centuries. *ca.* 9000 pcs.

A large and growing collection containing photographs, engravings, lithographs, paintings, etc., on a number of topics including Native Americans. In this supplement, references to the print collection employ the following code:

A—Regular File, Persons
B—Regular File, Places and Things
C—Oversize File, Persons

D—Oversize File, Places and Things
E—Regular File, Group Pictures
F—Regular File, Collections
G—Oversize File, Collections

The above letters indicate major divisions within the collection. A letter may be amplified with a number or a letter-number combination to specify the location of items within a division.

4017. MASON, JOHN ALDEN. Papers; 1926-1967. D., photographs. *ca.* 5000 items.

Includes: correspondence; notes; drafts of papers; photographs; etc. Correspondence concerns: *American Anthropologist;* various professional organizations; Native American languages; archeology; ethnography; etc. Correspondents include: C. M. Barbeau, Ruth Benedict, Franz Boas, Frederica de Laguna, John P. Harrington, George G. Heye, Diamond Jenness, Alfred V. Kidder, Alfred L. Kroeber, Gertrude Kurath, Robert H. Lowie, Gladys A. Reichard, William A. Ritchie, Edward Sapir, Morris Swadesh, Ruth M. Underhill, Benjamin L. Whorf, and many others. Languages include: Pima Bajo, Papago, Northern Tepehuan, Southern Tepehuan, Tepecano, and others. Areas include: southwestern United States, Mexico, South America.

Donors, John Alden Mason, 1967; Mason Estate, Apr. 1968; Department of Anthroplogy, University of Pennsylvania through Anthony F. C. Wallace, July 1972.

[Call No. B:M384]

4018. MCQUOWN, NORMAN A. Totonac texts; n.d. T.D. *ca.* 400 pp.

Includes: Totonac texts; Spanish translations; some English translation.

Donor, grantee, Apr. 1956.

[Call No. 497.3:M24]

4019. MURPHY, ROBERT CUSHMAN. Choco expedition; 1937. D. 1 v.

Primarily concerned with collection of water samples from the Pacific, meteorological data, etc. Some notes and discussion of Indians of Colombia and Ecuador. Groups mentioned: Choco, Citara, Noanama, Cholo, Paparo, Tucura, and Cuna.

Donor, Grace E. B. Murphy, May 1973.

[Call No. B:M957, v. 38]

4020. RHOADS, CHARLES JAMES. Papers; 1929. D. *ca.* 300 pp., newspaper clippings.

Re: Rhoads's appointment as Commissioner of Indian Affairs by President Hoover.

Donor, Brown Brothers, Harrimann and Co. through Mrs. Thatcher M. Brown III, Mar. 1965.

[Call No. B:R34]

4020*a*. SINGER, ERNESTINE H. WIEDER, comp. Anthropological reading notes; 1935. D.S. *ca.* 150 pp.

Includes: course notes on primitive economics (Incan) with A. Irving Hallowell; notes from seminars with Linton Satterthwaite (Mayan architecture), E. B. Howard (Problems of the Clovis, New Mexico, Site), and others; notes taken at the 1936 meeting of the American Anthropological Association of papers by Ruth Benedict, Frederica de Laguna, Walter Dyk, William N. Fenton, Alfred V. Kidder, David G. Mandelbaum, George P. Murdock, Arthur C. Parker, Elsie Clews Parsons, Gladys A. Reichard, William A. Ritchie, Linton Satterthwaite, Gene Weltfish, and others regarding Cree, Flatheads, Iroquois, Kaingang (S. Brazil), Kiowa, Mayan, Natchez, Navajo, Ojibwa, Pawnee, Pueblos, Sahaptin, Saulteaux, Siouan, Tarascan, Tonowanda (Seneca), Zuni, etc.

[Call No. 970.1:S16]

4020*b*. SPECK, FRANK G. Collection of photographs, drawings, etc.; mid-1800s through mid-1900s. Photographs, D. *ca.* 5000 pcs.

A collection of photographs, sketches, drawings, engravings, postal cards, proof sheets, lantern slides, etc., primarily from Speck's personal collection; some items from other sources. Photographs, drawings, etc., were produced by Speck and numerous others. Engravings are based on works by Karl Bodmer, George Catlin, Seth Eastman, and others. Geographically, the greater part of the material concerns the United States and Canada, but there are items relating to Mexico and South America. Table of contents available.

[170]

4020*c*. SPECK, FRANK G., comp. Catawba texts; n.d. *ca.* 500 pp.

Includes: myths; texts regarding history, birds, reptiles, signs and omens, remedies, marriage, poverty, industry, food, charms, taboos, etc.; English-free and interlinear literal translations.

[Call No. 497.3:Sp3]

4020*d*. Spokane primer; 1976, n.d. T.L.S. and photocopy of D. 58 pp.

Words, phrases, and sentences in Spokane and English. Includes letter to Carl F. Miller from Elénor C. Kelly (Mrs. William M.)

[Call No. 497.3:Sp5]

4020*e*. VOEGELIN, CARL F. Papers; 1934-1952, n.d. T. and A.D., T. and A.L.S. *ca.* 3200 pp., *ca.* 1600L.

Re: Algonquian languages and linguistics; Delaware; Potawatomi; Seneca; Shawnee. Includes: correspondence; Walam Olum; Shawnee law.

Donor, Carl F. Voegelin, Feb. 1979.

[Call No. B:V86p]

4021. WALLACE, PAUL A. W. Papers; 1920-1967. D. *ca.* 12,000 pcs.

Includes: correspondence; notes; clippings; photographs; etc. Primary topics are: Six Nations; John Heckewelder; Conrad Weiser; and the Muhlenbergs. Correspondents include: Edward Ahenakew, C. M. Barbeau, Jesse J. Cornplanter, Ray Fadden, William N. Fenton, S. H. Gapp, Diamond Jenness, Charles B. Montgomery, Arthur C. Parker, William A. Ritchie, Frank G. Speck, Matthew W. Stirling, Carl F. Voegelin, and others.

Donor, Wallace family, June 1967.

[Call No. B:W15p]

4022. WERNER, OSWALD. The Navaho ethnomedical domain: prolegomena to a componential semantic analysis; n.d. Ditto of T.D. 34 pp.

Re: terms for diseases; the dimensions of intensity, temporal duration, and spatial extension.

Donor, author, Mar. 1964.

[Call No. 497.3:W50]

4023. WERNER, OSWALD. A typological comparison of four trader Navaho speakers; 1963. T.D. 167 pp.

Doctoral dissertation in anthropology, Indiana University.

[Call No. 497.3:W50.1]

4023*a*. WHITING, ALFRED F., comp. Hopi tape-recording transcripts; 1964-1969, 1976. 257 pp.

Contents and transcriptions of recordings in No. 4363*a*. **Restricted research use only**: may not be reproduced until June 1986.

*Cf.* No. 4363*a*.
Donor, Department of Anthropology, Northern Arizona University through P. David Seaman, 1976.

[Call No. 497.3:W58]

## MICROFILMS

4024. ARCHIVO GENERAL DE INDIAS, SEVILLE: Reina-Jimenez Collection; n.d. 129 reels of film. Film No. 1337.

Re: post-conquest social and cultural processes in Guatemala. From originals in the AGI, Seville.

Donor, Ruben E. Reina, Dec. 1974.

4025. BERKHOFER, ROBERT F. Protestant missionaries to the American Indians, 1787-1862; 1960. 1 reel of film. Film No. 1157.

Doctoral dissertation, Cornell University.

4026. BOAS, FRANZ. Correspondence; 1885-1909. 1 reel of film. Film No. 372.3.

Re: work among the Eskimos and on Northwest Coast languages. From originals in possession of the Office of Anthropology, Smithsonian Institution.

Donor, Smithsonian Institution, Apr. 1967.

4027. CANADA, PUBLIC ARCHIVES; n.d. 2 reels of film. Film No. 426.

Includes materials from the Public Record Office, London, and Bibliothèque nationale, Paris. Some of the materials pertain to the Six Nations during the Revolutionary War era.

Donor, Barbara Graymont, 1965.

4028. Cherokee medicine book; n.d. 22 frames of microfilm. Film No. 1125.

Material to be edited and published by J. F. Kilpatrick. Written in the Cherokee syllabary.

4029. Collection of materials on American Indian sign language; 1966. 1 reel of film. Film No. 1226.

Includes: a Nez Perce hymnal; discussion and illustrations on the meaning of symbols and on the use of sign language; etc. From materials in possession of Miss Jean Rumsey.

4030. DALHOUSIE MUNIMENTS: papers relating to America, 1748-59: James Glen (governor of South Carolina), and John Forbes and his expedition in the French and Indian War. 2 reels of film. Film No. 1231.

Re: South Carolina politics and government; Indian policy; French and Indian War; etc. From originals in Scottish Record Office, Edinburgh.

4031. DE LAGUNA, FREDERICA, and MARIE FRANÇOISE GUÉDON. Atna of the Copper River Valley; 1960, 1968. 2 reels of film. Film No. 1278.

Re: Atna, Copper River, Totlin, Upper Tanana, Southern Tuchone, Burwash Landing, and Yukon.

4032. DE LAGUNA, FREDERICA, and CATHERINE MCCLELLAN, comps. Field notes on the ethnology of the Tlingit and Copper River Atna; 1949-1960. 6 reels of film. Film No. 1127.

Includes notes on archaeological investigations; transcripts of interviews with informants. Tlingit material taken primarily from Yakutat and Angoon; Copper River Atna (Ahtena) from Chitina, Copper Center, and Chistochina, Alaska. From originals in possession of the compilers.

*Cf.* Nos. 263-267.

4033. DU PONCEAU, PETER S. Correspondence with John G. E. Heckewelder; 1816-1822. 18 items on film. Film No. 1162.

Re: Zeisberger's Onondaga grammar and dictionary; Heckewelder's writings on the Indians; publications; question of whether or not any of the Lenape can pronounce the letter *r*. From originals in possession of the State Historical Society of Wisconsin.

4034. EDEL, MAY MANDELBAUM. American Indian linguistic materials; n.d. 4 reels of film. Film No. 1275.

Re: Salishan languages and dialects with emphasis on Tillamook. From originals in the University of Washington libraries.

4035. FLOYD, TROY S., coll. Archivo nacional, Guatemala City, Guatemala; 1961. 2 reels of film. Film No. 1155.

Selections from collections pertaining to the history of Guatemala, 1568-1806.

Donor, grantee, 1963.

4036. FREEMAN, JOHN F., comp. Guide to American Indian manuscripts in the Library of the American Philosophical Society; 1962. 2 reels of film. Film No. 1126.

From typed manuscripts produced in preparation of a guide for publication.

4037. History of Science Film No. 8; n.d. 1 reel of film.

Re: Algonquian, Choctaw, Illinois, and Narraganset. Includes letters of: B. A. Gould, F. R. Hassler, Gauss, Sir Joseph Banks, J. F. Blumenbach. From originals in the possession of the Niedersächische Staats und Universitätsbibliothek, Göttingen.

4037*a*. MCQUOWN, NORMAN A., comp. Quiché Maya texts; n.d. 1 reel of film. Film No. 1295.

Includes: vocabulary with Spanish glosses; texts recorded by Manuel J. Andrade (1935), transcribed and translated by Remigio Cochojil-González (1964-1971); orthography developed by Norman A. McQuown.

4038. Michigan Indians: celebration; 1967. 1 reel of movie film, 24 color slides. Film No. 1257.

Includes: stomp dance; war dance; partridge dance; dance to the four winds; round dance; snake dance; corn dance; audience and parade; crafts.

*Cf.* Nos. 4071, 4605, and Negative No. 475.
Donor, Gertrude P. Kurath, July 1968.

4039. MORAVIAN CHURCH ARCHIVES: records of the Moravian mission among the Indians of North America; n.d. 40 reels of film. Film No. 1279.

Includes: language materials in Delaware, Creek, Mohawk, and Onondaga; materials pertaining to the Chippewa, Cherokee, Nanticoke, and Shawnee; diaries (travel and other); reports; letters; conference minutes; various other materials relating to missionary activities and relations with the Indians. Materials from: New York, Connecticut,

Pennsylvania, Ohio, Michigan, Indiana, Kansas, Georgia, Oklahoma, and Ontario. Table of contents available. From originals in Bethlehem, Pa.

4039*a*. OLSON, RONALD L. American Indian linguistic materials; n.d. 1 reel of film. Film No. 1276.

Includes: vocabularies in several Native languages; material in the Quinault dialect of Lower Chelhalis; material in Quileute. From originals in the University of Washington libraries.

4040. RIGSBY, BRUCE, comp. Sahaptin field notes; 1963-1969. 2 reels of film. Film No. 1261.

Includes: vocabulary, paradigms, sentences, texts, and English translations collected at the Umatilla Indian Reservation; list of Umatilla speakers; vocabulary, sentences, etc., from dialects other than Umatilla; some material on Molale. Permission necessary for publication. From originals in possession of the compiler.

4041. SHEEHAN, BERNARD W. Civilization and the American Indian in the thought of the Jeffersonian era; 1965. 1 reel of film. Film No. 1241.4.

Doctoral dissertation in history, University of Virginia.

4042. SMILEY FAMILY: papers of the conferences at Lake Mohonk; 1885-1930. 1 reel of film. Film No. 1246.

Table of contents for the collection which is primarily concerned with the Indian conferences. From originals in possession of Haverford College.

4043. SOCIETY OF JESUS: the Oregon Province Archives, Indian Language Collection: the Alaska Native languages; 1976. 28 reels of film. Film No. 1364.

Includes: dictionaries; vocabularies; texts (primarily Christian religious materials); grammatical notes; sermons; hymns; etc. Languages include: Central Alaskan Yupik, Iñupiaq (Inuit), Koyukon, and Ingalik (Ingalit). From originals produced in the late nineteenth and twentieth centuries, on deposit at the Pacific Northwest Indian Center, Spokane, Washington.

4044. SOCIETY OF JESUS: the Oregon Province Archives, Indian Language Collection: the Pacific Northwest tribal languages; 1976. 21 reels of film. Film No. 1365.

Includes: dictionaries; vocabularies; texts (primarily Christian religious materials); grammars; etc. Languages include: Assiniboin (Dakota); Blackfoot; Chelan (Columbian); Coeur d'Alene; Colville (Okanagan); Columbian; Crow; Gros Ventre (Arapaho); Kalispel; Kutenai; Nez Perce; Yakima (Sahaptin). From originals produced in the late nineteenth and twentieth centuries, on deposit at the Pacific Northwest Indian Center, Spokane, Washington.

4046. SUE, HIROKO, comp. Materials collected among the Hare Indians, Fort Good Hope, N.W.T., Canada; 1962-1963. 1 reel of film. Film No. 1175.

Material to accompany No. 4236, reels 7-19.

*Cf.* No. 4238 for table of contents.
Donor, grantee.

4047. UNITED CHURCH BOARD FOR WORLD MINISTRIES: North American Indian papers; 1817-1883. 64 reels of film. Film No. 1223.

Re: missions among the Cherokee, Choctaw, Dakota, Osage, Chickasaw, Mackinaw, Creek, Ojibwa, Pawnee, Stockbridge, Maumee, Abenaki, and Penobscot. From originals in Houghton Library, Harvard University.

## RECORDINGS

4047*a*. ADAMS, WALTER R., coll. Recordings concerning religious practices of southeastern Chiapas, Mexico; 1977. 7 cassette tapes. Recording No. 108.

Informants include: Tzeltal: Francisco Calvo Perez-Romerias; Tojolabal: Hermalindo Jimenez; probable Tzeltal: Jose Hernandez, Ramiro Garcia, and Francisco Aguilar.

*Cf.* No. 4498*a*.
Donor, grantee, Nov. 1977.

4047*b*. BAHR, DONALD M., coll. Papago and Pima oral literature; 1977-1978. 132 reels of tape. Recording No. 111.

Includes: a variety of songs; discussions of curing practices and sand paintings; war orations and other speeches; myths; etc. Papago informants: Jose Manol, Juan Gregorio, Lupe Antone, Rosana Ventura, Ligali (Mrs. Masi Loin), B. Lopez family, Maila Kelaila, Frances Ventura, Mendes Lopez, Arturo Mendez, Listo Antone, Chico Moreno, Jose Hillman Ventura, Jose Pancho, Baptisto Lopez. Pima informant: Paul Manuel. Recorded at: Ak Cin and Sikol Himadk, Papago Reservation, Arizona; Santa Rosa, Arizona; Phoenix, Arizona. **Restricted access and duplication.**

*Cf.* No. 4622*a* for partial abstract.
Donor, grantee, 1978.

4048. BARTHOLOMEW, DORIS, coll. Matlatzinca verbs; 1966. 2 reels of tape. Recording No. 60.

Includes: verb paradigms; texts; translation of an Otomi primer. Informant: Ezequiel Hernández.

*Cf.* No. 4495.
Donor, grantee.

4049. BERNARD, H. RUSSELL, coll. Otomi stories; 1972. 3 reels of tape. Recording No. 90.

Includes: texts in Otomi with Spanish translations; discussion, in Spanish, of the meaning of each text. Informant: Jesús Salinas Pedraza.

*Cf.* Nos. 4050, 4617-4619, 4621-4622
Donor, grantee, Sept. 1972.

4050. BERNARD, H. RUSSELL, coll. Otomi stories and songs; 1971. 2 reels of tape. Recording No. 86.

Includes: folk tales; anecdotes; local history of the area around Ixmiquilpan, Hidalgo, Mexico; songs, etc.

*Cf.* Nos. 4049, 4617-4620, 4622.
Donor, grantee, 1972.

4051. BLACK, ROBERT A., coll. Hopi Indian songs; 1965. 4 reels of tape. Recording No. 56.

For table of contents, *cf.* No. 4346.

*Cf.* Nos. 4052, 4347-4349.
Donor, grantee.

4052. BLACK, ROBERT A., coll. Hopi songs; 1960. 10 reels of tape. Recording No. 47.

Includes: Kachina, clown, hunting, Hopi-Apache masked dance, Paiute, Walapai, and other songs. Informants include: Walter Albert, Irving Charley, Lester Charley, Alfred Joshongiva, Glenn Joswaytewa, Jimmy Kay, Kelnimtewa, Elridge Masa, Mary Maypi, Sylvin Nash, Poli Payestewa, Mrs. Sekwakwaptiwa, Charlie Talawepi, Paul Talawepi, and Mr. and Mrs. David Talawietema. Villages include: Bacavi, Moenkopi, New Oraibi, Old Oraibi, Shongopovi, Shupawlavi, and Sichomovi.

*Cf.* Nos. 4051, 4347-4349.
Donor, grantee.

4053. BOWERS, ALFRED W., coll. Mandan-Hidatsa cultural change and language studies; 1967-1972. 11 reels of tape. Recording No. 84.

Includes: texts, vocabulary, etc.; letter to Whitfield J. Bell, Jr.; table of contents.

*Cf.* No. 4054.
Donor, grantee, 1972.

4054. BOWERS, ALFRED W., coll. Mandan-Hidatsa ethnohistory and linguistics, Fort Berthold Reservation; 1967-1969. 19 reels of tape. Recording No. 81.

Includes: texts; vocabulary; some translations; table of contents.

*Cf.* No. 4053.
Donor, grantee.

4055. BRANDT, ELIZABETH A., coll. Linguistic data in the Sandia dialect of Tiwa; n.d. 29 reels of tape. Recording No. 72.

Includes: vocabulary; texts; analysis of the Sandia material by an Isleta informant; household items; foods; directions; natural phenomena; buildings; fruits; time expressions; verbs; adverbs; checking George L. Trager's material; pronominal reference; greetings; animal names (including domesticated); festivals; other ethnographic information.

Donor, grantee, Nov. 1969, June 1970.

4056. CORNELL, JOHN R., coll. Pima Bajo materials; 1970. 17 reels of tape. Recording No. 83.

Includes: word lists; history; texts, some with translation. Informants: Pedro Estrella Tánori and María Córdova, both of Ónabas, Sonora, Mexico.

Donor, grantee.

4057. DE LAGUNA, FREDERICA, coll. Materials recorded at Copper Center, Alaska; 1968. 17 reels of tape. Recording No. 68.

Includes: interviews; wide variety of songs and texts. Informants include: Andy Brown, Annie Ewan, Pete Ewan, Bacile George, Nancy George, Arthur Jackson, Martha Jackson, Billy Joe, Elizabeth Pete, Mentasta Pete, Jenny Peters, Kate Sanford, Fanny Stanfield, and others. Also includes some Upper Tanana.

4057*a*. DEMERS, RICHARD, coll. Lummi recordings; 1974. 20 reels of tape. Recording No. 105.

Includes: texts, sentences, etc. Re: greetings; meal preparation; preparing salmon, clams, duck; history; description of artifacts (baskets, arrowheads, canoes, etc.); syntactic analysis (negation, embedding, wh- questions); etc. Informant: Al Charles.

Donor, grantee, 1975.

4057*b*. DIEHL, H. C., coll. Hopi and Navajo recordings; 1955-1957, 1959, n.d. 21 reels of tape. Recording No. 103.

Re: Hopi words, phrases, texts, counting, and grammar (particles), some with English equivalents; Navajo (one reel) words and phrases with English glosses and Navajo literacy lessons. Also includes duplicates of Hopi recordings of Carl F. Voegelin; restatement of some material in the Voegelin recordings. Hopi informants include: Willie Coin, Jimmy Kewanwaytiwa, Bennie Nuvanisa, and Albert Yava. **Restricted research use only**: may not be reproduced until June 1986.

*Cf.* No. 4349*b*.
Donor, Department of Anthropology, Northern Arizona University through P. David Seaman, May 1976.

4058. DUNNIGAN, TIMOTHY, coll. Pima Bajo recordings; 1965. 12 reels of tape. Recording No. 55.

Recorded at Yecora, Sonora, Mexico. Informant: Leonardo Duarte O.

*Cf.* No. 4677.
Donor, grantee.

4059. GARCIA, ANTONIO, recorder. *Senshare* Man Ceremony: Kiva ritual of San Juan Pueblo, New Mexico; 1964-1965. 3 reels of tape. Recording No. 69.

Includes: *Senshare* songs by Juanito Trujillo and Peter Garcia; announcements and spirit calls by Antonio Garcia; songs for the *Xoxeye* Corn Dance by Juanito Trujillo. **Restricted access.**

*Cf.* Nos. 4834, 4839.

4060. GARRISON, EDWARD R., coll. Navajo texts; 1969. 7 reels of tape. Recording No. 79.

Recorded at the Navajo Indian Reservation, northeastern Arizona.

*Cf.* Nos. 4560-4561.
Donor, grantee, Oct. 1970.

4061. GOODMAN, LINDA, coll. San Juan Pueblo music; 1967. 5 reels of tape. Recording No. 62.

Includes: songs for Kachina, rain, green corn, yellow corn, buffalo, butterfly, deer, turtle, cloud, dog, and basket dances; peace song; some Tewa vocabulary; discussion of the dances and music. Informants include: Marie Cata, Nettie Cata, Ralph Cata, David Garcia, Jerry Garcia, Peter Garcia, Seriano Montoya, Stephen Trujillo.

*Cf.* Nos. 4836-4837.
Donor, grantee, May 1968.

4062. GREENE, CHIEF ELTON. Tuscarora language; n.d. 1 cassette tape. Recording No. 96.

Recording to accompany *Tuscarora Indian Language* published by the Johnson Publishing Co., Murfeesboro, North Carolina, 1969.

*Cf.* Nos. 4076, 4863.
Donor, F. Roy Johnson, Apr. 1973.

4063. HAMP, ERIC P., coll. Quileute recordings; n.d. 14 reels of tape. Recording No. 80.

*Cf.* No. 4064.
Donor, grantee, 1971.

4064. HAMP, ERIC P., coll. Quileute texts; 1969. 5 reels of tape. Recording No. 73.

Informant: Beatrice Black(?).

*Cf.* No. 4063.
Donor, grantee, Dec. 1969.

4065. HARBECK, WARREN A., coll. Siouan texts: mutual intelligibility survey; n.d. 1 reel of tape. Recording No. 71.

Recording to accompany No. 4204. Texts are from: Eagle Butte, South Dakota; Sintaluta, Saskatchewan; Fort Totten, North Dakota; Griswold, Manitoba; and Alberta.

Donor, grantee, 1969.

4066. HARDMAN-DE-BAUTISTA, M. J., coll. Kawki texts; n.d. 12 reels of tape. Recording No. 78.

Primarily Kawki, but includes some Huantan and Jaqaru. Numerous informants.

*Cf.* No. 4119 for transcription.
Donor, grantee, 1970.

4067. HEATH, JEFFREY G., coll. Mississippi Choctaw texts; n.d. 2 reels of tape. Recording No. 97.

Includes: anecdotes; descriptions of insects; descriptions of illustrations in children's books; etc.

*Cf.* No. 4181.
Donor, grantee, June 25, 1973.

4067*a*. HOIJER, HARRY, coll. Loucheux recordings; n.d. 4 reels of tape.

Words and brief phrases given in response to English.

[4012(21)]

4068. KEALIINOHOMOKU, JOANN WHEELER, coll. Hopi-Tewa recordings; 1965. 3 reels of tape. Recording No. 59.

Re: interviews with Tewas who are bilingual Hopi-Tewa. For transcript of the Hopi, *cf.* Nos. 4354, 4838; the Tewa has not been transcribed. **Restriction on reproduction and on publication of informants' names.**

Donor, grantee.

4069. KENDALL, MARTHA B., coll. Yavapai linguistic material; 1973. 3 reels of tape. Recording No. 100.

Re: phonology; modals; etc. Informant: Harold Sine.

*Cf.* No. 4866.
Donor, grantee, Sept. 1974.

4070. KINKADE, MARVIN DALE, coll. Wenatchee language recordings; 1965. 6 reels of tape. Recording No. 53.

Vocabulary in Wenatchee elicited by collector. Informants: Jerome and Agnes Miller.

*Cf.* No. 4185.
Donor, grantee.

4071. KURATH, GERTRUDE P., coll. Observations of Michigan Indians; 1953-1968. 9 reels of tape. Recording No. 63.

Includes: "Red Man in Michigan," an educational series narrated by Edwin Burrows; comparisons of Chippewa revival hymns (Michigan and Ontario); Lansing powwow; Kiowa songs; dances; speeches; comparisons of Calumet dances of Michigan, Muskwaki, Wisconsin (Lac du Flambeau Chippewa and Menomini), and Narraganset.

*Cf.* Nos. 4038, 4605, and Negative 475.
Donor, grantee, July 1968.

4072. KURATH, GERTRUDE P., coll. Songs from Lac du Flambeau Reservation, Wisconsin; n.d. 2 reels of tape. Recording No. 75.

Includes: a variety of Wisconsin Ojibwa songs and dances; four Ponca peyote songs. Informants include: Willie Catfish, Fred Lacasse, John Martin, George Brown, and James Howard (Ponca).

*Cf.* No. 4608 for a transcription of Willie Catfish's songs.
Donor, collector.

4073. LANGDON, MARGARET H., coll. Diegueño texts; n.d. 3 reels of tape. Recording No. 76.

*Cf.* No. 4233.
Donor, grantee, 1970.

4074. LONG, RONALD W., coll. Isleta Tiwa materials; 1965. 2 reels of tape. Recording No. 57.

Includes: story about informant's father; myth texts with translations. Informant: Mrs. Jojola.

Donor, grantee.

4075. MCQUOWN, NORMAN A., coll. Quiché Maya texts; 1972. 3 reels of tape. Recording No. 89.

Rerecorded from aluminum discs which were recorded Jan. 19, 1935, under the direction of Manuel Andrade.

*Cf.* No. 4693*a*.
Donor, grantee, July 1972.

4076. MITHUN, MARIANNE, coll. Tuscarora language materials narrated by Chief Elton Greene; 1971-1972. 6 reels of tape. Recording No. 88.

Includes: verbs; grammar; numbers; months; seasons; greetings; weather; body parts; etc.

*Cf.* No. 4062.
Donor, grantee, June 1972.

4077. OLSON, DONALD, coll. Cheyenne stories; 1963-1964. 1 reel of tape. Recording No. 51.

Informants include: Yellow Eagle, Howling Crane, Bearbow, Flying Out, and others.

*Cf.* No. 4173.
Donor, grantee.

4078. PARKS, DOUGLAS, coll. Pawnee texts; n.d. 1 reel of tape. Recording No. 67.

Texts in the South Band and Skiri dialects. Informants: Harry Cummings, Sam Allen, and Phillip Jim.

*Cf.* No. 4647.
Donor, grantee.

4079. POULTE, WILLIAM, coll. Oklahoma Cherokee paradigms and texts; n.d. 2 reels of tape. Recording No. 92.

Includes: paradigms; suffix forms; prepronominal prefixes; texts.

4080. ROARK-CALNEK, SUE N., coll. Delaware songs and texts; 1973-1974. 5 cassette tapes. Recording No. 106.

Re: dances; songs; prayers; vocabulary; medicine (herbal remedies); birds and fish; weather; Big House; false face; etc. Some English.

*Cf.* No. 4223 for table of contents. *Cf.* No. 4081.
Donor, grantee, June 1977.

4081. ROARK-CALNEK, SUE N., coll. Indian performances in Oklahoma; 1973-1974. 36 cassette tapes. Recording No. 107.

Re: songs; dances (including: Ponca wedding dance, war dances, gourd dances, snake dance, buffalo dance, stomps, Seneca-Cayuga green corn stomp); Oto hand game; etc. Includes: Arapaho, Delaware, Shawnee, Oto, Cheyenne, Ponca, Quapaw, Cherokee, Pawnee, Seneca-Cayuga.

*Cf.* No. 4223 for table of contents. *Cf.* No. 4080.
Donor, grantee, 1977.

4082. ROOD, DAVID S., coll. Wichita language materials; 1969. 1 reel of tape. Recording No. 77.

*Cf.* 4899 for transcript and dissertation based on this material.
Donor, grantee, 1970.

4083. SHETTER, WILLIAM Z., coll. Radio program, Holbrook, Arizona; Aug. 1, 1968. 1 reel of tape. Recording No. 64.

Autobiographical remarks by Mrs. Elsie Benally, Navajo Reservation, Bellemont, Ariz.

Donor, grantee, Sept. 1968.

4084. SIMEON, GEORGE, coll. Mam, Xinca, and Pocomam Central linguistics; n.d. 1 cassette tape. Recording No. 91.

A portion of the material which he collected in Guatemala.

*Cf.* Nos. 4482, 4684, 4914.
Donor, grantee, Oct. 1972.

4085. SIMONCSICS, PETER, coll. Yavapai language materials; n.d. 3 cassette tapes. Recording No. 99.

Donor, grantee, Aug. 1974.

4086. SPECK, FRANK G., coll. Recordings of Cherokee, Naskapi, Penobscot, Sioux (Santee), and Winnebago; 1964. 4 reels of tape. Recording No. 49.

Rerecorded from discs made in the 1930s. Originals in possession of the Museum of Primitive Art, New York.

*Cf.* No. 9, Speck, Frank G., table of contents . . . ; n.d.

4087. SUE, HIROKO, coll. Legends, etc., collected among the Hare Indians, Fort Good Hope, N.W.T., Canada; July-Sept. 1961. 19 reels of tape. Recording No. 38.

Includes: vocabulary, phrases, songs, texts, etc. Informants include: Berthy Boniface, Jane Boniface, Marie Rose Clement, Noel Kakfwi, Naura Masuzumi, Gregory Shae, Paul Voudrach, and others.

*Cf.* No. 4238 for contents of reels 7-19. *Cf.* No. 4237.
Donor, grantee.

4088. SWANSON, RICHARD A., coll. Hopi ethnoanatomy; 1972. 5 reels of tape. Recording No. 95.

Re: internal and external body parts; division of the body into parts; reproductive organs; sentences using anatomical terms; etc. Informant: Willard Sekiastewa.

Donor, grantee, Jan. 1973.

4089. SZABO, LASZLO, coll. Malecite stories; n.d. 6 reels of tape. Recording No. 85.

*Cf.* No. 4090.
Donor, grantee, 1972.

4090. SZABO, LASZLO, coll. Malecite stories; n.d. 3 reels of tape. Recording No. 102.

*Cf.* No. 4089.
Donor, grantee, May 1975.

4091. TAYLOR, ALLAN R., coll. Stoney (Assiniboine) texts taken at Stoney Reserve, Morley, Alberta; Jan. 1, 1968, Aug. 21-23, 1971. 3 reels of tape. Recording No. 87.

Informants include: Willie Good, Carl Simeon, and for the New Year's service, Lazarus Wesley, John Snow, and Dillon Rider.

*Cf.* No. 4209.
Donor, grantee, 1972.

4092. TEDLOCK, DENNIS, coll. Finding the center; n.d. 4 reels of tape. Recording No. 93.

Includes Zuni Indian stories which can also be found in the collector's published work of similar title.

Donor, grantee, Dec. 1972.

4093. TURNER, PAUL R., coll. Highland Chontal ethnohistorical materials; 1968. 4 reels of tape. Recording No. 66.

Recorded at San Matias Petacaltepec, Oaxaca, Mexico. Informants: Damian Flores, Clemente Zarate, and Porfirio Nicolas Flores.

*Cf.* No. 4094.
Donor, grantee, 1969.

4094. TURNER, PAUL R., coll. Highland Chontal texts; 1965-1966. 3 reels of tape. Recording No. 52.

Includes: texts; grammar.

*Cf.* No. 4093.
Donor, grantee.

4095. VOORHIS, PAUL, coll. Musquakie texts; n.d. 9 reels of tape. Recording No. 94.

*Cf.* No. 4257.
Donor, grantee, Nov. 1972.

4096. WATKINS, DONALD, coll. Okanagan Salish stories and songs; n.d. 2 reels of tape. Recording No. 101.

*Cf.* No. 4611.
Donor, grantee, Jan. 1975.

4097. WEBSTER, DONALD H., and WILFRIED ZIBELL, colls. Canadian Eskimo dialects; n.d. 11 reels of tape. Recording No. 74.

Includes: sentences; phrases; texts. Informants: Jimmy Gibbons; David Uvinaiyak (Eskimo Point); Hugh Ungunga (Baker Lake); Thomas Kadlak (Eskimo Point); Naomi (Coppermine); Doris Kipan (Cambridge Bay). Other areas given: Baffin Island; Rankin Inlet.

*Cf.* No. 4256.
Donor, grantee, Jan. 1970.

4097*a*. WHITING, ALFRED F., coll. Hopi and Tewa recordings; 1964-1965, 1969. 14 reels of tape. Recording No. 104.

Data are primarily Hopi but include some Tewa. Re: names of plants, birds, reptiles, and other animals (including domesticated); costumes (including Kachina); Migration Legend; place-names; kinship terms; numerals; weaving; pottery; Hopi, Huichol, and Tarahumara belts; medicine man; etc. Informants include: Frank Capella (Hopi and Tewa), Grace Chapella (Tewa), Ralph Charlie (Hopi?), George Cochase (Hopi and Tewa), Jim Kewanwytewa (Hopi), Donald Mahkewa (Tewa), Nettie Masayumptewa (Hopi?), Edmund Nequatewa (Hopi), Garnet Pavatea (Hopi?), Frank Sehma (Hopi), Henry Sheldon (Hopi), Annette Silas (Hopi), Albert Sinquah (Hopi), Dennis Sinquah (Hopi and Tewa), David Tawameiniwa (Hopi?), Joe Tevenyouma (Hopi?), Barton Wright (Hopi?), and Margaret Wright (Hopi?). **Restricted research use only**: may not be reproduced until June 1986.

*Cf.* No. 4363*b*.
Donor, Department of Anthroplogy, Northern Arizona University through P. David Seaman, 1976.

4098. WOLFART, H. CHRISTOPH, coll. Plains Cree texts from the province of Alberta; n.d. 5 reels of tape. Recording No. 65.

Texts and English translations.

*Cf.* No. 4193 for transcription and table of contents.
Donor, grantee, 1968.

## PART VI

# LANGUAGES, TRIBES, AND AREAS

## ABIPON

(Guaycurú / Macro-Panoan)

4099. NAJLIS DE KREYNESS, ELENA. Descripcion del Abipon; 1967. T.D. 41 pp. In Spanish.

Re: phonology, morphology, and syntax. Forwarded with letter to Carl F. Voegelin. [9]

Donor, Carl F. Voegelin.

## ACHUMAWI

(Hokan)

4100. ANGULO, JAIME DE. Conversational texts in Achumawi; n.d. A.D. 72 pp.

Includes: sentences in English; Achumawi equivalents; literal English translations; some paradigms and notes on grammatical points; notes on dialectal differences (Atwamdzini, Hammawi, Adzumawi). [30(Hla.1)]

4101. ANGULO, JAIME DE, coll. Reminiscences of an Achumawi youth; n.d. T. and A.D. 22 pp.

An autobiographical text with numbered English translations corresponding to the Achumawi sentences. Dictated by Willard Carmony, an Achumawi. [30(Hla.5)]

4102. ANGULO, JAIME DE, and LUCY S. FREELAND. Parallel Achumawi and Atsugewi texts; n.d. 11 pp.

Includes: texts; free English translation; literal translations for some sentences; references to an Achumawi grammar (*cf.* No. 433). [30(Hla.2)]

## AHTENA

(Athapascan)

4103. DAVIDSON, GEORGE. Letter to Newell Wardle, Philadelphia; San Francisco, Nov. 17, 1901. T.L.S. 3 pp. and add.

Re: the Copper River and the name "Atna" given it by the natives. [9]

4104. DE LAGUNA, FREDERICA, coll. Materials recorded at Copper Center, Alaska; 1968. 17 reels of tape. Recording No. 68.

Includes: interviews; wide variety of songs and texts. Informants include: Andy Brown, Annie Ewan, Pete Ewan, Bacile George, Nancy George, Arthur Jackson, Martha Jackson, Billy Joe, Elizabeth Pete, Mentasta Pete, Jenny Peters, Kate Sanford, Fanny Stanfield, and others. Also includes some Upper Tanana. [4057]

4105. DE LAGUNA, FREDERICA, comp. Atna Indians, Copper River, Alaska; 1958. T.D. 8 pp. c.c.

Includes: names of informants, contents of reels, and comments for the recordings in No. 266. [9]

Donor, compiler, June 1962.

4106. DE LAGUNA, FREDERICA, and MARIE FRANÇOISE GUÉDON. Atna of the Copper River Valley; 1960, 1968. 2 reels of film. Film No. 1278.

Re: Atna, Copper River, Totlin, Upper Tanana, Southern Tuchone, Burwash Landing, and Yukon. [4031]

4106*a*. DE LAGUNA, FREDERICA, and CATHERINE MCCLELLAN, comps. Field notes on the ethnology of the Tlingit and Copper River Atna; 1949-1960. 6 reels of film. Film No. 1127.

Includes: notes on archaeological investigations; transcripts of interviews with informants. Tlingit material taken primarily from Yakutat and Angoon; Copper River Atna (Ahtena) from Chitina, Copper Center, and Chistochina, Alaska. From originals in possession of the compilers. [4032]

*Cf.* Nos. 263-267.

## ALASKA

4107. MASON, JOHN ALDEN. Totem poles; 1941. T.D. 7L. c.c.

Re: the description, history, and disposition of two totem poles from Sukkwan, Prince of Wales Island, Alaska. [4017(C37)]

4107*a*. SOCIETY OF JESUS: the Oregon Province Archives, Indian Language Collection: the Alaska Native languages; 1976. 28 reels of film. Film No. 1364.

Includes: dictionaries; vocabularies; texts (primarily Christian religious materials); grammatical notes; sermons; hymns; etc. Languages include: Central Alaskan Yupik, Iñupiaq (Inuit), Koyukon, and Ingalik (Ingalit). From originals produced in the late nineteenth and twentieth centuries, on deposit at the Pacific Northwest Indian Center, Spokane, Washington. Guide book included. [4043]

## ALGONQUIAN

4108. AMERICAN PHILOSOPHICAL SOCIETY: verbal communication by Mr. Du Ponceau; Feb. 5, 1841. 1 p.

Re: a manuscript found on the coast of Labrador which Peter S. Du Ponceau presented to the Society in facsimile and which he believed to be Algonquian. [3]

4109. BAILEY, A. G. Letter to Frank G. Speck, Gloucester, Mass.; Fredericton, N. B., Canada, n.d. T.L.S. 1 p.

Sending a copy of his book on Algonquians to Speck. [170(26)]

4109*a*. BLOOMFIELD, LEONARD. Correspondence with Carl F. Voegelin; 1938, 1940. A.L.S., T.L. 5 pp.

Re: Algonquian linguistics; possible Sauk-Fox-Kickapoo inscription on a bracelet. [4020*e*(1)]

Donor, Carl F. Voegelin, Feb. 1979.

4109*b*. VOEGELIN, CARL F. Comments on the Linguistic Institute, 1937-1940; 1940. A.D. 21 pp.

Re: teaching methods; Algonquian languages. Mentions Edward Sapir, Leonard Bloomfield, Zellig Harris, and others. [4020*e*(2)]

Donor, Carl F. Voegelin, Feb. 1979.

4109*c*. VOEGELIN, CARL F., coll. Potawatomi notebooks; n.d. A.D. 146L. in 3 notebooks.

Includes: paradigms; texts; English translations for some material. [4020*e*(2)]

Donor, Carl F. Voegelin, Feb. 1979.

4109*d*. VOEGELIN, CARL F., comp. Vocabularies; n.d. T. and A.D. 58 pp.

Includes: comparative vocabularies for Ojibwa, Potawatomi, and Delaware(?); Delaware(?) vocabulary. [4020*e*(1),(2)]

Donor, Carl F. Voegelin, Feb. 1979.

## ARCHAEOLOGY

4110. MATTHEW, WILLIAM D. Letter concerning the Snake Creek artifacts; n.d. A.D.S. 6 pp.

Expresses opinion that the "artifacts" were produced by natural processes rather than by men. Believes that man did not come to the New World until long after the time of the "artifacts." [9]

## ATHAPASCAN

4111. GILLESPIE, BERYL C. Athapascans who have Cree for neighbors; 1971. Photocopy of T.D. 58 pp.

Re: influences of contact with Whites. The study concerns territory now associated with the Chipewyan, Slave, and Beaver Indians for the period 1700-1830. [10(112)]

Donor, grantee, June 1971.

4112. HOIJER, HARRY. Comparative Athapascan: prefixes; n.d. D. 29 pp.

Partially completed lists of prefixes taken from thirty-three Athapascan languages and dialects.

[4012(21)]

4113. HOIJER, HARRY. Comparative Athapascan: Sarsi, Chipewyan, Navajo; n.d. A.D. *ca.* 400 slips.

Cognates in the three languages filed alphabetically by English glosses. [4012(18)]

4113*a*. KRECH, SHEPARD III. Letter to Whitfield J. Bell, Jr., Philadelphia; Fairfax, Va., Feb. 28, 1978. T.L.S. 1 p.

Re: Krech's archival research on Northern Athapascan ethnohistory. [10(166)]

4114. LIBBY, DOROTHY. Ethnographic consequences of Sir John Franklin's Northern explorations; Feb. 23, 1965. T.L.S. to Richard H. Shryock. 2 pp.

Very brief sketch of results of research at the Library of Congress. [10(30)]

4115. SAPIR, EDWARD. Comparative Na-Dene dictionary. n.d. A.D. 4 v. of *ca.* 500 pp. each.

Volumes 1, 3, and 4 are comparative Na-Dene with provision for various Athapascan languages and dialects, Haida, and Tlingit. Volume 2 is comparative Sino-Tibetan-Na-Dene with provision for entries in Sino-Tibetan languages, Athapascan, Haida, and Tlingit. Most pages in all volumes have only a few entries. [30(Na20a.3)]

4116. SAPIR, EDWARD. Letter to Harry Hoijer; Nov. 2, 1935. A.L.S. 6 pp.

Re: comparative Athapascan linguistics.

[4012(21)]

## ATSUGEWI

### (Hokan)

4117. ANGULO, JAIME DE, and LUCY S. FREELAND. Conversational text in Atsugewi; n.d. T.D. 19 pp.

Includes: English sentences; Atsugewi equivalents; literal English translations; some grammatical notes; references to the Atsugewi grammar (*cf.* No. 433) of which it seems to have been a part originally. [30(H1b.2)]

4118. ANGULO, JAIME DE, and LUCY S. FREELAND. Parallel Achumawi and Atsugewi texts; n.d. 11 pp.

Includes: texts; free English translation; literal translations for some sentences; references to an Achumawi grammar (*cf.* No. 433).

[30(H1a.2)]

## AYMARA

### (Andean)

4119. HARD-DE-BAUTISTA, M. J., coll. Kawki texts; n.d. Photocopy of T.D. *ca.* 200 pp.

Texts in Kawki with Spanish translations. Also includes some Huantan and Jaqaru.

[10(91)]

*Cf.* Nos. 4119*a*, 4120, 4121.
Donor, grantee, June 1970.

4119*a*. HARDMAN-DE-BAUTISTA, M. J., coll. Kawki texts; n.d. 12 reels of tape. Recording No. 78.

Primarily Kawki, but includes some Huantan and Jaqaru. Numerous informants. [4066]

*Cf.* 4119 for transcription.
Donor, grantee, 1970.

4120. HARDMAN-DE-BAUTISTA, M. J. Letter to Gertrude D. Hess; June 16, 1970. T.L.S. 2 pp.

Re: linguistic work on Kawki, Jagaru, and Huantan. [10(94)]

*Cf.* Nos. 4119, 4119*a*, 4121.

4121. HARDMAN-DE-BAUTISTA, M. J. Reconstruction of Jaqi personal verbal suffixes; n.d. Photocopy of T.D. 4 pp.

Summarizes geographical distribution, social factors affecting the languages, and typological characteristics as prefatory to the reconstruction problem. [10(90)]

*Cf.* Nos. 4119, 4119*a*, and 4120.
Donor, grantee, Aug. 10, 1970.

## BIBLIOGRAPHY

4122. Bibliography of South American Indians; n.d. D. *ca.* 1000 slips. c.c.

Concerned primarily with South American languages. Many entries are not included in the *Handbook of South American Indians.* [4017(6)]

4123. FREEMAN, JOHN F., comp. Guide to American Indian manuscripts in the Library of the American Philosophical Society; 1962. 2 reels of film. Film No. 1126.

From typed manuscripts produced in preparation of a guide for publication. [4036]

4124. HALLOWELL, A. IRVING. Letter to John Witthoft, Harrisburg; Philadelphia, July 14, 1950. T. and A.D. 35 items.

Includes materials for Speck bibliography which is to be published. [170(29)]

4125. HARRIS, ZELLIG S. American Philosophical Society Indian linguistic material: Central America, Mexico; 1945. T.D. and L.S. 17 pp. c.c.

Includes: bibliographies of books and a few manuscripts on Indians of Central America, Mexico, and South America; letter from Harris to Mason; Mason's reply. [4017(ling. #2)]

4126. MASON, JOHN ALDEN. Andean civilization; June 1, 1960. T.D. 25 pp. c.c.

Includes: bibliography and two copies of the article for the *Encyclopaedia Britannica.* [4017(C7)]

4127. MASON, JOHN ALDEN. Language: South American handbook; 1947. T.D. and L. *ca.* 125L.

Includes: correspondence, bibliography, draft of introduction, etc., relating to his contribution to the *Handbook of South American Indians.* [4017(ling. #2)]

4128. NEVIN, BRUCE E. Transformational relations and discourse structure in Yana: a beginning; 1969-1970. T.D., photocopy of T.D., ditto of T.D. 60 pp.

Re: syntax, morphophonemics, and internal reconstruction. Also includes: letter to Whitfield J. Bell, Jr. (as report on Phillips Fund grant); bibliography of manuscripts relating to Yahi and Yana. [10(85)]

Donor, grantee, Feb. 1970.

4129. SPECK, FRANK G. Bibliography; *ca.* 1942. T.D. 4 pp.

Bibliography of Speck's publications in three versions (through early 1942). [170(30)]

4130. STEELE, SUSAN. Uto-Aztecan bibliography; n.d. T.D. *ca.* 600 slips. c.c.

Includes: books; articles; manuscripts. [10(142)]

Donor, grantee, Nov. 1974.

## BLACKFOOT

### (Algonquian)

4130*a*. Blackfoot; 1914, n.d. 6 postal cards, 1 photograph.

Pictures include: Henry Between Lodge, Chief Luke Big Turnips, Chief Turned-Up-Nose, Black Plume (Blood), two unidentified chiefs, Piegan squaw, and Piegan camp. One postal card is a note from Frank G. Speck to Mrs. Frank G. Speck (postmarked Old Town, Maine). [4020*b*(1),(8)]

## CALIFORNIA

4131. ALLIOT, HECTOR. Letter to De Moss Bowers; Sept. 22, 1915. T.L.S. 1 p.

Acknowledges the receipt of De Moss Bowers's father's papers; diaries; manuscript of "Archaeological explorations in southern California"; notes; pictures. [4004]

4132. BAIRD, SPENCER F. Letter to Stephen Bowers, Santa Barbara; Woods' Hole, July 13, 1875. A.L.S. 3 pp.

Inquires about the possibility of Bowers's exploring Santa Rosa in preparation for a monograph on the aboriginal inhabitants and requests his assistance in preparing an exhibit on California ethnology for the Centennial. [4004]

4132*a*. California Indians; 1907, n.d. 12 photographs.

Includes: Hupa, Little Lake Pomo, Wintun, Yana, Yuki, and Yurok portraits; sweathouse pit (Shasta Co.). [4020*b*(1)]

4132*b*. California: Mount Shasta; *ca.* 1873. Engraving. 1 pc.

Engraving by E. P. Brandard after J. D. Smillie showing Mount Shasta with Indian camp in foreground. [4016*a*(B)]

4133. FORBES, R. H. Letter to Stephen Bowers, Los Angeles; Tucson, Feb. 11, 1904. T.L.S. 1 p.

Requests a copy of Bowers's publication on Indian fish weirs in Salton Basin. [4004]

4134. HAYDEN, FERDINAND V. Letter to Stephen Bowers; Washington, Dec. 19, 1876. A.L.S. 1 p.

Re: the possible publication of articles on archaeological treasures of the West Coast. Mentions a volume on the Hidatsa language which Hayden was in the process of publishing. [4004]

4135. HENSHAW, HENRY W. Letter to Stephen Bowers, San Buenaventura; Sept. 14, 1884. A.L.S. 2 pp.

Re: the collection of vocabularies from the "Santa Barbara Indians" and in the "San Antonio language." Mentions Alphonse Pinart. [4004]

4136. HRDLICKA, ALES. Letter to Stephen Bowers, Los Angeles; Washington, Aug. 5, 1904. T.L.S. 1 p.

Inquires whether or not the decoration on a human skull from Santa Cruz Island, California, was of Indian origin. [4004]

4137. MAYNE, W. T. Letter to Stephen Powers, Ventura; Brentwood, July 6, 1889. A.L.S. 2 pp.

Re: the authenticity of the Calaveras skull. [4004]

4137*a*. OKRAND, MARC. Report on fieldwork on Bodega Miwok; 1977. T.L.S., T.D. 3 pp.

Re: collection of linguistic data. Includes letter to Whitfield J. Bell, Jr. [10(170)]

4137*b*. Oregon and California photographs; 1906, n.d. 35 pcs.

Includes photographs by [Edward Sapir]; two postal cards. Re: Takelma (Francis Johnson, John Punzie); Yana (Betty Brown, Tom Grapevine, Frank Wilkes and children, Stonewall Jackson, Dick Gere, Sam Batwi, Ishi); Chasta Costa (Jack, Wolverton, and Stanley Orton); Montgomery Creek (Milford and Ralph Hill); Coast Athapascan (John Spencer and sons); Achumawi (Lena Patterson, Bessie Mike); Miwok (unidentified woman, Lake County). [4020*b*(7)]

4138. PILLING, JAMES, and OTIS T. MASON. Letters to Stephen Bowers; Washington, Apr. 4, 1888 and Apr. 6, 1888. A.L.S. 2 pp.

Expressing appreciation for copies of Bowers's pamphlet on the Conchilla Valley and the Cahuillo Indians. [4004]

4139. POWERS, STEPHEN. Letter to Stephen Bowers; Waterford, Ohio, May 29, 1878. A.L.S. 4 pp.

Re: the proposed publication of Bowers's work on California archeology; the accuracy of the California part of Powers's map; linguistic affinities between the " 'Santa Barbara' stock" and the " 'Santa Cruz' Indians." [4004]

4140. PUTNAM, FREDERICK W. Letters to Stephen Bowers; Cambridge, May 17 and July 2, 1886. A.L.S. 3 pp.

Re: the purchase from Bowers by the Peabody Museum of some artifacts from a cave. [4004]

4141. RAU, CHARLES. Letter to Stephen Bowers; Washington, April 30, 1886. A.L.S. 2 pp.

Re: Bowers's article on relics found in a cave in the San Martin Mountains, Los Angeles County; functions of some of the artifacts. [4004]

4142. WILMOT, MRS. ARTHUR X. Letter to De Moss Bowers, Santa Monica; Santa Monica, Dec. 22, 1915. A.L.S. 3 pp.

Expresses appreciation for specimens which Bowers had brought to the Wilmots and invites the Bowerses for an evening visit to discuss the "Indian curios." [4004]

## CAMPA

(Arawakan)

4143. JOHNSON, JACOB B. Correspondence with John Alden Mason; Nov. 29, 1942, and Feb. 26, 1943. T.L.S. 7 pp.

Re: the Campa language and other languages and/or tribes in their area (Piro, Machiguenga, Amuexia, Chama, Conibo, Shipibo, Cocama, and Cashibo). [4017(ling. #2)]

## CANADA

4143*a*. Canada and New England; n.d. 26 pcs.

Pictures include: people; town and country scenes; map of Newfoundland; Micmac encampment (Nova Scotia); etc. May contain some Montagnais-Naskapi. [4020*b*(1),(13:1)]

4143*b*. Canadian scenes; 1912-1913, n.d. 7 photographs, 5 postal cards.

Pictures from Athabasca River: natives tracking on the river (with very brief note from [J. Alden] Mason to Frank G. Speck). From Chipewyan area: people of Ft. Chipewyan and Fond du Lac, a steamer, and a forest fire. From Quebec: Abenaki village, Pierreville; Batiscan River; Batiscan Summit. [4020*b*(1),(2)]

4144. Dictionary of Canadian biography; Oct. 1961–Feb. 1966. T. and A.L.S., A.D. *ca*. 90 pcs., 52 pp.

Re: biographies of Indians; comments by Paul A. W. Wallace on Indian biographies. Wallace's correspondents include: George W. Brown, André Vachon, Francess G. Halpenny, and Elizabeth W. Loosley. [4021(2)]

4145. HUDSON'S BAY COMPANY. Letters to Frank G. Speck, Gloucester, Mass.; July 16–Aug. 2, 1937. T.L.S. 3 pp.

Re: unavailability of birch-bark articles at Longlac, Ontario, and Pointe Bleue, Lake St. John, Quebec; availability of five baskets and one canoe for purchase at Montreal. [170(26)]

4146. REHNSTRAND, JANE. Letters to Frank G. Speck, Philadelphia; Superior, Wis., Jan. 23–Mar. 16, 1943. A.L.S. 5 pp.

Re: Speck's article on the Indian crafts of Canada for *School Arts Magazine*. [170(30)]

4147. SARGENT, R. W. Letter to Frank G. Speck, Gloucester, Mass.; Hazelton, B.C., July 21, 1937. T.L.S. 1 p.

Re: Indian birch-bark baskets with scratched floral and geometric designs available for purchase from R. S. Sargent, Ltd. [170(26)]

4148. SPECK, FRANK G. Letter to [Foster?] Bennett, River Desert, Que.; Feb. 15, 1927. T.L. 1 p. c.c.

Re: the purchase of and shipping instructions for three birch-bark canoes and two pairs of paddles. [170(26)]

## CATAWBA

(Macro-Siouan)

4148*a*. Catawba; 1906-1942, n.d. *ca*. 250 pcs.

Pictures include: people, activities, medicine, material culture, etc., collected and produced in conjunction with Frank G. Speck's work on the Catawba. A few photographs are Machapunga and possibly Cherokee. [4020*b*(1),(13:1)]

4148*b*. SPECK, FRANK G., comp. Catawba texts; n.d. *ca*. 500 pp.

Includes: myths; texts regarding history, birds, reptiles, signs and omens, remedies, marriage, poverty, industry, food, charms, taboos, etc.; English free and interlinear literal translations. [4020*c*]

4149. SWANTON, JOHN R. Letter to Frank G. Speck, Philadelphia; Washington, June 11, 1937. T.L.S. 1 p.

Re: Speck's paper, "Catawba Medicines and Curative Practices." [170(30)]

## CENTRAL AMERICA

4149*a*. Central and South America; n.d. 6 photographs.

Includes: people, houses, etc., in Panama, Peru, and the Amazon basin. [4020*b*(2)]

4149*b*. Cuna; 1947. 1 photograph.

Shows Nils M. Holmer, Dr. Wassen, and the wife and children of Manitinali, chief of Rio Caimán group of Cuna Indians. [4020*b*(2)]

4150. FLOYD, TROY S., coll. Archivo nacional, Guatemala City, Guatemala; 1961. 2 reels of film. Film No. 1155.

Selections from collections pertaining to the history of Guatemala, 1568-1806. [4035]

Donor, grantee, 1963.

4151. HARRIS, ZELLIG S. American Philosophical Society Indian linguistic material: Central America, Mexico; 1945. T.D. and L.S. 17 pp. c.c.

Includes: bibliographies of books and a few manuscripts on Indians of Central America, Mexico, and South America; letter from Harris to Mason; Mason's reply. [4017(ling. #2)]

4152. JOHNSON, FREDERICK. Linguistic groupings in Middle America; 1939. T.D. and L.S. 14 pp.

Paper sent to Mason to be read at the meeting of the American Anthropological Association. Discusses Hokan-Siouan Phylum, Tarascan, Macro-Otomanguean Phylum, Macro-Penutian Phylum, and Macro-Chibchan Phylum. [4017(ling. #2)]

4152*a*. KIDDER, ALFRED V. Correspondence with John Alden Mason; 1926-1956. A.L.S., T.L. and L.S. 180 pp.

Re: linguistic, archaeological, and ethnological work in Mexico and Guatemala; publications; meetings; etc. [4017(C22)]

4153. MASON, JOHN ALDEN. Article for [Lilly de Jongh] Osborne's handbook of Guatemala; n.d. T.D. 4 pp. c.c.

Re: the ruins of Piedras Negras, Guatemala. [4017(C8)]

4154. MASON, JOHN ALDEN. Los cuatro grandes filones linguisticos de Mexico y Centroamerica; 1939. T.D. 22 pp. c.c. In Spanish.

Two versions of a paper for the International Congress of Americanists, Mexico, August 1939. [4017(ling. #2)]

4155. MASON, JOHN ALDEN. Middle American languages; Dec. 1938. T.D. 8 pp.

Paper read at meeting of the American Anthropological Association, Dec. 1938, on the genetic classification of Middle American languages. [4017(ling. #2)]

4156. MASON, JOHN ALDEN. Middle American languages; n.d. T.D. *ca.* 60 pp.

Notes on genetic relationships and geographic distribution. Mostly from published sources. A compilation and juxtaposition of various opinions. [4017(ling. #2)]

4157. MASON, JOHN ALDEN. Talk given before Sociedad de geografia e historia de Guatemala; June 1938. T.D. 18 pp. c.c.

Regarding the architecture of Piedras Negras. English original which was translated into Spanish for publication in *Anales* 15 (Dec. 1938): pp. 202-216. [4017(C36)]

4157*a*. MERRILL, ROBERT H. Correspondence with John Alden Mason; 1933-1947. A.L.S., T.L. and L.S. 125 pp.

Re: archaeological work in Guatemala, Mexico, and Panama. [4017(C25)]

4158. Middle American linguistics; 1955. T.D. and L.S. 35 pp.

Includes: carbon copy of the paper "Middle American Linguistics 1955" by Norman A. McQuown; draft of a paper by Mason discussing that of McQuown; a copy of Mason's paper as delivered at the meeting of the American Anthropological Association, Nov. 17, 1955, Boston; a copy of Mason's paper as corrected for publication; correspondence with Robert J. Weitlaner and Gordon R. Willey. [4017(ling. #2)]

4158*a*. MORLEY, SYLVANUS G. Correspondence with John Alden Mason; 1927-1938. T.L. and L.S. *ca.* 100 pp.

Re: Piedras Negras, Guatemala; Chichen Itza; archaeological work in Guatemala and Mexico. [4017(C26)]

4159. SATTERTHWAITE, LINTON, JR. Correspondence with John Alden Mason; Oct. 27, 1929–May 13, 1953. D. and L.S. *ca.* 300L.

The bulk of the material is from 1933-1939 and concerns archeological work at Piedras Negras, Guatemala. Some discussion of the

Mayan calendar, the ruins at Yaxchilan, Mexico, and a 1953 expedition to the Caracol Ruins, Honduras. [4017(C32)]

4159*a*. SAYLES, E. B. Correspondence with John Alden Mason; 1929-1954. A.L.S., T.L. and L.S. 43 pp.

Re: archaeological work in Guatemala, Mexico, and Texas. [4017(C32)]

4159*b*. THOMPSON, J. ERIC S. Correspondence with John Alden Mason; 1927-1955. A.L.S., T.L. and L.S. 86 pp.

Re: Pima; Yaqui; Piedras Negras, Guatemala; Maya glyphs and architecture; archeological work in Guatemala, Mexico, and British Honduras. [4017(C37)]

## CHATINO

### (Zapotecan)

4160. ANGULO, JAIME DE. Brevisimas notas sobre el idioma Chatino para el uso de los textos; n.d. A.D. *ca.* 30 pp. In Spanish.

Primarily concerned with an analysis of verbs; some discussion of noun declension. [30(Z5.1)]

## CHEROKEE

### (Iroquois)

4161. BARTON, BENJAMIN SMITH. Letter to John Heckewelder; Aug. 29, 1796. Photocopy of A.L.S. 2 pp. and add.

Inquires whether any Indians ever have a sickly white color or white spots on them. Mentions Cherokee belief that their ancestors found a race of "develish white-people" when they came to the area then inhabited. From original in the Gilbert Collection, College of Physicians, Philadelphia. [4003]

4162. BUTLER, ELIZUR. Address to the Cherokee Nation; Oct. 10, 1855. A.D.S. 4 pp.

Address given at the Female Seminary, Cherokee Nation, before his move to Arkansas. [9]

4162*a*. Cherokee; 1915-1948, n.d. *ca.* 150 pcs.

Pictures include: people, activities, material culture, etc. [4020*b*(2),(13:1)]

4163. Cherokee medicine book; n.d. 22 frames of microfilm. Film No. 1125.

Material to be edited and published by J. F. Kilpatrick. Written in the Cherokee syllabary. [4028]

4164. CUSHING, FRANK HAMILTON. Letter to Isaac Minis Hays; Washington, D.C., Jan. 20, 1899. A.L.S. 7 pp.

Inquires about a William Bartram manuscript once in possession of Samuel G. Morton according to notes of E. G. Squier, and asks about a J. H. Payne manuscript on Cherokees. [3]

4164*a*. DRUKE, MARY A. Seventeenth and eighteenth century manuscripts in England pertaining to the Iroquois; 1977. T.D.S. and photocopy of A.D. 22 pp.

Report on search for primary documents. Includes an English-Mohawk-Cherokee word list. [10(161)]

Donor, grantee, Oct. 1977.

4165. GILLESPIE, JOHN DOUGLAS. Miscellaneous items pertaining to the American Indian; 1947-*ca.* 1961. D. and printed items. *ca.* 350 manuscripts, *ca.* 75 photographs, *ca.* 75 newspaper clippings, and *ca.* 70 printed items.

Primarily regarding Cherokee (North Carolina and Oklahoma) ethnography, folklore, linguistics, archaeology, history, music, etc. Also contains material on: Apache, Calusa, Chippewa, Choctaw, Delaware, Eskimo, Fox, Iroquois, Karankawa, Kuchin, Louchens, Mattaponi, Muskogee, Navajo, Onondaga, Pueblo, Sauk, Seminole, Seneca, Shawnee, Sioux, Slave, Timucua, Tuscarora, Tutelo, and Wyandot. [4010]

4166. HENRY, JAMES W., and SAMUEL HODGDON. Letter to John Harris; War Department, Feb. 15, 1799. 1 p. and end.

Notification of authorization to purchase a United States flag for the use of the Cherokee Nation. [9]

4167. MOONEY, JAMES. Letter to Isaac Minis Hays; Washington, Dec. 16, 1899. A.L.S. 1 p.

Asks about the location of John Howard Payne's manuscript on the Cherokee which was cited in Ephraim G. Squier's *Serpent Symbol* (1851). [3]

4168. POULTE, WILLIAM, coll. Oklahoma Cherokee paradigms and texts; n.d. 2 reels of tape. Recording No. 92.

Includes: paradigms; suffix forms; prepronominal prefixes; texts. [4079]

4169. SPECK, FRANK G., coll. Recordings of Cherokee, Naskapi, Penobscot, Sioux (Santee), and Winnebago; 1964. 4 reels of tape. Recording No. 49.

Rerecorded from discs made in the 1930s. Originals in possession of the Museum of Primitive Art, New York. [4086]

*Cf.* No. 9, Speck, Frank G., table of contents . . . ; n.d.

4170. WALSER, RICHARD. Letter to Frank G. Speck, Philadelphia; Raleigh, July 25, 1947. T.L.S. 1 p.

Re: the accuracy of material in Robert Strange, *Eoneguski, or the Cherokee Chief* (1939); the title as a variation of *Yonaguska* in the works of Mooney and Hodge. [170(26)]

4171. WITTHOFT, JOHN. Letter to John Alden Mason; Cherokee, N.C., July 23, 1945. A.L.S. 3 pp.

Re: problems in Cherokee archaeology; nature of earlier work. [4017(ling. #2)]

## CHEYENNE

(Algonquian)

4171*a*. Cheyenne; n.d. 2 photographs.

Includes John Wicks Okestehei; woman and child. [4020*b*(2)]

4172. OLSON, DONALD, coll. Cheyenne stories; 1963-1964. 1 reel of tape. Recording No. 51.

Informants include: Yellow Eagle, Howling Crane, Bearbow, Flying Out, and others. [4077]

*Cf.* No. 4173.
Donor, grantee.

4173. OLSON, DONALD, comp. Cheyenne texts; 1964. T.D. 99 pp.

Includes: explanation of orthography; Cheyenne texts; literal and free translations. Collected in Norman, Oklahoma. [10(20)]

*Cf.* No. 4172.
Donor, grantee.

## CHINOOK JARGON

4174. BOAS, FRANZ. Indian legends of the North Pacific coast of North America; 1974. Photocopy of T.D. 600 pp.

Legends in English from the German translation of Chinook Jargon, Kwakiutl, Tsimshian, and Shuswap. Translated by Dietrich Bertz from the original edition (*cf.* Boas 1895). **Permission necessary for reproduction.** [30(74)]

Donor, British Columbia Indian Language Project, Jan. 1975.

## CHIRICAHUA

(Navajo D.)

4175. HOIJER, HARRY, coll. Chiricahua and Mescalero texts: fieldnotes; 1934. D. 1 notebook of *ca.* 60L.

Includes texts and translations. Number VII of the series in No. 4176. [4012(6)]

4176. HOIJER, HARRY, coll. Chiricahua texts: fieldnotes; 1930, 1934. D. 5 notebooks of *ca.* 60L. each.

Includes texts and English translations. Notebooks are numbered I-IV and VI. [4012(5)]

*Cf.* No. 4175.

4177. HOIJER, HARRY. Chiricahua texts in translation; n.d. T.D. 23 pp.

Texts are taken from notebooks I, II, and VI of No. 4176. [4012(21)]

## CHIWERE

(Siouan)

4177*a*. GOOD TRACKS, JIMM G. Report on Iowa-Oto Indian language dictionary; 1978, n.d. 8 pp.

Discusses data collection, form of the dictionary entries, etc. Includes: letter to Whitfield J. Bell, Jr.; photocopies of a few dictionary entry cards. [10(172)]

Donor, grantee, Mar. 1978.

4178. MARSH, GORDON H., comp. Materials for a study of the Iowa Indian language; n.d. D. *ca.* 1000L., *ca.* 4000 cards, *ca.* 75 bluebooks of 4L. each, several photographs.

Cards are in three subdivided sections: parts of speech (containing cognates from Osage, Dakota, Santee, Teton, Ponca, Kansa, and Winnebago); English-Iowa; Iowa-English. Also included: Iowa texts with interlinear English translations; manuscript grammar of Ponca based on material in Dorsey (1890, 1891); grammatical notes on Winnebago taken from Lipkin (1945). [30(X4a.2)]

Donor, compiler (now Rev. Priestmonk Innocent), Aug. 1971.

4178*a*. Oto; 1904, n.d. 2 photographs.

Includes unidentified woman and man in full dress. [4020*b*(7)]

4179. SMITH, RONDAL B. Report on a study of the Ioway-Oto language; Feb. 1, 1965. T.L.S. to Richard H. Shryock. 3 pp.

Includes: report on fieldwork in Oklahoma; kinds of data elicited; status of processing of data. [10(32)]

## CHOCTAW

### (Muskogean)

4179*a*. Ball playing among the Choctaw Indians; Indian game of ball; n.d. 2 engravings.

The latter apparently is taken from plate 225 of Catlin's *North American Indians;* the source of the other is unidentified. [4020*b*(2)]

4179*b*. Choctaw beaded belts; 1941, 1946. 4 photographs.

Photos of belts obtained from Stella, Emma, and Louisa Celestine, Bayou La Combe, La. [4020*b*(2)]

4180. HEATH, JEFFREY G. Choctaw cases; 1973. Mimeo. D. 7 pp.

Paper to be read at the meeting of the American Anthropological Association, New Orleans, Nov.–Dec. 1973. Discusses case forms and functions of nouns and of pronominal affixes to verbs. [9]

4181. HEATH, JEFFREY G. Letter to the Phillips Fund, Philadelphia; Exeter, N.H., May 28, 1973. T.L.S. 3 pp.

Re: linguistic fieldwork on (Mississippi) Choctaw. [10(132)]

*Cf.* No. 4182.

4182. HEATH, JEFFREY G., coll. Mississippi Choctaw texts; n.d. 2 reels of tape. Recording No. 97.

Includes: anecdotes; descriptions of insects; descriptions of illustrations in children's books; etc. [4067]

*Cf.* No. 4181.
Donor, grantee, June 25, 1973.

## CHOLON

### (Andean)

4183. HARRINGTON, JOHN P. Affiliation of the Cholon language; n.d. T.D. 85 pp.

Includes: grammatical sketch of the language; some "comparisons" with Quechua, Pomo, and Chimariko; one page of John Alden Mason's comments. [4017(ling. #2)]

## COLUMBIAN

### (Salish)

4184. KINKADE, MARVIN DALE. A study of the structure of the Wenatchee language; 1966. T.D. 3 pp.

Includes report on field activities; brief discussion of phonology. [10(27)]

*Cf.* Nos. 4185, 4185*a*.

4185. KINKADE, MARVIN DALE, comp. Wenatchee language material; 1965. D. 272 pp. in 3 v.

Wenatchee with English translation: transcripts of recordings in No. 4185*a*. [10(41)]

*Cf.* No. 4184.
Donor, grantee.

4185*a*. KINKADE, MARVIN DALE, coll. Wenatchee language recordings; 1965. 6 reels of tape. Recording No. 53.

Vocabulary in Wenatchee elicited by collector. Informants: Jerome and Agnes Miller. [4070]

*Cf.* No. 4185 for transcript.
Donor, grantee.

## CONIBO

### (Pano)

4186. LAURIAULT, ERWIN H. Shipibo myths; 1940-1941. T.D. and L.S. 31 pp.

Includes: correspondence with John Alden Mason; Shipibo myths with interlinear English translation; grammatical analysis of the myths. [4017(ling. #2)]

## CREE

### (Algonquian)

4187. AHENAKEW, EDWARD. Correspondence with Paul A. W. Wallace; Aug. 25, 1922–July 31, 1961. A. and T.L.S. 60L.

Re: Ahenakew's manuscripts; the desirability of his collecting ethnographic material and tales; personal matters; etc. [4021(1)]

4188. AHENAKEW, EDWARD. Genealogical sketch of my family; Apr. 27, 1948. T.D. and L. 85 pp. Orig. and 2 c.c.

Includes autobiographical sketch; biographical sketch of parents and grandparents and some of their collateral relatives. [4021(1)]

*Cf.* No. 779.

4188*a*. Cree; 1908, 1910, 1925, 1940, n.d. 43 photographs, 5 postal cards.

Pictures include people, activities, etc. Primarily regarding Quebec and Ontario with a few from Manitoba. Includes notes to Frank G. Speck from A. Skinner (1908), Edward Sapir (1910), and Ralph S. Palmer (1940). [4020*b*(2)]

4188*b*. Montagnais-Naskapi; 1908-1941, n.d. *ca.* 900 pcs.

Re: people, activities, material culture, dogs, scapulimancy and divination devices, habitat, etc. Consists primarily of photographs, but includes some drawings and proof sheets and a few postal cards. Many items appear in publications, but the majority do not. Areas include Ontario, Quebec, and Newfoundland. Bands include: Barren Ground, Bersimis, Lake St. John, Michikamau, Moisie, Natasquam, Nichikun, Rupert House, St. Augustine, Ste. Marguerite, Têtes de Boule, and Ungava. Frederick Johnson photographs pertaining to material culture, people, etc., are probably Montagnais-Naskapi. Rupert House, James Bay, shows a beach encampment. [4020*b*(4),(5),(6),(9),(13:3)]

4189. SPECK, FRANK G. Letter to Martin Gusinde, Saint Gabriel-bec, Vien.; Oct. 30, 1926. T.L. 1 p. c.c.

Sending a manuscript, "Family Hunting Territories of the Lake St. John Montagnais," to be considered for publication. [170(26)]

4190. SPECK, FRANK G., coll. Recordings of Cherokee, Naskapi, Penobscot, Sioux (Santee), and Winnebago; 1964. 4 reels of tape. Recording No. 49.

Rerecorded from discs made in the 1930s. Originals in possession of the Museum of Primitive Art, New York. [4086]

*Cf.* No. 9, Speck, Frank G., table of contents . . . ; n.d.

4190*a*. Têtes de Boule; n.d. 28 photographs.

Re: people, dwellings, habitat, bark containers. [4020*b*(10)]

4191. WOLFART, H. CHRISTOPH. Report on linguistic fieldwork among the Plains Cree; Nov. 1968. T.D. 5 pp.

Re: the distribution, status, etc., of Plains Cree; informants; Cree classifications of texts. [10(63)]

Donor, grantee, 1968.

4192. WOLFART, H. CHRISTOPH, coll. Plains Cree texts from the province of Alberta; n.d. 5 reels of tape. Recording No. 65.

Texts and English translations. [4098]

*Cf.* No. 4193 for transcription and table of contents.
Donor, grantee, 1968.

4193. WOLFART, H. CHRISTOPH, coll. Plains Cree texts from the province of Alberta; n.d. T.D. 50 pp.

Table of contents and transcriptions for recordings in No. 4192. [10(68)]

Donor, grantee, 1968.

4194. YOUNG, EGERTON RYERSON, coll. Rossville Mission Indian vocabularies; April 15, 1872. Photocopy of D. 15 pp.

Cree vocabulary collected at the Rossville Mission near Norway House, Manitoba. [9]

Donor, Harcourt Brown, Feb. 27, 1970.

## DAKOTA

### (Siouan)

4194*a*. Assiniboin, Oglala, and Santee; n.d. 11 photographs.

Includes: woman wringing skin and woman with grandchild and dog travois, Assiniboins of Ft. Belknap Reservation, Montana; Oglalas in full dress (Spotted Tail, Leading Charger, Lays Hard, Nellie Lays Hard, Philip Iron Elk, and others); six Santee men (William Hoffman, Joe Williams, James Wabasha, Joseph Winegro, Jacob Walker, and Thomas Williams) from Prairie Island, Minnesota (copy of a photograph made at Redwing, Minnesota, probably before 1880). [4020*b*(1),(7),(10)]

4195. BOAS, FRANZ. Teton lexical file; n.d. D. *ca.* 2500 slips.

Includes: vocabulary items with English glosses; other formations on the same root; paradigms; cross references; etc. [30(X8a.30)]

Donor, Norman F. Boas, Jan. 26, 1976.

4196. CARTER, RICHARD T., JR., comp. Dakota linguistic materials; 1969-1970. Photocopy of A.D. 76 pp.

Includes: Dakota words and sentences elicited using English; words elicited using Dakota (from Boas-Deloria grammar and Deloria texts); volunteered words with English translation; letter to Whitfield J. Bell, Jr. (June 2, 1971), reporting on fieldwork. [10(100)]

Donor, grantee, June 1971.

4197. DELORIA, ELLA CARA. Dakota games; n.d. T.D. 35 pp.

Includes: text in Dakota with free English translation; grammatical notes. [30(X8a.8)]

4198. DELORIA, ELLA CARA. A Dakota greeting; n.d. T.D. 5 pp.

Includes: short text and translation in which the greeting involves saying the name of a dead person; discussion of the context and social acceptability of the naming; relating an incident in which naming a dead person was not considered appropriate; discussion of a short prayer said before drinking water. [30(X8a.9)]

4199. DELORIA, ELLA CARA. Dakota play on words; n.d. T.D. 19 pp.

Includes text in Dakota with literal and free translations; grammatical notes. [30(X8a.12)]

4200. DELORIA, ELLA CARA. A Dakota proverb; n.d. T.D. 2 pp.

Includes: text with literal and free translations; discussion of prohibition against a man's traveling with/being alone with a woman not his wife and of aversion to open attempts by a woman to gain a man's attention. [30(X8a.13)]

4201. DELORIA, ELLA CARA. Dialect pun in Dakota; n.d. T.D. 9 pp.

Includes: text with literal and free translations; explanatory comments; grammatical notes. [30(X8a.19)]

4202. DELORIA, ELLA CARA. Special expressions in Dakota; n.d. T.D. 13 pp.

Includes: new expressions; odd words; sayings; jokes with literal and free translations; explanatory comments; grammatical notes. [30(X8a.22)]

4203. DELORIA, ELLA CARA. Woodmen from Bear Creek; n.d. T.D. 13 pp.

Includes: illustration of some old traditions through the reported conversation in Dakota connected with the offer and acceptance of food and honoring the dead; English translations; discussions of the customs involved; notes on various Dakota words. [30(X8a.23)]

4204. HARBECK, WARREN A. A study in mutual intelligibility and linguistic separation among five Siouan languages; 1969. T.D. 38 pp.

Re: Lakota, Dakota, Nakota, Assiniboine, and Stoney. Includes: modified 100-word diagnostic list; cognates in the five dialects/languages. Author feels that his study shows greater separation than previously noted. [10(74)]

*Cf.* No. 4204*a*.
Donor, grantee, 1969.

4204*a*. HARBECK, WARREN A., coll. Siouan texts: mutual intelligibility survey; n.d. 1 reel of tape. Recording No. 71.

Recording to accompany No. 4204. Texts are from: Eagle Butte, South Dakota; Sintaluta, Saskatchewan; Fort Totten, North Dakota; Griswold, Manitoba; and Alberta. [4065]

Donor, grantee, 1969.
*Cf.* No. 4204.

4205. MATTHEWS, G. HUBERT. A phonemic analysis of a Dakota dialect; 1954. T.D. 13 pp.

Based on the speech of one man whose parents were Yankton speakers and whose schoolmates were mostly Teton speakers. [30(X8c.4)]

4206. MELODY, MICHAEL E. Letter to Murphy D. Smith, Philadelphia; Notre Dame, Mar. 21, 1976. T.L.S. 2 pp.

Re: Rev. Luke Walker, a full-blooded Santee Dakota; J. R. Walker, M.D.; Dr. Walker's "The Sun Dance and Other Ceremonies of the Oglala Division of the Teton Dakota" *(Anthropological Papers of the American Museum of Natural History)*; possibility that Dr. Walker is the source of Deloria's "Legends of the Oglala Sioux." [3]

4207. POWERS, WILLIAM K. Contemporary Oglala music and dance: Pan-Indianism versus Pan-Tetonism; report on field trip to Pine Ridge, South Dakota; 1967. Photocopy of T.D. 42 pp.

Re: definition of Pan-Tetonism; characteristic elements of Oklahoma Pan-Indianism and of Pan-Tetonism (i.e., dances, songs, styles, etc.); Oklahoma elements in Pan-Tetonism and vice versa; collection of material pertaining to the Bushotter texts; Oglala music vocabulary; sweat lodge ceremony; Memorial Feast of the Dead; *Yuwipi;* contemporary music and dance of western Sioux. [10(47)]

*Cf.* No. 4682*f*.
Donor, grantee.

4208. SPECK, FRANK G., coll. Recordings of Cherokee, Naskapi, Penobscot, Sioux (Santee), and Winnebago; 1964. 4 reels of tape. Recording No. 49.

Rerecorded from discs made in the 1930s. Originals in possession of the Museum of Primitive Art, New York. [4086]

*Cf.* No. 9, Speck, Frank G., table of contents . . . ; n.d.

4209. TAYLOR, ALLAN R. Fieldwork done at the Stoney Reserve, Morley, Alberta; Aug. 1971. T.D. and photocopy of T.D. and D. 38 pp.

Includes: Stoney texts with English translation; two-page report on Phillips Fund grant; contents of Willie Good Stoney tape. [10(116)]

*Cf.* No. 4210.
Donor, grantee, 1972.

4210. TAYLOR, ALLAN R., coll. Stoney (Assiniboine) texts taken at Stoney Reserve, Morley, Alberta; Jan. 1968, Aug. 1971. 3 reels of tape.

Informants include: Willie Good, Carl Simeon, and for the New Year's service, Lazarus Wesley, John Snow, and Dillon Rider. [4091]

*Cf.* No. 4209.
Donor, grantee, 1972.

## DELAWARE

## (Algonquian)

4211. ALDERFER, E. GORDON. Correspondence with Paul A. W. Wallace; Oct. 26–Dec. 27, 1954. T.L.S. and L. 8 pp.

Re: a proposed literary history of Pennsylvania and the desirability of including Indian oral literature; validity of Walam Olum. [4021(1)]

4212. BARTON, BENJAMIN SMITH. Letter to John G. E. Heckewelder; Dec. 2, 1795. Photocopy of A.L.S. 1 p. and add.

Re: whether words for "earthquake" exist in Delaware or other Indian languages; whether there is an "earthquake theme." From original in the Gilbert Collection, College of Physicians, Philadelphia. [4003]

4213. BARTON, BENJAMIN SMITH. Letter to John G. E. Heckewelder; Mar. 23, 1796. Photocopy of A.L.S. 1 p. and add.

Re: whether certain objects are unequivocally Indian; whether any species of birds is venerated or held in particular esteem by the Delawares or other Indians. From original in the Gilbert Collection, College of Physicians, Philadelphia. [4003]

4213*a*. Delaware; *ca.* 1910, 1929, 1932, 1940-1945, n.d. 71 pcs.

Pictures include: people, activities, items of material culture; several photographs and one painting of War Eagle (*wi'tapanóxwe* "Walks by Daylight"); photograph of Munsees with a mortar, Six Nations Reserve, Ontario (photograph by M. R. Harrington). [4020*b*(2),(6)]

4214. EWERS, JOHN C. Correspondence with Paul A. W. Wallace; Dec. 10-15, 1959. T.L.S. 4 pp.

Re: the true national identity of the Indian in "Portrait of a Delaware Indian" by C. B. J. F. de St. Mémin. (Original in the New York Historical Society.) [4021(2)]

4215. GODDARD, R. H. IVES III. James C. Weber's 1928 recordings of Delaware songs and speeches from the Frank G. Speck Collection (American Philosophical Society); 1970. T.D. 23 pp.

Includes: transcript of the Delaware texts with comments; comments by three Delawares on the songs. [10(84)]

*Cf.* No. 289.
Donor, grantee.

4216. GREYWACZ, KATHRYN B. Correspondence with Frank G. Speck; Nov. 9 and Nov. 12, 1929. T.L.S., A.L. 4L.

Re: possible purchase from Speck of some modern Delaware items; request for pictures of those pieces; Speck's reply. [170(26)]

4217. Letters to Frank G. Speck, Philadelphia; 1928-1932. D. 7 pp.

Re: Speck's *Delaware Indian Big House Ceremony*. [170(30)]

4218. Letters to Frank G. Speck, Philadelphia; 1937. D. 7 pcs.

Re: Speck's "Oklahoma Delaware Ceremonies, Dances, and Feasts." [170(30)]

4218*a*. LILLY, ELI. Correspondence with Carl F. Voegelin; 1936, 1940, 1945, 1950. T.L. and L.S. 17 pp.

Re: Walam Olum; translation of names; other routine matters. [4020*e*(2)]

Donor, Carl F. Voegelin, Feb. 1979.

4219. LILLY, ELI. Letters to Frank G. Speck; July 22–Aug. 24, 1948. T.L.S. and A.L.S. 4L.

Re: financial support by Indiana Historical Society for Speck's work on Delaware; receipt of Delaware Big House drawing; appreciation for items of Delaware material culture and copies of publications. [170(26)]

4220. MONTOUR, ANDREW. Extract from the account of the success of the Embassy of Scarrooyady and Montour to the Delaware Indians; Apr. 1756. A.D. 2 pp. copy. [9]

Re: events during a trip to Wyoming and along the Susquehanna River above Wyoming.

4221. MONTOUR, CHIEF JOSEPH. Correspondence with Paul A. W. Wallace; Mar. 28–July 14, 1936. T.L. and A.L.S. 25L.

Re: visit with Montour. [4021(8)]

4221*a*. ROARK-CALNEK, SUE N. Indian way in Oklahoma: transactions in honor and legitimacy; 1977. D. 945 pp.

Unpublished doctoral dissertation, Bryn Mawr College. [10(157)]

*Cf.* Nos. 4222, 4616.
Donor, grantee, June 1977.

4222. ROARK-CALNEK, SUE N., coll. Delaware songs and texts; 1973-1974. 5 cassette tapes. Recording No. 106.

Re: dances; songs; prayers; vocabulary; medicine (herbal remedies); birds and fish; weather; Big House; false face; etc. Some English. [4080]

*Cf.* No. 4223 for table of contents. *Cf.* No. 4221*a*.
Donor, grantee, June 1977.

4223. ROARK-CALNEK, SUE N., comp. Delaware songs and texts, 1973-74; Indian performances in Oklahoma, 1973-74. D. 32 pp.

Tables of contents for recordings of the same titles. [10(156)]

*Cf.* Nos. 4222, 4616.
Donor, grantee, June 1977.

4223*a*. SIEBERT, FRANK. Letters to Carl F. and Erminie W. Voegelin; Sept. 15–Oct. 3, 1939. A.L.S. 7L.

Re: Walam Olum; Delaware dialects; Penobscot mortuary customs; Frank G. Speck's work on Penobscot. [4020*e*(2)]

Donor, Carl F. Voegelin, Feb. 1979.

4224. SPECK, FRANK G. Letter to F. A. Godcharles, Harrisburg; March 25, 1929. T.L. 1 p. c.c.

Re: the shipment to Godcharles of Delaware Indian specimens received from War Eagle. [170(26)]

4225. SPECK, FRANK G. Letter to state of Pennsylvania; Mar. 17, 1928. T.L. 1 p. cc.

Re: Speck's expenses while gathering information on the Delaware language and religious ceremonies from Chief James Weber, Oklahoma. [170(26)]

4225*a*. SWADESH, MORRIS. Letter to Carl F. Voegelin; Sept. 11, 1937. A.L.S. 2 pp.

Re: Delaware vocabulary obtained from some Stockbridge Indians. [4020*e*(2)]

Donor, Carl F. Voegelin, Feb. 1979.

4225*b*. VOEGELIN, CARL F., coll. Delaware songs and texts; n.d. A.D. *ca.* 150 pp.

Includes: variety of songs; myths; ethnographic texts; some English translations. [4020*e*(1)]

Donor, Carl F. Voegelin, Feb. 1979.

4225*c*. VOEGELIN, CARL F., coll. Munsee notes; June 1938. A.D. 6 pp.

Re: names for various tribes; Walam Olum. Informant: Nickodemus Peters, Smoothtown, Six Nations Reserve, Ontario, Canada. [4020*e*(1)]

Donor, Carl F. Voegelin, Feb. 1979.

4225*d*. VOEGELIN, CARL F., comp. Delaware linguistic material; 1937, 1939, n.d. *ca.* 425 pp.

Re: phonology, phonotactics, morphology. Includes: materials for teaching the Delaware language at the Linguistic Institute; manuscript grammar of Delaware. [4020*e*(1)]

Donor, Carl F. Voegelin, Feb. 1979.

4225*e*. VOEGELIN, CARL F., comp. Walam Olum; n.d. T. and A.D. *ca.* 450 pp.

Includes: Walam Olum in English from Daniel G. Brinton and Constantine S. Rafinesque-Schmaltz; explanation and parsing of Delaware words; Walam Olum in Delaware (with interlinear English translation) after Frank G. Speck with corrections by James C. Weber; discussion of dialectal differences. [4020*e*(1)]

Donor, Carl F. Voegelin, Feb. 1979.

4226. WAINWRIGHT, NICHOLAS B. Correspondence with Paul A. W. Wallace; Dec. 18, 1958–Jan. 2, 1959. T.L.S. 3 pp.

Re: the Delawares-as-women problem. [4021(10)]

4227. WALLACE, PAUL A. W. Chief Joseph Montour: the last king of the Delawares; n.d. T.D. 12 pp.

Draft of article includes: relations between the Delawares and the Six Nations; a few events in the chief's life. [4021(1)]

4228. WALLACE, PAUL A. W. The Delawares-as-women problem; Oct. 1952. T.D. 79 pp.

Drafts, with corrections, of a paper read at the Iroquois Conference, Red House. [4021(10)]

4229. WALLACE, PAUL A. W. An Indian preacher; n.d. T.D. 6 pp. cc.

Report on a visit with Chief Joseph Montour (Delaware) at the Six Nations Reserve, Ontario. [4021(6)]

4230. WALLACE, PAUL A. W. We are the Six Nations; n.d. T.D. 18 pp.

Re: relations between the Delawares and Iroquois. Includes three copies. [4021(11)]

4231. WITTHOFT, JOHN. Polly Heckewelder's Indian doll; n.d. T.D. 3 pp.

Re: the age and origin of the doll. [4021(11)]

## DHEGIHA

### (Siouan)

4231*a*. Kansa (Kaw), Omaha, and Osage; 1904-1908, 1936, n.d. 37 pcs.

Pictures include: Kaw man and woman (Oklahoma); Washunga, Chief of the Kaws (Oklahoma): *Exákaská* "White Horn (Elk)" (Omaha), taken at Elkton; people, dances, camps, etc., of the Osage (Oklahoma) with a note from [Frank G. Speck] to Florence Insley. [4020*b*(4),(7),(11:10)]

4232. MARSH, GORDON H., comp. Materials for a study of the Iowa Indian language; n.d. D. *ca.* 1000L., *ca.* 4000 cards, *ca.* 75 bluebooks of 4L. each, several photographs.

Cards are in three subdivided sections: parts of speech (containing cognates from Osage, Dakota, Santee, Teton, Ponca, Kansa, and Winnebago); English-Iowa; Iowa-English. Also included: Iowa texts with interlinear English translations; manuscript grammar of Ponca based on material in Dorsey (1890, 1891); grammatical notes on Winnebago taken from Lipkin (1945). [30(X4a.2)]

Donor, compiler (now Rev. Priestmonk Innocent), Aug. 1971.

## DIEGUEÑO

### (Yuman)

4233. LANGDON, MARGARET H. Report on comparative study of Diegueño dialects; n.d. T.D. 56 pp.

Re: collection of dialectal material (word lists and texts). Includes: list of English and Spanish words to be obtained in Diegueño; announcement and tentative program for conference on Hokan languages; a review by Margaret Langdon of Alan Campbell Wares, *A Comparative Study of Yuman Consonantism.* [10(83)]

*Cf.* No. 4234.
Donor, grantee, Feb. 1970.

4234. LANGDON, MARGARET H., coll. Diegueño texts; n.d. 3 reels of tape. Recording No. 76. [4073]

*Cf.* No. 4233.
Donor, grantee,1970.

## DOGRIB

### (Athapascan)

4234*a*. Hare Indians; 1961-1962. 119 contact proof sheets.

Photographs to accompany Phillips Fund reports of Hiroko Sue. [4020*b*(3)]

*Cf.* Nos. 1546-1548, 4236-4238.
Donor, grantee.

4235. HOWREN, ROBERT, coll. Dogrib field notes; 1967. Photocopy of D. 151 pp.

Includes: words; sentences; paradigms; English glosses. [10(86)]

Donor, grantee, 1970.

4236. SUE, HIROKO, coll. Legends, etc., collected among the Hare Indians, Fort Good Hope, N.W.T., Canada; July–Sept. 1961. 19 reels of tape. Recording No. 38.

Includes: vocabulary, phrases, songs, texts, etc. Informants include: Berthy Boniface, Jane Boniface, Marie Rose Clement, Noel Kakfwi, Naura Masuzumi, Gregory Shae, Paul Voudrach, and others. [4087]

*Cf.* No. 4238 for contents of reels 7-19.
*Cf.* Nos. 4234*a*, 4237.
Donor, grantee.

4237. SUE, HIROKO, comp. Materials collected among the Hare Indians, Fort Good Hope, N.W.T., Canada; 1962-1963. 1 reel of film. Film No. 1175.

Material to accompany No. 4236, reels 7-19. [4046]

*Cf.* No. 4238 for table of contents.
*Cf.* No. 4234*a*.
Donor, grantee.

4238. SUE, HIROKO, comp. Materials on the Hare Indians, Fort Good Hope, N.W.T., Canada; 1962-1964. D. *ca.* 1500L.

Includes: notes about informants; myths, stories, etc., obtained from informants; copies of public documents; Hare-English word and phrase lists; contents of reels 7-19 of No. 4236. [10(19)]

*Cf.* Nos. 4234*a*, 4237.
Donor, grantee.

## EASTERN NORTH AMERICA

4238*a*. DU PONCEAU, PETER S. Correspondence with John G. E. Heckewelder;

1816-1822. 18 items on film. Film No. 1162.

Re: Zeisberger's Onondaga grammar and dictionary; Heckewelder's writings on the Indians; publications; question of whether or not any of the Lenape can pronounce the letter *r*. From originals in possession of the State Historical Society of Wisconsin. [4033]

4239. GREYWACZ, KATHRYN B. Letter to Frank G. Speck, Philadelphia; Trenton, Apr. 29, 1947. T.L.S. 1 p.

Re: proposed sale of some of Speck's baskets from eastern American Indian groups. [170(26)]

4240. LAUNER, PHILIP. Letter to Frank G. Speck; New York, Jan. 28, 1947. A.L.S. 1 p.

Re: Speck's "Eastern Algonkian Block-Stamp Decoration"; Harold Thompson's (Westfield, N.J.) collection of eastern splitwood baskets. [170(26)]

4241. RATHBONE, PERRY T. Letter to Frank G. Speck, Philadelphia; St. Louis, July 24, 1942. T.L.S. 1 p.

Re: interest in purchase of eastern American Indian material. [170(27)]

4242. CONRAD WEISER; n.d. T.L. and L.S., A.L.S., T. and A.D., photostats. *ca.* 700 pcs.

Correspondence, notes, etc., as part of research for publications and speeches by Paul A. W. Wallace. [4021]

4243. DALHOUSIE MUNIMENTS: Papers relating to America, 1748-59: James Glen (governor of South Carolina), and John Forbes and his expedition in the French and Indian War. 2 reels of film. Film No. 1231.

Re: South Carolina politics and government; Indian policy; French and Indian War; etc. From originals in Scottish Record Office, Edinburgh. [4030]

4244. GAPP, S. H. Correspondence with Paul A. W. Wallace; Sept. 15, 1948-June 12, 1956. T. and A.L.S. 80L.

Re: Wallace's research on John Heckewelder; etc. Mentions William N. Fenton and his work on the political history of the Six Nations. [4021(3)]

4244*a*. Heckewelder illustrations; 1955, n.d. 8 photographs, 1 drawing.

Includes: photographs from New Fairfield, Ontario (woman and child, Indian church); photographs of the restored Moravian village, Schönbrunn, Ohio, and the Christian Indian monument, Gnadenhütten, Ohio; drawing by Mrs. Charles Macmillan for Paul A. W. Wallace's *Thirty Thousand Miles with John Heckewelder.* [4020*b*(3)]

4245. John Heckewelder; n.d. T.L. and L.S., A.L.S., photostats, T. and A.D. *ca.* 1800 pcs.

Correspondence, notes, drafts, etc., as part of research for publications and speeches by Paul A. W. Wallace. [4021]

4245*a*. Menomini; n.d. 4 photographs.

Includes: Dewey Necomish, Howard Rain, Louis Thunder, and Mitchell Weso. Published in J. S. Slotkin, "Menomini Peyotism," *Trans. Amer. Philos. Soc.* **42**, 4 (1952): pp. 565-700. [4016*a*(A:In22P)]

4246. MONTGOMERY, CHARLES B. Correspondence with Paul A. W. Wallace; Sept. 1935–Oct. 1942. A. and T.L. and L.S. *ca.* 700 pp.

Re: Conrad Weiser; Six Nations; Delawares; Pennsylvania history; personal matters; etc. [4021(7,8)]

4246*a*. Tutelo; 1870, 1937-1938, n.d. 80 pcs.

Includes: photograph of Nikonha, "The Last Tutelo"; drawings, photographs, proofs, sheet music, and plans for Frank G. Speck's *Tutelo Spirit Adoption Ceremony.* [4020*b*(10)]

4247. WHEELER, GEORGE. Correspondence with Paul A. W. Wallace; Oct. 13, 1935–Dec. 30, 1940. T.L., A.L.S. 38 pp.

Re: Wallace's research on Indian trails; Conrad Weiser; etc. [4021(11)]

## ESKIMO

### (Eskimo-Aleut)

4248. BOAS, FRANZ. Correspondence; 1885-1909. 1 reel of film. Film No. 372.3.

Re: work among the Eskimos and on Northwest Coast languages. From originals in possession of the Office of Anthropology, Smithsonian Institution. [4026]

Donor, Smithsonian Institution, Apr. 1967.

4249. BOAS, FRANZ. Drawings for "Property Marks of Alaskan Eskimo"; 1899. D. 18 items.

Drawings from which the illustrations in Boas (1899) were reproduced. [30(Ela.5)]

Donor, Frederica de Laguna, Oct. 1964.

4250. DE LAGUNA, FREDERICA. An Arctic summer; 1930. Photocopy of T.D. 345 pp.

Report on archaeological expedition to the island of Inugsuk (north of Upernivik, Greenland). Taken from letters to her family. [10(23)]

*Cf.* No. 4251.
Donor, author.

4251. DE LAGUNA, FREDERICA. Greenland photographs; 1929. Prints, negatives, T.D. *ca.* 110 pcs., 6 pp.

Re: archaeological expedition reported in No. 4250. Includes: identification, exposure data, time of day, and weather conditions for each photograph. Subjects include: artifacts, terrain, Eskimo people, etc. [4016*a*(B)]

Donor, grantee.

4251*a*. Eskimo; 1901, 1909, 1932-1935, 1947, n.d. *ca.* 350 pcs.

Pictures include: a variety of people and activities; masks; dwellings; etc. Photographs from E. W. Curtis volumes (presented by Stewart A. Eastwood) concern Yupik and Alaskan Eskimo. Canadian Eskimo photographs are from Baffin Land, Keewatin, Labrador, and Southampton Island. Postal cards include notes to Frank G. Speck from Sam (mentions G. Heye) (1934), Edward Sapir (1909), and Duke (192-). [4020*b*(3),(I3:1)]

4252. GUNTHER, ERNA. Letter to Richard H. Shryock; Jan. 28, 1969. T.L.S. 2 pp.

Re: visits to Eskimo and Northwest Coast exhibits in European museums; visits to two manuscript collections in the Soviet Union. [10(70)]

4253. LIBBY, DOROTHY. Ethnographic consequences of Sir John Franklin's northern explorations; Feb. 23, 1965. T.L.S. to Richard H. Shryock. 2 pp.

Very brief sketch of results of research at the Library of Congress. [10(30)]

4254. MANNING, E. W. (Mrs. T. H.) Letters to Frank G. Speck; Ottawa, July 30 and Sept. 19, 1943. T.L.S. 2 pp.

Will forward copies of notes on her husband's Eskimo work. Expresses interest in northern Indians sharing cultural traits with the Eskimo. [170(27)]

4254*a*. Under the midnight sun; Aug. 11-12, 1869, n.d. 1 v. of 92 photographs, 1 map.

Includes some photographs of people, activities, scenery, etc., in Newfoundland and Greenland. [Call No. 919.8:D73U]

4255. WEBSTER, DONALD H., and WILFRIED ZIBELL, colls. Canadian Eskimo dialects; n.d. 11 reels of tape. Recording No. 74.

Includes: sentences; phrases; texts. Informants: Jimmy Gibbons; David Uvinaiyak (Eskimo Point); Hugh Ungunga (Baker Lake); Thomas Kadlak (Eskimo Point); Naomi (Coppermine); Doris Kipan (Cambridge Bay). Other areas given: Baffin Island; Rankin Inlet. [4097]

*Cf.* No. 4256.
Donors, grantees, Jan. 1970.

4256. WEBSTER, DONALD H., and WILFRIED ZIBELL, comps. Report of Canadian Eskimo language survey; 1968. Photocopy of D. 38 pp.

Re: phonemic inventories in the various dialects studied; various orthographic systems used. Includes comparative lists of words, phrases, and sentences. [10(82)]

*Cf.* No. 4255.
Donors, grantees, Jan. 1970.

## FOX

### (Algonquian)

4256*a*. Kickapoo, Musquakie, and Sauk; 1870, 1932, n.d. 10 pcs.

Pictures include: Kickapoo house near McCloud, Oklahoma; three postal cards showing Musquakie Indians; Sauk children outside a bark house, Ottawa, Kansas (photograph by Joseph Romig). [4020*b*(4),(6),(10)]

4257. VOORHIS, PAUL. Report on fieldwork among the Musquakie; 1969. T.D. 3 pp.

Re: collection of linguistic data near Tama, Iowa; expense account. [10(79)]

*Cf.* No. 4258.
Donor, grantee, 1969.

4258. VOORHIS, PAUL, coll. Musquakie texts; n.d. 9 reels of tape. Recording No. 94. [4095]

*Cf.* No. 4257.
Donor, grantee, Nov. 1972.

## GALICE

### (Athapascan)

4259. Galice record; n.d. A.D. 16 pp.

Includes nouns and verbs with various person markers, but no complete paradigms. [4012(21)]

## GENERAL

4260. BAIRD, SPENCER FULLERTON. Letter to J. T. Ames; Washington, Dec. 31, 1882. A.L.S. 1 p. and end.

Expresses appreciation for Ames's gift of three busts of Indians and promises gift to Ames of some shell and mineral specimens. [9]

4261. BALL, CARL C. Letter to Frank G. Speck, Philadelphia; Okmulgee, Okla., June 9, 1942. T.L.S. 1 p.

Re: purchase of Indian artifacts from Speck; appreciation for Speck's papers on the Yuchi; desire to obtain items of Cherokee, Creek, and Choctaw material culture. [170(30)]

4262. BARTON, BENJAMIN SMITH. Letter to John G. E. Heckewelder; Mar. 22, 1794. Photocopy of A.L.S. 2 pp. and add.

Wants Heckewelder's opinion on the strength of body and age of Indians in comparison to Whites. From original in the Gilbert Collection, College of Physicians, Philadelphia. [4003]

4263. BARTON, BENJAMIN SMITH. Letter to John G. E. Heckewelder; Sept. 6, 1795. Photocopy of A.L.S. 2 pp.

Inquires what Indian nations in Heckewelder's knowledge compress heads of children and how it is done. Also seeks information on health, nursing, menstruation, etc. From original in the Gilbert Collection, College of Physicians, Philadelphia. [4003]

4264. BARTON, BENJAMIN SMITH. Letter to John G. E. Heckewelder; Dec. 28, 1795. Photocopy of A.L.S. 2 pp. and add.

Asks the Indian name of a particular bird. From original in the Gilbert Collection, College of Physicians, Philadelphia. [4003]

4265. BARTON, BENJAMIN SMITH. Letter to John G. E. Heckewelder; Jan. 13, 1796. Photocopy of A.L.S. 2 pp. and add.

Wants to know the Indians' feelings and beliefs about the opossum. From original in the Gilbert Collection, College of Physicians, Philadelphia. [4003]

4266. BARTON, BENJAMIN SMITH. Letter to John G. E. Heckewelder; May 17, 1796. Photocopy of A.L.S. 1 p. and add.

Expresses belief that some Indian nations formerly had a hieroglyphic writing system and asks Heckewelder's opinion. Inquires whether Indian chiefs have more or less power now than formerly. From original in the Gilbert Collection, College of Physicians, Philadelphia. [4003]

4267. BARTON, BENJAMIN SMITH. Letter to John G. E. Heckewelder; Feb. 11, 1798. Photocopy of A.L.S. 1 p. and add.

Pursues his inquiry into the relations of North American and Asiatic languages. Asks about accuracy of G. H. Loskiel's "History of the Mission of the United Brethren among the Indians in North America," which mentions the Moshkos Indians; Barton had never heard of them before. Also mentions study of the Nanticoke. From original in the Gilbert Collection, College of Physicians, Philadelphia. [4003]

4268. BARTON, BENJAMIN SMITH. Letter to John G. E. Heckewelder; Mar. 14, 1805. Photocopy of A.L.S. 1 p. and add.

Expresses appreciation for materials and information on Indians. [4003]

4268*a*. BELL, ROBERT. Papers; 1880-1908. A.L.S. 77 items.

Correspondence from Franz Boas, Elliot Coues, William Isbister, J. M. LeMoine, James C. Pilling, and E.F.S.J. Petitot regarding Canada, geography, geology, geological survey of Canada, Indians of North America, and paleontology. [4003*a*]

4268*b*. BERKHOFER, ROBERT F. Protestant missionaries to the American Indians, 1787-1862; 1960. 1 reel of film. Film No. 1157.

Doctoral dissertation, Cornell University. [4025]

4268*c*. BOAS, FRANZ, coll. Anthropometric data; 1892, 1897, n.d. A.D. *ca.* 3000 pp.

Includes data on: Apache, Bella Bella, Bella Coola, Caddo, Cherokee, Chickasaw, Chilcotin, Chippewa, Comanche, Crow, Delaware, Haida, Kiowa, Lillooet, Mississagua, Mohawk, Munsee, Nez Perce, Oglala, Ojibwa, Oka, Omaha, Oneida, Santee, Shuswap, Sioux, Teton, Tlingit, Wichita, Winnegabo, Yankton, and others. [4003*b*]

Donor, Northwestern University Library.

4269. BOAS, FRANZ. Letter to members of the Executive Section and the Advisory Section of the Committee on Research in Native American Languages; New York, Nov. 20, 1934. T.L.S. 1 p. c.c.

Re: criticism of the work of the Executive Section. [170(30)]

4270. BOAS, FRANZ. Letter to Waldo G. Leland, Washington; New York, Jan. 26, 1932. T.L.S. c.c. to Frank G. Speck. 7 pp.

Report of Committee on Research in Native American Languages, listing vanishing languages studied, by whom, publications, materials to be published, work to be done, and expenditures. [170(28)]

4271. BURGESSE, J. ALLAN. Letter to Frank G. Speck, Gloucester, Mass.; Arvida, P.Q., Aug. 5, 1945. T.L.S. 1 p.

Re: difficulty of obtaining crooked knives, birch-bark baskets, etc., for Speck; Burgesse's work on the translation from the French of Eugene Roy's diary (including Sumner's battle with Cheyennes and descriptions of other Indians). [170(26)]

4272. CALDWELL, CHARLES. Letter to Benjamin Horner Coates, Philadelphia; Lexington, Ky., Aug. 11, 1834. A.L.S. 3 pp. and add., end.

Discusses speculations on the origin of the American Indian and the futility of such speculations. Points out difficulty with Coates's hypothesis. [9]

4273. CHASE, FANNIE S. (MRS. WALTER G.) Letters to Frank G. Speck; Wiscasset, Me., Jan. 13, 1934 and earlier. T.L.S. 3 pp.

Re: Speck's manuscript on the Penobscot Indians; her work on the Wawenock tribe. Mentions Henry Masta, Dr. Kohl, Cyrus Curtis, J. Franklin Jameson, Pemaquid Indians. [170(30)]

4273*a*. CHOATES, J. N., photographer. Photographs from the Indian Training School, Carlisle Barracks, Pennsylvania; 1879-1880, n.d. 30 positive prints, 18 negatives.

Groups represented in the pictures include: Cheyenne, Creek, Lipan, Peoria, Pueblo (Laguna, San Felipe, unidentified), Sioux, Ute, and Zuni. Individuals include: Mad Wolf (Cheyenne), Man on Cloud (Cheyenne), Spotted Tail (Sioux Chief), and others. Also includes: boys at work in shoemaker's and saddler's shops, Indian students' brass band, native costumes, etc. [4020*b*(14)]

4274. COBB, RODNEY D. Letters to Frank G. Speck, Philadelphia; Fresno, Jan. 27 & Mar. 15, 1944. A.L.S. 2 pp. and add.

Request for copies of some of Speck's publications and other references on the birch-bark technique. [170(30)]

4274*a*. DE LAGUNA, FREDERICA. Correspondence with John Alden Mason; 1930-1949. A.L.S., T.L. and L.S. 86L.

Re: archeological work in Alaska; the Eskimo; southwestern United States; Northwest Coast; Mexico. [4017(C13)]

4275. DOUGLAS, FREDERIC H., and FRANCES RAYNOLDS. Letters to Frank G. Speck, Philadelphia and Gloucester, Mass.; Denver, 1939-1943. T.L.S. 10 pp.

Re: acquisition by the Denver Art Museum of items of material culture of Malecite, Penobscot, Pamunkey, Chickahominy, Rappahannock, Tunica, Creek, Nanticoke, Yuchi, Northwest Coast, Mattaponi, Catawba, Naskapi, and Micmac. [170(30)]

4276. DRAKE, NOAH FIELDS. Letter to the American Philosophical Society; Stanford University, Jan. 4, 1898. A.L.S. 2 pp. Enc. wanting.

Requests additional copies of his paper, "A Geological Reconnaissance of the Coal Fields of the Indian Territory" [*Proc. Amer. Philos. Soc.* 36 (1897): pp. 326-419]. [3]

4277. DRAKE, NOAH FIELDS. Letter to Isaac Minis Hays, Philadelphia; Stanford University, Jan. 5 and Apr. 14, 1898. A.L.S. 2 pp.

Re: the paper in No. 4276. [3]

4278. DUNNACK, HENRY E. Letter to Frank G. Speck, Phila.; Augusta, Me., Dec. 18, 1935. T.L.S. 1 p.

States that the Maine State Library has *Symbolism in Penobscot Art* and *Wawenock Myth Texts* and has ordered *Naskapi.* Anticipates Speck's new volume on Maine Indians. [170(27)]

4279. EDGERTON, FRANKLIN. Letter to Frank G. Speck; Phila., Nov. 20, 1915. A.L.S. 1 p.

Expresses appreciation for copies of some of Speck's publications. [170(25)]

4280. ESKEW, JAMES W. Letters to Frank G. Speck; Findlay, Ill., Aug. 8, 1943, and Nov. 4, 1944. T. and A.L.S. 2 pp.

Requests information on publications relating to American Indians, e.g., about the mounds of the Mississippi and Ohio valleys and about the Cliff Dwellers and Pueblos of the Southwest. [170(27)]

4281. FIELD, CLARK. Letters to Frank G. Speck, Philadelphia; Tulsa, Apr. 2, 1946, and May 12, 1947. A.L.S. 2 pp.

Re: purchase from Speck of Malecite storage basket; Penobscot carrying basket; possible procurement for Field of Tunica-Louisiana baskets. Mentions Arthur Langer and Frederic Douglas. [170(30)]

4282. GALLATIN, ALBERT. Letter to ----; Washington, May 29, 1826. A.L.S. 1 p. and end.

Requests that enclosed letters be forwarded to E. Lincoln, J. Pickering, S. Wood, Ebenezer Harris, James Rochelle, and Peter S. Du Ponceau with documents for collection of vocabularies. [9]

4283. GODMAN, JOHN DAVIDSON. Letter to Reuben Haines, New York; Germantown, Nov. 18, 1828. Photocopy of A.L.S. 3 pp. and add.

Expresses intention to give Haines an Indian pipe and stem ornamented with porcupine quills. From original in the Gilbert Collection, College of Physicians, Philadelphia. [Call No. 509:L56.26]

4284. GUSINDE, MARTIN. Letter to Frank G. Speck; Laxenburg bei Wien, Mar. 13, 1939. T.L.S. 1 p. In German.

Requests a copy of Speck (1933). Mentions Gusinde's *Anthropologie der Feuerland-Indianer.* [170(30)]

4285. HALLOWELL, A. IRVING. Letter to John Witthoft, Harrisburg; Philadelphia, July 14, 1950. T. and A.D. 35 items.

Includes materials for Speck bibliography to be published. [170(29)]

4286. HALLOWELL, A. IRVING. The nature and function of property as a human institution; n.d. T.D. 33 pp. cc.

Prepublication manuscript with additions and corrections. [170(30)]

4287. HEYE, GEORGE G. D. and L. S. *ca.* 225L.

Re: Heye's obituary and biography. [4017(ling. #2)]

4288. HILLER, WESLEY R. Letter to Frank G. Speck; Minneapolis, March 26, 1946. A.L.S. 2 pp.

Re: obtaining copies of publications by Speck and others. [170(26)]

4289. History of Science Film No. 8; n.d. 1 reel of film.

Re: Algonquian, Choctaw, Illinois, and Narraganset. Includes letters of: B. A. Gould, F. R. Hassler, Gauss, Sir Joseph Banks, J. F. Blumenbach. From originals in the possession of the Niedersächische Staats und Universitätsbibliothek, Göttingen. [4037]

4289*a*. HOWARD, EDGAR B. Correspondence with John Alden Mason; 1929-1943. A.L.S., T.L. and L.S. 46 pp.

Re: "Pygmy Race of Durango"; archaeological work in western United States, Saskatchewan, Mexico; Hrdlicka's archaeological work in Alaska. [4017(C20)]

4290. HUMBOLDT, ALEXANDER VON. Letter to Rembrandt Peale; Paris, Sept. 15, 1810. A.L.S. 1 p. In French.

Requests that Indian material be forwarded. Refers to C. W. Peale. [91(H88.54)]

4291. Indian medicine; 1958, 1965. T.L. and L.S. 9 pp.

Correspondence of Paul A. W. Wallace with Francisco Guerra and R. Jerrel Williams regarding references pertaining to Indian medicine. [4021(6)]

4291*a*. Indian races of North and South America: illustrations; 1855. 37 engravings.

Hand colored engravings like those published in Charles DeWolf Brownell's *The Indian Races of North and South America*. Includes: Montezuma, Osceola, Pocahontas, Samoset, Tisquantum (or Squanto), King Philip, Joseph Brant, Red Jacket, Tecumseh, Black Hawk, and others. [4020*b*(4)]

4291*b*, Indians of North and South America: miscellaneous illustrations; n.d. 78 pcs.

Mostly engravings (some hand colored). Subjects include: King Philip (Metacomet), Powhatan, Pontiac, Pocahontas, Sitting Bull, Tecumseh, Osage warrior, Kickapoo chief, Iowa chief, Cherokee, Pequot, etc. Artists include: J. R. Chapin, A. Chappel, E. H. Corbould, F.O.C. Darley, J. M. Nevin, J. A. Oertel, H. Warren, A. H. Wray, and others. Engravers include: J. C. Armytage, J. C. Buttre, A. B. Durand, A. W. Graham, A. Heath, T. Knight, W. Ridgway, John Rogers, J. Sartain, J. Stephenson, and others. [4020*b*(4)]

4292. KAYE, S. A. Letter to Frank G. Speck, Swarthmore; New York, Sept. 16, 1946. T.L.S. with 3 enclosures. 6 pp.

Re: Speck's biography for the *Biographical Encyclopedia of the World;* includes a partial bibliography through early 1942. [170(26)]

4293. KEALIINOHOMOKU, JOANN W. Dance data guide; 1966. T.D. 6 pp.

Guide for collection of data on dances by anthropologists who are non-dancers. [10(24)]

Donor, grantee, 1966.

4293*a*. KROEBER, ALFRED L. Correspondence with John Alden Mason; 1926-1957. A.L.S., T.L. and L.S. *ca*. 200L.

Re: migration routes from Asia to North America; Mason's archeological work in Mexico; Mason's work on Papago and Uto-Aztecan; South America; Franz Boas; John P. Harrington. Mention of numerous colleagues. Includes correspondence between Mason and Carl Sauer. [4017(C22)]

4294. LARUE, MABEL G. (MRS. DANIEL W.) Letter to Frank G. Speck; East Stroudsburg, Pa., Sept. 5, 1947. T.L.S. 2 pp.

Re: methods used by Indians of New England to suspend pots over fire; preparation of educational materials (supplementary readers) pertaining to American Indians. [170(26)]

4295. LINGELBACH, WILLIAM E. Correspondence with Paul A. W. Wallace; Dec. 1939–Mar. 1962. T.L. and L.S. *ca*. 250 pp.

Regarding Wallace's research on: John Heckewelder; the Muhlenberg family; Indians of Pennsylvania; the Six Nations; collections in the Library of the American Philosophical Society; Cree; Blackfoot; etc. [4021(7)]

4295*a*. MASON, JOHN ALDEN. American Anthropological Association: correspondence; 1927-1964. *ca*. 3000 pp.

Re: matters concerning Mason as editor of the *American Anthropologist*. Correspondents include: Burt W. Aginsky, Ethel G. Aginsky, Ralph L. Beals, Ruth Benedict, Douglas S. Byers, Frederica de Laguna, Henry Field, A. Irving Hallowell, John P. Harrington, Melville J. Herskovits, Harry Hoijer, Clyde Kluckhohn, Alfred L. Kroeber, Weston La Barre, Ralph Linton, Robert H. Lowie, Margaret Mead, George P. Murdock, Leslie Spier, Julian H. Steward, Sol Tax, Carl F. Voegelin, Erminie W. Voegelin, Leslie White, et al. [4017(C1-C6)]

4296. MASON, JOHN ALDEN. Class notes; 1908-1910. D. 1 notebook of *ca*. 70L., *ca*. 400L.

Notes from courses taken at the University of Pennsylvania with Edward Sapir, Frank G. Speck, et al. Topics include: ethnology, archeology, linguistics, Iroquois religion, and Takelma. [4017]

4297. MASON, JOHN ALDEN. Correspondence with Franz Boas; 1927-1940. T. and A.L.S. *ca.* 130 pp.

Includes: professional correspondence on various topics; copy of letter from Boas, Leonard Bloomfield, and Edward Sapir on proposed organization of a Society for American Indian Linguistics and an *International Journal of American Indian Languages;* carbon of letter to Edward Sapir; a few letters between Frans Blom and Mason. [4017(C10)]

4298. MASON, JOHN ALDEN. Liaisons between linguistics and archeology; 1939. T.D. 10 pp.

Paper delivered at the meeting of the American Anthropological Association, Chicago, 1939. [4017(ling. #2)]

4299. MASON, JOHN ALDEN. Fifty years of American anthropology; Oct. 1, 1956–Feb. 19, 1957. T. and A.D. and T.L.S. *ca.* 85 pcs.

Re: Mason's 1957 Wenner-Gren talk. Includes: list of invitees; guest list; abstract; correspondence with Paul Fejos; notecards. [4017(ling. #2)]

4300. MAZZEI, FILIPPO. Letter to Giovanni Fabroni; Pisa, July 6, 1803. A.L.S.: Pippo. 1 p. In Italian.

Re: Jefferson and a quote from a translation he made referring to Indians. Mentions Appleton. [Call No. B:F113.m]

4301. MEIER, EMIL F. Letters to Frank G. Speck, Philadelphia and Gloucester; Chicago, Feb. 27–July 13, 1937. T.L.S. 4 pp.

Re: difficulties in obtaining Indian masks; purchase of two Eskimo masks and one Naskapi mask from Speck; Eskimo masks and masks from Mexico and Guatemala, in his own collection. [170(27)]

4301*a*. Miscellaneous photographs and drawings; 1966, n.d. 18 pcs.

Pictures include: Aztec drawings (*cf.* Nos. 58 and 2140); front and rear views of silver statuette from Peru; church and roundhouse at Isleta Pueblo, New Mexico. [4016*a*(D)]

4301*b*. Miscellaneous photographs and sketches; 1907, 1909, 1924, 1933, 1940, 1943, n.d. 128 pcs.

Includes: Labrador sketches by Frank Stanford Speck; petroglyphs; Sauk and Fox; Wichita; Seminole; Creek; Piegan; Delaware; Minnehaha, Sacajawea, and Pocahontas by Georgianna Marbeson; Iroquois false face; Weasel Tail; Lottie Welsh and daughter; portraits by L. T. Alexander; unidentified people and scenes; Choctaw belt and Ojibwa(?) cradle board; splint basket; birch-bark baskets; cave-scene diorama (Guernsey and Pitman); notes to Florence Insley from C. L. Brooke and Frank G. Speck; note to Frank G. Speck from (Pvt.) Claude E. Schaeffer; map showing distribution of southeastern tribes; Indian children in school; Machapunga (North Carolina); Choctaw village, La. (from D. I. Bushnell, Choctaw, Bayou La Combe, La.); unidentified people, scenes, and objects (eastern U.S. and Canada). [4020*b*(5),(11:4,5,6,7,8),(13:2)]

4302. MOONEY, JAMES. Letter to Frank G. Speck, Ottawa; Wash., D.C., Nov. 1, 1915. A.L.S. 1 p.

Expresses appreciation for copies of some of Speck's publications. [170(25)]

4303. MORTON, SAMUEL GEORGE. Letter to Joseph N. Nicollet, Washington; Philadelphia, Mar. 8, 1840. A.L.S. 1 p. and add.

Acknowledges receipt of shipment of Indian skulls from west of the Mississippi. [127(B:M843.2)]

4303*a*. MORTON, SAMUEL G. Sketches of human skeletons; n.d. D. 12 pcs.

Includes: drawing of an Aymara tomb (Peru); drawings of skeletons and skulls of American Indians from burial sites in Kentucky, Massachusetts, Mississippi, Ohio, Rhode Island, and Tennessee. [127(M843.s)]

4304. MYERS(?), JOHN L. Letters to Frank G. Speck; Oxford, May 5 and May 7, 1943. A.L.S. 4 pp.

Expresses appreciation for a copy of *Montagnais-Naskapi Bands.* Some discussion of ethical sanctions on personal rights (e.g., game taken in traps) and Speck's papers on Algonquian and Iroquois society. [170(27)]

4305. NELSON, DOROTHY M. Letter to Frank G. Speck; Moorestown, N.J., n.d. A.L.S. 1 p.

Re: payment for purchase of Indian materials from Speck. [170(26)]

4306. NORTON, JEANETTE YOUNG. Correspondence with Frank G. Speck; Dec. 3 and Dec. 6, 1926. T.L.S. 2 pp.

Re: information on Indians' foods; tribes other than Navajo who do silver work; a wampum "memory chain"; northwestern tribes. [170(26)]

4307. NUTTALL, ZELIA MARIA MAGDALENA. Summary of paper "Fresh Light on Ancient American Civilizations and Calendars"; 1926. T.D. 5 pp.

Re: means by which ancient American cultures situated between 20°N. and 20°S. of the equator learned the true length of the solar year; various features of art, architecture, and religion in light of her hypothesis. Read at the meeting of the British Association for the Advancement of Science, Oxford, Aug. 11, 1926. [9]

4308. OAK, LISTON M. Letter to Frank G. Speck, Philadelphia; New York, Apr. 2, 1931. T.L.S. 2 pp.

Re: purchase of Chitimacha baskets, Catawba pottery, Cherokee baskets, or other articles suitable for the Exposition of Indian Tribal Arts, Inc. [170(28)]

4309. OAK, LISTON M. Letter to Frank G. Speck, Philadelphia; New York, Apr. 21, 1931. T.L.S. 5 pp.

Includes: informal report on activities and progress of Exposition of Indian Tribal Arts, Inc., New York; estimated budget. [170(28)]

4310. OWEN, SIR RICHARD. Letter to Mrs. Denman; May 23, 1865. A.L.S. 4 pp.

Re: animal specimens from Panama; Indians' skinning of sea otters. [Call No. B:Ow2.18]

4311. PARSONS, ELSIE CLEWS. Correspondence; 1921-1941. L., postal cards, pictures, etc. *ca.* 750 pcs.

Re: the publication of her own and others' work; American Folklore Society; American Anthropological Association; etc. Correspondents include: Bernard W. Aginsky, Ruth Benedict, Frank Calcott, John W. Cooper, D. S. Davidson, Fred Eggan, Aurelio M. Espinosa, Jr., Ann H. Grayton, A. Irving Hallowell, Melville J. Herskovits, George Herzog, Hamilton Holt, Dorothy L. Keur, Clyde Kluckhohn, Paul S. Martin, J. Alden Mason, H. Scudder Mekeel, Cornelius Osgood, Juan B. Rael, Robert Redfield, F. M. Setzler, Marian Smith, Leslie Spier, Bernhard J. Stern, William Duncan Strong, Stith Thompson, George C. Vaillant, Bella Weitzner, Edward M. Weyer, Leslie A. White, and Clark Wissler. [137(4)]

4312. PARSONS, ELSIE CLEWS. Letter to Leslie A. White; May 4, 1931. Photocopy of T.L.S. 2 pp.

Re: Parsons's recent return from Mexico; her popular books; anthropological laboratory at Santa Fe. [137]

4313. PAUL WILHELM, DUKE OF WURTEMBURG. Letter to "Monsieur le President"; Oct. 30, 1856. A.L.S. 2 pp. In French.

Expresses appreciation for publications. Discusses eating of horse meat and dogs by Indians. [Call No. 509:L56.f]

4314. PEALE, BENJAMIN FRANKLIN. Letter to Titian Ramsay Peale; Philadelphia, Mar. 31, 1855. A.L.S. 2 pp.

Re: the sending of Indian artifacts and skulls to Dr. Davis of Shelton, England. [140(10)]

4315. PEALE, BENJAMIN FRANKLIN. Letter to Titian Ramsay Peale; Feb. 15, 1861. A.L.S. 3 pp.

Re: his cabinet of Stone Age artifacts; catalog; possible additions to the collection. [140(10)]

4316. PEALE, BENJAMIN FRANKLIN. Letter to Titian Ramsay Peale; Philadelphia, July 12, 1861. A.L.S. 4 pp.

Forwarding copies of a paper read before the American Philosophical Society; speculations on means employed in making stone tools. [140(10)]

4317. PEALE, BENJAMIN FRANKLIN. Letter to Titian Ramsay Peale; March 28, 1862. A.L.S. 2 pp.

Re: shipment of two boxes of Stone Age implements to Henry; photographing his cabinet of Stone Age artifacts. [140(10)]

4318. PEALE, BENJAMIN FRANKLIN. Letter to Titian Ramsay Peale; April 20, 1862. A.L.S. 6 pp.

Asks whether or not two boxes of Stone Age implements reached the Smithsonian Institution. [140(10)]

4319. PHILLIPS, HENRY, JR. Letter to Hugo von Meltzel, Kolozsvor, Hungary; Philadelphia, n.d. Photocopy of A.L.S. 2 pp.

Re: some American Indian songs sent to von Meltzel. From original in Magyar Indomanyou Akademie [9]

4319*a*. Photographs of Franz Boas; 1866-1932, n.d. *ca.* 160 pcs.

Re: Boas as child, student, and adult; Boas with wife, children, other relatives, friends, and colleagues; Boas on Arctic trip and in Eskimo costume; Boas in various activities and groups; his seventieth birthday. Also includes photographs of: Wilhelm Weike and wife; George Hunt and family (Kwakiutl Indians); Eskimo family; Boas's Arctic sketches and pictures; some of Boas's maternal ancestors. [4016*a*(B:B61 in F & G)]

4320. PIKE, ZEBULON MONTGOMERY. Letter to Thomas Jefferson; Washington, Feb. 3, 1808. Photocopy of A.L.S. 4 pp., end.

Acknowledges receipt of Jefferson's letter and answers Peale's inquiry about some grizzly bears captured by Indians. From original in Edward Wanton Smith Collection, Haverford College Library. [9]

Donor, Whitfield J. Bell, Jr., 1969.

4321. PRESCOTT, WILLIAM HICKLING. Letter to Peter S. Du Ponceau, Philadelphia; Boston, Mar. 14, 1839. A.L.S. 2 pp. and add., end.

Re: a copy of Du Ponceau's "Memoir on the Indian Languages." Mentions J. Vaughan and J. Pickering. [9]

4322. PRIESTLEY, JOSEPH. Letter to Benjamin Smith Barton, Philadelphia; Northumberland, June 16, 1796. Copy of A.L.S. 3 pp. and add., end.

Re: printing of Barton's paper on Indian antiquities. [Call No. B:P931.7]

4323. RAFINESQUE-SCHMALTZ, CONSTANTINE SAMUEL. Letter to John Quincy Adams, Washington City; Lexington, Ky., July 8, 1824. 3 pp. and add., end.

Re: Rafinesque's interest in the ancient history, antiquities and languages of America; vocabularies deposited in the State or War Department, particularly of Lewis and Clark, Pike, and Dunbar. [151]

4324. Review of Dean Pittman, *Practical Linguistics;* 1950. T.L.S. 10 pp.

Re: John Alden Mason's review of the book. Includes: copy of letter from George L. Trager to Melville J. Herskovits criticizing Mason's review; letter from Herskovits to Mason enclosing copy of Trager's letter for rejoinder; three versions of Mason's reply. [4017(ling. #2)]

4325. RHOADS, CHARLES JAMES. Papers; 1929. D. *ca.* 300 pp. and newspaper clippings.

Re: Rhoads's appointment as Commissioner of Indian Affairs by President Hoover. [4020]

Donor, Brown Brothers, Harrimann and Co. through Mrs. Thatcher M. Brown III, Mar. 1965.

4326. SCHOOLCRAFT, HENRY R. Letter to Messrs. Carey, Lea, & Blanchard, Philadelphia; Michilimackinac, Feb. 9, 1835. A.L.S. 1 p.

Inquires whether or not they would be interested in publishing his projected volumes on Indians. [9]

4327. SHEEHAN, BERNARD W. Civilization and the American Indian in the thought of the Jeffersonian era; 1965. 1 reel of film. Film No. 1241.4.

Doctoral dissertation in history, University of Virginia. [4041]

4327*a*. SINGER, ERNESTINE H. WIEDER, comp. Anthropological reading notes; 1935. D.S. *ca.* 150 pp.

Includes: course notes on primitive economics (Incan) with A. Irving Hallowell; notes from seminars with Linton Satterthwaite (Mayan architecture), E. B. Howard (Problems of the Clovis, New Mexico, Site), and others; notes taken at the 1936 meeting of the American Anthropological Association from papers given by Ruth Benedict, Frederica de Laguna, Walter Dyk, William N. Fenton, Alfred V. Kidder, David G. Mandelbaum, George P. Murdock, Arthur C. Parker, Elsie Clews Parsons, Gladys A. Reichard, William A. Ritchie, Linton Satterthwaite, Gene Weltfish, and others regarding Cree, Flatheads, Iroquois, Kaingang (S. Brazil), Kiowa, Mayan, Natchez, Navajo, Ojibwa, Pawnee, Pueblos, Sahaptin, Saulteaux, Siouan, Tarascan, Tonowanda (Seneca), Zuni, etc. [4020*a*]

4328. SMILEY FAMILY: papers of the conferences at Lake Mohonk; 1885-1930. 1 reel of film. Film No. 1246.

Table of contents for the collection which is primarily concerned with the Indian conferences. From originals in possession of Haverford College. [4042]

4329. SMITH, EDGAR F. Letters to Frank G. Speck; Philadelphia, Aug. 2, 1915–Sept. 25, 1916. T.L.S. 3 pp.

Expresses appreciation for copies of some of Speck's publications. [170(25)]

4330. SPECK, FRANK G. The American Indian as a factor in American history; n.d. T.D. 8 pp.

Chapter and heading outline for book. [170(30)]

4331. SPECK, FRANK G. Letters to E. S. Gauthier, Maniwaki, P.Q.; Feb. 16, 1928, and May 4, 1929. T.L. 2 pp. c.c.

Re: the meaning of the Indian name *Pizendawach;* purchase of a bow and arrow by Speck. Mentions Andre Cayer. [170(26)]

4331*a*. SPIER, LESLIE. Correspondence with John Alden Mason; 1928-1944. A.L.S., T.L. and L.S., T.D. 65 pp.

Re: Yuman tribes of the Gila River; Pima; Yaqui; Papago; South American languages; archeological work in Colombia, Venezuela, Guatemala, Mexico, Panama, Puerto Rico; *American Anthropologist;* transportation of artifacts by migratory animals. Mentions Alfred L. Kroeber, Melville Jacobs, Edward Sapir, Franz Boas, Elsie Clews Parsons, Frank G. Speck. [4017(C35)]

4332. STAUB, PETER. Letter to Frank C. [*sic*] Speck, Philadelphia; Johannesburg, July 11, 1941. T.L.S. and A.D. 2 pp.

Re: obtaining North Carolina Cherokee masks and masks in general; list of masks sent to Peter Staub: two Eskimo, one Cherokee, one Tsimshian, one Iroquois, one Seneca, and one Cayuga. [170(27)]

4333. SWADESH, MORRIS. Correspondence with John Alden Mason; 1954. T.L. and L.S. 26L.

Re: disagreement between Mason and Swadesh as to whether there were one or two phonemic stop series in Papago. Includes: Mason's correspondence with Swadesh, Fr. Regis Rohder, O.F.M., and Dean F. Saxton; copy of "Amerindian Non-Cultural Vocabularies" (8pp.) for Tunica, Muysca, Dakota, Chitimacha, and Calcasien and Hiyekit. [4017(ling. #1)]

4333*a*. SWANTON, JOHN R. Correspondence with John Alden Mason; 1940-1953. T.L. and L.S., T.D. 27 pp.

Re: Papago place-names; Haida totem poles from Old Kasaan, Alaska; proposed linguistic relationships involving Uto-Aztecan, Hokan, Quechua, and others; parapsychology. [4017(C36)]

4334. TURNER, G.E.S. Letter to Frank G. Speck, Philadelphia; Oxford, Aug. 24, 1942. T.L.S. 3 pp.

Description of some moccasins in the Pitt Rivers Museum, Oxford University, for possible identification by Speck. Discussion of other items in the museum and comparison of moose hair embroidery with quillwork. [170(27)]

4334*a*. VOEGELIN, CARL F. Correspondence with John Alden Mason; 1941-1964. A.L.S., T.L. and L.S. 46 pp.

Re: bibliography of American Indian linguistics; classification of Central and South American languages; Uto-Aztecan; Papago. Mentions Morris Swadesh, George Trager, and others. [4017(C38)]

4335. WALLACE, PAUL A. W. A debt we owe the Indian; June 24, 1949, and Apr. 21, 1950. T. and A.D. 83 pp.

Notes and different versions of talks given at Farmers' Forum, York, Pa., Madison Historical Society, N.J., etc. [4021(1)]

4336. WALTERS, EDWIN. Letter to De Moss Bowers, Los Angeles; Kansas City, Mo., Sept. 27, 1909. A.L.S. 1 p.

Re: Walters's intention to publish a book on Indian sign language possibly with an appendix or second part on Indian picture writing or Indian art. [4004]

4337. WASHINGTON, GEORGE. Letter to Richard Henry Lee; March 15, 1785. A.L.S. 3 pp.

Re: a treaty with the Western Indians; the Shawnees in Ohio. [108(L51)]

4338. WHEELER, GEORGE M. Letter to Stephen Bowers, Santa Barbara; Washington, Nov. 6, 1879. A.L.S. 2 pp.

Inquires about an Indian woman who was "rescued" from San Nicholas Island in 1851 by a Mr. Nidever and taken to Santa Barbara. [4004]

4339. WHORF, BENJAMIN LEE. Remarks on Utaztecan and Macro-Penutian; Jan. 1939. T.D. 9 pp.

Discussion of Utaztecan, Penutian, and Mayan and probable linguistic relationship. [150]

Donor, Mrs. Paul Radin through Dell Hymes; May 1972.

4339*a*. WISSLER, CLARK. Correspondence with John Alden Mason; 1927-1941. T.D., T.L. and L.S. 70 pp.

Re: routine affairs of the American Anthropological Association, the American Museum of Natural History, and the University Museum (University of Pennsylvania); publications; Central and South American archaeology. [4017(C40)]

4340. WISSLER, CLARK. Letter to Frank G. Speck, Philadelphia; New York, July 1, 1935. T.L.S. 1 p.

Invites Speck to become a member of editorial committee for new enlarged edition of the *Handbook of American Indians*. Sapir, Stirling, Kidder also invited. [170(26)]

4341. YARDLEY, T. W. Letter to John L. LeConte; Wyandotte, Kans., Dec. 23, 1866. A.L.S. 3 pp.

Re: plans for railroad across the Rockies; Indian disapproval of railroads. [107(B:L493.3)]

## HAIDA
## (Na-Dene)

4341*a*. BLACKMAN, MARGARET B. Ethnohistory and the life history of a northern Haida woman; 1978. T.L.S., T.D., photocopy of D. *ca.* 160 pp.

Re: work on a biography of Florence Edenshaw Davidson, a Haida woman. Includes: letter to Whitfield J. Bell, Jr.; project report; History of the Queen Charlotte Islands, British Columbia, by Charles Harrison (from the *Queen Charlotte Islander*). [10(175),(175a)]

Donor, grantee.

4341*b*. EDWARDS, ELIZABETH A. Topic and topic marking particles in Haida; 1978. T.L.S., T.D. 44 pp.

Unpublished masters thesis, University of Washington. Includes letter to Whitfield J. Bell, Jr. [10(174)]

Donor, grantee.

4342. SAPIR, EDWARD, comp. Comparative Na-Dene dictionary; n.d. A.D. 4 v. of *ca.* 500 pp. each.

Volumes 1, 3, and 4 are comparative Na-Dene with provision for various Athapascan languages and dialects, Haida, and Tlingit. Volume 2 is comparative Sino-Tibetan-Na-Dene with provision for entries in Sino-Tibetan languages, Athapascan, Haida, and Tlingit. Most pages in all volumes have only a few entries. [30(Na20a.3)]

## HIDATSA
## (Siouan)

4343. BOWERS, ALFRED W., coll. Mandan-Hidatsa cultural change and language studies; 1967-1972. 11 reels of tape. Recording No. 84.

Includes: texts, vocabulary, etc.; letter to Whitfield J. Bell, Jr.; table of contents. [4053]

*Cf.* No. 4344.
Donor, grantee, 1972.

4344. BOWERS, ALFRED W., coll. Mandan-Hidatsa ethnohistory and linguistics,

Fort Berthold Reservation; 1967-1969. 19 reels of tape. Recording No. 81.

Includes: texts, vocabulary; some translations; table of contents. [4054]

*Cf.* No. 4343.
Donor, grantee.

## HOPI

### (Uto-Aztecan)

4345. BLACK, ROBERT A. A content analysis of 81 Hopi chants; 1964. T.D. *ca.* 500 pp. c.c.

Includes: introductory statement of form, content, etc., of chants; detailed analysis of the chants; tables showing distribution of chants; general content by village; content categories within chants. Doctoral dissertation in anthropology, Indiana University. [10(21)]

Donor, grantee.

4346. BLACK, ROBERT A. Report of field work among the Hopi Indians and catalogue of Hopi tapes; 1965. T.D. 9 pp.

Includes: preliminary reclassification of song domains; contents of the recordings in No. 4348. [10(40)]

Donor, grantee, 1966.

4347. BLACK, ROBERT A. Report on a study to determine stylistic changes of meaningful words in Hopi song-texts, as compared with words in spoken Hopi; 1960. T.D. 2 pp.

Summary of procedures for obtaining material to systematically delineate variation in songs for both the individual singer's style and song content and to study distinctions between spoken and sung occurrences of words. [10(15)]

*Cf.* No. 4349.

4348. BLACK, ROBERT A., coll. Hopi Indian songs; 1965. 4 reels of tape. Recording No. 56.

For table of contents, *cf.* No. 4346. [4051]

*Cf.* No. 4349.
Donor, grantee.

4349. BLACK, ROBERT A., coll. Hopi songs; 1960. 10 reels of tape. Recording No. 47.

Includes: Kachina, clown, hunting, Hopi-Apache masked dance, Paiute, Walapai, and other songs. Informants include: Walter Albert, Irving Charley, Lester Charley, Alfred Joshongiva, Glenn Joswaytewa, Jimmy Kay, Kelnimtewa, Elridge Masa, Mary Maypi, Sylvin Nash, Poli Payestewa, Helen Sekaquaptewa, Charlie Talawepi, Paul Talawepi, and Mr. and Mrs. David Talawietema. Villages include: Bacavi, Moenkopi, New Oraibi, Old Oraibi, Shongopovi, Shipaulovi, and Sichomovi. [4052]

*Cf.* Nos. 4051, 4347-4348.
Donor, grantee.

4349*a*. DIEHL, H. C., coll. Hopi and Navajo recordings; 1955-1957, 1959, n.d. 21 reels of tape. Recording No. 103.

Re: Hopi words, phrases, texts, counting, and grammar (particles), some with English equivalents; Navajo (one reel) words and phrases with English glosses and Navajo literacy lessons. Also includes: duplicates of Hopi recordings of Carl F. Voegelin; restatement of some material in the Voegelin recordings. Hopi informants include: Willie Coin, Jimmy Kewanwaytiwa, Bennie Nuvanisa, and Albert Yava. **Restricted research use only**: may not be reproduced until June 1986. [4057*b*]

*Cf.* No. 4349*b*.
Donor, Department of Anthropology, Northern Arizona University through P. David Seaman, May 1976.

4349*b*. DIEHL, H. C., comp. Hopi language materials; 1955-1959. Photocopy of D. 600 pp.

Contents and transcripts of Hopi recordings in No. 4349*a*. **Restricted research use only**: may not be reproduced until 1986. [4006*a*]

Donor, Department of Anthropology, Northern Arizona University, through P. David Seaman, May 1976.

4350. HODGE, CARLETON T. Indian summer; n.d. Photocopy of T.D. 3 pp.

Regarding feasibility of a Hopi dictionary. [10(71)]

4351. HODGE, CARLETON T. Report on the Hopi dictionary project: letter to Whitfield J. Bell, Jr.; Dec. 22, 1969. T.L.S. 2 pp.

Re: collection of textual material; involving young Hopis in production of the dictionary. [10(81)]

4351*a*. Hopi; 1908, 1938, n.d. 6 postal cards, 2 photographs.

Pictures include: women in formal hairdos, woman in wedding dress, Moki man, architecture, snake dance. Includes: notes to Frank G. Speck from Edward Sapir (1908) and "Roop" (1938). [4020*b*(3)]

4351*b*. JEANNE, LAVERNE M. Hopi workshop sessions, 1-15; n.d. Photocopy of D. *ca.* 75 pp.

Introductory linguistic analysis of Hopi morphology and syntax. Includes Hopi vocabulary with English glosses. [10(154)]

Donor, grantee, Apr. 1977.

4352. KEALIINOHOMOKU, JOANN WHEELER. The folklore of Hopi pottery makers; 1968. Photocopy of T.D. 18 pp.

Paper read at annual meeting of the American Folklore Society, Nov. 8, 1968, Bloomington, Ind. [10(61)]

Donor, grantee, 1968.

4353. KEALIINOHOMOKU, JOANN WHEELER. Hopi and Polynesian gesture codes; 1965. T.D. 8 pp.

Re: cross-cultural comparison of types of dance gestures; meanings of gestures; ways used; objectives of dance; etc. [10(29)]

Donor, grantee, 1966.

4354. KEALIINOHOMOKU, JOANN WHEELER, coll. Interviews with Hopis; 1965. T.D. 29 pp.

Transcript of Hopi for recording in Nos. 4068, 4356, 4838*a*. Tewa on the tapes is not transcribed. **Restriction on reproduction and on publication of informants' names.** [10(52)]

Donor, grantee.

4355. KEALIINOHOMOKU, JOANN WHEELER. Notes on Hopi pottery makers; n.d. T.D. 36 pp., 11 photographs.

Includes: notes from interviews and correspondence with pottery makers; observations and descriptions of materials and implements. **Restriction on reproduction and on publication of informants' names.** [10(60)]

Donor, grantee, 1968.

4356. KEALIINOHOMOKU, JOANN WHEELER, coll. Hopi-Tewa recordings; 1965. 3 reels of tape. Recording No. 59.

Re: interviews with Tewas who are bilingual Hopi-Tewa. For transcript of the Hopi, *cf.* Nos. 4354, 4838; the Tewa has not been transcribed. **Restriction on reproduction and on publication of informants' names.** [4068]

Donor, grantee.

4357. MASAYESVA, LAVERNE. Letter to Whitfield J. Bell, Jr.; July 30, 1970. T.L.S. 1 p.

Re: work on the Hopi language. [10(93)]

4358. PARSONS, ELSIE CLEWS. Letter to Leslie A. White; Oct. 28, 1933. Photocopy of T.L.S. 2 pp.

Re: return of dance pictures to White; her work on the Hopi clan for an appendix to Alexander M. Stephen's Journal; her future trip to Mexico. [137]

4359. PARSONS, ELSIE CLEWS. Letter to Leslie A. White; Dec. 7, 1933. Photocopy of A.L.S. 1 p.

Re: exogamy as criterion of the composition of the Hopi clan; Santo Domingo *naiya* as compared with Cochiti *nahia;* her coming trip to Mexico. [137]

4360. SCHEPERS, E. M. Hopi ethnoanatomy: summary of work to date; Dec. 1968. T.D. 8 pp.

Re: collection of ethnoanatomical data to recover the hierarchical classificatory system for comparison with that of the Navajo (by O. Werner). [10(64)]

Donor, grantee, 1968.

4361. SEAMAN, P. DAVID. Letter to Whitfield J. Bell, Jr., Philadelphia; Flagstaff, Apr. 30, 1976. T.L.S. 1 p. 7 pp. encs.

Re: Hopi fieldwork; work on Hopi dictionary. [10(148)]

Donor, grantee.

4362. SWANSON, RICHARD A., coll. Hopi ethnoanatomy; 1972. 5 reels of tape. Recording No. 95.

Re: internal and external body parts; division of the body into parts; reproductive organs; sentences using anatomical terms; etc. Informant: Williard Sakiestewa. [4088]

Donor, grantee, Jan. 1973.

4362*a*. VOEGELIN, CARL F., and FLORENCE M. Syntactic uses of Hopi conjunct mode occurring and non-occurring in Kennard's texts; 1977. Photocopy of T.D., ditto of T.D. 17 pp.

Discusses syntactic and semantic features, relative infrequency of occurrence in folkloristic texts. Paper given at the annual meeting of the American Anthropological Association. [10(165)]

Donors, grantees, Dec. 1977.

4363. WHITE, LESLIE A. Letter to Elsie Clews Parsons; September 3, 1937. Photocopy of T.L.S. with handwritten additions by E.C.P. 1 p.

Re: the Journal of Alexander M. Stephen; whether Stephen was a trader in Hopi country; how Stephen supported himself. [137]

4363*a*. WHITING, ALFRED F., coll. Hopi and Tewa recordings; 1964-1965, 1969. 14 reels of tape. Recording No. 104.

Data are primarily Hopi but include some Tewa. Re: names of plants, birds, reptiles, and other animals (including domesticated); costumes (including Kachina); Migration Legend; place-names; kinship terms; numerals; weaving; pottery; Hopi, Huichol, and Tarahumara belts; medicine man; etc. Informants include: Frank Capella (Hopi and Tewa), Grace Chapella (Tewa), Ralph Charlie (Hopi?), George Cochise (Hopi and Tewa), Jim Kewanwytewa (Hopi), Donald Mahkewa (Tewa), Nettie Masayumptewa (Hopi), Edmund Nequatewa (Hopi), Garnet Pavatea (Hopi and Tewa), Frank Sehma (Hopi), Henry Sheldon (Hopi), Annette Silas (Hopi), Albert Sinquah (Hopi), Dennis Sinquah (Hopi and Tewa), David Tawameiniwa (Hopi?), and Joe Tevenyouma (Hopi?). Mentions Barton Wright and Margaret Wright. **Restricted research use only**: may not be reproduced until June 1986. [4097*a*]

*Cf.* No. 4363*b*.
Donor, Department of Anthropology, Northern Arizona University through P. David Seaman, 1976.

4363*b*. WHITING, ALFRED F., comp. Hopi tape-recording transcripts; 1964-1969, 1976. 257 pp.

Contents and transcriptions of recordings in No. 4363*a*. **Restricted research use only**: may not be reproduced until June 1986. [4023*a*]

*Cf.* No. 4363*a*.
Donor, Department of Anthropology, Northern Arizona University through P. David Seaman, 1976.

4364. WHORF, BENJAMIN L. The Hopi language; n.d. T.D. 59 pp. c.c.

A grammatical sketch of the dialect of Mishongnovi pueblo. [30(U3a.3)]

## HOUMA

## (Muskogean)

4364*a*. Houma; 1936, 1938, 1941, n.d. *ca*. 300 photographs.

Pictures include: people, activities, daub and wattle houses, other dwellings, thatched roofs, boats, blowguns, etc. Louisiana places include: Bayou Blue, Bayou Grand Caillou, Bayou La Combe, and Pointe du Chien. Includes letter to Frank G. Speck from "Stu" [Stuart Neitzel]; mentions Gordon Willey. May contain some Tunica and Chitimacha. [4020*b*(4),(11:3),(13:1)]

4365. MCCASKILL, J. C. Letter to Frank G. Speck, Philadelphia; Washington, D.C., Feb. 11, 1941. T.L.S. 1 p.

Re: report which Speck is to write on the Houma situation. [170(30)]

## HUAVE

## (Penutian)

4366. RADIN, PAUL. Huave word list and miscellaneous notes; n.d. A.D. 19 pp.

Huave-English word lists. Mentions Yalalag, Abijones, Alaapa, and Ixtlan. [150]

Donor, Mrs. Radin through Dell Hymes, May 1972.

## HUICHOL

## (Uto-Aztecan)

4367. CUSHING, FRANK HAMILTON. Letters to Isaac Minis Hays and the American Philosophical Society; Jan. 23–Feb. 18, 1898. A.L.S. 12 pp.

Re: a lecture to be given by Carl Lumholtz on the Huichol Indians of Mexico. [3]

4368. WEIGAND, PHIL C. Correspondence with John Alden Mason; Dec. 15, 1966–Jan. 16, 1967. T.L.S. and L. 6L.

Re: acculturation, history, relations with Whites in San Sebastian and Azqueltan, Mexico (northern). [4017(ling. #1)]

## HUPA

## (Athapascan)

4369. SAPIR, EDWARD. Hupa texts and slip file; 1927. A.D.S. and A.D. 11 notebooks of *ca.* 125 pp. each; *ca.* 5000 slips.

Hupa texts with English translation. Slip file is vocabulary with grammatical notes filed alphabetically Hupa-English. [30(Na20a.4)]

## INDIANA

4370. MERCER, HENRY CHAPMAN. Letter to George Henry Horn; Doylestown, Nov. 22, 1895. A.L.S. 1 p. and end.

Notice of having sent a manuscript, "Jasper and Stalagmite Quarried by Indians in the Wyandotte Cave." [*Cf. Proc. Amer. Philos. Soc.* 34 (1895): pp. 396-400.] [3]

## IROQUOIS

4371. BOYCE, DOUGLAS W. The Iroquoian tribes of the Virginia–North Carolina coastal plain; n.d. Photocopy of T.D. 32 pp.

Article written for the *Handbook of North American Indians* 14: *Northeast.* [10(140)]

*Cf.* Nos. 4860, 4861.
Donor, grantee, Sept. 1974.

4372. CANADA, PUBLIC ARCHIVES; n.d. 2 reels of film. Film No. 426.

Includes: materials from the Public Records Office, London, and Bibliothèque nationale, Paris. Some of the materials pertain to the Six Nations during the Revolutionary War era. [4027]

Donor, Barbara Graymont, 1965.

4373. CARRINGTON, HENRY BEEBEE. Notes on the Six Nations of New York, successors of the Five Nations of the Iroquois Confederacy, as of Jan. 1, 1890. D. 1 v. of 251 pp.

Taken for the eleventh Census of the U.S., 22nd Division. Lists chiefs, crops, population, diseases, houses, other property, and values. [4005]

Donor, William N. Fenton, Sept. 1971.

4374. CHALMERS, HARVEY, 2nd. Letter to Paul A. W. Wallace, Annville; Amsterdam, N.Y., Apr. 7, 1954. T.L.S. 1 p.

Re: Heckewelder's prejudice against the Six Nations and its effect on Cooper; prejudice aroused by Cooper's novels. [4021(1)]

4375. COMRIE, HOWARD F. Correspondence with Paul A. W. Wallace; Feb. 26–Apr. 18, 1958. T.L. and L.S. 3 pp.

Re: the Iroquois Confederacy as an inspiration for the Constitution and Bill of Rights. [4021(1)]

4376. CONGDON, CHARLES E. Correspondence with Paul A. W. Wallace; Aug. 22, 1946–Sept. 12, 1952. T.L. and L.S. 5 pp.

Re: arrangements for conferences on Iroquoian studies. [4021(1)]

4377. CORNPLANTER, JESSE J. Drawings; 1937. D.S. 5 pcs.

Includes: "Two Friends," "Mortise," and three untitled. [4021(1)]

4377*a*. CORNPLANTER, JESSE J. Drawings; 1937, n.d. D.S. 11 pcs.

Includes: corn husk dolls, the three sisters, utensils, clan symbols, Naked Bear drawings. [4020*b*(2)]

4378. DESKAHEH, CHIEF. Correspondence with Paul A. W. Wallace; Aug. 3–Sept. 20, 1947. T.L. and A.L.S. 3 pp.

Re: additional copies of Wallace's *White Roots of Peace.* [4021(2)]

4378*a*. DRUKE, MARY A. Seventeenth and eighteenth century manuscripts in England pertaining to the Iroquois; 1977. T.D.S. and photocopy of A.D. 22 pp.

Report on search for primary documents. Includes an English-Mohawk-Cherokee word list. [10(161)]

Donor, grantee, Oct. 1977.

4379. DURSTON, HARRY C. Correspondence with Paul A. W. Wallace; June 1945–Nov. 1949. T.L. and L.S. 12 pp.

Re: the date and place of the founding of the Five Nations Confederacy; possible influences of the Six Nations on the U.S. Constitution. [4021(2)]

4380. EINHORN, ARTHUR (SKARONIATE). Correspondence with Paul A. W. Wallace; May 31–Oct. 8, 1956. A.L.S., T.L. and L.S. 4 pp.

Re: copies of publications; misinformation about the Iroquois; plans for building an "Indian village." [4021(2)]

4381. FADDEN, JOHN (KA-HON-HES). The persecuted Iroquois; n.d. 1 pc.

Three-step woodcut. Reinterpretation of Chagall's(?) Christ. [4021]

4382. FADDEN, RAY (AREN AKWEKS). Correspondence with Paul A. W. Wallace; Mar. 20, 1947–Jan. 23, 1967. T. and A.L.S. *ca.* 450L.

Re: publications; the Six Nations; Akwesasne Mohawks; personal matters; etc. [4021(2,3)]

4383. FADDEN, RAY (AREN AKWEKS). Stories for good children and bad; Nov. 23, 1962. T.D. 12 pp. c.c. In English.

Includes: "How an Indian punished his children," "Why the Bear Clan knows the medicine," and "Why the hermit thrush is so shy." [4021(3)]

4384. FADDEN, RAY (AREN AKWEKS). The visions of Handsome Lake; Apr. 1955. T.D. *ca.* 75 pp.

An interpretation of Fadden's wampum belt. Includes two drawings by John Fadden. [4021(3)]

4385. FENTON, WILLIAM N. Collecting materials for a political history of the Six Nations; 1948. T.D. 14 pp. c.c.

Re: published and manuscript sources relating to the history of political institutions and laws of the Six Nations, particularly with regard to ethnological sources; procedural methods to reach the desired goal; expected results. Published in *Proc. Amer. Philos. Soc.* 93 (1949): pp. 233-238. [4021(3)]

4386. FENTON, WILLIAM N. Correspondence with Paul A. W. Wallace; Apr. 6, 1945–Mar. 23, 1965. T.L. and L.S., A.L.S. *ca.* 200 pp.

Re: the Six Nations; different versions of the Deganawidah legend; meanings of Indian names; archeological work in the area to be flooded by the Kinzua Dam; political history of the Iroquois; Seth Newhouse; publications, research, fieldwork; etc. [4021(3)]

4387. FENTON, WILLIAM N. A newsletter to the Second Conference on Iroquois Research; 1946. Ditto of T.D. 9 pp.

Tentative program and list of persons expected to attend. [170(30)]

4388. FREEMAN, JOHN F. Correspondence with Paul A. W. Wallace; Nov. 3–Dec. 22, 1961. T.L.S. 5 pp.

Re: Ray Fadden and the Akwesasne Mohawk Counsellor Organization. Mentions Seth Newhouse, Bernice Loft, and Edward Ahenakew. [4021(3)]

4388*a*. GABOR, RAY, and ROBERT GABOR. Handsome Lake drawings; 1952. 3 pcs.

Includes: "The Three Messengers appear to Handsome Lake"; "Handsome Lake preaching in the Long House"; "The Great Feather Dance." [4020*b*(3)]

4389. GABOR, ROBERT (SAGOTAOALA). Correspondence with Paul A. W. Wallace; June 23, 1954–Aug. 30, 1955. T.L.S. 22 pp.

Re: Gabor's interest in and research on the effects of the adoption complex on the Iroquois Confederacy; his art work for Ray Fadden; circumstances under which the Delawares entered the League; etc. [4021(3)]

4390. GENERAL, ALEXANDER (CHIEF DESKAHEH), Letters from Paul A. W. Wallace to; Sept. 11, 1940–Nov. 3, 1955. T.L. 4 pp.

Re: the identity of a Mohawk chief; meaning of some names; Wallace's trip for the Seventh Annual Pageant at Ohnedagowah. [4021(3)]

4391. GENERAL, EMILY. Correspondence with Paul A. W. Wallace; Sept. 19, 1952–Oct. 20, 1959. T. and A.L.S. 12 pp.

Re: possible genealogical studies of chiefs of the Six Nations; the annual pageant at Ohnedagowah; vital statistics of Deskaheh (Hi-wyi-iss, Levi General). [4021(3)]

4392. GRAYMONT, BARBARA. Primary sources relating to the Iroquois in the American Revolution; n.d. T.D. 9 pp.

Includes: locations of manuscript collections and summary of contents of the more notable items; some published manuscript collections; an abstract, "The Border War: The Iroquois in the American Revolution." [10(72)]

Donor, grantee, 1969.

4393. GRIDLEY, MARION E. Correspondence with Paul A. W. Wallace; Mar. 7, 1953–June 1955. T.L. and L.S. 7 pp.

Re: *The Amerindian: American Indian Review;* a picture of Maria Tallchief; role of the Delawares, Tuscaroras, and Oneidas in the American Revolution. [4021(4)]

4394. GROSSMAN, JULIAN A. One lying across: Lewis Henry Morgan. The birth of American ethnology; 1965. T.D. 29 pp., ill.

Re: Morgan's interest in and study of the Iroquois. Some details of development of Morgan's interest. [4011]

Donor, author, 1966.

4395. GUTHE, ALFRED R. Correspondence with Paul A. W. Wallace; Aug. 22–Nov. 9, 1955. T.L. and L.S. 6 pp.

Re: old photos of Iroquois costumes in the Rochester Museum of Arts and Sciences. [4021(4)]

4396. HORSFORD, EBEN NORTON. Letter to John W. Jordan; Cambridge, Oct. 7, 1892. A.L.S. 1 p.

Expresses appreciation for the Onondaga grammar. Discusses census of the Iroquois. [9]

4397. Interview with Chief William Dewaseragech Loft; Dec. 1942. T. and A.D. 46 pp.

Re: the Six Nations. [4021(7)]

4397*a*. Iroquois; 1913, 1934, 1939, 1949-1952, n.d. 93 pcs.

Pictures include: Iroquois (Seneca and Upper Cayuga) longhouses, Six Nations Reserve, Ontario; Ray Fadden (Aren Akweks), his son (John Fadden), scenes of the Lake George (New York) Indian Village; men in false faces (oil painting by Frank G. Speck); Six Nations portraits (Charles A. Cooke, Chief Joseph Logan, Mrs. Joseph Logan, John Alexander, Chief David Thomas); wampum beads used in the Tutelo adoption rite; wampum belts from the Six Nations Reserve, Ontario, and Oka, P. Q.; Huron silkwork; a Huron with birch-bark canoe. [4020*b*(2),(4),(7),(10),(13:2)]

4398. JAMES, EDWARD T. Correspondence with Paul A. W. Wallace; Feb. 28–Mar. 27, 1961. T.L.S. 4 pp.

Re: biographical sketch of Madam Montour for *Notable American Women, 1607-1950.* [4021(6)]

4399. JAMIESON, M. J. Correspondence with Paul A. W. Wallace; Oct. 12, 1956–Jan. 15, 1957. A. and T.L.S. 6 pp.

Re: attendance by Wallace at the Condolence to the Dead and the Great Feast for the Dead. [4021(6)]

4400. LOFT, BERNICE M. (DAWENDINE). Correspondence with Paul A. W. Wallace; [Dec. 1936]–Sept. 1937. T.L. and A.L.S. 8L.

Re: the Six Nations; the health of her father, Chief William Loft (Mohawk). [4021(7)]

4401. MAD BEAR. Correspondence with Paul A. W. Wallace; Aug. 29–Sept. 3, 1959. A.L.S., T.L. 3 pp.

Re: a parcel of land in Philadelphia reportedly owned by the Six Nations. [4021(7)]

4402. MILLER, P. SCHUYLER. Correspondence with Paul A. W. Wallace; May 6-12, 1946. T.L.S. and L. 3 pp.

Re: the Deganawidah legend. [4021(7)]

4403. MONTOUR, E. T. Correspondence with Paul A. W. Wallace; Apr.–May 1952. A. and T.L. and L.S. 9 pp.

Re: the Handsome Lake religion. [4021(8)]

4404. MONTOUR, ETHEL BRANT. Correspondence with Paul A. W. Wallace; Oct.

1, 1951–June 17, 1955. T. and A.L. and L.S. 28 pp.

Re: the Six Nations; the Brant and Montour families. [4021(8)]

4405. NEWHOUSE, SETH. Letter to Arthur C. Parker; Ka-ryen-geh P.O., Brant County, Ont., Canada, Nov. 11, 1913. Photocopy of A.L.S. 2 pp.

Requests return of his manuscript history of the "Five Nations Union" for correction and reading before the Privy and General Councils of Mohawk chiefs. Requests twelve copies of the circular about the "society of American Indians." [9]

*Cf.* No. 4408.

4405*a*. NEWHOUSE, SETH. Mohawk-Onondaga; 1897, *ca.* 1914, n.d. 4 pcs.

Includes: photographs of Seth Newhouse by J.N.B. Hewitt, by John Brostup after F. W. Waugh, and by Arthur C. Parker (postal card); part of a letter from Seth Newhouse to J.N.B. Hewitt. All but Parker photograph published in William N. Fenton, "Seth Newhouse's Traditional History and Constitution of the Iroquois Confederacy," *Proc. Amer. Philos. Soc.* 93, 2 (1949): pp. 141-158. [4016*a*(A:In22P)]

4406. PARKER, ARTHUR C. Correspondence with Paul A. W. Wallace; Sept. 1936–Aug. 1954. T.L. and L.S. 39L.

Re: the Six Nations; Conrad Weiser. [4021(9)]

4407. PARKER, ARTHUR C. Letter to Frank G. Speck, Philadelphia; Rochester, Nov. 10, 1945. T.L.S. 1 p.

Re: Speck's "The Iroquois and their Cultural Development"; Paul A. W. Wallace's work on Conrad Weiser; the Iroquois seminar at Allegany State Park. [170(27)]

4408. PARKER, ARTHUR C. Letter to Seth Newhouse, Ontario, Canada; Albany, N.Y., Nov. 20, 1913. Photocopy of T.L. 1 p.

Promises to send the manuscript and circulars requested in No. 4405 and suggests starting a "Society of Canadian Indians." From original in the archives of the New York State Museum and Science Service. [9]

4409. PARKER, ELY S. List of "errors" concerning the League of the Iroquois; n.d. A.D. 1 p.

Apparently suggested corrections to a manuscript. [135]

4410. PARKER, ELY S. Short essays; n.d. A.D. 4L.

Re: Iroquois religion and political organization. [135]

4411. RICHMOND, DONALD. Correspondence with Paul A. W. Wallace; Dec. 8-10, 1958. T.L.S. 2 pp.

Re: copying the Seth Newhouse version of Deganawidah sent to the St. Regis Mohawks. [4021(9)]

4412. RITCHIE, WILLIAM A. Correspondence with Paul A. W. Wallace; July 26, 1947–Apr. 26, 1948. A.L.S., T.L. and L.S. 12L.

Re: a meeting at the American Philosophical Society; Indian trails in the Delaware Valley; the probable date of the founding of the Five Nations Confederacy. [4021(9)]

4413. SERRES, JOHN. Correspondence with Paul A. W. Wallace; Sept. 22–Dec. 15, 1961. A. and T.L.S. 10 pp.

Re: the dedication of an Iroquois monument at Scarboro, Ontario; attempts to preserve Native culture. [4021(9)]

4414. Six Nations journal; 1936, 1937, 1955. T.D. 60 pp.

Includes: notes on interviews with Nick Peters, Chief Joseph Montour, J.N.B. Hewitt, Isaiah Williams, Chief Hess, Chief William Loft, Alec General, and Jerry Aaron. [4021(10)]

4415. SNYDERMAN, GEORGE S. Ethnohistory: amalgam of anthropology and history; *ca.* 1952. T.D. 19 pp.

Re: the interest of the American Philosophical Society in the American Indian; the method used by historians to evaluate source materials; value of fieldwork; the Parker Collection at the American Philosophical Society; availability of materials pertaining to Indian studies at the Historical Society of Pennsylvania, the Quaker Historical Association, and the Haverford College Library. [9]

4416. WALLACE, ANTHONY F. C. Cornplanter's talk—cosmogony, history of relations with Whites; n.d. Photo. 5 pp.

Transcript of document (*ca.* 1822) in the Draper Collection, Princeton University. Includes a one-page letter from "MHD" with some corrections to the transcript. [4021(1)]

4417. WALLACE, PAUL A. W. De-Ka-Nah-Wi-Deh; *ca.* 1961. T. and A.D., T.L.S. *ca.* 50 pcs.

Re: biography written for the *Dictionary of Canadian Biography.* Includes: draft of the article; correspondence; etc. [4021(10)]

4418. WALLACE, PAUL A. W. The Iroquois: a brief outline of their history; n.d. T. and A.D. 45 pp.

Includes: notes and draft of an article. [4021(11)]

4419. WALLACE, PAUL A. W. Letters to Jesse J. Cornplanter; Mar. 24–Sept. 8, 1952. T.L. 5 pp.

Re: the purchase of drawings from Cornplanter. [4021(1)]

4420. WALLACE, PAUL A. W. The return of Hiawatha; n.d. T.D. *ca.* 30 pp.

Re: reasons for Iroquois ascendancy. [4021(11)]

4421. WARGON, ALLAN. Letter to Paul A. W. Wallace; Nov. 5, 1951. T.L.S. 1 p.

Re: the film "The Longhouse People." [4021(11)]

4422. WILSON, PETER. Talk given before the New York Historical Society; May 28, 1847. A.D. 2 pp.

An abstract by Ely S. Parker: contrasts the part played by the Iroquois in the development and history of New York with their unhappy position in the mid-nineteenth century. [135]

4423. WINSLOW, BERNICE LOFT (DAWENDINE) (MRS. ARTHUR H.) Correspondence with Paul A. W. Wallace; June 22, 1943–May 4, 1956. A.L.S., T.L., T.D. 81 pp.

Re: the Six Nations; publications; etc. Includes some of Mrs. Winslow's poetry. [4021(11)]

4424. WOOLEY, PETER. Receipt to James Burd; July 18, 1767. 1 pc.

On the account of John Penn for purchase of vermilion for the use of the Six Nation Indians. [33]

4425. WYLER, BARBARA. Report on grant to study Iroquois masks; Sept. 14, 1964. T.L.S. to Richard H. Shryock. 4 pp. c.c.

Reports lack of success in obtaining information on masks during field trip; indicates change of topic to cultural change among the Seneca. [10(34)]

## JICARILLA

(Navajo D.)

4426. HAILE, FATHER BERARD, OFM, coll. Jicarilla texts; n.d. T. and A.D. *ca.* 250 pp.

Texts with free and interlinear literal English translations. [4012(1)]

*Cf.* No. 4427.

4427. HAILE, FATHER BERARD, OFM, coll. Jicarilla texts: fieldnotes; n.d. A.D. 5 notebooks of *ca.* 60L. each.

Includes: texts in Jicarilla; interlinear English translation; many explanatory notes of ethnographic interest; notes added by "J.J.V." [4012(2)]

*Cf.* No. 4426.

4428. HAILE, FATHER BERARD, OFM, comp. Jicarilla texts in translation; n.d. D. *ca.* 100L.

Free translation of Jicarilla texts collected by the compiler. Translation is keyed to page numbers in No. 4427 for pp. 17-242 and 248-250. [4012(3)]

4429. HAILE, FATHER BERARD, OFM. Pliny Earle Goddard's Jicarilla texts rewritten; n.d. D. 1 notebook of *ca.* 70L.

Reworking and addition of pitches to Goddard's (1911) texts numbers 22 and 80 with some differences in transcription and translation. [4012(4)]

4430. HOIJER, HARRY, coll. Jicarilla texts (#1); n.d. T.D. *ca.* 350 pp.

Texts are the same as in No. 4433. [4012(7)]

4431. HOIJER, HARRY. Jicarilla texts (#2); n.d. T.D. and photocopy of T.D. *ca.* 250 pp.

Includes: texts; photocopies of the texts; literal translations. Jicarilla texts are same as those in No. 4430, but in a more modern orthography. [4012(8)]

4432. HOIJER, HARRY. Jicarilla texts (#3); n.d. A.D. *ca.* 250 pp.

Apparently a transcription in preparation for typing No. 4431. [4012(21)]

4433. HOIJER, HARRY, coll. Jicarilla texts; fieldnotes; 1934. A.D. 5 notebooks of 60L. each.

Includes: texts in Jicarilla with interlinear English translation; explanatory notes of ethnographic interest. [4012(9)]

## JIVARO

### (Andean-Equatorial)

4434. HARRINGTON, JOHN P. Jibaro epitome; n.d. T.D. 12 pp.

Re: the orthography used in the grammar by Father Juan Ghinassi; the name *Jibaro;* the accent in *Jivaro.* [4017(ling.#2)]

## KERES

### (language isolate)

4436. BEALS, RALPH. Quote from Alegre with comments; Oct. 1933. Photocopy of T.D. 1 p.

Reference mentioned in No. 4455. [137]

4437. BOAS, FRANZ. Letter to Edward Sapir; May 7, 1926. Photocopy of T.L.S. 1 p.

Re: financial support of White's fieldwork; possible alternatives to working at Acoma. [137]

4438. DAVIS, IRVINE, comp. Preliminary material for an Acoma (Keresan) dictionary; n.d. T.D. 137 pp.

Acoma-English. Based on data from compiler's field notes and from Wick Miller, *Acoma Grammar and Texts.* [10(69)]

Donor, grantee, Feb. 1969.

4439. MARING, JOEL, coll. Acoma Keresan texts; 1959, n.d. D. 228 pp.

Includes: Acoma texts, most with English translation; sixty-two sentences given in each of: Acoma, Laguna, Zia, Santa Ana, San Felipe, Santo Domingo, and Cochiti for comparison; translations of Keresan stories. [10(13)]

Donor, grantee.

4440. PARSONS, ELSIE CLEWS. Letter to Mischa Titiev; May 7, 1941. Photocopy of T.L.S. 1 p.

Re: White's and Stirling's Acoma manuscripts. [137]

4441. PARSONS, ELSIE CLEWS. Letter to Edward Sapir; December 26, 1925. Photocopy of A.L.S. 2 pp.

Re: possible fieldwork by White on Acoma; financial support thereof. [137]

4442. PARSONS, ELSIE CLEWS. Letter to Leslie A. White; May 17, 1926. Photocopy of A.L.S. 2 pp.

Re: White's Acoma fieldwork; financing thereof; difficulty of getting Acoma informants; requests that he cultivate any Isletan he finds. [137]

4443. PARSONS, ELSIE CLEWS. Letter to Leslie A. White; May 27, 1926. Photocopy of A.L.S. 4 pp.

Re: difficulty of getting Acoma, San Felipe, and Santo Domingo informants; necessity of working with informant away from his town. Suggests Pima as an alternative. Mentions Sapir and Boas. [137]

4444. PARSONS, ELSIE CLEWS. Letter to Leslie A. White; June 3, 1926. Photocopy of A.L.S. 2 pp.

Re: Acoma fieldwork; publications sent (Laguna, Zuni); picking out Keresan ceremonial terms to encourage informants; caution against letting any Pueblo Indian see the publications. Asks for outlines of Acoma material as he gets it. [137]

4445. PARSONS, ELSIE CLEWS. Letter to Leslie A. White; June 18, 1926. Photocopy of A.L.S. 2 pp.

Re: Acoma fieldwork; request for outline of data obtained, using Keresan terms where possible, so that she can give further direction. [137]

4446. PARSONS, ELSIE CLEWS. Letters to Leslie A. White; July 14 and 31, 1926. Photocopy of A.L.S. 2 pp.

Re: financial support of White's fieldwork. [137]

4447. PARSONS, ELSIE CLEWS. Letter to Leslie A. White; July 17, 1926. Photocopy of A.L.S. 7 pp.

Re: Acoma fieldwork; characteristics which seem to be peculiar to Acoma; prayer sticks; prediction; war chiefs and *opi* or scalptakers; maps; Corn people's ceremony; ceremonial functions of other clans; medicine societies; ceremonial calendar; possibility of a Mother *(yaya)*; Kachina organization; mask design. [137]

4448. PARSONS, ELSIE CLEWS. Letter to Leslie A. White; Aug. 8, 1926. Photocopy of A.L.S. 6 pp.

Re: financial support; necessity of comparative study particularly in Pueblo work; painting of Fire and Hunt societies; Water people (Isleta); tobacco; crystal for second sight; Winock rag ball with corn grains (also used at Laguna); offerings to stillborn and dead (in general); *Kabina* medicine society (also at Laguna); *estufa* and comparison to Zuñi use; how *cazique* (town chief) is chosen; succession to office in medicine societies. [137]

4449. PARSONS, ELSIE CLEWS. Letter to Leslie A. White; Aug. 23, 1926. Photocopy of A.L.S. 2 pp.

Re: White's notes; choice of *cazique* by the Antelope clan; whether *cazique* is an Antelope; whether Antelope clan has a special relation to the *Kachina* cult (as suggested at Laguna). [137]

4450. PARSONS, ELSIE CLEWS. Letter to Leslie A. White; October 8, 1926. Photocopy of A.L.S. 2 pp.

Re: possible publications of White's Acoma monograph. [137]

4451. PARSONS, ELSIE CLEWS. Letter to Leslie A. White; Oct. 22, 1926. Photocopy of T.L.S. 1 p.

Re: meeting White in Chicago to review his Acoma manuscript before she goes to New Mexico. [137]

4452. PARSONS, ELSIE CLEWS. Letter to Leslie A. White; Oct. 5, 1927. Photocopy of A.L.S. 2 pp.

Re: Laguna report; trip to the Keres; Acoma summary or comparative Keres for the meeting of the American Anthropological Association. [137]

4453. PARSONS, ELSIE CLEWS. Letter to Leslie A. White; May 3, 1930. Photocopy of T.L.S. 3 pp.

Re: White's San Felipe manuscript; pictures of San Felipe prayer sticks collected by Kidder; her collecting Taos folk tales and an account of social organization from three groups of informants. [137]

4454. PARSONS, ELSIE CLEWS. Letter to Leslie A. White; Aug. 28, 1933. Photocopy of T.L.S. 3 pp.

Re: White's Santo Domingo manuscript; archeological evidence for Kachina masks in the fourteenth or fifteenth century; Aztec use of masks; Kachina cult in Sahagun; paper on Aztec-Pueblo parallels. [137]

4455. PARSONS, ELSIE CLEWS. Letter to Leslie A. White; Oct. 10, 1933. Photocopy of T.L.S. 4 pp.

Re: identifying White's Keresan mask *Nyenyek'a* with reference in Alegre (1841); White's Santo Domingo manuscript; *Gowawaima Kachina* from Mexico; destruction of masks during the great rebellion; *gowatcanyi* (in Mexico, *topiles*); picture of the Santo Domingo *Koshare.* [137]

*Cf.* No. 4436.

4456. PARSONS, ELSIE CLEWS. Letter to Leslie A. White; [before Mar. 14, 1934]. Photocopy of A.L.S. 2 pp.

Re: White's Zia paper; proposed laboratory bulletin on Spanish sources. Mentions Kroeber. [137]

4457. PARSONS, ELSIE CLEWS. Letter to Leslie A. White; July 27, 1935. Photocopy of T.L.S. 2 pp.

Re: Acoma and the "autobiography." [137]

4458. PARSONS, ELSIE CLEWS. Letter to Leslie A. White; Dec. 14, 1935. Photocopy of T.L.S. 2 pp.

Re: Santa Ana paper; Acoma papers; "An Autobiographic Sketch" and comments. [137]

4459. PARSONS, ELSIE CLEWS. Letter to Leslie A. White; Aug. 3, 1937. Photocopy of A.L.S. 3 pp.

Re: Stirling's Acoma manuscript; suggestion that she, White, and Boas edit it. [137]

4460. PARSONS, ELSIE CLEWS. Letter to Leslie A. White; April 23, 1938. Photocopy of T.L.S. 1 p.

Re: the possibility of finding a Keresan reference (particularly Acoma) other than Laguna for laying out a deer as if it were a dead person. [137]

4461. PARSONS, ELSIE CLEWS. Letter to Leslie A. White; May 27, 1938. Photocopy of T.L.S. 1 p.

Re: the Stirling manuscript; work on it by Parsons and Boas; White's Acoma manuscript; two papers on ethnobotany by Jones. [137]

4462. PARSONS, ELSIE CLEWS. Letter to Leslie A. White, [1938?]. Photocopy of T.L.S. 1 p.

Re: Acoma manuscripts; translation of Acoma songs collected by Boas; letter from Stirling. [137]

4463. PARSONS, ELSIE CLEWS. Letter to Leslie A. White; Jan. 6, 1939. Photocopy of T.L.S. 1 p.

Re: Stirling's Acoma manuscript; White's Zia manuscript; Santa Ana prospects. Mentions Boas and Spier. [137]

4464. PARSONS, ELSIE CLEWS. Letter to Leslie A. White; Sept. 15, 1940. Photocopy of A.L.S. on postal card. 1 p.

Re: book on Keres; Santa Ana manuscript; field notes on Andean Indians of Ecuador. [137]

4465. PARSONS, ELSIE CLEWS. Letter to Leslie A. White; Jan. 16, 1941. Photocopy of T.L.S. 2 pp.

Re: White's Santa Ana monograph and cutting down size for publication; White's memoirs on San Felipe and Santo Domingo. [137]

4466. PARSONS, ELSIE CLEWS. Letter to Leslie A. White; Jan. 30, 1941. Photocopy of T.L.S. 2 pp.

Re: White's Santa Ana monograph; myths; tales. Mentions Linton and Archer Taylor. [137]

4467. PARSONS, ELSIE CLEWS. Letter to Leslie A. White; Apr. 14, 1941. Photocopy of T.L.S. 1 p.

Re: fake Acoma *cacique;* work on Acoma manuscript; Stirling. [137]

4468. PARSONS, ELSIE CLEWS. Letter to Leslie A. White; May 17, 1941. Photocopy of T.L.S. 1 p.

Re: lists of fauna (Acoma and Santa Ana); illustrations for the Acoma manuscript. [137]

4469. PARSONS, ELSIE CLEWS. Letter to Leslie A. White; June 20, 1941. Photocopy of T.L.S. on postal card. 1 p.

Re: Santa Ana; possibility of publishing Stevenson collection. [137]

4470. KURATH, GERTRUDE P., comp. Songs by Celestino Quintana, Cochiti Pueblo: Keresan recording; n.d. T.D. with sheet music. 23L.

Transcription of songs with brief discussion of choreography, music, and similarities between Hopi and Keresan styles. [9]

*Cf.* No. 275.

## KOKAMA
### (Equatorial)

4471. HARRINGTON, JOHN P. Cocama epitome; n.d. T.D. 5 pp.

Gives phonetic inventory and discusses some features of phonetics, nouns, and pronouns without any examples. [4017(ling. #2)]

## KWAKIUTL

(Wakashan)

4472. BOAS, FRANZ. Indian legends of the North Pacific coast of North America; 1974. Photocopy of T.D. 600 pp.

Legends in English from the German translation of Chinook Jargon, Kwakiutl, Tsimshian, and Shuswap. Translated by Deitrich Bertz from the original edition (see Boas 1895). Permission necessary for reproduction. [30(74)]

Donor, British Columbia Indian Language Project, Jan. 1975.

## LIPAN

(Navajo D.)

4473. HOIJER, HARRY. The history and customs of the Lipan, as told by Augustina Zuazua; 1975 and n.d. T.D. 14 pp., and one offprint.

Offprint of and part of draft for an article in *Linguistics* **161**: pp. 5-38. [4012(21)]

4474. HOIJER, HARRY. Lipan Apache: fieldnotes; n.d. A.D. 1 notebook of *ca.* 60L.

Lipan texts with interlinear English translation. [4012(10)]

4475. Lipan texts; n.d. T.D. 8 pp.

Three short texts in Lipan with literal English translation. [4012(21)]

## LOCONO

(Equatorial)

4476. SCHULZ, THEODORE. Letter to Peter S. Du Ponceau, Philadelphia; Schoeneck, Sept. 25, 1821. Photocopy of A.L.S. 3 pp., and add., end.

Re: men's and women's speech in the Arawak language. From original in the College of Physicians, Philadelphia. [9]

## LOUCHEUX

(Athapascan)

4477. HOIJER, HARRY, coll. Loucheux recordings; n.d. 4 reels of tape.

Words and brief phrases given in response to English. [4067*a*]

## MAINE

4478. SPECK, FRANK G. Letter to Charles E. Bond, White Plains, N.Y.; Nov. 3, 1925. T.L. 1 p. cc.

Re: references for information on the Indians of Maine. Mentions Chief Frances and A. V. Kidder. [170(26)]

## MALECITE

(Passamaquoddy D.)

4479. SZABO, LASZLO, coll. Malecite stories; n.d. 6 reels of tape.

Recording No. 85. [4089]

*Cf.* No. 4480.
Donor, grantee, 1972.

4480. SZABO, LASZLO, coll. Malecite stories; n.d. 3 reels of tape.

Recording No. 102. [4090]

*Cf.* No. 4479.
Donor, grantee, May 1975.

## MAM

(Mayan)

4481. CANGER, UNA. Report on a study of the Todos Santos dialect of Mam. T.D.S. 2 pp.

Re: fieldwork in Todos Santos, Guatemala. [10(57)]

4482. SIMEON, GEORGE. Letter to Whitfield J. Bell, Jr., Philadelphia; Waimea, Kauai, Hawaii, Sept. 21, 1972. T.L.S. 2 pp.

Brief list of materials recorded in Pocomam Central, Mam, and Xinca. [10(126)]

*Cf.* No. 4483.

4483. SIMEON, GEORGE, coll. Mam, Xinca, and Pocomam Central linguistics; n.d. 1 cassette tape. Recording No. 91.

A portion of the material which he collected in Guatemala. [4084]

*Cf.* Nos. 4482, 4684, 4914.
Donor, grantee, Oct. 1972.

## MANDAN

### (Siouan)

4484. BOWERS, ALFRED W., coll. Mandan-Hidatsa cultural change and language studies; 1967-1972. 11 reels of tape. Recording No. 84.

Includes: texts, vocabulary, etc.; letter to Whitfield J. Bell, Jr.; table of contents. [4053]

*Cf.* No. 4485.
Donor, grantee, 1972.

4485. BOWERS, ALFRED W., coll. Mandan-Hidatsa ethnohistory and linguistics, Fort Berthold Reservation; 1967-1969. 19 reels of tape. Recording No. 81.

Includes: texts; vocabulary; some translations; table of contents. [4054]

*Cf.* No. 4484.
Donor, grantee.

4486. HOLLOW, ROBERT C., JR. A Mandan dictionary; 1970. Photocopy of T.D. 496 pp.

Mandan-English and English-Mandan. In the Mandan-English section, Mandan forms are listed by underlying phonological form. Includes: sketch on phonology; section on grammatical morphemes. [10(92)]

Donor, grantee, Sept. 1970.

## MARATIN

### (Uto-Aztecan)

4487. Maratin; Mar. 8-25, 1925. D. 22 pcs.

Includes: letter from William E. W. MacKinlay to J. Alden Mason; Maratin song and fragment as given by Fr. Santa Maria with Spanish and English interlinear translations; a Tonkawa word list with English glosses (mostly names of other tribes); Mason's reply. [4017(C23)]

## MASSACHUSETT

### (Algonquian)

4488. AMERICAN PHILOSOPHICAL SOCIETY LIBRARY COMMITTEE. Report on the loan of the Eliot Indian Bible to A. J. Holman and Co.; 1876. 1 p. and end.

Recommendation that the loan of the Eliot Indian Bible be approved. Committee: D.S.B.H. Coates, Eli K. Price, George H. Horn. [3]

4489. BEVER, MARION G. (MRS. MICHAEL). Letter to Frank G. Speck, Philadelphia; Salt Lake City, Jan. 29, 1938. T.L.S. 1 p.

Requests references on the Indians around Mashpee, Mass. Mentions Simeon L. Deyo, *History of Barnstable County* and Mary Farwell Ayer, *Richard Bourne, Missionary to the Mashpee Indians.* [170(30)]

4490. EAMES, WILBURFORCE. Letter to Isaac Minis Hayes [*sic*]; New York, February 4, 1899. T.L.S. 1 p.

Sending copy of his monograph on the Eliot Indian Bible. [3]

4490*a*. Eliot Oak; 1925. 1 photograph.

Photograph by H. Hey(?) showing the white oak where John Eliot preached to the Indians, Brookline, Massachusetts. [4016*a*(B)]

4491. HOLMAN, A. J., and CO. Correspondence; Feb. 17–Mar. 28, 1876. L. 5 pp.

Re: the loan of the Eliot Indian Bible to the company for display at the Centennial Exposition. Includes letters to: the American Philosophical Society; J. Peter Lesley; Joseph Carson; and Eli K. Price. [3]

4491*a*. Narraganset and Wampanoag; 1870, 1885, n.d. 11 pcs.

Pictures include: Narragansets Henry Harris, Jim Harris, Abigail Maumee(?), Rachel Maumee(?), unidentified woman and child; Wampanoags Simon Thompson (Gay Head, Mass.), *Ti•wi•lí•ma* "Child of Woods" and two unidentified women (Betty's Neck, Mass.), unidentified man. [4020*b*(6),(10)]

4492. PRICE, ELI KIRK. Letter to Benjamin Hornor Coates; Mar. 31, 1876. A.L.S. 1 p.

Regarding the loan of the Eliot Indian Bible. Mentions G. H. Horn. [3]

4493. SPECK, FRANK G. Letter to Mrs. Charles Ryan, Gay Head, Mass.; May 3, 1928. T.L. 1 p. cc.

Re: accommodations for Speck and family while Speck works with the Gay Head Indians (Martha's Vineyard). [170(26)]

4494. WELSH, JOHN. Letter to the American Philosophical Society; Mar. 25, 1876. A.L.S. 1 p.

Letter of recommendation certifying the trustworthiness of A. J. Holman & Co. in regard to the loan of the Eliot Indian Bible. [3]

## MATLATZINCA

### (Otomian)

4495. BARTHOLOMEW, DORIS. Matlatzinca; n.d. T.D. 44 pp.

Re: phonology with considerable emphasis on tones. Includes: reproduction of visual displays of pitch and intensity; lists of verbs with Spanish and English translations; texts with interlinear Spanish translation. [10(53)]

Donor, grantee.

4496. BARTHOLOMEW, DORIS, coll. Matlatzinca verbs; 1966. 2 reels of tape. Recording No. 60.

Includes: verb paradigms; texts; translation of an Otomi primer. Informant: Ezequiel Hernández. [4048]

Donor, grantee.

## MAYA

### (Mayan)

4497. BAER, PHILLIP, and WILLIAM R. MERRIFIELD. Lacandone subsistence and culinary arts; the recent history of the Southern Lacandones; n.d. T.D. *ca.* 275 pp. cc.

Re: social context; physical context; daily round; yearly round; agriculture; means and methods of food preparation; gathering; hunting and fishing; domestic animals; wine and drunkenness; household furnishings; tools; history covering the past one hundred years; kinship. [10(73)]

Donors, grantees, 1969.

4498. HELLMUTH, NICHOLAS M. Some notes on the Ytza, Quejache, Verapaz Chol, and Toquegua Maya: a progress report on ethnohistory research conducted in Seville, Spain, June–August 1971; 1971. Mimeograph of T.D. and L.S., photo. 60 pcs.

Re: population; distribution; settlements; government; kinship and marriage; subsistence; religion. Includes: outline of a descriptive ethnography of the Cholti-Lacandon Maya of the settlement of Sac Balam . . . , Chiapas, Mexico. [10(115)]

Donor, grantee, Nov. 1971.

## MAYAN

4498*a*. ADAMS, WALTER RANDOLPH. Religious practices of southeastern Chiapas, Mexico; 1976-1977, n.d. T.D., c.c. of T.D., photocopy of D., T.L.S., photographs. *ca.* 425 pcs.

Includes: discussion and photographs of religious pilgrimages and concomitant religious practices; discussion of prayers (with emphasis on the *Rezo Tzeltal*), the cargo system, and the Coxoh colonial project; report on pilgrimages by the Tzeltal and Tojolabal; copies of papers on the Coxoh (Chicomuceltec) coauthored by Thomas A. Lee, Jr., and Sidney D. Markham (given at the Society for Historic Archaeology and the Forty-second International Congress of Americanists); transcripts of Spanish manuscripts; field notes. [10(162),(162*a*),(162*b*)]

*Cf.* Nos. 4047*a*, 4498*b*.
Donor, grantee.

4498*b*. ADAMS, WALTER R., coll. Recordings concerning religious practices of southeastern Chiapas, Mexico; 1977. 7 cassette tapes. Recording No. 108.

Informants include: Tzeltal: Francisco Calvo Perez-Romerias; Tojolabal: Hermalindo Jimenez; probable Tzeltal: Jose Hernandez, Ramiro Garcia, and Francisco Aguilar. [4047*a*]

*Cf.* No. 4498*a*.
Donor, grantee, Nov. 1977.

4498*c*. ANDRADE, MANUEL J. Correspondence with John Alden Mason; 1930-1939. T.L. and L.S. 6 pp.

Re: Andrade's work on Maya and Huastec; Mason's query concerning subgrouping of Mayan languages. [4017(C7)]

4499. ARCHIVO GENERAL DE INDIAS, SEVILLE: Reina-Jimenez Collection; n.d. 129 reels of film. Film No. 1337.

Re: post-conquest social and cultural processes in Guatemala. From originals in the AGI, Seville. [4024]

Donor, Ruben E. Reina, Dec. 1974.

4500. John Alden Mason photographs: Mexico (Mayan) photographs; 1917. Prints, negatives. ca. 120 pcs.

Re: Uxmal, Chichen Itza, etc. [4017]

## MAZATEC

### (Popolocan)

4501. KIRK, PAUL L. The development of Jalapa Mazatec voiced aspirantes; 1969. Photocopy of T.D. 9 pp.

Paper presented at the meeting of the Linguistic Society of America, Dec. 29-31, San Francisco, California. [10(104)]

Donor, grantee.

## MESCALERO

### (Navajo D.)

4502. HOIJER, HARRY, coll. Chiricahua and Mescalero texts: fieldnotes; 1934. D. 1 notebook of *ca.* 60L.

Includes: texts; translations. Labeled number VII in the series described in No. 4176. [4012(6)]

4503. HOIJER, HARRY, coll. Mescalero texts: fieldnotes (#1); n.d. D. 3 notebooks of *ca.* 60L. each.

Texts in Mescalero, some with English translation. Informants include: Sam Chino, Horace Torres, Leon Pariko, Arnold K., and John Shanta. [4012(11)]

4504. HOIJER, HARRY, coll. Mescalero texts: fieldnotes (#2); 1934. D. 2 notebooks of 46L. each.

Texts with interlinear English translations. Informant: Charles Smith(?). [4012(12)]

## MEXICO

4504*a*. ABBOT, G. E. Photographs of Mexican and Central American antiquities; n.d. 123 photographs.

Re: architecture and people. Photographs identified with the following groups and places: Museum of Mexico, Tula, Teotihuacan, Iztaccihuatl, Oaxaca, Chichen Itza, Tabasco, Comalcalco, Yucatan, Palenque, Aztec, · Toltec, Lacandon, Yucatec, Maya, Mixtec, etc. [Call No. 913.72:Ab23]

4504*b*. BOAS, FRANZ, coll. Language data; n.d. A.D. 1 notebook, 22 pp.

Includes: Chatino vocabulary and texts; Nahuatl vocabulary; discussion of Spanish elements in modern Nahuatl. [4003*b*]

Donor, Northwestern University Library.

4505. BRUGGE, DAVID M. Brugge-Annon trip to Sonora; Nov. 1955. T.D. 20 pp. c.c.

Includes: log of trip; itinerary of pack trip from Yecora to Maicoba; lists of photographs; journal. [4017(ling. #1)]

4506. BRUGGE, DAVID M. Some archeological sites near Rancho Guiracoba, Sonora, Mexico; n.d. T.D. 7 pp. c.c.

Report on surface collections at six sites in southern Sonora. [4017(ling. #1)]

4507. HOWARD, AGNES MCCLAIN. Correspondence with John Alden Mason; 1948-1960. A.L.S., T.L. and L.S. *ca.* 125L.

Re: internal strife in local (Durango) Indian tribe (including murders); archaeology in Durango; collection of specimens of material culture; work at Schroeder pyramid; cliff dwellings near Mezquital. Mentions Alex Krieger. [4017(C20),(ling. #1)]

4508. HUMBOLDT, ALEXANDER VON. Letter to ———; n.d. A.L.S. with initials. 3 pp. In French.

Re: publication on Indians of Mexico. [91(H88.86)]

4509. KROEBER, ALFRED L. Letter to John Alden Mason, Philadelphia; Berkeley, Dec. 10, 1942. T.L.S. and D. 3 pp.

Re: Mason's Subtiaba-Hokan-Caduveo-Mataco comparative vocabulary. Kroeber is not much impressed with the possible resemblances in Mason's list (included). [4017(ling. #2)]

4510. LEON, NICOLAS. Familias linguisticas de Mexico: idiomas y dialectos a ellas pertencientes; n.d. T.D. 6 pp. original and 2 c.c.

A list of the families with subdivisions: for Museo nacional de arqueologia, historia y etnologia, Anales. [4017(ling. #2)]

4511. MACLURE, WILLIAM. Letter to Samuel G. Morton; Mexico, Apr. 3, 1830. A.L.S. 10 pp.

Re: the local situation; innate capabilities of the Indians; educating the Indians. Also includes a typescript (1946). [127]

4512. MASON, JOHN ALDEN. Cave investigations in Durango and Coahuila; Apr. 1963. T.D. 19 pp. c.c.

Report on search conducted with Robert H. Merrill for traces of early man, particularly on the Folsom horizon. Written for Weitlaner volume. [4017(ling. #1)]

4513. MASON, JOHN ALDEN. *Los cuatro grandes filones linguisticos de Mexico y Centroamerica;* 1939. T.D. 22 pp. c.c. In Spanish.

Two versions of a paper for the International Congress of Americanists, August 1939, Mexico. [4017(ling. #2)]

4514. MASON, JOHN ALDEN. *Cucurbita moschata* in Sonora, Mexico; n.d. T.D. 5 pp. c.c.

Includes: description of three varieties of *cucurbita moschata;* evidence in conflict with the theory that *cucurbita moschata* was introduced into southern Arizona in late prehistoric or early historic times from the north and east. [4017(ling. #1)]

4515. MASON, JOHN ALDEN. Durango expedition: photographs and list of photographs; 1935-1936. T.D. and photographs. 31 pp. and *ca.* 105 photographs.

Includes: list of photographs; *"Informes hacerca de la Sierra de la Candela";* notes from Tarayre, pp. 184-185 "Ruins of an agricultural colony near Zape"; possible routes of migration into Mexico; Everardo Gamiz "La Raza Pigmea," Durango, April 1934; an incomplete set of numbered photos enumerated in above list (all duplicates from museum set). [4017(ling. #1)]

4516. MASON, JOHN ALDEN. Mexican linguistics: comparative vocabularies, etc.; n.d. A. and T.D. 17 pp.

Includes: short comparative vocabularies for Comecrudo, Papago-Tepecano, Nahua, Huaxtec, Choctaw, Coahuiltec, Karankawa, Torkana, Atakapa, Chitimacha, Tunica; notes on Sapir's classification; other miscellaneous notes. [4017(ling. #2)]

4517. MASON, JOHN ALDEN. Notes on the northern extension of the Chalchihuites culture; Aug. 1948. T.D. 3 pp.

Written for the Mexican Historical Congress, Zacatecas. [4017(ling. #1)]

4518. MASON, JOHN ALDEN. Photographs; 1917, 1919, 1934. Prints, negatives. 102 pcs.

Re: Mexico; the Papago; a dig at Slayton Creek, Delaware. [4017]

4519. MASON, JOHN ALDEN. Photographs; 1935-1966. *ca.* 400 pcs.

Includes: Mexico (Chihuahua, Durango, Sonora, etc.); some Peru. [4017(ling. #1)]

4520. MASON, JOHN ALDEN. Photographs: Mexico; 1913-1917. Prints, negatives. *ca.* 400 pcs.

Unidentified photographs showing people, dwellings, terrain, etc. [4017]

4520*a*. Mexico; 1894, 1911, 1923, n.d. 7 pcs.

Pictures include: two calendar stones and a sacrificial stone (donated to the Society by Charles A. Rutter through I. C. Morris, Dec. 4, 1894); postal cards with notes to Frank G. Speck from J. Alden Mason regarding work on a Nahuatl dictionary, Uto-Aztecan studies, and imminent departure for Tepecano country with Franz Boas; Pyramid of the Sun, San Juan de Teotihuacan (photograph by W. H. M. Hauser). [4020*b*(5)]

4520*b*. MITCHELL, MARY-ELIZABETH B. An analysis of 16th century tribute documents from the Juzgado Archives of Teposcolula in the Mixteca Alta; 1976-1977. T.L.S., photocopy of T.D., printed D. 29 pp., 1 book.

Re: history of the tribute system; effects of the Spanish tribute system on the indigenous culture; litigation with respect to the tribute system. Includes a copy of *Indice del Archivo del Juzgado de Teposcolula, Oaxaca: epoca colonial.* [10(163)]

Donor, grantee, Dec. 1977.

4521. NUTINI, HUGO G. Report on the syncretic and pre-Hispanic components of Tlaxcalan ritual kinship and folk Catholicism; Oct. 1, 1970. T.L.S. to Whitfield J. Bell, Jr. 3 pp.

Report on cataloging and microfilming of documents (four collections) in archives (public and private) in Mexico. [10(96)]

4521*a*. Palenque photographs and drawings; 1951, n.d. *ca.* 100 photographs.

Re: temple, excavation, crypt, jade work, etc. Includes a photograph of John Alden Mason and Burton W. Bascom. [4016*a*(B:M384 in F)]

4522. PARRY, FRANCIS. Letter to Henry Phillips; New York, May 1, 1894. A.L.S. 1 p. and end.

Re: copy of Brinton's paper on Nagualism. [3]

4523. PARSONS, ELSIE CLEWS. Letter to Leslie A. White; Oct. 29, 1940. Photocopy of T.L.S. 2 pp.

Re: Bandelier's letters; confusion of Bandelier and Means on clanship in early Mexico and Peru. [137]

4524. ROSENGARTEN, JOSEPH GEORGE. Letter to Isaac Minis Hays, Philadelphia; Apr. 17, 1899. A.L.S. 1 p.

Re: "Mexican Picture Chronicle" to be sold at Quartritch's; Crawford manuscripts. [3]

4524*a*. VAILLANT, GEORGE C. Correspondence with John Alden Mason; 1927-1945. A.L.S., T.L. and L.S. 165 pp.

Re: Maya pottery; Piedras Negras, Guatemala; archeological work in Mexico and Guatemala; publications; the University Museum (University of Pennsylvania); Vaillant's obituary. Includes correspondence between Mason and Sue Vaillant (Mrs. George C.) and between Mason and Charles Marius Barbeau. [4017(C38)]

4525. WEITLANER, ROBERT J. Comparative vocabulary; 1942. T.D. and L.S. 19 pp.

Includes: letter from Frederick Johnson to J. Alden Mason; comparative vocabulary which is number-keyed to a list of twenty-two languages and arranged in columns headed by Spanish glosses. Words lacking in some languages for almost all items. Languages include: Otomi, Mazahua, Matlatzinca, Ocuiltec, Pame, Chichimeca, Cuitlateco, Mazatec, Popoloca, Chocho (Tlapanec), Ichcateco, Trique, Chiapanec, Manque, Mixtec, Cuicatec, Amuzgo, Zapotec, Chatino, Chinantec, Tarasco, and Tlapanec. [4017(ling #2)]

*Cf.* No. 2203.

4525*a*. WEITLANER, ROBERT J. Correspondence with John Alden Mason; 1935-1957. T.L. and L.S. 37 pp.

Re: archeological, ethnological, and linguistic work in Mexico; genetic classification of languages of Central America and Mexico. [4017(C39)]

4526. WEITLANER, ROBERT J. Hokano:Otomangue:Yuto-Azteca:Mayance; n.d. T.D. 1 p. c.c.

Includes: lexical items in the various languages arranged in columns; Spanish glosses. [4017(ling. #2)]

## MICMAC

### (Algonquian)

4527. BOCK, PHILIP K. Fieldwork at Restigouche; 1971. T.D. 3 pp.

Re: political, economic, and educational changes during the period 1961-1971. [10(109)]

4527*a*. Micmac; 1913-1914, 1947, n.d. 48 pcs.

Pictures include: people, habitat, material culture, etc. Includes photographs from Nova Scotia, New Brunswick, and Newfoundland. [4020*b*(5)]

4528. PROULX, PAUL. Letter to Whitfield J. Bell, Jr.; Antigonish, N.S., Canada, Apr. 4, 1975. T.L.S. and enc. 13 pp.

Re: Peter Perro's telling of the legend *saagub* "Jacob." In Micmac with English translation. [10(144)]

Donor, grantee.

## MIXTEC

(Mixtecan)

4529. TROIKE, NANCY P. Report on the Codex Zouche-Nuttal at the British Museum; n.d. 26 pp., ill.

Re: establishing the relative order in which the two sides of the pages in the Codex were printed. Includes: color photographs; 2 pp. letter to Whitfield J. Bell, Jr. [10(101)]

Donor, grantee, 1971.

## MOHAWK

(Iroquois)

4530. Adoption into Akwesasne Mohawk Nation; July 1949. T.D., 1 p., 5 photos, 1 newspaper.

Re: adoption of Paul A. W. Wallace. Includes Ray Fadden's speech. [4021(1)]

4531. BONVILLAIN, NANCY. Report on fieldwork carried out at the St. Regis Mohawk Indian Reserve; 1969. T.D. 5 pp.

Re: factors affecting language use (political, religious, etc.); work toward a synchronic description. [10(78)]

Donor, grantee, 1969.

4532. COOK, CHIEF JULIUS. Correspondence with Paul A. W. Wallace; Jan. 14-22, 1948. T.L.S. and L. 2 pp.

Requesting Wallace's aid in defeating some unspecified Senate bills which he felt would be bad for the Indians. [4021(1)]

4532*a*. DRUKE, MARY A. Seventeenth and eighteenth century manuscripts in England pertaining to the Iroquois; 1977. T.D.S. and photocopy of A.D. 22 pp.

Report on search for primary documents. Includes an English-Mohawk-Cherokee word list. [10(161)]

Donor, grantee, Oct. 1977.

4533. FADDEN, JOHN (KA-HON-HES). Correspondence with Paul A. W. Wallace; Mar. 23, 1962–Mar. 17, 1963. T.L. and L.S., A.L.S. 20L.

Re: the exhibition and sale of John Fadden's paintings. [4021(2)]

4534. FADDEN, JOHN (KA-HON-HES). Paintings; [1962]. Gouache. 3 items.

Includes: "Hunting Party Surprised by Bear"; "Iroquois Delegation to the Aztecs"; "Youth Dreams of his Guardian *Manito* (an eagle)." [4021]

4535. JONES, LOUIS C. Letter to Frank G. Speck, Philadelphia; Cooperstown, N.Y., May 23, 1947. T.L.S. 1 p.

Returning Speck's manuscript "The Mohawk Folk Tale." [170(26)]

4536. MICHAEL, GLYNN. Correspondence with Paul A. W. Wallace; June 28–July 5, 1943. A.L.S., T.L. 2 pp.

Re: the death of Chief William Loft. [4021(7)]

4536*a*. Mohawk; 1925, 1944-1945. 6 pcs.

Includes photographs of: Chief Split Cloud(?) [Cook] and his son, Tommy Cook; Iroquois crooked knife; Mohawk village, Oka, P. Q. [4020*b*(5)]

4537. PARKER, ELY S. Ancient rites of the Condoling Council, Mohawk dialect; n.d. A.D. 20L.

A. C. Parker felt this was probably from Horatio Hale, "Iroquois Book of Rites." In Mohawk with English translation. [135]

4538. POSTAL, PAUL M. Some syntactic rules in Mohawk; 1962. D. 1 v. of 429 pp.

A partial treatment of Mohawk syntax in a transformational-generative grammar. Doctoral dissertation, Yale University. [10(12)]

## MOHEGAN TRIBES

## (Algonquian)

4539. MOCHON, MARION J. The Stockbridge-Munsee community; Sept. 10, 1965. T.D. and L.S. to Richard H. Shryock. 5 pp.

Re: acculturation, economic problems, etc., of the Stockbridge-Munsee community (near Bowler, Wisconsin). [10(36)]

*Cf.* No. 4540*a*.
Donor, grantee.

4539*a*. Mohegan; 1909, 1914, 1921, 1931-1932, n.d. 40 pcs.

Re: people, material culture, etc. Includes: four photographs of Charles Mathews (Mohegan-Nehantic); note to Frank G. Speck from Mrs. Henry Mathews; letters to Frank G. Speck from George G. Heye and Mary M. Chappelle. [4020*b*(5),(13:2)]

4539*b*. Pequot; 1921, 1941, n.d. 5 pcs.

Photographs of two women and a carved wooden mortar. [4020*b*(9)]

4540. PRINCE, JOHN DYNELEY. Letter to G. B. Gordon; New York, Mar. 15, 1907. T.L.S. 1 p.

Recommending Speck for scholarship; discusses Speck's work, as a student, on the Pequot dialect of Mohegan-Pequots, Algic, and Yuchee. [170(25)]

4540*a*. Stockbridge-Munsee Indian community (Wisconsin); 1965. 29 photographs.

Re: people, dwellings, etc. Photographs by Marion J. Mochon to accompany No. 4539. [4020*b*(10)]

Donor, grantee.

4541. WARD, CHRISTOPHER L. Correspondence with Frank G. Speck; Dec. 2-10, 1927. T.L. and L.S. 4 pp.

Requesting offprints of Speck's monograph on the Nanticokes. [170(30)]

## MOUNTAIN TEQUISTLATECO

## (Hokan)

4542. TURNER, PAUL R. Grammar of Highland Chontal, Oaxaca, Mexico; Sept. 14, 1965. T.L.S. to Richard H. Shryock. 1 p. and newspaper clipping.

Very brief report on research activities. [10(37)]

*Cf.* No. 4544.

4543. TURNER, PAUL R. Highland Chontal dialect survey; n.d. D. 22 pp. Photocopy of D., c.c.

Re: procedures; major isoglosses. Includes: maps; noncultural vocabulary list in Spanish. [10(59)]

Donor, grantee, 1968.

4544. TURNER, PAUL R. Highland Chontal grammar; 1966. T.D. *ca.* 350 pp. c.c.

Dissertation at the University of Chicago; grammar is in tagmemic framework. [10(42)]

Donor, grantee, 1966.
*Cf.* No. 4542.

4545. TURNER, PAUL R., coll. Highland Chontal ethnohistorical materials; 1968. 4 reels of tape. Recording No. 66.

Recorded at San Matias Petacaltepec, Oaxaca, Mexico. Informants: Damian Flores, Clemente Zarate, and Porfirio Nicolas Flores. [4093]

*Cf.* No. 4546.
Donor, grantee, 1969.

4546. TURNER, PAUL R., coll. Highland Chontal texts; 1965-1966. 3 reels of tape. Recording No. 52.

Includes: texts; grammar. [4094]

*Cf.* No. 4545.
Donor, grantee.

## MUSKOGEE

## (Muskogean)

4546*a*. Creek, Yuchi, and Shawnee; 1904, 1932, 1941, n.d. *ca.* 150 pcs.

Pictures include: people, activities, churches, etc. Includes: photos of Yuchi Annual Harvest Ceremony, Creek Nation, Oklahoma, 1904; photos in area of Atmore, Alabama; portraits. [4020*b*(2),(10),(13:1,4)]

4547. FIFE, SHARON A. *Thlewarle Mekko Sapkv Coko* (House of Prayer); 1970. Photocopy of T.D. 24 pp., ill.

Re: history and ceremonies of Thlewarle Indian Baptist Church; description of ceremonies, participants, accoutrements, etc. [10(105)]

*Cf.* Nos. 4613-4614.
Donor, grantee, July 1971.

4548. MCNICKLE, D'ARCY. Letter to Frank G. Speck, Philadelphia; Washington, June 4, 1941. T.L.S. 1 p.

Re: Speck's report on and pictures of Creek Indians of Atmore, Alabama. [170(30)]

4548*a*. NATHAN, MICHELE. Report on fieldwork amóng the Florida Seminole Indians; 1978. T.L.S., T.D. 4 pp.

Re: fieldwork on the Florida Seminole dialect of Creek. Includes letter to Whitfield J. Bell, Jr. [10(169)]

Donor, grantee, Apr. 1978.

4549. SADIGA, SALLY. Creek Indian land dispute to the Supreme Court of Alabama: Sally Sadiga vs. Richard DeMarcus and Peter Hufman; n.d. A.D. 5 pp.

Legal brief by the plaintiff's attorney. [9]

4549*a*. Seminole; 1927, 1930, 1937, 1939-1940, n.d. 71 pcs.

Pictures include: people, dwellings, activities, etc., of Seminoles in Florida. [4020*b*(10),(13:4)]

4550. SPECK, FRANK G., coll. Yuchi and Creek dances; July 17, 1904(?). A.D. 6L. and 1 notebook of 8L.

Includes: sheet music for songs to accompany dance; choreography; a few items with translation. [170(15)]

4551. SPECK, FRANK G., coll. Yuchi and Creek songs; n.d. A.D. *ca.* 25L.

Includes: Yuchi and Creek songs; twelve vocabulary slips. [170(15)]

## NA-DENE

4552. SAPIR, EDWARD. Comparative Na-Dene dictionary; n.d. A.D. 4 v. of *ca.* 500 pp. each.

Volumes 1, 3, and 4 are comparative Na-Dene with provision for various Athapascan languages and dialects, Haida, and Tlingit. Volume 2 is comparative Sino-Tibetan-Na-Dene with provision for entries in Sino-Tibetan languages, Athapascan, Haida, and Tlingit. Most pages in all volumes have only a few entries. [30(Na20a.3)]

## NAHUA

### (Uto-Aztecan)

4553. CAMPBELL, LYLE, coll. Aztec manuscript and Xinca linguistic material; 1972, n.d. Photocopy of D. 221 pp.

Includes: copy of an Aztec manuscript in possession of the *Sindico* of Santa Maria Ixhuatan, Guatemala; Xinca vocabulary with Spanish glosses from collector's fieldnotes. [10(128)]

*Cf.* No. 4913.
Donor, grantee, Nov. 1972.

4554. CULIN, ROBERT STEWART. Letter to Isaac Minis Hays; Philadelphia, Dec. 17, 1898. A.L.S. 1 p. enc. wanting.

Sends letter from M. H. Saville about Culin's paper on the Montezuma Tribute Role. [3]

*Cf.* No. 4557 for enclosure.

4555. HIGGINS, F. R. A preliminary sketch of the morphology and phonology of the Zacapoaxtla dialect of Nahuat; 1970. Photocopy of T.D. 82 pp.

Re: phonology (in taxonomic phonemic terms); morphology of the noun and verb and associated phonological processes (transformational-generative). Includes a three-page report on fieldwork. [10(98)]

Donor, grantee, Jan. 1971.

4556. KNAB, TIM. American Philosophical Society report; n.d. Photocopy of A.L.S. and T.D. 10 pp.

Re: a phonological analysis of San Miguel Nahuat; differences in tone and stress patterns of prayers from those of the vernacular mode. [10(150)]

*Cf.* No. 4556*a*.
Donor, grantee, 1976.

4556*a*. KNAB, TIM. Dialect survey of Nahuatl in the state of Puebla; 1975-1976. Photocopy of D. *ca.* 500 pp.

Includes: vocabulary, phrases, and sentences in Spanish and Nahuatl. [10(153)]

*Cf.* No. 4556.
Donor, grantee, Mar. 1977.

4557. SAVILLE, MARSHALL HOWARD. Letter to Robert Stewart Culin; New York, Dec. 16, 1898. A.L.S. 1 p.

Re: Culin's paper on Montezuma Tribute Roll; relationship of Philadelphia fragments to manuscripts in Berlin (*cf. Trans. Amer. Philos. Soc.* 17: pp. 53-61). Mentions E. Seler. [3]

*Cf.* No. 4554.

## NANTICOKE

## (Mohegan D.)

4558. BARTON, BENJAMIN SMITH. Letter to John G. E. Heckewelder; Nov. 20, 1797. Photocopy of A.L.S. 2 pp.

Re: whether the Pampticangs and Nanticokes are the same people; suggested comparison of their languages with possible aid from Zeisberger; sending publications for Zeisberger and others. From original in the College of Physicians, Philadelphia. [4003]

4558*a*. Nanticoke; 1912, n.d. 13 pcs.

Pictures include: woman with wooden mortar and pestle and man with corn sheller, Indian River, Delaware; woman identified only as Nanticoke, Delaware; Sam Patterson and his daughter (possibly Tuscarora); unidentified Nanticoke woman (Ontario); Chief Josiah Hill and brother; Council House (Ontario); etc. [4020*b*(6),(13:3)]

4559. SPECK, FRANK G. Nanticoke and Tuscarora; 1914, 1915-1917. D. 8 pcs., 1 notebook of *ca.* 30L.

Includes: names for the Nanticokes in Cayuga, Tuscarora, Mohawk, Seneca, Onondaga, and Oneida; notes on wampum, folklore, and the Canadian Tuscarora; some Nanticoke vocabulary. [170(7)]

## NAVAJO

## (Athapascan)

4560. GARRISON, EDWARD R. Spaces, objects, and figures in Navajo: from labeling to perception and cognition; 1970. Photocopy of T.D. 26 pp.

Two copies of a paper presented at the meeting of the Central States Anthropological Society, Indiana University, Bloomington, Indiana. [10(89)]

*Cf.* No. 4561.
Donor, grantee, Aug. 1970.

4561. GARRISON, EDWARD R., coll. Navajo texts; 1969. 7 reels of tape. Recording No. 79.

Recorded at the Navajo Indian Reservation, northeastern Arizona. [4060]

*Cf.* No. 4560.
Donor, grantee, Oct. 1970.

4562. HAMMOND, BLODWEN, and MARY SHEPARDSON. Report on work with the Navajo; 1965, n.d. D. and Printed D. 12 pp., chart, 2 photographs.

Re: Navajo kinship. Includes: chart showing those descendants of Whiteman Viller and his wife, Salt Woman, who are still part of the Navajo Mountain community; photographs of Elsa Liza Greymountain and Jackson Greymountain. [10(50)]

4563. HILL, JENNIE-KEITH. Letter to Richard H. Shryock, Philadelphia; Evanston, Ill., Feb. 1966. T.L.S. 2 pp.

Re: research in Navajo syntax; locations; personnel; general method of fieldwork. [10(44)]

*Cf.* No. 4564.

4564. HILL, JENNIE-KEITH. A transformational-generative sketch of two problems in Navajo syntax; 1966. T.D. 14 pp.

Re: use of transformational-generative grammar (with informant's enhanced perception of his language) as a heuristic device; the enclitic *-go;* the closely related verb forms *oolghe* and *wolghe.* [10(26)]

Donor, grantee, 1966.

4565. HOIJER, HARRY. Navajo lexicon; n.d. A.D. *ca.* 300L.

Manuscript of the lexicon published in *University of California Publications: Linguistics* 78 (1974). [4012(20)]

4566. HOIJER, HARRY, coll. Navaho night chant; Feb. 25–Mar. 8, 1930. A.D. 5 notebooks of *ca.* 60L. each.

In Navajo with very little English translation. [4012(13)]

4567. HOIJER, HARRY, coll. Navaho songs; 1930. A.D. 11 notebooks of *ca.* 60L. each.

In Navajo with some English translation. [4012(14)]

4568. KAUFMAN, ELLEN S. Navajo complementizers and semantic subordination; 1974. Photocopy of T.D. 52 pp.

Re: subordinate clauses marked by *go* and *ikii.* [10(135)]

Donor, grantee, Mar. 1974.

4569. Navajo conversations; n.d. A.D. 9 pp.

Includes: conversations; English translations. In the hand of Edward Sapir with additions by Harry Hoijer. [4012(21)]

4570. Navaho texts; Nov. 21 and Dec. 12, 1956. A.D. 32 pp.

One narrative of a childhood experience and one coyote story both with English translation. Some explanatory and analytical notes added. [4012(21)]

4571. PERKINS, ELLAVINA. The Navajo particle of constituent negation; Nov. 1973. Photocopy of T.D. 15 pp.

Re: the particle *hanii.* [10(134)]

Donor, grantee, Mar. 1974.

4572. SANDOVAL, CHIC. Navajo texts; 1937-1939. A.D. and L., T.L.S. *ca.* 200 pp.

Includes: Navajo texts with free and interlinear literal English translations; letters from H. J. Ostrander to the University of Chicago and E. G. Conklin; letter from Frederic Woodward to H. J. Ostrander; letter from Sandoval to Harry Hoijer. [4012(21)]

4573. SAPIR, EDWARD, coll. Navajo conversations; n.d. A.D. 9 slips.

Short conversations with two participants. In Navajo with English translation. [4012(21)]

4574. SAPIR, EDWARD. Navajo texts, field notes, and word lists; n.d. A.D. 17 notebooks of *ca.* 125 pp. each and *ca.* 11,000 slips.

Notebooks contain Navajo texts with English translations. Slip files include: verb paradigms with divisions according to stem class; nouns; prefixes; particles; syllable types; etc. [30(Na31.5)]

4575. SAPIR, EDWARD, and HARRY HOIJER. Navajo grammatical notes; n.d. A.D. *ca.* 100 slips.

Includes: notes on various aspects of Navajo grammar and phonology; some comparisons with other Athapascan languages; some reconstructions for Proto-Athapascan. [4012(19)]

4575*a*. Scenes in Arizona and New Mexico; Mar. 1926. 11 photographs.

Re: people, activities, dwellings. Includes view on Papago reservation. Photographs from Fred F. Russell in the Flexner Collection, American Philosophical Society. [B:F365(174)]

4576. SHETTER, WILLIAM Z. Report on summer work on Navajo; 1968. T.D., photocopy of T.D. 8 pp.

Re: methods of elicitation; materials obtained. [10(65)]

Donor, grantee, 1968.

4577. SHETTER, WILLIAM Z., coll. Radio program, Holbrook, Arizona; Aug. 1, 1968. 1 reel of tape. Recording No. 64.

Autobiographical remarks by Mrs. Elsie Benally, Navajo Reservation, Bellemont, Ariz. [4083]

Donor, grantee, Sept. 1968.

4578. TAPTTO, MARY H. Ranking in Navajo nouns; 1972. T.D. 12 pp.

Re: subject-object inversion in Navajo. [10(121)]

Donor, grantee, 1972.

4579. WERNER, OSWALD. The Navaho ethnomedical domain: prolegomena to a componential semantic analysis; n.d. Ditto of T.D. 34 pp.

Re: terms for diseases; the dimensions of intensity, temporal duration, and spatial extension. [4022]

Donor, author, Mar. 1964.

4580. WERNER, OSWALD. Report on edition of the Young and Morgan Navaho dictionary; Feb. 4, 1965. T.L.S. to Richard H. Shryock. 3 pp.

Re: editing and keypunching the dictionary. [10(33)]

4581. WERNER, OSWALD. A typological comparison of four trader Navaho speakers; 1963. T.D. 167 pp.

Doctoral dissertation in anthropology, Indiana University. [4023]

4582. WERNER, OSWALD, et al. The anatomical atlas of the Navaho; Navaho food taxonomies; taxonomy and paradigm; pragmatics and ethnoscience; a note on the passive in English; 1966, n.d. T., mimeo, and photocopy D. 286 pp.

Re: Navajo anatomical classification, including diagrams and Navajo terms with English glosses; Navajo classifications of foods; semantics; pragmatics. [10(46)]

Donor, grantee.

## NOOTKA

## (Wakashan)

4583. KLOKEID, TERRY J. The source of prepositional phrases in Nootka; 1970. Photocopy of T.D. 12 pp.

Re: derivation of prepositional phrases from underlying sentences. [10(88)]

Donor, grantee, 1970.

4584. KLOKEID, TERRY J. An introduction to the West Coast [Nootka] language of Vancouver Island; n.d. T.D. and photocopy of T.D. 75 pp.

Re: phonetics, phonology, and orthography. Written for use in teaching the language; includes some exercises. [10(118)]

Donor, grantee, May 1972.

4585. KLOKEID, TERRY J. The West Coast [Nootka] text manuscripts held by the National Museum of Man and the American Philosophical Society; Sept. 1971. T.D. 20 pp.

Description and history of the manuscripts. [10(119)]

Donor, grantee, May 1972.

4586. SAPIR, EDWARD. Miscellaneous Nootka material; n.d. T. and A.D. *ca.* 1600L., 19 notebooks of *ca.* 100 pp. each, 5 notebooks of *ca.* 200 pp. each, and *ca.* 750 slips.

Includes: ethnographic notes, often with Nootka terms; some drawings by a Nootka; census data. Notebooks are the source of material in the typed notes. Slips are alphabetical lists of Nootka personal and place names. Table of contents available. [30(W2a.18)]

Donor, Sapir family, May 1972.

## NORTH AMERICA

4586*a*. BARBEAU, CHARLES MARIUS. Correspondence with John Alden Mason; 1941, 1949-1954. A.L.S., T.L. and L.S. 24 pp.

Re: Barbeau's work on North Pacific coast and Eskimo art. [4017(C8)]

4587. BARBEAU, CHARLES MARIUS. Correspondence with Paul A. W. Wallace; June 22, 1920–Dec. 5, 1958. A. and T.L.S., T.L. 59L.

Re: French-Canadian folklore; Edward Ahenakew's Manebogo manuscript; Conrad Weiser and the Delawares; American Philosophical Society; Barbeau's Huron-Wyandot work; filming of the Contrecoeur papers and Huron grammars at Seminaire de Quebec; Richard Pilant and the founding of an international Institute of Iroquoian Studies. [4021(1)]

4587*a*. Canada and New England; n.d. 26 pcs.

Includes people, town and country scenes, map of Newfoundland, Micmac encampment (Nova Scotia), etc. May contain some Montagnais-Naskapi. [4020*b*(1),(13:1)]

4587*b*. CATLIN, GEORGE; n.d. 6 photographs.

Photographs of Catlin paintings including: children of a Comanche chief, Sioux ball-player, and four unidentified. [4020*b*(11:1)]

4588. Collection of materials on American Indian sign language; 1966. 1 reel of film. Film No. 1226.

Includes: a Nez Perce hymnal; discussion and illustrations on the meaning of symbols and on the use of sign language; etc. From materials in possession of Miss Jean Rumsey. [4029]

4588*a*. EASTMAN, SETH; n.d. 11 engravings.

Includes: dances, shamans, hunting, etc. Engravings by John C. McRae, C. E. Wagstaff and J. Andrews, R. Amshelwood, and C. K. Burt after Eastman. [4020*b*(11:2)]

4589. GALLATIN, ALBERT. Letter to Peter S. Du Ponceau [*ca.* May 20, 1826]. A.L.S. 2 pp., end.

Sending transcribed vocabularies of Yuchi, Natchez, and Muskogee; also sending a Sioux grammar to Col. Thomas L. McKenny, Office of Indian Affairs, via James Barbour, Secretary of War. [9]

4589*a*. Indians of North America: American Philosophical Society Print Collection; 1827, 1838, n.d. 14 pcs.

Includes: reproductions of "The Smoke Signal" (Frederic Remington) and "The Big Soldier" (Karl Bodmer) (3 copies); Shau-Hau-Napo-Tinia (Iowa) (uncolored lithograph); petroglyphs in Pennsylvania and West Virginia. Also includes hand colored lithographs showing: Ong Pa Ton Ga (Omaha chief); Osages (Myhangah, Washingasbha, Marchanthitahtoongah, Minckchatahooh, Grétomih, and Kishagashugah) (L. Boilly, Nos. 89 and 90); Peah-Mus-Ka (Musquakie chief); and Pet-A-Le-Shar-Ro (Pawnee). [4016*a*(C:In22E),(C:In22P)]

4589*b*. JENNESS, DIAMOND. Correspondence with John Alden Mason; 1928-1943. A.L.S., T.L. and L.S. 48 pp.

Re: possible migration routes into North America from Asia; remains of early man in North America; Frederica de Laguna's archeological work in Alaska; Edgar B. Howard's work on early man in North America. [4017(C21)]

4590. MERRILL, WILLIAM L. An investigation of ethnographic and archaeological specimens of mescalbeans *(sophora secundiflora)* in American museums; 1976. Photocopy of T.D.S. 106 pp.

Re: cultural and geographical use of mescalbeans; range of uses; relationship between use of mescalbeans and peyote and between use of mescalbeans and *erythrina flabelliformis.* [10(149)]

Donor, grantee, May 1976.

4590*a*. Miscellaneous photographs and sketches; 1907, 1909, 1924, 1933, 1940, 1943, n.d. 128 pcs.

Includes: Labrador sketches by Frank Stanford Speck; petroglyphs; Sauk and Fox; Wichita; Seminole; Creek; Piegan; Delaware; Minnehaha, Sacajawea, and Pocahontas by Georgianna Marbeson; Iroquois false face; Weasel Tail; Lottie Welsh and daughter; portraits by L. T. Alexander; unidentified people and scenes; Choctaw belt and Ojibwa(?) cradle board; splint basket; birch-bark baskets; cave-scene diorama (Guernsey and Pitman); notes to Florence Insley from C. L. Brooke and Frank G. Speck; note to Frank G. Speck from (Pvt.) Claude E. Schaeffer; map showing distribution of southeastern tribes; Indian children in school; Machapunga (North Carolina); Choctaw village, La. (from D. I. Bushnell, Choctaw, Bayou La Combe, La); unidentified people, scenes, and objects (eastern U.S. and Canada). [4020*b*(5),(11:4,5,6,7,8),(13:2)]

4591. MORAVIAN CHURCH ARCHIVES: records of the Moravian mission among the Indians of North America; n.d. 40 reels of film. Film No. 1279.

Includes: language materials in Delaware, Creek, Mohawk, and Onondaga; materials pertaining to the Chippewa, Cherokee, Nanticoke, and Shawnee; diaries (travel and other); reports; letters; conference minutes; various other materials relating to missionary activities and relations with the Indians. Materials from: New York, Connecticut, Pennsylvania, Ohio, Michigan, Indiana, Kansas, Georgia, Oklahoma, and Ontario. Table of contents available. From originals in Bethlehem, Pa. [4039]

4592. OLSON, RONALD L. American Indian linguistic materials; n.d. 1 reel of film. Film No. 1276.

Includes: vocabularies in several Native languages; material in the Quinault dialect of Lower Chelhalis; material in Quileute. From originals in the University of Washington libraries. [4039*a*]

4592*a*. Shindler Collection of North American Indians; 1858, 1868, n.d. 95 photographs, 8 pp.

Includes: Yankton, Brule, Cherokee, Ponca, Sauk and Fox, Chippewa, Seminole, Pawnee, Osage, Cheyenne, Choctaw, Ute, and others. [Call No. 970.1:Sh6]

4592*b*. SOCIETY OF JESUS. The Oregon Province Archives, Indian Language Collection: the Pacific Northwest tribal languages; 1976. 21 reels of film. Film No. 1365.

Includes: dictionaries; vocabularies; texts (primarily Christian religious materials); grammars; etc. Languages include: Assiniboin (Dakota); Blackfoot; Chelan (Columbian); Coeur d'Alene; Colville (Okanagan); Columbian; Crow; Gros Ventre (Arapaho); Kalispel; Kutenai; Nez Perce; Yakima (Sahaptin). From originals produced in the late nineteenth and twentieth centuries, on deposit at the Pacific Northwest Indian Center, Spokane, Washington. Guide book included. [4044]

4592*c*. UNITED CHURCH BOARD FOR WORLD MINISTRIES: North American Indian papers; 1817-1883. 64 reels of film. Film No. 1223.

Re: missions among the Cherokee, Choctaw, Dakota, Osage, Chickasaw, Mackinaw, Creek, Ojibwa, Pawnee, Stockbridge, Maumee, Abenaki, and Penobscot. From originals in Houghton Library, Harvard University. [4047]

4593. WHORF, BENJAMIN L. Linguistic realignment north of Mexico; 1940, n.d. T.D. 7 pp.

Gives six phyla, one "broken phylum," and two uncertain languages (for presentation at the meeting of the American Anthropological Association, Chicago, 1940) and a detailed outline of five phyla plus several unaffiliated languages. [4017(ling. #2)]

## NORTHEAST

4594. BARNSLEY, THOMAS. Letter to Horatio Gates; Fort London, Oct. 20, 1764. Photostat of A.L.S. 2 pp.

Re: attacks by Indians; his concern for convoys to Fort Pitt. From original in William L. Clement Library. [9]

Donor, Edward R. Barnsley, Feb. 1963.

4595. BARTON, BENJAMIN SMITH. Letter to John G. E. Heckewelder; Philadelphia, Feb. 22, 1796. Photocopy of A.L.S. 2 pp. and add.

Asks questions about Indian artifacts, mica, color of Indian children at birth, etc. [9]

4595*a*. Beothuk-Micmac; 1911. 10 pcs.

Pictures of: Santu, "The Last of the Beothuks," and her son, daughter-in-law (Micmac), and granddaughter. [4020*b*(1),(13:1)]

4596. DIXON, JEREMIAH. Letter to James Bird [Burd], Paxton; Near the Great Meadows, August 21, 1767. Photocopy of A.L.S. 1 p. and add., end.

Authorizes two Indians to return home. Refers them to Sir William Johnson for pay. [9]

Donor, Whitfield J. Bell, Jr., 1971.

4597. Fort William Henry, copy of a journal kept during the siege of; Aug. 2-10, 1757. A.D. 1 bound v. of 8L. of which 6L. are used.

Re: the participation of Indians in the siege; atrocities committed by the Indians; failure of the French to attempt any control; receipt of plunder by the French from the Indians. [4008]

4598. GATES, HORATIO. Letter to Capt. Thomas Barnsley, Carlisle; New York, Apr. 6, 1765. Photostat of L. 1 p.

Re: seizure of goods of Croghan, et al., by country people. From original in William L. Clement Library. [9]

Donor, Edward R. Barnsley, Feb. 1963.

4598*a*. Northeast; 1940-1941, 1955, n.d. 55 pcs.

Pictures include: Annawan's Rock (near Taunton, Massachusetts); photographs by

Charles Marius Barbeau of items in the Ashmolean Museum, Oxford University; photograph of beadwork of Iroquois, Micmac, Passamaquoddy, and Penobscot origins; "Indian Scene," an engraving by J. C. Armytage after W. H. Bartlett; Nipmuc people, baskets, and Herring Pond Indian Church on Martha's Vineyard; Pokagon (Potawatomi) family at their birchbark wigwam (Hartford, Mich.); Chief Frank Coggswell (Scatticook), his house, and an unidentified man (Scatticook Indian Reservation, Kent, Conn.); "Weetamoo Swimming the Matapoiset," an engraving by S. A. Schoff after C. S. Reinhart; Indian melodrama; Mohegan boy in headdress; Micmac camp (Nova Scotia); Mashpee Indians; Sachem John Neptune; Cree medicine man.
[4020*b*(1),(4),(7),(9),(10),(13:2,3)]

## NORTHWEST COAST

4599. AMOSS, PAMELA T., comp. Catalogue of the Marian Smith Collection in the Library of the Royal Anthropological Institute of Great Britain and Ireland; 1975, n.d. T.D. 25 pp. c.c.

The catalog lists: documents on the Salish, the Kwakiutl, and Indian Shakers; correspondence between Smith and Ernest Bertelson; typewritten notes of Arthur Ballard on Salish; photographs on various topics. [10(145)]

Donor, grantee, July 1975.

4599*a*. BOAS, FRANZ, coll. Northwest Coast language materials; 1889-1897, n.d. A.D. 8 notebooks.

Includes: vocabulary in Bella Coola, Haida, Kutenai, Kwakiutl, Lillooet, Nitinat, Nootka, Okanagan, Shuswap, Tlingit, Tsimshian, and others; texts in Bella Coola, Haida, Kwakiutl, Shuswap, Tlingit, and Tsimshian. Shorthand used extensively. [4003*b*]

Donor, Northwestern University Library.

4600. BOAS, FRANZ. Correspondence; 1885-1909. 1 reel of film. Film No. 372.3.

Re: work among the Eskimos and on Northwest Coast languages. From originals in possession of the Office of Anthropology, Smithsonian Institution. [4026]

Donor, Smithsonian Institution, Apr. 1967.

4600*a*. DEMERS, RICHARD, coll. Lummi recordings; 1974. 20 reels of tape. Recording No. 105.

Includes: texts, sentences, etc. Re: greetings; meal preparation; preparing salmon, clams, and duck; history; description of artifacts (baskets, arrowheads, canoes, etc.); syntactic analysis (negation, embedding, wh- questions); etc. Informant: Al Charles. [4057*a*]

Donor, grantee, 1975.

4601. GUNTHER, ERNA. Letter to Richard H. Shryock; Jan. 28, 1969. T.L.S. 2 pp.

Re: visits to Eskimo and Northwest Coast exhibits in European museums; visits to two manuscript collections in the Soviet Union.
[10(70)]

4601*a*. Northwest Coast; 1910, 1917, n.d. 5 postal cards, 1 photograph.

Includes: photograph of Louis Shotridge, Tlingit chief; Queen Johnnie, Indian squaw, British Columbia; Alaskan costumes and totems; note to Frank G. Speck from Edward Sapir regarding fieldwork in British Columbia.
[4020*b*(7)]

4602. ROHNER, RONALD P. Franz Boas: ethnographer of the Northwest Coast; [1966]. T.D. 60 pp.

An account of Boas's activities while in the field, his attitudes toward the work, his relations with the Indians; based primarily on Boas's letters, diaries and, to some extent, on what the Indians said about him. [10(25)]

Donor, grantee, 1966.

4602*a*. Spokane primer; 1976, n.d. T.L.S. and photocopy of D. 58 pp.

Includes: words, phrases, and sentences in Spokane and English; letter to Carl F. Miller from Elenor C. Kelly (Mrs. William M.).
[4020*d*]

## OJIBWA

### (Algonquian)

4602*b*. Algonquin; 1924-1937; n.d. 6 photographs.

Re: people and activities. [4020*b*(1)]

4603. ETTAWAGESHIK, JANE E. W. Changing patterns of Ottawa kinship and social organization; correlated changes in Ottawa kinship and social organization; 1948. T.D. 190 pp. c.c.

Re: the modern kinship system and comparison with earlier usage; analysis according to kinship group, sex, age, descent, generation; change, borrowing, effects of contact on social organization, agents of contact. Includes: lists of Ottawa kinship terms as collected by the Jesuit Fathers Andre (1688?) and du Jaunay (1741?), by Lewis H. Morgan (1870?), and by the author (1946); map of Indian houses in Harbor Springs, Michigan. [10(16)]

Donor, grantee.

4603*a*. JONES, WILLIAM. Ethnographic and linguistic field notes on the Ojibwa Indians; n.d. *ca.* 250 pp., 42 photographs.

Re: government, mythology, festivals, customs, games, etc. Also includes: comments on the language; vocabulary, some items with English glosses; lists of bands and locations; photographs of people, activities, dwellings, canoes, etc. [4012*a*]

Donor, Ruth Landes, Dec. 1977.

4604. KAH-GE-GA-GAH-BOWH (alias GEORGE COPWAY). Letter to F. W. Porter; Philadelphia, June 29, 1847. A.L.S. 2 pp.

Re: Chippewa education efforts. [9]

4605. KURATH, GERTRUDE P. Observations of Michigan Indians; 1967-1968. D., photographs, clippings. 30 pp., 47 pcs.

Re: dance, music, powwows, contents of recordings, interviews, etc. Concerned primarily with the Chippewa of northern Michigan. Mentions Oklahoma, Kiowa, Winnebago, Mashpee, Narraganset, etc. [10(55)]

*Cf.* Nos. 4038, 4606, and Negative 475.
Donor, grantee, July 1968.

4606. KURATH, GERTRUDE P., coll. Observations of Michigan Indians; 1953-1968. 9 reels of tape. Recording No. 63.

Includes: "Red Man in Michigan," an educational series narrated by Edwin Burrows; comparisons of Chippewa revival hymns (Michigan and Ontario); Lansing powwow; Kiowa songs; dances; speeches; comparisons of Calumet dances of Michigan, Muskwaki, Wisconsin (Lac du Flambeau Chippewa and Menomini), and Narraganset. [4071]

*Cf.* Nos. 4038, 4605, and Negative 475.
Donor, grantee, July 1968.

4607. KURATH, GERTRUDE P., coll. Songs from Lac du Flambeau Reservation, Wisconsin; n.d. 2 reels of tape. Recording No. 75.

Includes: a variety of Wisconsin Ojibwa songs and dances; four Ponca peyote songs. Informants include: Willie Catfish, Fred Lacasse, John Martin, George Brown, and James Howard (Ponca). [4072]

*Cf.* No. 4608 for a transcription of Willie Catfish's songs.
Donor, collector.

4608. KURATH, GERTRUDE P., comp. Songs by Willie Catfish; 1956. T.D. with sheet music. 8 pp.

Transcription of the Ojibwa songs by Willie Catfish from the recordings in No. 4607. [9]

Donor, compiler.

4609. Michigan Indians: celebration; 1967. 1 reel of movie film, 24 color slides. Film No. 1257.

Includes: stomp dance; war dance; partridge dance; dance to the four winds; round dance; snake dance; corn dance; audience and parade; crafts. [4038]

*Cf.* Nos. 4071, 4605, and Negative No. 475.
Donor, Gertrude P. Kurath, July 1968

4609*a*. Ojibwa; 1913-1914, 1936, n.d. 93 pcs.

Pictures of: people, activities, life in the bush, canoes, etc. Includes: White Bear, first chief of the Temagami Indians; photographs from Bear Island, Lake Temagami, Ontario; etc. [4020*b*(7)]

4609*b*. Ottawa; 1930, 1946, n.d. 24 pcs.

Pictures of: people, ceremonies, material culture. Includes photographs from Ontario and Michigan. [4020*b*(7)]

4610. RADIN, PAUL. Ojibway miscellany; n.d. A.D. *ca.* 200L.

Includes: two outlines for works on Ottawa culture and history; a comparative and contrastive discussion of "The Two Boys" and "Twin

Myth"; text of an interview with Jim Pontiac including the description of thirty-two dreams; Ojibwa villages of the Upper Peninsula in English or French and Ojibwa; etc. [150]

## OKANAGAN

## (Salish)

4611. WATKINS, DONALD. Letter to Whitfield J. Bell, Jr., Philadelphia; Red Deer, Alberta, Dec. 26, 1974. T.L.S. 5 pp.

Includes: report on fieldwork; contents of Okanagan tape recordings of vocabulary, stories, and songs. [10(143)]

*Cf.* Nos. 4096, 4612.
Donor, grantee, Jan. 1975.

4612. WATKINS, DONALD, coll. Okanagan Salish stories and songs; n.d. 2 reels of tape. Recording No. 101. [4096]

*Cf.* No. 4611.
Donor, grantee, Jan. 1975.

## OKLAHOMA

4612*a*. Indian village (Oklahoma); n.d. 1 pc.

Painting by Frank G. Speck. [4020*b*(4)]

4613. RACHLIN, CAROL K. Study on Negro-Indians; July, 1971. T.L.S. to Whitfield J. Bell, Jr. 2 pp.

Re: whether individuals identify with the Black community or with the Indian; folklore. [10(103)]

*Cf.* Nos. 4547, 4614.

4614. RACHLIN, CAROL K., and ALICE L. MARRIOTT. Negro Indians; 1971. Photocopy of T.D. 22 pp.

Re: persons of mixed blood (Native American with Black and/or White); groups with which they identify; social, economic, and political factors; folklore among those who identify with the Native American community, with the Black community. [10(110)]

*Cf.* No. 4613.
Donors, grantees, 1971.

4615. ROARK-CALNEK, SUE N. Indian way in Oklahoma: transactions in honor and legitimacy; 1977. D. 945 pp.

Unpublished doctoral dissertation, Bryn Mawr College. [10(157)]

*Cf.* Nos. 4222, 4616.
Donor, grantee, June 1977.

4616. ROARK-CALNEK, SUE N., coll. Indian performances in Oklahoma; 1973-1974. 36 cassette tapes. Recording No. 107.

Re: songs; dances (including: Ponca wedding dance, war dances, gourd dances, snake dance, buffalo dance, stomps, Seneca-Cayuga green corn stomp); Oto hand game; etc. Includes: Arapaho, Delaware, Shawnee, Oto, Cheyenne, Ponca, Quapaw, Cherokee, Pawnee, Seneca-Cayuga. [4081]

*Cf.* No. 4616*a* for table of contents.
Donor, grantee, 1977.

4616*a*. ROARK-CALNEK, SUE N., comp. Delaware songs and texts, 1973-74; Indian performances in Oklahoma, 1973-74. D. 32 pp.

Tables of contents for recordings of the same titles. [10(156)]

*Cf.* Nos. 4222, 4616.
Donor, grantee, June 1977.

## OTOMI

## (Otomian)

4617. BERNARD, H. RUSSELL. Letter to Whitfield J. Bell, Jr., Philadelphia; La Jolla, July 10, 1972. T.L.S. and enc. 47 pp.

Re: linguistic work on Otomi. Includes: contents of tape recording; copy of article on Otomi orthography submitted to the *International Journal of American Linguistics;* five Otomi texts with free and literal English translations. [10(131)]

*Cf.* Nos. 4049-4050, 4618-4622.
Donor, grantee, 1972.

4618. BERNARD, H. RUSSELL. Letter to Whitfield J. Bell, Jr.; La Jolla, July 25, 1972. A.L.S. and enc. 6 pp.

Re: support of work on Otomi language orthography. Includes: letter to Whitfield J. Bell,

Jr., from Jesús Salinas Pedraza, July 13, 1972 (in Otomi with English translation). [10(130)]

*Cf.* Nos. 4049-4050, 4617, 4619-4622.
Donor, grantee, July 1972.

4619. BERNARD, H. RUSSELL. Letter to Whitfield J. Bell, Jr., Philadelphia; La Jolla, Aug. 30, 1972. T.L.S. 1 p.

Re: collection and analysis of Otomi data. [10(125)]

*Cf.* Nos. 4049, 4620.

4620. BERNARD, H. RUSSELL, coll. Otomi stories; 1972. 3 reels of tape. Recording No. 90.

Includes: texts in Otomi with Spanish translations; discussion, in Spanish, of the meaning of each text. Informant: Jesús Salinas Pedraza. [4049]

*Cf.* Nos. 4050, 4617-4619, 4621-4622.
Donor, grantee, Sept. 1972.

4621. BERNARD, H. RUSSELL, coll. Otomi stories and songs; 1971. 2 reels of tape. Recording No. 86.

Includes: folk tales; anecdotes; local history of the area around Ixmiquilpan, Hidalgo, Mexico; songs, etc. [4050]

*Cf.* Nos. 4049, 4617-4620, 4622.
Donor, grantee, 1972.

4622. BERNARD, H. RUSSELL. Preliminary remarks on Otomi sexual humor; 1973. Copy of T.D. 10 pp.

Re: collection, taxonomy, etc., of sexual humor. Includes: four Otomi jokes in English translation. Paper given at the meeting of the American Folklore Society, Nashville, November 3, 1973. [9]

*Cf.* Nos. 4617-4621.
Donor, author, Dec. 1973.

## PAPAGO

### (Pima D.)

4622*a*. BAHR, DONALD M. Abstract of Papago recordings; 1977-1978. T.L.S., photocopy of T.D. 135 pp.

Abstract in English of the Papago. Includes letter to Whitfield J. Bell, Jr. [10(171)]

*Cf.* No. 4622*b*.
Donor, grantee, July 1978.

4622*b*. BAHR, DONALD M., coll. Papago and Pima oral literature; 1977-1978. 132 reels of tape. Recording No. 111.

Includes: a variety of songs; discussions of curing practices and sand paintings; war orations and other speeches; myths; etc. Papago informants: Jose Manol, Juan Gregorio, Lupe Antone, Rosana Ventura, Ligali (Mrs. Masi Loin), Baptisto Lopez and family, Maila Kelaila, Frances Ventura, Mendes Lopez, Arturo Mendez, Listo Antone, Chico Moreno, Jose Hillman Ventura, Jose Pancho, Baptisto Lopez. Pima informant: Paul Manuel. Recorded at: Ak Cin and Sikol Himadk, Papago Reservation, Arizona; Santa Rosa, Arizona; Phoenix, Arizona. Restricted access and duplication. [4047*b*]

*Cf.* No. 4622*a* for partial abstract.
Donor, grantee, 1978.

4623. DOLORES, JUAN. Papago grammatical notes; n.d. A.D. 3 notebooks of *ca.* 50L. each.

Notes on various items of Papago grammar; apparently in hand of Juan Dolores with some additional notes by Mason. Each notebook has table of contents; notebooks are numbered 10, 11, and 12. [4017(ling. #1)]

4624. DOLORES, JUAN. Papago texts; n.d. Photocopy of D., T.D. 138 pp. c.c.

Papago texts with interlinear English translations. [4017(ling. #1)]

4625. ENOS, SUZIE, comp. Papago stories narrated by Jose Ventura; n.d. Photocopy of T.D. 31 pp.

Papago texts with indication of syntactic function of elements in sentences, other grammatical notes, and English translations. [4007]

Donor, Dean Saxton, 1968.

4626. GARCIA, MIGUEL. Papago text; 1919. A.D. 21L.

Includes: Papago text (in ink) without translation; Dolores's corrections (in pencil). [4017(ling. #1)]

4627. HERZOG, GEORGE. Letters to John Alden Mason; Apr. 17–Nov. 16, 1947. T.L.S. and D. 14L.

Includes: several pages of comments on Mason's Papago grammar. [4017(ling. #2)]

4628. KROEBER, ALFRED L. Correspondence with John Alden Mason; Nov. 23, 1942–Jan. 4, 1943 and Mar. 26–Apr. 12, 1947. T.L.S. 7L.

Re: Mason's Papago grammar. [4017(ling. #2)]

4629. MASON, JOHN ALDEN. Morphological data on coyote story; n.d. T.D. 1 p.

Includes: Papago text with morph boundaries marked; English translations. [4017(ling. #2)]

4630. MASON, JOHN ALDEN. Papago field notes; n.d. A.D. Notebook of *ca.* 60L.

Notes on kinship terms, other vocabulary, some texts, and comparisons with Tepecano. [4017(ling. #1)]

4631. MASON, JOHN ALDEN. Papago: general characteristics; n.d. T.D. 4 pp.

Apparently part of a larger manuscript. Summary of the salient features of Papago without examples. [4017(ling. #2)]

4632. MASON, JOHN ALDEN. Papago linguistics; n.d. D. *ca.* 3500 cards.

Papago with English glosses, many with grammatical or other explanatory notes. [4017(2)]

4633. MASON, JOHN ALDEN. Papago miscellaneous notes; 1918-1919, n.d. D. *ca.* 125 pcs.

Includes: kinship terms; paradigms; various other grammatical notes. [4017(ling. #1)]

4634. MASON, JOHN ALDEN. Papago songs and ethnographic notes; 1919. A.D. 9 pcs., notebook of 36L.

Includes: songs with English interlinear translations; ethnographic and archeological notes; Tepecano and Papago comparisons. [4017(ling. #1)]

4635. MASON, JOHN ALDEN, coll. Papago texts; 1919. A.D. 23 pp.

Includes: Papago texts; interlinear translations in English; some Spanish translations. [4017(ling. #1)]

4636. MASON, JOHN ALDEN. Papago words with *p* and *t;* n.d. T. and A.D. 4 pp.

Lists of words with English glosses. [4017(ling. #2)]

4637. MASON, JOHN ALDEN. William Kurath, a brief introduction to Papago; n.d. T.D. 9 pp. c.c.

Comments on Kurath's orthography for Papago. [4017(ling. #2)]

4638. Notebook No. 14 of Juan Dolores; n.d. T.D. 1 p.

Table of contents listing myths and songs in the notebook. Notebook wanting. [4017(ling. #2)]

4639. Papago grammatical notes; 1941, n.d. T. and A.D. *ca.* 105L.

Includes: drafts of an article by Mason giving Dolores's verb conjugations and a letter giving George Herzog's comments on same; various notes, lists, analyses, etc., on Papago adjectives, nouns, verbs, pronouns, etc., much of it from Dolores. [4017(ling. #2)]

4640. Papago nominal stems ending in *l, li,* or *t;* n.d. T.D. 1 p.

Lists stems from Dolores (Mason), Hearst Memorial Volume, pp. 22-31 with cognates from Pima, Northern Tepehuan, and Tepecano. [4017(ling. #2)]

4641. Papago stops; Jan. 8, 1954–Feb. 7, 1955. T.L.S. 18L.

Correspondence regarding Mason's Papago grammar and the dispute with Morris Swadesh on whether there is one or two stop series in Papago. Correspondents include: Joe Grimes; Burton W. Bascom, Jr.; George Herzog; Rev. Fr. Regis Rohder, O.F.M.; and Dean Saxton. [4017(ling. #2)]

4641*a*. UNDERHILL, RUTH M. Correspondence with John Alden Mason; 1931-1959. A.L.S., T.L. and L.S. 30 pp.

Re: work on the Papago language. [4017(C37)]

## PASSAMAQUODDY

### (Algonquian)

4642. KNECHT, LAURA. Field notes on the Passamaquoddy language; 1975. Photocopy of A.D. *ca.* 150 pp.

Includes: words; sentences; paradigms; English translations. [10(146)]

Donor, grantee, Sept. 1975.

4642*a*. LE SOURD, PHILIP S., coll. Field notes on Passamaquoddy; 1976. Photocopy of D. *ca.* 500 pp.

Includes: vocabulary, paradigms, sentences, etc., in Passamaquoddy; English glosses. [10(155)]

*Cf.* No. 4642*b*.
Donor, grantee, May 1977.

4642*b*. LE SOURD, PHILIP S., coll. Passamaquoddy field notes; 1977. Photocopy of A.D. *ca.* 200L.

Includes: sentences, paradigms, etc., in Passamaquoddy; English glosses. [10(164)]

*Cf.* No. 4642*a*.
Donor, grantee, Feb. 1978.

4642*c*. Passamaquoddy; n.d. 4 pcs.

Pictures include: Pleasant Point Indian Village near Eastport, Maine; portraits of Lola Mohawk and Mary Selmore; unidentified group (photograph by M. F. Knight). [4020*b*(8),(13:3)]

4643. PRINCE, JOHN DYNELEY. Letters to the American Philosophical Society; New York, Jan. 10, Mar. 11, and Apr. 14, 1898. T.L.S. 3 pp.

Requesting copies of his article "Passamaquoddy Wampum Records" (*cf. Proc. Amer. Philos. Soc.* **36** (1897): pp. 479-495) and acknowledging receipt thereof. [3]

4644. PRINCE, JOHN DYNELEY. Letter to the American Philosophical Society; New York, Nov. 7, 1899. T.L. with MS corrections S. 1 p. Enc. wanting.

Re: paper on Passamaquoddy witchcraft tales; his article on Passamaquoddy wampum records (*cf.* No. 4643); his study of the language and traditions of the eastern Algic tribes, particularly, Abenakis, Passamaquoddies, and Penobscots. Mentions Daniel G. Brinton. [3]

4645. SPECK, FRANK G. Malecite bird names; n.d. D. 3 pp. and end.

Includes: list of bird names in Malecite; English glosses. [9]

Donor, Frank Siebert, Sept. 1970.

## PATAGONIAN
### (Andean?)

4646. DU PONCEAU, PETER S. *Vocaboli de' Patagoni del Medesimo;* n.d. D. in a bound v. 1L.

Vocabulary in Spanish and Patagonian. Includes some items identical to those of Pigafetta in Daniel G. Brinton, "Studies in South American Native Languages," *Proc. Amer. Philos. Soc.* **30** (1892): pp. 45-105; others are not included in Brinton. [60(55)]

## PAWNEE
### (Caddoan)

4647. PARKS, DOUGLAS. Report of field work on Pawnee; 1966. T.D. 1 p.

Summary of work accomplished. [10(48)]

*Cf.* No. 4648.

4648. PARKS, DOUGLAS, coll. Pawnee texts; n.d. 1 reel of tape. Recording No. 67.

Texts in the South Band and Skiri dialects. Informants: Harry Cummings, Sam Allen, and Phillip Jim. [4078]

*Cf.* No. 4647.
Donor, grantee.

4648*a*. Pawnee; 1904, 1912, n.d. 3 postal cards, 2 photographs, 1 painting.

Includes: Tom Morgan (Pawnee chief) and four unidentified persons; group picture and dance at camp near Black Bear Creek, Oklahoma Territory; view of a Pawnee camp as painted by Frank G. Speck. [4020*b*(8)]

4649. WELTFISH, GENE. Morphology of the Pawnee language; n.d. T. and A.D. 88L.

Includes: outline for a Pawnee grammar (South Band dialect); partial treatment of verb morphology according to the plan of the outline. [30(C1.1)]

## PENNSYLVANIA

4650. Indian height; Apr. 23–May 31, 1962. T.L. and L.S. 8 pp.

Re: the average height of Indians of Pennsylvania. Includes correspondence between Paul A. W. Wallace and J. E. Anderson, W. Laughlin, William A. Ritchie, T. D. Stewart, and Charles Wray. [4021(6)]

4650*a*. Indian massacre at Wilkesbarre; n.d. 1 engraving.

Engraving by John Rogers after F.O.C. Darley. [4020*b*(10)]

4651. MASON, JOHN ALDEN. The Indians of Pennsylvania; Sept. 1957. T.D. 20 pp. c.c.

Re: the Delaware, Susquehannock, Erie, Wenrohronon, Honniasont, and the transitory Mohegan, Seneca, Oneida, Wyandot, Ottawa, Tuscarora, Saponi, Tutelo, Nanticokes, Conoy, Shawnee, and Munsee. Written for the Pennsylvania Historical Commission. [4017(C20)]

4652. MORTON, GEORGE. Permit for wagons to pass to Ft. Pitt; July 4, 1760. A.D.S. 1 p.

Re: two loads of "Indian stores." [33]

4652*a*. Pennsylvania; 1941, n.d. 2 pcs.

Pictures include: petroglyphs from rocks in the Susquehanna River; Chief Running Wolf using divining rod of willow to find water. [4020*b*(8)]

4653. WALLACE, PAUL A. W. Indian highways; n.d. T.D. *ca.* 65 pp.

Description of some Indian paths (primarily in Pennsylvania), purposes for which they were used, and their later use by Whites. [4021(6)]

4654. WALLACE, PAUL A. W. Indian trails and Pennsylvania travelers; 1951. T. and A.D. *ca.* 125 pp.

Drafts, etc., of an article for the *Northumberland County Historical Society Proceedings.* [4021(10)]

4655. WALLACE, PAUL A. W. Sakayenkwarahton and General Sullivan travel the Great Warriors Path; July 4, 1966. T. and A.D. *ca.* 50 pp.

Re: the military use of Indian trails by Whites, particularly with respect to the Battle of Wyoming. Includes: two copies, synopsis, and preliminary notes. [4021(10)]

## PENOBSCOT

### (Algonquian)

4656. DAY, GORDON M. Letter to Frank G. Speck, Philadelphia; New Brunswick, N.J., May 23, 1947. T.L.S. 1 p.

Re: obtaining a copy of Speck's *Penobscot Transformer Texts.* [170(26)]

4657. ECKSTORM, FANNIE H. Letters to Frank G. Speck and to Henry E. Dunnack; Brewer, Me., Nov. 13, 1935. T.L.S. and L. 2 pp.

Re: financial support for publication of Speck's manuscript on Penobscot social and economic life. [170(27)]

4658. GANDY, ETHEL. Letter to Charles Marius Barbeau; Nov. 12, 1926. T.L. 1 p. c.c.

Expressing appreciation for names of chiefs and their clans. Regarding the reproduction by Wissler of plates for Gandy's forthcoming monograph on Penobscot art. [170(26)]

4659. GORDON, EUGENE S. Miscellaneous notes of Penobscot words and materials; 1956. D. 83 pp.

Includes: paradigms; grammatical notes; texts. [10(17)]

*Cf.* No. 271.
Donor, grantee.

4660. Letters to and from Frank G. Speck; May 30, 1913–Dec. 7, 1917. T.L. 9 pp.

Re: publication of Speck's *Life and Culture of the Penobscot Indians.* [170(30)]

4661. Letters to Frank G. Speck; Nov. 23, 1938–Nov. 27, 1943, and n.d. T. and A.L.S. 23L.

Expressing appreciation for copies of and giving comments on *Penobscot Man.* [170(27)]

4662. NASSAU, R. H. Letters to Frank G. Speck; Ambler, Pa., May 21 and Sept. 10, 1913. A.L.S. 4L.

Re: Speck's manuscript of Penobscot stories and ethnological notes. [170(25)]

4663. OSGOOD, CORNELIUS. Letter to Frank G. Speck, Philadelphia; New Haven, Nov. 26, 1937. T.L.S. 1 p.

Re: possible sales of Speck's *Penobscot Man.* Mentions Murdock. [170(30)]

4663*a*. Penobscot; 1906-1907, 1910-1917, 1926, 1929, 1937-1938, 1941, n.d. *ca.* 650 pcs.

Includes photographs, drawings, and postal cards. Some photographs and drawings published in Frank G. Speck's *Penobscot Man.* Primarily concerned with Maine, but a few photographs are from Quebec (St. Francis Abenaki). Subjects include people, activities, material culture, habitat, etc. A few items pertain to other groups: Passamaquoddy, Malecite, Micmac, Lake George Abenaki, and Musquakie. Postal cards include the following notes: to Mrs. Florence Speck from Mrs. Neptune, to D. Scribner Hyler from Mae (resident of Old Town, Me.), to Frank G. Speck from E., to Frank G. Speck from C. F. Paul, and to Mrs. Florence Speck from Frank G. Speck (2). One tintype shows Clara Paul in native dress of *ca.* 1840 with war bow and silver brooches (*Penobscot Man,* p. 144). [4020*b*(8),(9),(13:1)]

4664. SPECK, FRANK G. Notes on Penobscot manuscript; n.d. A.D. 3 pp.

Re: progress on the manuscript; proportion of expenses to be borne by the University Museum, G. G. Heye, and himself. [170(30)]

4665. SPECK, FRANK G., coll. Recordings of Cherokee, Naskapi, Penobscot, Sioux (Santee), and Winnebago; 1964. 4 reels of tape. Recording No. 49.

Rerecorded from discs made in the 1930s. Originals in possession of the Museum of Primitive Art, New York. [4086]

*Cf.* No. 9, Speck, Frank G., table of contents . . . ; n.d.

## PENUTIAN

4666. WHORF, BENJAMIN L. Macro-Penutian; Jan. 1939. T.D. 6 pp.

List, in outline form, of divisions and subdivisions of Macro-Penutian as far as Whorf felt certain at the time. Refers to table I, Utaztecan. [4017(ling. #2)]

## PIMA

### (Uto-Aztecan)

4667. PARSONS, ELSIE CLEWS. Letter to Edward Sapir; May 19, 1920 [1926]. Photocopy of A.L.S. 2 pp.

Re: financial support of White's fieldwork; Boas's suggestion that White go to the Pima; "going over" Russell; study of possible relations between Pima and Pueblo. [137]

## PIMA BAJO

### (Uto-Aztecan)

4668. BRUGGE, DAVID M. Correspondence with John Alden Mason; 1955-1960. T.D., A.L.S., T.L. and L.S. 175 pp.

Re: Brugge's work on Pima Bajo and Navajo; problems arising from mistreatment of Maicoba Pimas by Whites. Includes: log, itinerary, list of photographs, and journal of Brugge-Annon trip to Sonora; correspondence with the Wenner-Grenn Foundation and Paul Fejos; essay on distribution, religion, fiestas, social structure, economy, houses and furnishings, handicrafts, etc., of the Pima Bajo. [4017(C10),(ling. #1)]

4669. BRUGGE, DAVID M. History of the Pima Bajo of the mountains; May 1960. T.D. 10 pp.

Discusses information from historical and archeological sources regarding the Pima in the villages of Yecora and Maicoba, Sonora, and Yepachic and Moris, Chihuahua. [4017(ling. #1)]

4670. BRUGGE, DAVID M. Letter to John Alden Mason; Gallup, N. Mex., Feb. 28, 1956. T.L.S., photographs. 5 pcs.

Gives identification for two photographs showing pottery and baskets and for two showing terrain near Rancho Los Tepalcates. [4017(ling. #1)]

4671. BRUGGE, DAVID M. Letter to John Alden Mason; Gallup, N. Mex., Mar. 1, 1956. T.L.S., photographs. 3 pcs.

Gives information about baskets shown in four photos (two photos wanting). [4017(ling. #1)]

4672. BRUGGE, DAVID M. Letter to John Alden Mason; Gallup, N. Mex., June 30, 1958. A.L.S., T.L. 21 pp.

Concerning mistreatment of Maicoba Pimas by Whites: taking of land, cattle, church offerings, etc. [4017(ling. #1)]

4673. BRUGGE, DAVID M. Lower Pima notes; n.d. T.D. 10 pp.

Brugge's contribution to an article coauthored with J. Alden Mason. [4017(ling. #1)]

*Cf.* No. 4682.

4674. BRUGGE, DAVID M., coll. Nevome word lists; Jan. 1954. T. and A.D. 13 pp.

Notes from three informants at Santa Ana rancheria near Onavas, Sonora. [4017(ling. #1)]

*Cf.* No. 4681.

4675. BRUGGE, DAVID M. Tepehuan and Pima Bajo recording logs; Pima Bajo texts; 1958-1965. D. 25 pp.

Includes: notes on Yaqui and Northern Tepehuan recordings to be sent to Indiana University; contents of Southern Tepehuan recordings (in hand of J. Alden Mason); two Pima Bajo texts; Spanish translations for four texts; phonetic key for Pima Bajo. [4017(C36)]

4676. CORNELL, JOHN R., coll. Pima Bajo materials; 1970. 17 reels of tape. Recording No. 83.

Includes: word lists; history; texts, some with translation. Informants: Pedro Estrella Tánori and María Córdova, both of Ónabas, Sonora, Mexico. [4056]

Donor, grantee.

4677. DUNNIGAN, TIMOTHY. A report on linguistic field work among the Pima Bajo of eastern Sonora, Mexico; n.d. T.D. 3 pp.

Report on fieldwork in the highland dialect; very brief discussion concerning phonology and syntax. [10(43)]

*Cf.* No. 4678.

4678. DUNNIGAN, TIMOTHY, coll. Pima Bajo recordings; 1965. 12 reels of tape. Recording No. 55.

Recorded at Yecora, Sonora, Mexico. Informant: Leonardo Duarte O. [4058]

*Cf.* No. 4677.
Donor, grantee.

4679. Lower Pima linguistic notes; 1956-1957. D., L.S. *ca.* 1000 cards, 4 pp.

Cards are probably by David M. Brugge. Most items have English translation. Some items are keyed to informant. Includes three letters between Brugge and J. Alden Mason discussing the language and Brugge's work. [4017(4)]

4680. MASON, JOHN ALDEN. Nevome grammatical notes; n.d. T. and A.D. 2 pp.

Primarily a listing of locative particles and adverbs. From an unspecified source. [4017(ling. #2)]

4681. MASON, JOHN ALDEN. Nevome (Lower Pima Expedition) 1953; 1953-1954. D. *ca.* 100L., notebook of *ca.* 20L.

Includes: correspondence, draft reports on, and expenses for trip to Sonora, Mexico. Correspondents include: Dale S. King, James McConnell, Edward H. Spicer, Fernando Pesqueira, David Lopez Molina, Robert J. Weitlaner, John E. Heimnick, and Robert J. Drake. [4017(ling. #1)]

*Cf.* No. 4674.

4682. MASON, JOHN ALDEN, and DAVID M. BRUGGE. Notes on the Lower Pima; 1956. T.D. and L.S. *ca.* 85 pp.

Includes: drafts of an article (one complete, two incomplete); letters; notes; bibliographic items; linguistic map of northwestern Mexico. [4017(ling. #1)]

*Cf.* No. 4673.

## PLAINS

4682*a*. Comanche war shield; 1925. 1 photograph.

Showing a buffalo-hide shield taken in western Texas, 1868. [4020*b*(2)]

4682*b*. Crow; 1938, 1948, n.d. 5 postal cards, 2 photographs.

Re: people, sun dance, war dance. Includes notes to Frank G. Speck from Claude [E. Schaeffer] (3) and Dorothy (1). [4020*b*(2)]

4682*c*. Kiowa Apache; n.d. 1 postal card.

Three Kiowa Apache in costume with horse travois, Craterville Park, Oklahoma. [4020*b*(4)]

4682*d*. Kutenai; 1947-1948. 13 postal cards.

Portraits of Kutenai, Blackfoot (including Piegan), Shoshoni, etc. All include notes to Frank G. Speck from Claude [E. Schaeffer] regarding fieldwork near Polson and Browning, Montana, and Bonners Ferry, Idaho. [4020*b*(4)]

4682*e*. Plains; 1935, n.d. 67 pcs.

Pictures include: engravings after the work of Karl Bodmer regarding Sauk, Fox, Punka (Dhegiha?), Mannitarri (Hidatsa), Mandan, Dakota, Assiniboin, Fort Mackenzie scene; Iowa and Ponca (Dhegiha) dancers; shields (painting by Robert Riggs and photographs), people, camps, and dances with regard to the Gros Ventre, Assiniboin, and others; portraits of Red Cloud (Dakota), White Eagle (Ponca chief), Wades-in-the-Water, and Chief Bull; photograph of "Buffalo Hunt on Snowshoes" by Peter Rindisbacher. [4020*b*(1),(4),(9),(11:11)]

4682*f*. POWERS, WILLIAM K. At the Pine Ridge Indian Reservation, South Dakota: photographs; Aug. 1966. 64 color slides. Negative No. 456.

Re: people; dwellings; *Yuwipi* meeting; sweat lodge; Memorial Feast of the Dead. Includes: Mr. and Mrs. George Plenty Wolf and family; Mr. and Mrs. Charles Red Cloud; Mrs. Melvin Red Cloud; Mr. and Mrs. William Horn Cloud; Oglala and Arapaho; others. Table of contents available.

*Cf.* No. 4207.
Donor, grantee.

4683. POWERS, WILLIAM K. Indians of the Northern Plains; n.d. T.D. 205 pp. c.c.

Re: Arapaho, Arikara, Assiniboin, Blackfoot, Cheyenne, Crow, Gros Ventre, Hidatsa, Mandan, Plains Cree, Plains Ojibwa, Sarsi, and Sioux with the topics: before Whites, dwellings, transportation, communication, subsistence, warfare, naming, religion, music, dance, games, sports. [10(54)]

Donor, grantee.

4683*a*. Sitting Bull and Shahaka; n.d. 4 photographs.

Includes: photograph by O. S. Goff of Sitting Bull (Sioux chief) seated; three copies of photo by C.B.J.F. de St. Mermin of Shahaka (Mandan chief). [4016*a*(A:In22P),(A:Sh22P)]

4683*b*. The Rocky Mountains; *ca.* 1871. Engraving. 1 pc.

Engraving by R. Hinshelwood after W. Whitteredge showing distant mountains and an Indian camp in foreground. [4016*a*(B)]

## POCOMAM

## (Mayan)

4684. SIMEON, GEORGE. Letter to Whitfield J. Bell, Jr., Philadelphia; Waimea, Kauai, Hawaii, Sept. 21, 1972. T.L.S. 2 pp.

Brief list of materials recorded in Pocomam Central, Mam, and Xinca. [10(126)]

*Cf.* Nos. 4685-4687.

4685. SIMEON, GEORGE, coll. Mam, Xinca, and Pocomam Central linguistics; n.d. 1 cassette tape. Recording No. 91.

A portion of the material which he collected in Guatemala. [4084]

*Cf.* Nos. 4482, 4684, 4914.
Donor, grantee, Oct. 1972.

4686. SIMEON, GEORGE. Pocomam Central linguistics; 1968-1969. T.D., T.L.S. to Richard H. Shryock. 4 pp.

Summary of material recorded in Guatemala. Also includes Xinca, Kekchi, Cakchiquel, and Mam. [10(117)]

*Cf.* Nos. 4482, 4685, 4914.

4687. SIMEON, GEORGE. Report on the Pocomam Central language and culture, Guatemala; 1969. T.D. 3 pp.

Re: the geographical distribution of Pocomam Central; study of native concepts of disease, medicinal plants, and sorcery. [10(77)]

*Cf.* Nos. 4684-4686.

## POWHATAN TRIBES

4687*a*. Chickahominy; 1939-1941, 1948, n.d. 70 photographs.

Re: people, some items of material culture. A few of the photos are by Theodore Stern. [4020*b*(2)]

4687*b*. Mattaponi; 1939-1940, n.d. 36 pcs.

Pictures include: people, material culture, etc. [4020*b*(5)]

4688. MUELLER, WERNER. Letter to University of Pennsylvania; Berlin, Sept. 4, 1947. A.L.S. 1 p.

Inquiring whether Speck's book on the Nansamond and Chickahominy Indians of Virginia was published. Mentions Speck's publications on the Rappahannock and Powhaton. [170(26)]

4688*a*. Nansemond; 1921, 1940-1941, n.d. 24 pcs.

Pictures include: views of Lake Drummond and the Dismal Swamp, Virginia; scenes on the Pasquotank River, North Carolina by Theodore Stern; people. [4020*b*(6)]

4688*b*. Pamunkey; 1921, 1932, 1939-1941, 1948, n.d. *ca.* 130 pcs.

Pictures concern: people, fishing, dances, dwellings, habitat, material culture, etc. Also includes Pamunkey vocabulary [partial duplication of list collected by E. A. Dalrymple] (Jno. Garland Pollard, "The Pamunkey Indians of Virginia," *Bull. Bur. Amer. Ethnol.* **17**) with some differences in phonetic detail. [4020*b*(8)]

4688*c*. Potomac; n.d. 5 photographs.

Includes: two unidentified girls; two unidentified men; two views of the Rappahannock River; Luther Newton. [4020*b*(9)]

4688*d*. Rappahannock; 1941, n.d. 14 pcs.

Pictures include: portraits of Chief Big Otter Nelson, wife of Little Otter Nelson, and Mrs. Sam Nelson, all of Indian Neck, Va.; types of squash grown by Sadie and Sam Nelson, Indian Neck, Va.; Rappahannock traps and hunting and fishing equipment; Catawba hunting and fishing equipment; photographs of Margaret Wiley Brown (Catawba) and Mrs. Sampson Owl (Catawba). [4020*b*(9),(11:9,12)]

## QUECHUA

(Andean)

4689. HARRINGTON, JOHN P. Adjective derivational suffixes of Quechua; n.d. T.D. 9 pp.

A listing of suffixes with brief comments; one slip of Mason's comments. [4017(ling. #2)]

4690. HARRINGTON, JOHN P. Correspondence with John Alden Mason; Nov. 6, 1941–Oct. 11, 1948. T.L.S. 33 pp.

Re: Harrington's work on the Hokan nature of Quechua; Pima-Papago. [4017(C19)]

4691. HARRINGTON, JOHN P. The nominal derivational suffixes of Quechua; 1944 (?). T.D. 32 pp.

Includes: a list of the suffixes with examples; a brief discussion by Harrington; Mason's comments. [4017(ling. #2)]

4692. HARRINGTON, JOHN P., and LUIS VALCARCEL. Grammarlets of the Quechua and Cocama languages; n.d. T.D. 50 pp.

Includes: grammatical sketch of Quechua; very brief sketch of Cocama. [4017(ling. #2)]

## QUICHÉ

(Mayan)

4693. MCQUOWN, NORMAN A., coll. Quiché Maya texts; 1972. 3 reels of tape. Recording No. 89.

Rerecorded from aluminum discs which were recorded Jan. 19, 1935, under the direction of Manuel J. Andrade. [4075]

*Cf.* No. 4693*a*.
Donor, grantee, July 1972.

4693*a*. MCQUOWN, NORMAN A., comp. Quiché Maya texts; n.d. 1 reel of film. Film No. 1295.

Includes: vocabulary with Spanish glosses; texts recorded by Manuel J. Andrade (1935), transcribed and translated by Remigio Cochojil-González (1964-1971); orthography developed by Norman A. McQuown. [4037*a*]

## QUILEUTE

(Chimakuan)

4694. HAMP, ERIC P. Quileute recordings; 1970, Jan. 7, 1971. T.D. and L. 5 pp.

Re: status of work on the language; techniques used in elicitation; some results of the fieldwork. Includes: letter from George W. Corner to Hamp regarding work on Quileute and Greenlandic Eskimo. [10(97)]

*Cf.* Nos. 4695-4697.
Donor, grantee, 1970.

4695. HAMP, ERIC P. Report on study of the Quileute language: letter to Whitfield J. Bell, Jr.; Nov. 7, 1969. T.L.S. 9 pp.

Re: collection and recording of texts; collection of ethnobotanical terms; correction of lists taken earlier. [10(80)]

*Cf.* Nos. 4694, 4696-4697.
Donor, grantee.

4696. HAMP, ERIC P., coll. Quileute recordings; n.d. 14 reels of tape. Recording No. 80.

Informant: Beatrice Black. [4063]

*Cf.* Nos. 4694-4695, 4697.
Donor, grantee, 1971.

4697. HAMP, ERIC P., coll. Quileute texts; 1969. 5 reels of tape. Recording No. 73.

Informant: Beatrice Black. [4064]

*Cf.* Nos. 4694-4696.
Donor, grantee, Dec. 1969.

4698. POWELL, J. V., and FRED WOODRUFF. A note on the Quileute entries of *Ethnobotany of Western Washington;* Aug. 17-18, 1970. Ditto of T.D. 7 pp.

Paper presented at the Fifth International Salish Conference, Spokane, Wash. Includes: corrected forms of ethnobotanical terms from Quileute; a few Chimakum ethnobotanical terms taken from notes of Franz Boas. [9]

Donor, J. V. Powell, Sept. 1970.

## RIVER YUMAN

## (Yuman)

4698*a*. HALPERN, ABRAHAM M. Coyote and Quail; 1976, 1978. T.L.S., photocopy of T.D. 14 pp.

Includes: letter to Whitfield J. Bell, Jr.; Quechan (Yuma) text with interlinear English translation; free English translation; grammatical notes. [10(168)]

Donor, grantee, Apr. 1978.

4698*b*. Maricopa man; n.d. 1 photograph.

Front view (waist up) of unidentified man. [10(122)]

4699. MUNRO, PAMELA. Letter to Whitfield J. Bell, Jr., Phila.,; La Jolla, June 19, 1972. T.L.S. 1 p.

Re: linguistic interaction between the Mohave and the Chemehuevi on the Colorado River Indian Reservation (Parker, Arizona). [10(122)]

## SAHAPTIN

## (Penutian)

4700. RIGSBY, BRUCE J. Report on Sahaptin linguistic field research; 1966. D. and photocopy of D. 39 pp.

Includes: Yakima (paradigms, kinship terms, etc.); Walla Walla (words and phrases); Tygh Valley. [10(49)]

Donor, grantee.

4701. RIGSBY, BRUCE J. A short practical dictionary of the Yakima Sahaptin language; myth texts; n.d. Photocopy of T.D. 12 pp.

Includes: numerals, pronouns, noun declension, kinship terms, etc. (English-Sahaptin); myths in Sahaptin without translation. [10(111)]

Donor, grantee, 1971.

4701*a*. RIGSBY, BRUCE, comp. Sahaptin field notes; 1963-1969. 2 reels of film. Film No. 1261.

Includes: vocabulary, paradigms, sentences, texts, and English translations collected at the Umatilla Indian Reservation; list of Umatilla speakers; vocabulary, sentences, etc., from dialects other than Umatilla; some material on Molale. Permission necessary for publication. From originals in possession of the compiler. [4040]

## SALINAN

### (Hokan)

4702. MASON, JOHN ALDEN. Salinan linguistics and ethnology; 1916-1917. A.D. 2 notebooks of *ca.* 100L. each.

Includes: grammatical notes; texts; ethnographic notes. Marked as "Work completed for Kroeber." [4017(10)]

## SAN CARLOS

### (Navajo D.)

4703. MANDELBAUM, DAVID G., coll. San Carlos Apache texts; Aug. 1933. A.D. 25 pp.

Texts with interlinear English translation. [4012(21)]

4703*a*. San Carlos Apache; 1946. 9 photographs.

Re: sweat lodge, people, beadwork, etc. Photographs by Theodore Stern. [4020*b*(10)]

4704. San Carlos texts; n.d. T.D. *ca.* 325 pp.

Includes: edited copy of each text; original and carbon copy of each text taken from the edited copy. In San Carolos. [4012(16)]

## SARSI

### (Athapascan)

4705. HOIJER, HARRY, comp. Sarsi slip file; n.d. A.D. *ca.* 900 slips.

Includes: postpositions, verb and noun paradigms, etc., taken from Sapir's notebooks (*Cf.* No. 4707). Slips are keyed to notebook and page. [4012(17)]

4706. JENNESS, DIAMOND, coll. Sarcee linguistics; n.d. (poss. 1937). A.D. 1 notebook of 50L.

Includes: vocabulary, paradigms, and one short text; English translations. [4012(15)]

4707. SAPIR, EDWARD, coll. Sarsi linguistics; 1922, n.d. A.D. 7 notebooks of *ca.* 100 pp. ea.

Includes: vocabulary; paradigms; texts with notes; English translations. [30(Na6.1)]

*Cf.* No. 4708.
Donor, Harry Hoijer, Jan. 1973.

4708. SAPIR, EDWARD, comp. Tales of the Sarcee Indians: texts and translations; n.d. T. and A.D. *ca.* 250 pp.

Includes: typed texts in Sarsi; English translation (for 7 of 25 texts) in Sapir's hand. [4012(21)]

*Cf.* No. 4707.

4708*a*. Sarsi; 1908, n.d. 4 postal cards.

Showing women and tipis. One includes note to [Frank G.] Speck. [4020*b*(10)]

## SENECA

### (Iroquois)

4709. ABLER, THOMAS S. Factional dispute and party conflict in the political system of the Seneca Nation (1845-1895): an ethnohistorical analysis; 1969. Photocopy of T.D. 274 pp.

Re: history and development of the Seneca political system; interaction between the Seneca Nation and the dominant White society; pressures on the Seneca political system. [10(107)]

*Cf.* Nos. 4710-4711.
Donor, grantee, July 1971.

4710. ABLER, THOMAS S. The political history of the Seneca Nation; 1965. T.D. 5 pp.

Report on research activities. [10(35)]

*Cf.* Nos. 4709, 4711.
Donor, grantee, 1966.

4711. ABLER, THOMAS S. Research report: Seneca Nation ethnohistory; n.d. T.D. 5 pp.

Re: the Seneca two-party system. Includes tentative outline for work on the origin of the two-party system. [10(45)]

*Cf.* Nos. 4709-4710.
Donor, grantee.

4712. BARBEAU, CHARLES MARIUS. Cayuga: an Iroquoian dialect; 1964. A.D.S. 82 pp.

Vocabulary includes: body parts; terms for people by age, function, etc.; foods; flora; fauna; kinship terms; other nouns; verbs; adjectives; pronouns; numerals; other expressions. Also includes some verb paradigms and noun paradigms with possessive person markers. Informants: Mr. and Mrs. Cuthbert Davey. [4001]

Donor, author, Oct. 1964.

4713. BARTON, BENJAMIN SMITH. Letter to John G. E. Heckewelder; May 23, 1796. Photocopy of A.L.S. 2 pp. and add.

Inquiring whether Heckewelder knows of the sacrifice of a large tortoise or other animal by the Onondaga. From original in the Gilbert Collection, College of Physicians, Philadelphia. [4003]

4714. BARTON, BENJAMIN SMITH. Letter to John G. E. Heckewelder; Feb. 14, 1798. Photocopy of A.L.S. 1 p. and add.

Re: an Onondaga vocabulary; an Indian Bible which Heckewelder is to send. From original in the Gilbert Collection, College of Physicians, Philadelphia. [4003]

4714*a*. Cayuga; 1949, n.d. 18 pcs.

Pictures include: portraits; masks; longhouse; a painting of the Cayuga Sour Springs Long House by Frank G. Speck. [4020*b*(1),(10)]

4715. CHAFE, WALLACE L. Toward a generative semantic description of Onondaga; n.d. Photocopy of T.D. 183 pp.

Re: simple sentences; phonological processes; etc. [10(66)]

Donor, grantee, 1968.

4716. CORNPLANTER, EDWARD. The code of Handsome Lake; Nov. 10, 1933. Photocopy of A.D. 102 pp.

From a manuscript by Edward Cornplanter. Copy is from a document in possession of Edna (Mrs. Nick) Bailey, Tonawanda Reservation. In the hand of and signed by Jesse J. Cornplanter. In Seneca. [4006]

Donor, Elizabeth Tooker, Sept. 1968.

4717. FELLOWS, JOSEPH. Letter to Ely S. Parker; Geneva, N.Y., Nov. 7, 1845. A.L.S. 1 p. and add.

Re: the Ogden Company's willingness to carry out the treaty with the Tonawandas and the wisdom of avoiding litigation. [135]

4718. JACKET, JOHN (chairman), and C. C. JIMESON (secretary). Minutes of "Old Party Caucus"; Cattaraugus Reservation, April 29, 1856. A.D. 4 pp.

Lists nominations for officers. [135]

4718*a*. JOHN, HAZEL V. DEAN. Letter to Whitfield J. Bell, Jr., Philadelphia; Tucson, Aug. 21, 1978. T.L.S. 3 pp.

Re: her work on the Seneca language materials preserved in the Library of the American Philosophical Society. [10(173)]

4719. JOHNSON, HENRY W. Letter to William Parker; Albany, Oct. 28, 1853. A.L.S. 1 p.

Returning Parker's report of Oct. 27, 1853, for completion. [135]

4720. Letters of Onondaga Indians; 1850-1855. L. 32 pcs.

Re: travel by Indians; land; education; difficulties on the reservation. Includes: letters to Ebenezer Meriam from Thomas La Fort, David Hill, L. A. Hill, and Jameson L. Thomas. [4016]

4721. Letters to John W. Jordan; June 9, [1888]-Mar. 27, 1889. A.L.S. 21 pp.

Re: Zeisberger's Onondaga grammar; Onondaga customs; inclusion of Mohawk words in Zeisberger's dictionary; etc. Letters from William M. Beauchamp, Daniel G. Brinton, Isaac Craig, Albert Cusick, Horatio Hale, and Da Cost Smith are mounted in the editor's copy of Zeisberger's *Essay of an Onondaga Grammar.* [Call No. 497.3:Z3e]

4722. MARTINDALE, J. H. Letter to William Parker; Rochester, Nov. 3, 1855. A.L.S. 1 p.

Advising publication of a communication from the chiefs without revision. [135]

4723. Mental elevator, No. 13; Dec. 24, 1846. Printed D. 8 pp.

Published by the Mission Press, Cattaraugus Reservation, N.Y. Mostly in Seneca. Report on the emigration to the West, including names of those who died. Summary of Seneca census for 1846. [135]

4724. PARKER, ELY S. Letter to Henry R. Schoolcraft, Washington; May 30, 1849. A.L.S. 1 p. and end.

Re: obtaining information from public documents on Indian affairs and intentions of government toward the Indians; Senecas; Tonawandas' (Senecas) remaining in their homes. [135]

4725. PARKER, ELY S. Letter to Henry R. Schoolcraft, Washington; Nunda, N.Y., May 30, 1849. A.L.S. 1 p.

Requesting copies of public documents regarding intentions and actions of the government toward Indians. Mentions Senecas and Tonawandas. [135]

4726. PARKER, ELY S. Letter to W. P. Angel, Tonawanda Reservation; Aug. 18, 1846. A.L.S. 1 p.

Re: number of Tonawandas entitled to annuity funds and goods under treaties. [135]

4727. PARKER, WILLIAM. Letter to Henry S. Randall; Alabama, N.Y., Oct. 27, 1853. A.L.S. with "x" and his mark witnessed by Ely S. Parker. 1 p.

An account of expenditures for education of Indian children at Tonawanda. [135]

4727*a*. Seneca; 1928, 1947, 1949, n.d. 24 pcs.

Pictures include: people, stone pipe, sun disc staff, and rattles. Includes photographs from New York, Ontario, and Oklahoma. [4020*b*(10)]

4728. STURTEVANT, WILLIAM C. Report on research on the ethnography of the Oklahoma Seneca-Cayuga; Washington, D.C. Aug. 12, 1963. T.D.S. 7 pp.

Emphasis on comparison with Iroquois in New York and Canada in area of ceremonialism; summarizes situation of Seneca-Cayuga in Oklahoma and briefly reports on fieldwork in Ontario and New York and on archival research; discusses contacts between Oklahoma Seneca-Cayuga and eastern Iroquois. [10(14)]

Donor, grantee, 1963.

4729. TWO GUNS, HENRY. Announcement in Seneca and English of a meeting of the General Council; n.d. Printed D. 1 p.

Re: an amendment to the constitution of the Seneca Nation. [135]

4729*a*. VOEGELIN, CARL F., coll. Seneca notebooks; n.d. A.D. 77L. in 2 notebooks.

Includes paradigms. Informant: Leroy Cooper. [4020*e*(2)]

Donor, Carl F. Voegelin, Feb. 1979.

4730. WRAY, CHARLES F. Correspondence with Paul A. W. Wallace; Apr. 30–May 3, 1962. A. and T.L.S. 2 pp.

Re: the average height of precontact Senecas. [4021(11)]

4731. WRIGHT, ASHER(?). Conjugation of the verbs "take" and "receive" in Seneca; n.d. A.D. 58 pp.

Paradigms with English glosses. [135]

4732. WYLER, BARBARA. The attitude of the Seneca Indians towards land from 1750-1965: an ethnohistorical study; 1965. T.D. 105 pp., 8 pp. of ill.

Participants include: the Senecas, Cornplanter, Handsome Lake, Quakers, federal government, New York state government, and Thomas Ogden. Discusses interactions, problems, etc., leading to changes in Seneca life-style and attitudes toward land. Illustrations include: houses and other buildings; maps; Allegheny River; Kinzua Dam. [10(22)]

Donor, grantee, 1965.

## SHAWNEE

## (Algonquian)

4732*a*. Creek, Yuchi, and Shawnee; 1904, 1932, 1941, n.d. *ca.* 150 pcs.

Pictures concern: people, activities, churches, etc. Includes: photos of Yuchi Annual Harvest Ceremony, Creek Nation, Oklahoma, 1904; photos in area of Atmore, Alabama portraits. [4020*b*(2),(10),(13:1,4)]

4733. SCHUTZ, NOEL W., JR. Shawnee sentence profiles in contrastive and noncontrastive syntax; Feb. 17, 1965. T.L.S. to Richard H. Shryock. 2 pp.

Very brief report on fieldwork. [10(39)]

4734. SCHUTZ, NOEL W., JR. Letter to Whitfield J. Bell, Jr., Philadelphia; Portland, Oregon, Nov. 15, 1972. T.L.S. and enc. 4 pp.

Re: fieldwork on Shawnee mythology. Includes inventory of narratives and translations on tape (recordings wanting). [10(133)]

*Cf.* No. 4733.

4734*a*. VOEGELIN, CARL F. Shawnee grammar; n.d. T. and A.D. *ca.* 175 pp.

Re: phonetics, phonology, morphology. Includes list of tribal names in Shawnee. [4020*e*(2)]

Donor, Carl F. Voegelin, Feb. 1979.

4734*b*. VOEGELIN, CARL F., coll. Shawnee texts; 1934, 1952, n.d. A. and T.D. *ca.* 1900 pp., *ca.* 1300L. in notebooks.

In Shawnee with English translations. Includes: myths; ethnographic texts on numerous topics; Shawnee law; autobiographical texts of [Mary Williams] with work sheets. [4020*e*(2)-(9)]

Donor, Carl F. Voegelin, Feb. 1979.

## SHUSWAP

### (Salish)

4735. BOAS, FRANZ. Indian legends of the North Pacific coast of North America; 1974. Photocopy of T.D. 600 pp.

Legends in English from the German translation of Chinook Jargon, Kwakiutl, Tsimshian, and Shuswap. Translated by Deitrich Bertz from the original edition (see Boas 1895). Permission necessary for reproduction. [30(74)]

Donor, British Columbia Indian Language Project, Jan. 1975.

## SIOUAN

4736. GARNER, BEATRICE MEDICINE. Analysis of comparative Siouan dialects of Canada; Feb. 8, 1965. T.D.S. 3 pp.

Brief report on exploratory trip to Ft. Q'uapple, Saskatchewan, type of information elicited, and plans for future research. [10(31)]

4737. Sioux; 1900, n.d. 5 photographs, 3 postal cards.

Includes: portraits of Broken Arm, Flying Hawk, Chief Hollow Horn Bear, Wander Horse, and an unidentified man; Plains Siouan diorama. [4020*b*(10)]

## SOUTH AMERICA

4738. Bibliography of South American Indians; n.d. D. *ca.* 1000 slips. c.c.

Concerned primarily with South American languages. Many entries are not included in the *Handbook of South American Indians.* [4017(6)]

4739. BRITTEN, MARIAN HALE. Letter to Frank G. Speck, Philadelphia; Washington, July 6, 1936. T.L.S. 1 p.

Re: Speck's reappointment to Committee on Survey of South American Indians, National Research Council. [170(26)]

4739*a*. Central and South America; n.d. 6 photographs.

Includes: people, houses, etc., in Panama, Peru, and the Amazon basin. [4020*b*(2)]

4740. Ecuadorian Oriente; Feb. 17, 1937. T.D. and L. 17 p. c.c.

Notes concerning a letter (included) from Harry B. Wright to Captain Colon Eloy Alfaro proposing that expeditions be sent to Ecuadorian Oriente for study in linguistics, ethnology, etc. [4017(ling. #2)]

4741. GARRO, J. EUGENIO. Geographical distribution of the Native languages and dialects of Peru; 1942. T.D. 16 pp. c.c.

An article submitted for the *Handbook of South American Indians* (marked "not printed in Handbook"). [4017(ling. #2)]

4742. GREEN, OTIS H. Correspondence with John Alden Mason; Feb. 27–Mar. 6, 1943. T.L.S. 3 pp.

Re: origin of the word *jivaro.* [4017(ling. #2)]

4743. HARRINGTON, JOHN P. Affiliation of Witoto, Miranya and Guaranian; 1944 (?). T.D. *ca.* 110 pp.

Includes: Harrington's text comparing vocabulary items (with Guaranian represented by Cocama); Mason's comments. [4017(ling. #2)]

4744. HARRINGTON, JOHN P. Correspondence with John Alden Mason; May 19, 1943–June 21, 1944. T.L. and L.S. *ca.* 55L.

Most are from Harrington to Mason in regard to Harrington's work for Mason on the *Handbook of South American Indians.* [4017(ling. #2)]

4745. HARRINGTON, JOHN P. South American linguistics: Miranya, Witoto, Tupi-Guarani affiliations; 1943. T.D. and L.S. 11 pp.

Discusses hypothesized relationships among the languages. [4017(ling. #2)]

4745*a*. Kagaba; n.d. T.D. 27 pp.

Includes: texts with interlinear Spanish translation; lists of animals, plants, body parts, natural phenomena, kinship terms, etc., with Spanish and English glosses. [4017(C23)]

4746. LEVI–STRAUSS, CLAUDE. Correspondence with John Alden Mason; Feb. 13–July 20, 1942. T. and A.L.S., map. 5L.

Re: locations of Parintintin, Rama-Rama, Tupi, and Nambikuara; Nambikuara dialects; Tupi-Kawahib; Kabixiana; Kep-kiri-uat; Rama-Rama. [4017(ling. #2)]

4747. MASON, JOHN ALDEN. Andean civilization; June 1, 1960. T.D. 25 pp. c.c.

Includes: bibliography; two copies of the text for the *Encyclopaedia Britannica.* [4017(7)]

4748. MASON, JOHN ALDEN. Handbook of South American Indians: correspondence; 1940-1943, 1950. T.L. and L.S. and A.L.S. 60L.

Correspondents include Zellig S. Harris, Harry Hoijer, Eugene A. Nida, et al. Soliciting contributions to the handbook, etc. [4017(ling. #2)]

4749. MASON, JOHN ALDEN. Handbook on the Andean region; n.d. T.D. 166 pp. c.c.

Re: preconquest history and culture of the Andean region, primarily with regard to Peru, through the medium of artifacts preserved in the University Museum (University of Pennsylvania). [4017(C18)]

4750. MASON, JOHN ALDEN. Language: South American handbook; 1947. T.D. and L. *ca.* 125L.

Includes: correspondence, bibliography, draft of introduction, etc., relating to his contribution to the *Handbook of South American Indians.* [4017(ling. #2)]

4751. MASON, JOHN ALDEN. Notes for the Handbook of South American Indians; n.d. A.D. 37 pp.

Notes on the distribution, relationships, etc., of South American languages. [4017(10)]

4752. MASON, JOHN ALDEN. Preface to the Spanish edition of *Ancient Civilizations of Peru;* n.d. T.D. 5 pp. c.c.

Includes: two copies of the preface; memorandum from Alfred Kidder II to Mason regarding recent developments in Central Andean archaeology. [4017(C7)]

4753. MASON, JOHN ALDEN. South American linguistics; 1940s. T. and A.D. and L.S. *ca.* 225 pcs.

Includes notes on: genetic relationships, subgrouping, etc., from published sources or giving his own impressions; Kamakan; Choroti; Ashluslay; Kaduveo; Mataco; Malali; Mashakali; Ge; Vejoz; Coropo; Motilon; Towothli; Kaingang; Subtiaba; Hokan; Coroado. [4017(ling. #2)]

4754. MASON, JOHN ALDEN. The status and problems of research in the Native languages of South America; n.d. T.D. 14 pp.

Primarily concerned with historical linguistics and genetic relationship. Incomplete. [4017(ling. #2)]

4755. MURPHY, ROBERT CUSHMAN. Choco expedition; 1937. D. 1 v.

Primarily concerned with collection of water samples from the Pacific, meteorological data, etc. Some notes and discussion of Indians of Colombia and Ecuador. Groups mentioned: Choco, Citara, Noanama, Cholo, Paparo, Tucura, and Cuna. [4019]

Donor, Grace E. B. Murphy, May 1973.

4755*a*. PARK, WILLARD Z. Correspondence with John Alden Mason; 1937-1948. A.L.S., T.L. and L.S. 53 pp.

Re: Park's ethnological work among the Kagaba in Colombia. [4017(C28)]

4756. PARSONS, ELSIE CLEWS. Letter to Leslie A. White; Sept. 15, 1940. Photocopy of A.L.S. on postal card. 1 p.

Re: book on Keres; Santa Ana manuscript; field notes on Andean Indians of Ecuador. [137]

4757. PARSONS, ELSIE CLEWS. Letter to Leslie A. White; Oct. 29, 1940. Photocopy of T.L.S. 2 pp.

Re: Bandelier's letters; confusion of Bandelier and Means on clanship in early Mexico and Peru. [137]

4758. RANKIN, LOUIS. Correspondence with John Alden Mason; July 28 and Aug. 6, 1942. T.L.S. 2 pp.

Re: the Cocama, Cocamilla, Chama, Campa, and Amuesha languages. [4017(ling. #2)]

4759. ROWE, JOHN H. Correspondence with John Alden Mason; 1942-1955. T.L. and L.S. 64 pp.

Re: South American languages and cultures; Quechua, Aymara, and Millcayac languages; early work of Max Uhle in Peru, Bolivia, etc. Mentions Alfred V. Kidder, Alfred L. Kroeber, and others. [4017(C31),(ling. #2)]

4759*a*. South America; 1922, 1932, n.d. *ca*. 100 pcs.

Includes: Mato Grosso (Brazil); photographs by V. M. Petrullo and William C. Farabee regarding the Araucanian (Mapuche), Macushi, Oakupovi(?), and possibly Witoto; Patagonian woman with dog; Flujensio Santana (San Miguel Salivan) and Pedro Encinales (San Antonio Salivan); Venezuela and Brazil, postal cards regarding the Orinoco, Rio Negro, and others; village in the Peruvian Andes; Parintintin Indians; unidentified people, terrain, material culture, etc. [4020*b*(1),(8),(10)]

4760. South American linguistic notes (#1); n.d. D. *ca*. 800 cards.

Re: genetic classification of South American languages. [4017(7)]

4761. South American linguistic notes (#2); n.d. D. *ca*. 3000 cards.

Re: South American languages and dialects; geographical distribution; etc. Includes some bibliographical items which are also included in No. 4738. [4017(8)]

4762. STOUT, DAVID B. Correspondence with John Alden Mason; Feb. 4-July 10, 1942. T.L.S. 10 pp.

Re: Stout's genetic classification of Chibchan, Cuna, and Choco. Includes one page of Mason's opinions on Stout's classification. [4017(ling. #2)]

## SOUTHEAST

4763. DRAKE, CHARLEY G. Letter to Frank G. Speck, Philadelphia; Union City, Georgia, Jan. 4, 1945. T.L.S. 1 p.

Requesting a copy of "Gourds of the Southeastern Indians"; payment enclosed. [170(27)]

4763*a*. Tunica; 1940-1941, n.d. 56 pcs.

Pictures include: people; blowguns; hide tanning; games; etc.; possibly some Houma. [4020*b*(10)]

## SOUTHERN PAIUTE

### (Uto-Aztecan)

4764. MUNRO, PAMELA. Letter to Whitfield J. Bell, Jr., Phila.; La Jolla, June 19, 1972. T.L.S. 1 p.

Re: linguistic interaction between the Mohave and the Chemehuevi on the Colorado River Indian Reservation (Parker, Arizona). [10(122)]

4765. PIA, J. JOSEPH. Report on pilot linguistic study of the Ute language; March 10, 1966. T.L.S. to Richard H. Shryock. 4 pp.

Report on field activities with some ethnographic observations. [10(28)]

4766. SAPIR, EDWARD. Ute and Kaibab Paiute linguistic material; 1909-1910, 1916, n.d. A.D. 5 notebooks of *ca*. 150 pp. each and 55L.

Notebooks include: paradigms, grammatical notes and texts for Uncompahgre and Uintah

Ute and for Kaibab Paiute; lists of kinship terms from Thompson River (Salish), Nootka, Nass River (Tsimshian), Kutenai, Uintah Ute, Yurok, and Kaibab Paiute. [30(U.5)]

Donor, Sapir family, May 1972.

4766*a*. Ute; n.d. 17 photographs.

Re: people; dwellings; activities; etc. Includes: Uintah; Uncompahgre; unspecified. [4020*b*(10)]

## SOUTHWEST

4767. BILLINGS, JOHN S. Letter to Stephen Bowers, Ventura; Washington, Jan. 27, 1890. T.L.S. 2 pp.

Re: possible publication of "an illustrated catalogue of skulls and skeletons of prehistoric North American Indians collected and presented to the Museum by the Hemenway Southwestern Arohaeological Expedition." [4004]

4768. HENRY, THOMAS CHARLTON. Letter to John L. Le Conte, Philadelphia; Fort Webster, April 16, 1853. A.L.S. 3 pp.

Re: Henry's work in the natural sciences. Mentions that the Gila and Jicarilla Apaches were quiet. [Call No. B:L493.3]

4769. KIDDER, ALFRED V. Correspondence with Neil Judd; 1920-1962. A.L.S., T.L. and L.S., printed D. 88 pp.

Re: archeological work in the Southwest at Pueblo Bonito, Chaco Canyon, etc.; *kivas;* the Alfred Vincent Kidder Award. [4014]

Donor, Neil M. Judd, Jan. 1965.

4770. PARSONS, ELSIE CLEWS. Letter to Leslie A. White; April 8, 1927. Photocopy of A.L.S. 1 p.

Re: White's "Southwest Medicine Societies" and Acoma manuscripts; proposed Santo Domingo-San Felipe field trip by White. [137]

4771. PARSONS, ELSIE CLEWS. Letter to Leslie A. White; April 27, 1927. Photocopy of A.L.S. 2 pp.

Re: Goldfrank's publication on Cochiti; Parsons's "Zuñi Scalp Ceremony." [137]

4772. PARSONS, ELSIE CLEWS. Letter to Leslie A. White; July 13, 1927. Photocopy of A.L.S. 2 pp.

Re: San Felipe; Acoma; Laguna; George Herzog's trip to record music for Boas (*kachina* songs; Santa Fe, Tewa, Zuñi). [137]

4773. PARSONS, ELSIE CLEWS. Letter to Leslie A. White; Aug. 16, 1927. Photocopy of A.L.S. 6 pp.

Re: Acoma; San Felipe; Santo Domingo; Laguna (migration of 1880); Tewa; Zuñi; Cochiti; *kachina; kiva; koshare; cacique;* scalps; war chieftain; outside chiefs. [137]

4774. PARSONS, ELSIE CLEWS. Letter to Leslie A. White; Oct. 28, 1927. Photocopy of T.L.S. 1 p.

Requests White's San Felipe notes and Southwest plan for next September through January. [137]

4775. PARSONS, ELSIE CLEWS. Letter to Leslie A. White; Nov. 13, 1927. Photocopy of T.L.S. 2 pp.

Re: White's San Felipe paper; *kachina* data; Turquoise and Squash groups; three *kachina* groups at Laguna; White's Acoma manuscript; White's proposed paper on Keresan medicine societies; Parsons's proposed paper on influence of the Keresan societies among other pueblos (Zuñi, Isleta, Hopi, Tewa). [137]

4776. PARSONS, ELSIE CLEWS. Letter to Leslie A. White; July 8, 1928. Photocopy of A.L.S. 2 pp.

Re: White's coming field trip; White's Acoma manuscript; Parsons's *Tewa Social Organization.* [137]

4777. PARSONS, ELSIE CLEWS. Letter to Leslie A. White; Jan. 28, 1929. Photocopy of T.L.S. 1 p.

Re: White's Acoma monograph; Zuni papers by Bunzel and Benedict; Parsons's Isleta paper; Stirling's Acoma material; Acoma recordings. [137]

4778. PARSONS, ELSIE CLEWS. Letter to Leslie A. White; Oct. 9, 1930. Photocopy of T.L.S. 2 pp.

Re: White's Acoma manuscript; White's notes on other Keresan towns and on Taos; Santa

Clara and Jemez masks; White's field trip to Taos; work of Parsons and Goldfrank at Isleta. [137]

4779. Parsons, Elsie Clews. Letter to Leslie A. White; May 3, 1932. Photocopy of T.L.S. 2 pp.

Re: student research projects at the laboratory, Santa Fe, New Mexico; difficulties connected with ceremonial studies among the Hopi; Barbara Aitken's discussion of a split at Santa Clara; White's Zia manuscript. Mentions Ruth Benedict. [137]

4780. Parsons, Elsie Clews. Letter to Leslie A. White; Oct. 26, 1932. Photocopy of T.L.S. 1 p.

Re: the ceremony of the Flute society in Oraibi. [137]

4781. Parsons, Elsie Clews. Letter to Leslie A. White; Oct. 19, 1933. Photocopy of T.L.S. 1 p.

Re: invalidation of the Alegre (1841) reference as added by Bustamente in 1841, not from Alegre (1764); reference to F. Starr (1901-1903) for a variant of White's Sundaro by Aztec Nahuatl speaking towns in Huaxteca, Mexico. [137]

4782. Parsons, Elsie Clews. Letter to Leslie A. White; Oct. 23, 1933. Photocopy of T.L.S. 2 pp.

Re: publication of White's Santo Domingo manuscript; White's notes on *kachinas;* title of volume on the Onate expedition. Requests that White pass the clown paper to Julian Steward for comment. [137]

4783. Parsons, Elsie Clews. Letter to Leslie A. White; Mar. 14, 1934. T.D., A.L.S. 3 pp.

Suggests sending White's Santo Domingo manuscript to Spier; asks White's opinion of her Hopi-Zuni ceremonialism memoir; mentions White's Zia paper; asks for complete citation for the royal decree of secular government for New Spain. [137]

4784. Parsons, Elsie Clews. Letter to Leslie A. White; Apr. 23, 1934. Photocopy of T.L.S. 2 pp.

Re: White's Santo Domingo memoir; Parsons's photograph of the Domingo *koshare;* Redfield's "Zepozthan"; Pueblo war captains. Mentions Spier and Titiev. [137]

4785. Parsons, Elsie Clews. Letter to Leslie A. White; May 21, 1934. Photocopy of T.L.S. 1 p.

Re: White's note on masks in the Southwest. [137]

4786. Parsons, Elsie Clews. Letter to Leslie A. White; June 9, 1935. Photocopy of T.L.S. 2 pp.

Re: her Taos manuscript, White's Keresan book. [137]

4787. Parsons, Elsie Clews. Letter to Leslie A. White; Aug. 8, 1935. Photocopy of T.L.S. 2 pp.

Re: "Pueblo Indian Religion"; *kapina* society; Acoma snake society; Hopi antelope society; Zuni shalako strings; Parsons and Beals's "Pueblo Mayo-Zoque Clowns"; Santa Ana; Zia. [137]

4788. Parsons, Elsie Clews. Letter to Leslie A. White; Sept. 23, 1935. Photocopy of T.L.S. 1 p.

Re: Keresan origin of Hopi Snake-Antelope societies corresponding to Acoma and Zia snake-*kapina* societies. [137]

4789. Parsons, Elsie Clews. Letter to Leslie A. White; Oct. 9, 1935. Photocopy of T.L.S. 4 pp.

Re: Keresan origin of Hopi snake-antelope societies; evidence to support her belief. [137]

4790. Parsons, Elsie Clews. Letter to Leslie A. White; Sept. 17, 1937. Photocopy of A.L.S. 3 pp.

Re: altar pictures given to Stirling; a *Mishongnovi* antelope sand painting and possible plagiarism by informant from a Bureau of American Ethnology publication; Antelope altar in Tusayan flute and snake ceremonies; *Chamahiya* snake swallowers; "A Campaign against the Moqui Pueblos" (Martinez, 1716), *New Mexico Historical Review* 6 (1931); Tewa of Hamo residing twenty years in Hopi land; Santo Domingo refugees at Laguna. [137]

4791. Parsons, Elsie Clews. Letter to Leslie A. White; Dec. 3, 1937. Photocopy of T.L.S. 1 p.

Re: "Pueblo Indian Religion" manuscript; possible existence of references to rhombus, bullroarer or whizzer in publications other than those on Zuñi and Hopi. [137]

4792. PARSONS, ELSIE CLEWS. Letter to Leslie A. White; Dec. 13, 1937. Photocopy of T.L.S. 1 p.

Re: "Pueblo Indian Religion" manuscript; whether or not scalps are used as rainmakers; asks for possible reference for Acoma on laying out a dead deer like a person. [137]

4793. PARSONS, ELSIE CLEWS. Letter to Leslie A. White; Mar. 10, 1938. Photocopy of T.L.S. 2 pp.

Re: "Pueblo Indian Religion"; animals associated with disease among the Keres; Santa Ana supernaturals *(maiyanyi, kopishtaiya)*; possible route by which ritual tobacco came to Isleta; archeological relations between southern Caddoans and northeastern Algonquians. [137]

4794. PARSONS, ELSIE CLEWS. Letter to Leslie A. White; Mar. 19, 1938. Photocopy of T.L.S. 1 p.

Re: *maiyanyi* notes from White; ditch opening; Isleta; Santo Domingo. [137]

4795. PARSONS, ELSIE CLEWS. Letter to Leslie A. White; Oct. 19, 1938. Photocopy of T.L.S. 1 p.

Re: Bandelier's journals and delight makers; suggested review by White of Densmore's Santo Domingo (possibly with Herzog); Stirling's Acoma manuscript. [137]

4796. PARSONS, ELSIE CLEWS. Letter to Leslie A. White; Mar. 22, 1941. Photocopy of A.L.S. 2 pp.

Re: David Hare's portfolio of Pueblo portraits; self-styled *cazique* (Acoma); work on Acoma. [137]

4796*a*. Southwest; 1910, n.d. 23 pcs.

Pictures include: Apache people and dance; Indians of the Rio Colorado, an engraving marked "LALY"; Mesa Verde cliff dwellings and Sun Temple; pueblo people, buildings, ruins, etc., of Acoma, Isleta, Laguna, etc.; on one pueblo postal card, a note to Frank G. Speck from Edward Sapir regarding Sapir's work on ethnogeography in British Columbia. [4020*b*(1),(5),(9)]

4797. WHITE, LESLIE A. Letter to Elsie Clews Parsons; July 12, 1928. Photocopy of T.L.S. (with handwritten additions by E.C.P.). 1 p.

Re: Parsons's Tewa Social Organization; White's Acoma paper; paintings of masks and altars; maps and diagrams. [137]

4798. WHITE, LESLIE A. Letter to Elsie Clews Parsons; Apr. 5, 1934. Photocopy of T.L.S. 3 pp.

Re: White's Santo Domingo paper; Parsons's *Hopi and Zuni Ceremonialism* and comments on it; possible trip to New Mexico for additional data on Santa Ana; White's Oraibi notes. [137]

4799. WHITE, LESLIE A. Letter to Elsie Clews Parsons; Sept. 20, 1940. Photocopy of T.L.S. 1 p.

Re: *Pioneers in American Anthropology;* work on Santa Ana; *The Pueblo of Santo Domingo;* Zia; Cochiti; general book on Keres. [137]

4800. WHITE, LESLIE A. Letter to Elsie Clews Parsons; Jan. 27, 1941. Photocopy of T.L.S. 1 p.

Re: White's Santa Ana monograph; Parsons's Tewa memoir; White's sample of *stcamun* ($Fe_3O_4$ magnetite and $Fe_2O_3$ hematite). [137]

## SPOKANE

## (Salish)

4801. CARLSON, BARRY F. Spokane linguistic material; 1974. Photocopy of T.D. *ca.* 160 pp.

Includes: report on Spokane fieldwork; tables of contents of notebooks and tapes; Spokane-English dictionary of words and phrases. [10(139)]

Donor, grantee, Sept. 1974.

## TAKELMA

## (Penutian)

4802. KENDALL, DAYTHAL L. A syntactic analysis of Takelma texts; 1977. Photocopy of T.D. 147 pp.

Re: decoding and generation of sentences (both simple and complex) and of texts; morphology. Doctoral dissertation in linguistics, University of Pennsylvania. [4013]

Donor, author, May 1977.

4803. SAPIR, EDWARD, coll. Takelma linguistic material and songs; [1903-1904], [1906]. D. 5 notebooks of *ca.* 120 pp. each, 6L. sheet music, 10L.

The notebooks contain myth texts with English translations, medicine formulas, etc. (published as Sapir, 1909) as well as paradigms and other grammatical notes. Sheet music contains transcriptions of four Takelma songs and one each for Chasta Costa, Shasta, and Chinook Jargon. Remaining leaves are vocabulary notes made by H. H. St. Clair. Informant: Francis Johnson. [30(Pn1.1)]

## TALAMANCA

## (Chibchan)

4804. JOHNSON, FREDERICK. Letters to John Alden Mason regarding the Talamanca; Apr. 13, 1942, and Apr. 21, 1943. T.L.S. and D. 8 pp.

Re: distribution, names, and synonyms for subdivisions of Talamanca. [4017(ling. #2)]

## TENNESSEE

4805. BUELL, IRA M. Letter to De Moss Bowers; Beloit, Feb. 8, 1916. A.L.S. 1 p.

Re: arranging a large collection of artifacts from Indian mounds in Tennessee. [4004]

## TEPECANO

## (Tepehuan D.)

4806. MASON, JOHN ALDEN. Escuela Internacional de Etnologia y Arqueologia Americanas, preliminary report as Fellow to the; 1912-1913. T.D. 32 pp. c.c.

Report on continued investigations in linguistics, religion, ethnology, and mythology of the Tepecanos and in the archaeology of their region. [4017(ling. #2)]

4807. MASON, JOHN ALDEN. Miscellaneous notes on Tepecano; 1911-1913. T. and A.D. *ca.* 300 pcs.

Re: ethnology; linguistics; religion; Piman comparisons; etc. Includes: prayers; interlinear English translation. With note "work done for Boas." [4017(9)]

4808. MASON, JOHN ALDEN. A sketch of Tepecano religion; n.d. A.D. 6 pp.

The description includes some comparison with religious beliefs of Huichols and Coras. [4017(ling. #2)]

4809. MASON, JOHN ALDEN. Tepecano trip; 1912-1913. A.D. 8 notebooks of 120L. each.

Includes: list of specimens purchased; texts; notes on the language, ethnology, and archaeology; etc. [4017(10)]

4810. Tepecano linguistic file; n.d. D. *ca.* 1000 cards.

Includes: Tepecano words and sentences; Spanish translations for most; some English translations. [4017(5)]

4811. Tepecano rain festival song; n.d. D. 1 p. sheet music.

Includes: music; Tepecano lyrics. [4017(ling. #2)]

4812. Tepecano verbal roots; n.d. T.D. 6 pp.

List of verbal roots with English glosses. [4017(ling. #2)]

## TEPEHUAN

## (Uto-Aztecan)

4813. BASCOM, BURTON W., JR., comp. Comparative lists from southern and northern dialects of Tepehuan; Dec. 1947. T.D. 5 pp.

Includes: Northern Tepehuan; Southern Tepehuan; English glosses; comments. From work in 1943-1944 under the auspices of the Summer Institute of Linguistics. [4017(ling. #2)]

4814. BASCOM, BURTON W., JR. Correspondence with John Alden Mason; 1947-1960. T.D., A.L.S., T.L. and L.S. *ca.* 100 pp.

Re: Northern Tepehuan with some mention of Tepecano, Pima, Papago, and Southern Tepehuan. Includes: short paper by Bascom on Northern Tepehuan possessive *-ga;* Northern Tepehuan verb list for comparison with Mason's Tepecano list; discussion of noun plural formation with examples. [4017(C9),(ling. #2)]

4815. DOLORES, JUAN. Northern Tepehuan myth; n.d. A. and T.D. 17 pp.

Includes: two copies of "The Sacred Case" in Northern Tepehuan; English translation. [4017(ling. #2)]

4816. HART, BRETE R. Correspondence with John Alden Mason; Apr. 30 and May 13, 1953. T.L.S. 3 pp.

Re: receipt of material on Utaztecan; work on alphabet for Southern Tepehuan; brief description of Fiesta for the Dead observed at Xoconoxtle, Durango, Mexico. [4017(ling. #2)]

4817. HOBGOOD, JOHN. Hobgood-Riley: visit to Santa María Ocotlán; Feb. 25–Apr. 24, 1959, n.d. T.D. and T.L.S. 9 pp.

Report of events transpiring during a visit by John Hobgood and Carroll L. Riley to Santa María Ocotlán: presentation of letters; request for permission to study the Tepehuan language and customs of the village; interactions with the villagers. Includes correspondence between Hobgood and J. Alden Mason regarding the report; mentions Agnes McClain Howard and Carroll L. Riley. [4017(C19),(ling. #1)]

4818. MASON, JOHN ALDEN. Digest of Rinaldini's *Tepehuane;* Mar. 1936. D. 1 notebook of 50L.

Taken from the book in the Ayer Collection, Newberry Library. [4017(10)]

4819. MASON, JOHN ALDEN, comp. Kinship terms: Southern Tepehuan, Northern Tepehuan, Tepecano; n.d. A. and T.D. 14 pp.

Includes: list of kinship terms in English; lists of kinship terms in Southern Tepehuan, Northern Tepehuan, and Tepecano with English glosses. [4017(ling. #2)]

4820. MASON, JOHN ALDEN. Northern Tepehuan linguistic expedition, Baborigame, Chihuahua, Mexico; 1951. T.D. 5 pp. c.c.

General report on his trip with itinerary. [4017(ling. #1)]

4821. MASON, JOHN ALDEN, comp. Northern Tepehuan linguistic file; n.d. D. 600 cards.

Includes: words, phrases, and sentences with Spanish glosses; some Tepecano and Papago cognates. [4017(3)]

4822. MASON, JOHN ALDEN, coll. Northern Tepehuan linguistics; Feb. 1936. A.D. 2 notebooks of 100 pp. each.

Includes: vocabulary and texts with Spanish glosses. Informant: Pedro Valencia. [4017(10)]

4823. MASON, JOHN ALDEN. Northern Tepehuan notebooks; 1951. A.D. 2 notebooks of *ca.* 100L. each.

Includes: grammatical notes and texts from wire recordings. [4017(10)]

4824. MASON, JOHN ALDEN, comp. Northern Tepehuan texts; n.d. T.D. 20 pp.

Texts with interlinear Spanish translation. [4017(ling. #1)]

4825. MASON, JOHN ALDEN. Notes on the linguistic and cultural affiliations of the Tepehuan and Tepecano; Aug. 1948. T.D. 5 pp.

Written for Mexican Historical Congress, Zacatecas. [4017(ling. #1)]

4826. MASON, JOHN ALDEN, comp. *Perdones Tepehuanes;* n.d. A.D. 11L.

Includes: lists of *perdones* and notes on same. [4017(ling. #2)]

4827. MASON, JOHN ALDEN. The primitive religions of Mexico; 1916. T.D. 3 pp.

Paper read at American Association for the Advancement of Science, Dec. 1, 1916. Tepecano prayers to accompany the paper wanting. [4017(ling. #2)]

4828. MASON, JOHN ALDEN, comp. Southern Tepehuan notebooks; 1948. A.D. 7 notebooks of 40L. each.

Includes: grammatical notes; texts; some transcriptions and translations of recordings at the American Philosophical Society (*cf.* No. 283). [4017(10)]

4829. MASON, JOHN ALDEN. The Tepehuan of northern Mexico; 1958. D. 47 pp.

Re: observations on the culture which were made incidental to linguistic fieldwork. Includes original and two copies with maps. [4017(C36)]

4830. Northern Tepehuan: miscellaneous notes; n.d. T. and A.D. 5 pp.

Includes: verb conjugation labeled "[Burton W.] Bascom"; map; other notes. [4017(ling. #2)]

4831. Northern Tepehuan: morphology; 1951, n.d. T. and A.D. 14 pp.

Concerned primarily with suffixes. Taken from the files of Burton W. Bascom. [4017(ling. #2)]

4832. Northern Tepehuan myths and other texts; 1936(?). T.D. 20 pp.

Includes: myths; official speeches; settling marital difficulties; interlinear Spanish translations. [4017(ling. #2)]

4833. WEIGAND, PHIL C. Correspondence with John Alden Mason; Dec. 15, 1966–Jan. 16, 1967. T.L. and L.S. 6L.

Re: acculturation; history; relations with Whites in San Sebastian and Azqueltan. [4017(ling. #1)]

## TEWA

## (Tanoan)

4834. GARCIA, ANTONIO. The man ceremony in San Juan Pueblo; 1970. T.D. 7 pp.

Includes: description of the *senshare* ceremony; transcription of No. 4835 with English translation. [9]

*Cf.* No. 4839.

4835. GARCIA, ANTONIO, recorder. *Senshare* man ceremony: Kiva ritual of San Juan Pueblo, New Mexico; 1964-1965. 3 reels of tape. Recording No. 69.

Includes: senshare songs by Juanito Trujillo and Peter Garcia; announcements and spirit calls by Antonio Garcia; songs for the *xoxeye* corn dance by Juanito Trujillo. **Restricted access.** [4059]

*Cf.* Nos. 4834, 4839.

4836. GOODMAN, LINDA S. The form and function of the basket dance of San Juan Pueblo; 1968. Photocopy of T.D. 194 pp.

Includes: background information on San Juan Pueblo; the ceremonial cycle; basket dance; songs with interlinear translation; sheet music; etc. M.A. thesis at Wesleyan University, Middletown, Conn. [10(56)]

*Cf.* Nos. 4061, 4837.
Donor, grantee, June 1968.

4837. GOODMAN, LINDA, coll. San Juan Pueblo music; 1967. 5 reels of tape. Recording No. 62.

Includes: songs for *kachina,* rain, green corn, yellow corn, buffalo, butterfly, deer, turtle, cloud, dog, and basket dances; peace song; some Tewa vocabulary; discussion of the dances and music. Informants include: Marie Cata, Nettie Cata, Ralph Cata, David Garcia, Jerry Garcia, Peter Garcia, Seriano Montoya, Stephen Trujillo. [4061]

*Cf.* Nos. 4836-4837.
Donor, grantee, May 1968.

4838. KEALIINOHOMOKU, JOANN WHEELER, coll. Interviews with Hopis; 1965. T.D. 29 pp.

Transcript of Hopi for recording in Nos. 4068, 4356, 4838*a*. Tewa on the tapes is not transcribed. **Restriction on reproduction and on publication of informants' names.** [10(52)]

Donor, grantee.

4838*a*. KEALIINOHOMOKU, JOANN WHEELER, coll. Hopi-Tewa recordings; 1965. 3 reels of tape. Recording No. 59.

Re: interviews with Tewas who are bilingual Hopi-Tewa. For transcript of the Hopi, *cf.* Nos. 4354, 4838; the Tewa has not been transcribed. **Restriction on reproduction and on publication of informants' names.** [4068]

Donor, grantee.

4838*b*. KROSKRITY, PAUL V. Coyote and Bullsnake; 1977-1978. T.L.S., photocopy of T.D. 12 pp.

Includes: letter to Whitfield J. Bell, Jr.; text of the story in Arizona Tewa with interlinear literal English translation; grammatical analysis; free English translation. [10(167)]

Donor, grantee, Mar. 1978.

4839. KURATH, GERTRUDE, comp. *Senshare* ceremony; 1964. T.D. 22 pp.

Includes: analysis; sheet music. From tapes made by Antonio Garcia, Juanito Trujillo, and Peter Garcia at San Juan Pueblo, New Mexico. **Restricted.** [Call No. 970.6:K96s]

*Cf.* Nos. 4834-4835.

## TILLAMOOK

### (Salish)

4841. EDEL, MAY MANDELBAUM, coll. American Indian linguistic materials; n.d. 4 reels of film. Film No. 1275.

Re: Salishan languages and dialects with emphasis on Tillamook. From originals in the University of Washington libraries. [4034]

## TIWA

### (Tanoan)

4842. BRANDT, ELIZABETH A. On the origins of linguistic stratification: the Sandia case; 1969. copy of T.D. 9 pp.

Discusses stratification by age group. Criterion is the extent to which stops are spirantized. Paper presented at the meeting of the American Anthropological Association, Nov. 1969, New Orleans. [10(76)]

*Cf.* Nos. 4055, 4843-4844.
Donor, grantee, 1969.

4843. BRANDT, ELIZABETH A. Sandia Pueblo, New Mexico: a linguistic and ethnolinguistic investigation; 1970. Photocopy of T.D. 142 pp.

Re: historical background; Sandia Pueblo as a modern community; phonology; morphology; changes in phonology and morphology across four generations; use of Sandia, Spanish, and English in the community. [10(95)]

*Cf.* Nos. 4055, 4842, 4844.
Donor, grantee, 1970.

4844. BRANDT, ELIZABETH A., coll. Linguistic data in the Sandia dialect of Tiwa; n.d. 29 reels of tape. Recording No. 72.

Includes: vocabulary; texts; analysis of the Sandia material by an Isleta informant; household items; foods; directions; natural phenomena; buildings; fruits; time expressions; verbs; adverbs; checking George L. Trager's material; pronominal reference; greetings; animal names (including domesticated); festivals; other ethnographic information. [4055]

*Cf.* Nos. 4842-4843.
Donor, grantee, Nov. 1969, June 1970.

4844*a*. LONG, RONALD W., coll. Isleta Tiwa materials; 1965. 2 reels of tape. Recording No. 57.

Includes: story about informant's father; myth texts with translations. Informant: Mrs. Jojola. [4074]

Donor, grantee.

4845. PARSONS, ELSIE CLEWS. Isleta pictures with notes; n.d. T.D. *ca.* 170 pp.

Two copies with additions and corrections of the captions and discussion for *Isleta Paintings*, Bull. Bur. Amer. Ethnol. **181** (1962). Pictures wanting. [137(67)]

*Cf.* Nos. 237, 1860-1861.
Donor, Esther Goldfrank, Mar. 1964.

4846. PARSONS, ELSIE CLEWS. Letter to Leslie A. White; July 14, 1930. Photocopy of T.L.S. 4 pp.

Regarding Miller's doctoral thesis; a Taos feud involving the Mirabal family; difficulty of doing further work on Taos; possibility of working with Lorenzo Martinez and his wife and difficulties therewith. [137]

4847. PARSONS, ELSIE CLEWS. Letter to Leslie A. White; June 5, 1937. Photocopy of T.L.S. 1 p.

Re: Stevenson's Taos manuscript; pictures of *chamahia* stones from Kidder (stones rubbed by soil contact versus weapon theory); words for Catholic priest—Nahuatl or Mexican-Spanish. Mentions Boas. [137]

4848. PARSONS, ELSIE CLEWS. Letter to Leslie A. White; May 3, 1930. Photocopy of T.L.S. 3 pp.

Re: White's San Felipe manuscript; pictures of San Felipe prayer sticks collected by Kidder;

her collecting Taos folk tales; an account of social organization from three groups of informants. [137]

## TLINGIT

## (Na-Dene)

4849. DE LAGUNA, FREDERICA. Tlingit recordings; 1950-1954. T.D. 18 pp.

Includes: comments by author on Tlingit recording (*cf.* No. 265); translations of story, songs, and comments by informants. Published in part: *Bull. Amer. Ethnol.* 172: pp.169-171. [9]

Donor, author, June 1962.

4850. DE LAGUNA, FREDERICA, and CATHERINE MCCLELLAN, comps. Field notes on the ethnology of the Tlingit and Copper River Atna; 1949-1960. 6 reels of film. Film No. 1127.

Includes: notes on archaeological investigations; transcripts of interviews with informants. Tlingit material taken primarily from Yakutat and Angoon; Copper River Atna (Ahtena) from Chitina, Copper Center, and Chistochina, Alaska. From originals in possession of the compilers. [4032]

*Cf.* Nos. 263-267.

4851. SAPIR, EDWARD. Comparative Na-Dene dictionary; n.d. A.D. 4 v. of *ca.* 500 pp. each.

Volumes 1, 3, and 4 are comparative Na-Dene with provision for various Athapascan languages and dialects, Haida, and Tlingit. Volume 2 is comparative Sino-Tibetan-Na-Dene with provision for entries in Sino-Tibetan languages, Athapascan, Haida, and Tlingit. Most pages in all volumes have only a few entries. [30(Na20a.3)]

## TOTONAC

## (Totonacan)

4852. MCQUOWN, NORMAN A. Totonac texts; n.d. T.D. *ca.* 400 pp.

Includes: Totonac texts; Spanish translations; some English translation. [4018]

Donor, grantee, Apr. 1956.

## TSIMSHIAN

## (Penutian)

4853. BARBEAU, CHARLES MARIUS, comp. Raven-Clan outlaws on the North Pacific Coast; n.d. T.D. 447 pp. c.c.

Includes: Tsimshian myths in translation; a few Haida myths in translation. [4002]

Donor, compiler, Apr. 1963.

4854. BOAS, FRANZ. Indian legends of the North Pacific Coast of North America; 1974. Photocopy of T.D. 600 pp.

Legends in English from the German translation of Chinook Jargon, Kwakiutl, Tsimshian, and Shuswap. Translated by Deitrich Bertz from the original edition (see Boas 1895). **Permission necessary for reproduction.** [30(74)]

Donor, British Columbia Indian Language Project, Jan. 1975.

4855. DUNN, JOHN A. Linguistic and demographic history of the Coast Tsimshian; n.d. T.D. 9 pp.

Includes: map; diagrams; tables; a few examples from the language. [10(75)]

Donor, grantee, 1969.

## TUALATIN

## (Kalapuyan / Penutian)

4856. ANGULO, JAIME DE, and LUCY S. FREELAND, colls. Autobiography in Tfalati Kalapuya; n.d. T.D. 53 pp.

More than 300 numbered sentences. The first 28 have interlinear literal and free translations; the remainder have only free translations on separate pages. Informant: Louis Kenoy. [30(Pn3.2)]

4857. ANGULO, JAIME DE, and LUCY S. FREELAND. Short grammatical analysis of Tfalati Kalapuya with appended comparison between Tfalati and Chinook jargon; n.d. T.D. 35 pp.

Re: phonology and morphology. Includes: comparative texts; interlinear literal translations; free translations in English and French. Informant: Louis Kenoy. [30(Pn3.3)]

4858. ANGULO, JAIME DE, and LUCY S. FREELAND, comps. The Tfalati dialect of Kalapuya: texts; n.d. T.D. 32 pp.

Includes: numbered sentences in Tfalati; interlinear literal translations; free translations. [30(Pn3.5)]

## TUPI

### (Equatorial)

4859. WAGLEY, CHARLES. Correspondence with John Alden Mason; May 3 and Nov. 19, 1942. T.L.S. 2 pp.

Re: Tapirape, Guajajara, Urubu, Tembe, Tenetehara. [4017 (ling. #2)]

## TUSCARORA

### (Iroquois)

4860. BOYCE, DOUGLAS W. Notes on Tuscarora political organization, 1650-1713; 1971. Reproduction of T.D. 69 pp.

M.A. thesis in anthropology, University of North Carolina. [10(141)]

*Cf.* Nos. 4371, 4861.
Donor, grantee, Sept. 1974.

4861. BOYCE, DOUGLAS W. Tuscarora political organization, ethnic identity, and sociohistorical demography, 1711-1825; n.d. Photocopy of T.D. 284 pp.

Doctoral dissertation in anthropology, University of North Carolina. [10(138)]

*Cf.* Nos. 4371, 4860.
Donor, grantee, Sept. 1974.

4862. GREENE, CHIEF ELTON. Tuscarora language; n.d. 1 cassette tape. Recording No. 96.

Recording to accompany *Tuscarora Indian Language* published by the Johnson Publishing Co., Murfeesboro, North Carolina, 1969. [4062]

*Cf.* Nos. 4076, 4863.
Donor, F. Roy Johnson, Apr. 1973.

4863. MITHUN, MARIANNE, coll. Tuscarora language materials narrated by Chief Elton Greene; 1971-1972. 6 reels of tape. Recording No. 88.

Includes: verbs; grammar; numerals; months; seasons; greetings; weather; body parts; etc. [4076]

*Cf.* Nos. 4062, 4862.
Donor, grantee, June 1972.

4864. SPECK, FRANK G. Nanticoke and Tuscarora; 1914, 1915-1917. D. 8 pcs., 1 notebook of *ca.* 30L.

Includes: names for the Nanticokes in Cayuga, Tuscarora, Mohawk, Seneca, Onondaga, and Oneida; notes on wampum, folklore, and the Canadian Tuscarora; some Nanticoke vocabulary. [170(7)]

4864*a*. Tuscarora; 1948, 1950, n.d. 7 pcs.

Pictures include: Anthony F. C. Wallace with Tuscarora informants; Daniel Smith and Nellie Cansworth; wooden carving by Daniel Smith of a mythological beast; Cassie Bennett Ninham, Grand River Reserve; Beullah Williams; Tuscarora school; Running Deer. [4020*b*(10),(13:4)]

## UNITED STATES

4865. HILLIARD, SAM B. Report on study of Indian land cessions; May 7, 1971. T.L.S. to Whitfield J. Bell, Jr. 2 pp.

Brief summary of activities. [10(102)]

4865*a*. Miscellaneous engravings, lithographs, photographs, etc.; n.d. 17 pcs.

Includes: Eliot, the First Missionary among the Indians (86); Jesuit Missionaries in California (99); The Death of Miantonomo (124); General Harrison and Tecumseh (130); William Penn's Treaty with the Indians (137); The Death of Philip Metacomet (141a); Pocahontas Saving the Life of Captain John Smith (144); The Murder of Major Waldron (161); Massacre of Wyoming (173); Landing of Roger Williams (178); Colonel Taylor at the Battle of O-Ke-Cho-Bee (186); Tecumseh Saving Prisoners (187); The Death Cry (202); A Medicine Man Curing a Patient (203); Photographs of George G. Heye and others (218). Artists include: J. R. Chapin, Benjamin West, C. S. Reinhart, J. A. Oertel, Alonzo Chappel, Seth Eastman, and others. Engravers include: W. Ridgway, J. Hall, C. K. Burt and C. H. Smith, J. C. Buttre, J. P. Davis, S. S. Smith, J. C. Armytage, and C. Schuesele. [4016*a*(E:86 . . . 218)]

4865*b*. North American Indians (Catlin): illustrations; n.d. 19 engravings.

Uncolored engravings, primarily portraits. All published in George Catlin's *North American Indians*. Groups included: Cherokee, Cheyenne, Chinook, Chippewa, Delaware, Flat Head, Kiowa, Menomini, Mohegan, Oneida, Osage, Seminole, Seneca, Shawnee, Tuscarora, and Winnebago. [4020*b*(7)]

## UPLAND YUMAN

## (Yuman)

4866. KENDALL, MARTHA B. Yavapai linguistic material; n.d. T.D. 33 pp.

Includes: Yavapai sentences; English translations. [10(136)]

*Cf.* No. 4866*a*.
Donor, grantee, Sept. 1974.

4866*a*. KENDALL, MARTHA B., coll. Yavapai linguistic material; 1973. 3 reels of tape. Recording No. 100.

Re: phonology; modals; etc. Informant: Harold Sine. [4069]

*Cf.* No. 4866.
Donor, grantee, Sept. 1974.

4867. REDDEN, JAMES E. Notes on Walapai verb root structure; 1976. Photocopy of D. 69 pp.

Re: some high frequency verb stems containing high frequency morphemes (paper given at 1976 Hokan-Yuman Languages Workshop). Also includes field notes containing sentences, paradigms, etc., in Walapai with English translations. [10(152)]

Donor, grantee, May 1977.

4867*a*. SIMONCSICS, PETER, coll. Yavapai language materials; n.d. 3 cassette tapes. Recording No. 99. [4085]

Donor, grantee, Aug. 1974.

4868. SLOANE, EMILY-SUE. A linguistic analysis of three versions of a Yavapai *ič-kiyuka* text; n.d. Photocopy of T.D. 97 pp.

Includes: an ethnographic description; salient features of the language; three versions of the text (creation myth) with literal and free English translations. [10(137)]

Donor, grantee, Sept. 1974.

## URU

## (Chipayan)

4869. HARRINGTON, JOHN P. Uru-Puquina; 1943. T.L. and D. 22 pp.

Expresses belief that Uru-Puquina is Arawakan, that Campa and Mojo are related to Uru-Puquina; discusses the position of the Uru in the Inca Empire, the distribution of Uru, and works on Uru and Arawak. [4017(ling. #2)]

## UTO-AZTECAN

4869*a*. BENEDICT, RUTH. Correspondence with John Alden Mason; 1927-1943. A.L.S., T.L. and L.S. 27 pp.

Re: work on Papago, Pima, and Yaqui languages; honorarium for Franz Boas; Ruth Underhill's *Papago Ceremonies*. [4017(C9)]

4869*b*. HERZOG, GEORGE. Correspondence with John Alden Mason; 1929-1958. T.L. and L.S. *ca.* 75 pp.

Re: Tepehuan music and language; Pima-Papago language. Mentions Franz Boas, Gene Weltfish, Edward Sapir, Ruth Underhill, Frank G. Speck, and others. [4017(C19)]

4870. Huichol-Cora comparisons; n.d. T. and A.D. 4 pp.

Includes: thirty-four items in English, Huichol, and Cora; notes on correspondences, etc. [4017(ling. #2)]

4871. KELLEY, DAVID H. Correspondence with John Alden Mason; Mar. 26–July 15, 1957. T.L.S. 9L.

Re: the section of his doctoral thesis dealing with Uto-Aztecan-Polynesian linguistic comparisons. [4017(ling. #2)]

*Cf.* No. 4872.

4872. KELLEY, DAVID H. Uto-Aztecan-Polynesian linguistic comparisons; n.d. T.D. 71 pp. c.c.

Part of a Harvard University doctoral thesis regarding the borrowing of Uto-Aztecan words into Polynesian. [4017(ling. #2)]

*Cf.* No. 4871.

4873. MASON, JOHN ALDEN, comp. Notes on Nahuatl, Tepehuan, Tepecano, and Ute; n.d. A.D. 40 pp. in 1 notebook.

Includes: vocabulary; other notes. Primarily concerned with Nahuatl. [4017(10)]

4874. MASON, JOHN ALDEN. Notes on numerical systems; n.d. T.D. 1 p.

Discussion of characteristics of numerical systems of twenty Uto-Aztecan languages without examples. [4017(ling. #2)]

4875. MASON, JOHN ALDEN. Some initial phones and combinations in Utaztecan stems; 1951. T.D. 20 pp.

Abstract and full text of paper delivered at the Philadelphia meeting of the American Association for the Advancement of Science. [4017(ling. #1)]

*Cf.* No. 4878.

4876. SAPIR, EDWARD. Correspondence with John Alden Mason; Aug. 15-29, 1914. T. and A.L.S. 32 pp.

Includes: examples from Tepehuan, Tepecano, Papago, Nahua; data from Mason for Sapir's use in Uto-Aztecan comparative work; Sapir's comments on Mason's data and analysis; additional data; Sapir's views on Uto-Aztecan historical phonology. [4017(ling. #2)]

4877. SAPIR, EDWARD. Correspondence with John Alden Mason; June 18, 1927–Sept. 29, 1938. T. and A.L.S. 35L.

Re: Mason's work on Tepehuan, Papago, Sonoran languages, and Yaqui; Sapir's work on Paiute and Hupa. Mentions Boas, Rivet, Speck, Spier, and Whorf. [4017(C32)]

4878. Some initial phones and combinations in Utaztecan stems: correspondence; May 28–Nov. 1, 1951, and Oct. 19-23, 1953. T.L.S. 19L.

Discussion, with data, of J. Alden Mason's 1951 paper for the American Association for the Advancement of Science. [4017(ling. #2)]

*Cf.* No. 4875.

4879. STEELE, SUSAN. Uto-Aztecan bibliography; n.d. T.D. *ca.* 600 slips. c.c.

Includes: books; articles; manuscripts. [10(142)]

Donor, grantee, Nov. 1974.

4880. SWADESH, MORRIS. Correspondence with John Alden Mason; 1941-1960. T.D., A.L.S., T.L. and L.S. 29 pp.

Re: establishing an official Aztec alphabet; Swadesh's glottochronological work in Uto-Aztecan; disagreement between Mason and Swadesh over number of stop series in Papago; Mosan; Macro-Penutian; Uto-Aztecan (Yutonahuan); Hokan. Includes: Swadesh's retraction (to be published in *Word*) of his criticisms of Mason's Papago grammar; copies of letters from Swadesh to [Dean] Saxton and Andre Martinet. [4017(C36),(ling. #2)]

4881. Tarahumara-Cahita comparisons; n.d. T. and A.D. 17L.

Includes: Spanish-Tarahumara-Cahita lists; notes of consonant correspondences. [4017(ling. #2)]

4882. Tepehuan-Tepecano-Huichol-Cora comparative vocabulary; n.d. T.D. 35 pp. c.c.

Spanish-Tepehuan-Tepecano-Huichol-Cora (=Pima Bajo) with sources indicated by initials. [4017(ling. #2)]

4883. Utaztecan sound shifts; 1951. D. 13 pp.

Includes: notes, correspondences, etc., on Uto-Aztecan historical phonology. [4017(ling. #2)]

4884. Uto-Aztecan comparative vocabularies: Nahua, Yaqui, Opata, Huichol, Tepecano, Papago; n.d. T.D. 10 pp.

Cognate sets with English glosses divided according to various vowel and consonant correspondences. [4017(ling. #2)]

4885. Uto-Aztecan comparative vocabularies: Tarahumara, Yaqui, Tepecano, Aztec; n.d. A.D. 4 pp.

Cognates with Spanish glosses. [4017(ling. #2)]

4886. Uto-Aztecan comparative vocabulary: Tubar, Heve, Tarahumara, Yaqui; n.d. T.D. 3 pp.

Cognates with English glosses. [4017(ling. #2)]

4887. Uto-Aztecan: lexicostatistical compilations and comparative vocabulary; n.d. T.D. 6 pp.

Re: Huichol, Cora, Papago, Arivechi Opata, Huepac Opata, Guaymas Yaqui, Mocoriba Yaqui, and Fuerte Yaqui. [4017(ling. #2)]

4888. WHORF, BENJAMIN L. Correspondence with John Alden Mason; 1928-1939. A.L.S., T.L. and L.S. 29 pp.

Re: Whorf's grant application to the Social Sciences Research Council to work on modern Nahuatl; Uto-Aztecan phonology; Maya glyphs; Nahuatl; Papago; Tepecano; Tepehuan; Yaqui; subgrouping. [4017(C39),(ling. #1)]

4889. WHORF, BENJAMIN L. Utaztecan; Jan. 1939. T.D. and photo. 15 pp.

Includes: table of relationships with explanation; genetic relationships of Mayan (reference to table III, Macro-Penutian); photo reproduction of Whorf's Azteco-Tanoan tree. [4017(ling. #2)]

## VIRGINIA

4890. WALKER, ABRAHAM M. Letter to Frank G. Speck, Philadelphia; Petersburg, Va., Oct. 22, 1943. T.L.S. 1 p.

Re: obtaining material on the Indians of Virginia. Mentions W. Carson Ryan. [170(27)]

## WASCO

### (Upper Chinook D./Penutian)

4891. HYMES, DELL H. Letter to Whitfield J. Bell, Jr., Phila., Dec. 5, 1971. T.L.S. 5 pp.

Report on linguistic fieldwork with Michael Silverstein among the Wasco Chinook. [10(120)]

4892. SAPIR, EDWARD, WALTER DYK, and DELL H. HYMES, comps. Wasco-Wishram Chinook linguistic material; 1905, 1930-1933, 1951, 1954. Photocopy and microfilm of A.D. *ca.* 22,000 slips and 5 reels.

Vocabulary, paradigms, etc., collected at White Swan and Spearfish, Washington, and Celilo and Warm Springs, Oregon. Includes photocopy of a one-page letter from Michael Silverstein to Whitfield J. Bell, Jr., Sept. 29, 1972. [30(Pn4a.10)]

4893. SILVERSTEIN, MICHAEL. Wishram-Wasco Chinook: report on field work; n.d. T.D. 2 pp.

Details concerning the collection of linguistic and ethnographic data at the Yakima Reservation, Washington. [10(58)]

4894. SILVERSTEIN, MICHAEL. Report on field work: Wishram and Wasco Chinook; n.d. T.D. 2 pp.

Re: work on syntax and semantics; collection of texts at the Yakima Reservation, Washington; trip to Warm Springs Reservation, Oregon. [10(67)]

## WEST INDIES

4896. HÜPSCH-LONTZEN, JOHANN WILHELM CARL ADOLPH VON HONVLEZ-ARDENN, FREIHERR VON. List of artifacts and animal specimens for collection; 1789(?). D. 6 pp.

Areas of collection: East and West Indies. [9]

## WICHITA

### (Caddoan)

4897. GARVIN, PAUL L., comp. Wichita paradigms; 1962. Ditto of T.D. 544 pp.

Includes: verb paradigms; a few noun paradigms with possessive person markers. [4009]

Donor, compiler, 1962.

4898. ROOD, DAVID S. Structure of the Wichita language; Sept. 25, 1965. T.L.S. to Richard H. Shryock. 4 pp.

Includes: report on fieldwork; some discussion of phonology. [10(38)]

4899. ROOD, DAVID S. Wichita grammar: a generative semantic sketch; Wichita language materials; 1969. T.D. and photocopy of T.D. 267 pp.

Includes: grammatical sketch; English-Wichita word lists; a few short texts. [10(87)]

Donor, grantee, 1970.

4900. ROOD, DAVID S., coll. Wichita language materials; 1969. 1 reel of tape. Recording No. 77. [4082]

*Cf.* No. 4899 for transcript and dissertation based on this material.
Donor, grantee, 1970.

4900*a*. Wichita man and grass house; n.d. 2 photographs.

From World's Columbian Fair, Chicago. Photograph by Jessie Tarbox Beals. [4020*b*(10),(13:4)]

## WINNEBAGO

### (Siouan)

4901. FRAENKEL, GERD, comp. Notes to accompany Winnebago recording; 1962. T.D. 38 cards.

Re: informant, date, place, contents, etc., of each tape. Some recordings were made with informant reading from texts published by Paul Radin, Memoirs 2 and 3, *International Journal of American Linguistics.* [9]

*Cf.* No. 270.
Donor, grantee, June 1962.

4902. RADIN, PAUL, comp. Winnebago card file; n.d. A.D. *ca.* 500 cards.

Winnebago-English vocabulary with cross-references to other items. [150]

Donor, Mrs. Radin through Dell H. Hymes, May 1972.

4903. SPECK, FRANK G., coll. Recordings of Cherokee, Naskapi, Penobscot, Sioux (Santee), and Winnebago; 1964. 4 reels of tape. Recording No. 49.

Rerecorded from discs made in the 1930s. Originals in possession of the Museum of Primitive Art, New York. [4086]

*Cf.* No. 9, Speck, Frank G., table of contents . . . ; n.d.

4904. WALKER, WILLARD. The Winnebago syllabary and the generative model; 1973. Copy of T.D. 45 pp.

Re: the Fox orthography and the derivation of the Winnebago orthography from it; Winnebago phonology; rules for conversion from phonemic transcription to the Winnebago orthography. [9]

4904*a*. Winnebago; 1929, n.d. 10 pcs.

Photographs of people, including Chief Black Snake. [4020*b*(10)]

## WINTU

### (Wintun/Penutian)

4905. RADIN, PAUL, comp. Wintu-English dictionary; n.d. T. and A.D. 114 pp.

Includes: Wintu-English; English-Wintu. [150]

Donor, Mrs. Radin through Dell Hymes, May 1972.

## WISHRAM

### (Upper Chinook D./Penutian)

4906. SAPIR, EDWARD. Wishram in early days; n.d. T.D. and A.D. *ca.* 50L.

Ethnographic notes in English with some vocabulary items. Five pages of place-names possibly by J. Wolf. [30(Pn4a.9)]

4907. SAPIR, EDWARD, WALTER DYK, and DELL H. HYMES, comps. Wasco-Wishram Chinook linguistic material; 1905, 1930-1933, 1951, 1954. Photocopy and microfilm of A.D. *ca.* 22,000 slips and 5 reels.

Vocabulary, paradigms, etc., collected at White Swan and Spearfish, Washington, and Celilo and Warm Springs, Oregon. Includes photocopy of a one-page letter from Michael Silverstein to Whitfield J. Bell, Jr., Sept. 29, 1972. [30(Pn4a.10)]

4908. SILVERSTEIN, MICHAEL. Report on field work: Wishram and Wasco Chinook; n.d. T.D. 2 pp.

Re: work on syntax and semantics; collection of texts at the Yakima Reservation, Washington; trip to Warm Springs Reservation, Oregon. [10(67)]

4909. SILVERSTEIN, MICHAEL. Wishram-Wasco Chinook: report on field work; n.d. T.D. 2 pp.

Details concerning the collection of linguistic and ethnographic data at the Yakima Reservation, Washington. [10(58)]

## WYANDOT

### (Iroquois)

4910. POTIER, PIERRE, comp. Huron-French vocabulary; n.d. Photo of A.D. 29 pp.

From a document possibly in the archives of St. Mary's College, Montreal. [4021(9)]

4911. WALLACE, PAUL A. W. Who were the Hurons' allies of 1615?; n.d. T.D. 8 pp.

Concludes that the unnamed allies who were to aid Champlain and the Hurons probably were Susquehannocks. [4021(11)]

## XINCA

### (Macro-Chibchan)

4912. CAMPBELL, LYLE, coll. Aztec manuscript and Xinca linguistic material; 1972, n.d. Photocopy of D. 221 pp.

Includes: copy of an Aztec manuscript in possession of the *Sindico* of Santa Maria Ixhuatan, Guatemala; Xinca vocabulary with Spanish glosses from collector's fieldnotes. [10(128)]

*Cf.* No. 4913.
Donor, grantee, Nov. 1972.

4913. CAMPBELL, LYLE. Letter to Whitfield J. Bell, Jr., Philadelphia; Columbia, Mo., Oct. 19, 1972. T.L.S. 2 pp., enclosure wanting.

Re: lack of success in finding a Chicomuceltec informant; fieldwork on Xinca in Guazacapan, Jumaytepeque, and Chignimulilla; a Nahuatl manuscript in Santa Maria Ixhuatan, in possession of the *Sindico.* [10(127)]

*Cf.* No. 4912.

4914. SIMEON, GEORGE. Letter to Whitfield J. Bell, Jr., Philadelphia; Waimea, Kauai, Hawaii, Sept. 21, 1972. T.L.S. 2 pp.

Brief list of materials recorded in Pocomam Central, Mam, and Xinca. [10(126)]

*Cf.* No. 4915.

4915. SIMEON, GEORGE, coll. Mam, Xinca, and Pocomam Central linguistics; n.d. 1 cassette tape. Recording No. 91.

A portion of the material which he collected in Guatemala. [4084]

*Cf.* Nos. 4482, 4684, 4914.
Donor, grantee, Oct. 1972.

## YANA

### (Hokan)

4916. NEVIN, BRUCE E. Transformational analysis of some grammatical morphemes in Yana; 1971. Photocopy of T.D. 27 pp.

Re: embedded sentences. [10(99)]

Donor, grantee, 1971.

4917. NEVIN, BRUCE E. Transformational relations and discourse structure in Yana: a beginning; 1969-1970. T.D., photocopy of T.D., ditto of T.D. 60 pp.

Re: syntax; morphophonemics; internal reconstruction. Also includes: letter to Whitfield J. Bell, Jr. (as report on Phillips Fund grant); bibliography of manuscripts relating to Yahi and Yana. [10(85)]

Donor, grantee, Feb. 1970.

## YAQUI

### (Uto-Aztecan)

4918. MASON, JOHN ALDEN. A preliminary sketch of the Yaqui language; n.d. T.D. and A.L.S. 28 pp.

Includes: Mason's manuscript; a note from Edward Sapir regarding the manuscript and Uto-Aztecan linguistics. [4017(ling. #2)]

4919. MASON, JOHN ALDEN, coll. Yaqui texts and song; 1954. A.D. 10L.

Material taken at Hermosillo, Sonora, Mexico. In Yaqui with Spanish translation. [4017(ling. #1)]

4920. Yaqui texts; n.d. T.D. 2 pp.

Includes: two short texts with interlinear Spanish translation; numerals one through ten. [4017(ling. #2)]

## YUCHI

### (Macro-Siouan)

4922. Creek, Yuchi, and Shawnee; 1904, 1932, 1941, n.d. *ca.* 150 pcs.

Pictures concern: people, activities, churches, etc. Includes: photos of Yuchi annual harvest ceremony, Creek Nation, Oklahoma, 1904; photos in area of Atmore, Alabama; portraits. [4020*b*(2),(10),(13:1,4)]

4923. SPECK, FRANK G., coll. Yuchi and Creek dances; July 17, 1904(?). A.D. 6L.

Includes: sheet music for songs to accompany dance; choreography; a few vocabulary items with translations. [170(15)]

4924. SPECK, FRANK G., coll. Yuchi and Creek songs; n.d. A.D. *ca.* 25L.

Includes: Yuchi and Creek songs; twelve vocabulary slips. [170(15)]

4925. WAGNER, GUNTER, comp. English-Yuchi dictionary; n.d. T. and A.D. 109 pp.

Includes: English-Yuchi dictionary; introductory and explanatory section; reference to a Yuchi-English section which is wanting. [30(Yu.1)]

## YUKI

### (Yukian)

4926. ULDALL, HANS J. Preliminary report on Yuki tones; Atlantic City, Dec. 31, 1932. T.D. 8 pp.

Discussion of syllable structure, stems, and suffixes and of the behavior of tones with stems and suffixes; list of stem forms. [30(Yk.1)]

## YUMAN

### (Hokan)

4927. UNDERHILL, RUTH M. Correspondence with John Alden Mason; Sept. 14-18, 1953. T.L.S. and D. 4L.

Re: linguistic relatives of the Yumans; the existence of warrior's purification in Mexico. [4017(ling. #2)]

## YUROK

### (Macro-Algonquian)

4928. ANGULO, JAIME DE, and LUCY S. FREELAND, colls. Short vocabulary in Yurok; n.d. A.D. 30 pp. c.c.

English-Yurok vocabulary with phonetic keys. Informant: Robert Nat, Lower Klamath River. [30(A7.1)]

## ZAPOTEC

### (Zapotecan)

4929. ANGULO, JAIME DE, coll. Zapotec text in the Miahuatec dialect; n.d. A.D. 34 pp. c.c.

Text with Spanish and English translations. [30(Z1.1)]

4930. PARSONS, ELSIE CLEWS. Letter to Leslie A. White; Feb. 7, 1931. Photocopy of A.L.S. 1 p.

Re: Parsons's study in a Zapotec-speaking town; White's trip to Taos. [137]

4931. ROSENBAUM, HARVEY. Constraints in Zapotec questions and relative clauses; 1971. Printed D. 25 pp.

Revised version of a paper presented at the meeting of the Linguistic Society of America, Dec. 1971. To appear in *Festschrift* for Archibald A. Hill. [10(129)]

## ZUNI

### (Penutian)

4931*a*. TEDLOCK, DENNIS. From prayer to reprimand: the inversion of stress and pitch in Zuni; n.d. Photocopy of T.D. 23 pp.

Discussion of some linguistic and cultural factors associated with "raised up" speech. Zuni examples have literal and free English translations. [10(159)]

Donor, grantee, Mar. 1973.

4932. TEDLOCK, DENNIS. In search of the miraculous at Zuni; n.d. Mimeograph of T.D. 17 pp.

Re: Zuni medicine societies. Paper prepared for the Ninth International Congress of Anthropological and Ethnological Sciences, Sept. 1973. [10(160)]

Donor, grantee, Mar. 1973.

4933. TEDLOCK, DENNIS. The story of how a story was made; n.d. Photocopy of T.D. 9 pp.

Recounts the telling of a new story (based in fact) in the form of a *telapnaawe* by a Zuni. [10(158)]

Donor, grantee, Mar. 1973.

4934. TEDLOCK, DENNIS. Zuni field notes; 1964-1968. A.D. and T.D. *ca.* 2000 pp.

Texts in Zuni with English translation, some in translation only; typed diary including notes on activities and interviews with Zunis. **Restriction on use.** [10(124)]

Donor, grantee, June 1972.

4935. TEDLOCK, DENNIS, coll. Finding the center; n.d. 4 reels of tape. Recording No. 93.

Includes Zuni Indian stories which can also be found in the collector's published work of similar title. [4092]

Donor, grantee, Dec. 1972.

# PART VII

# BIBLIOGRAPHY


ALEGRE, FRANCISCO JAVIER. 1841. *Historia de la Compania de Jesus en Nueva Espania* (3 v., Mexico).

BOAS, FRANZ. 1895. *Indianische Sagen von der Nord-Pacifischen Kuste Amerikas.* Berlin: Verhandlungen der Berliner Gesellschaft fur Anthropologie, Ethnologie und Urgeschichte 1891-1895.

———1899. "Property Marks of Alaskan Eskimo." *Amer. Anthropol.*, n.s., 1: pp. 601-613.

DORSEY, JAMES OWEN. 1890. *The Ȼegiha Language. U.S. Geographical and Geological Survey of the Rocky Mountain Region, Contributions to North American Ethnology* **6**.

———1891. *Omaha and Ponka Letters.* Bull. Bur. Amer. Ethnol. **11**.

DRAKE, NOAH FIELDS. 1897. "A Geological Reconnaissance of the Coal Fields of the Indian Territory." *Proc. Amer. Philos. Soc.* **36**: pp. 326-419.

FREEMAN, JOHN F., comp. 1966. *A Guide to Manuscripts Relating to the American Indian in the Library of the American Philosophical Society.* Mem. Amer. Philos. Soc. **65**.

GODDARD, PLINY EARLE. 1911. "Jicarilla Apache Texts." *Anthro. Papers Amer. Mus. Nat. Hist.* **8**: pp. 1-276.

LIPKIN, WILLIAM. 1945. *Winnebago Grammar* (New York: King's Crown Press).

MERCER, HENRY C. 1895. "Jasper and Stalagmite Quarried by Indians in the Wyandotte Cave." *Proc. Amer. Philos. Soc.* **34**: pp. 96-400.

MURDOCK, GEORGE P., and TIMOTHY J. O'LEARY. 1975. *Ethnographic Bibliography of North America* (4th ed., New Haven: Human Relations Area Files).

O'LEARY, TIMOTHY J. 1963. *Ethnographic Bibliography of South America* (New Haven: Human Relations Area Files).

PRINCE, JOHN DYNELEY. 1897. "Passamaquoddy Wampum Records." *Proc. Amer. Philos. Soc.* **36**: pp. 479-495.

SEBEOK, THOMAS A., ed. 1976. *Native Languages of the Americas* (New York: Plenum).

SPECK, FRANK G. 1933. "Notes on the Life of John Wilson: Revealer of Peyote." *Gen. Mag. and Hist. Chron.*

———1937. *Oklahoma Delaware Ceremonies, Dances, and Feasts.* Mem. Amer. Philos. Soc. 7.

———1940. *Penobscot Man, the Life History of a Forest Tribe in Maine* (Philadelphia).

STARR, F. 1901-1903. "Notes Upon the Ethnography of Southern Mexico." *Proc. Davenport Acad. of Sci.* 9: pp. 70-72.

STEWARD, JULIAN H., ed. 1950. *Handbook of South American Indians.* Bull. Bur. Amer. Ethnol. **143**.

VOEGELIN, C. F., and F. M. VOEGELIN. 1973. *Classification and Index of the World's Languages* (New York, Oxford, and Amsterdam: Elsevier).

WAUCHOPE, ROBERT, gen. ed. 1967. *Handbook of Middle American Indians* (Austin: University of Texas Press).

# PART VIII

# INDEX

NOTE: Items with asterisk include pictures of or relating to the topic, group, or area. Italicized numbers indicate the primary group of entries pertaining to a topic, e.g., recordings, specific languages, areas, etc.

Abbot, G. E., photographer(?), 4504*a*

Abenaki, 4644; Lake George, 4663*a**; missions to, 4047, 4592*c*; St. Francis, 4663*a**; village, Pierreville, P. Q., 4143*b**

Abijones, 4366

Abipon, *4099*

Abler, Thomas S., author, 4709-4711; donor, 4709-4711

Abnaki. *See* Abenaki

Acculturation, Azqueltan, 4368, 4833; Huichol, 4368; San Sebastian, 4368, 4833; Stockbridge-Munsee community, 4539; Tepehuan, 4833

Achumawi, *4100-4102*; **dialects**, 4100; **informant**, Willard Carmony, 4101; **language**, 4100-4102; **linguistics**, 4100, 4102, 4118; **paradigms**, 4100; **people**: Bessie Mike and Lena Patterson, 4137*b**; **texts**, 4100-4102, 4118

Acoma, N. Mex. 4437, 4441-4445, 4447, 4450-4452, 4457-4463, 4467-4468, 4770, 4772-4773, 4775-4778, 4795-4796, 4796*a**, 4797; archaeology, 4796*a**; dance songs, 4439; dictionary, 4438; dwellings, 4796*a**; fauna, 4468; *kapina* society, 4788; language, 4438-4439; laying out dead deer, 4792; linguistics, 4438; manuscripts, 4440; people, 4796*a**; snake society, 4787–4788; songs, 4462; texts, 4439

Adams, John Quincy, corres. with Constantine S. Rafinesque-Schmaltz, 4323

Adams, Walter R., author, 4498*a*; collector, 4047*a*, 4498*b*; donor, 4047*a*, 4498*a*, 4498*b*

Adoption, Paul A. W. Wallace by Mohawks, 4530; ceremony, Tutelo spirit, 4246*a**; complex, Iroquois, 4389

Adzumawi. *See* Achumawi

Aginsky, Bernard W., **corres.** with: John Alden Mason, 4295*a*; Elsie Clews Parsons, 4311

Aginsky, Ethel G., corres. with: John Alden Mason, 4295*a*

Agriculture, Lacandone, 4497; Mexico, 4514

Ahenakew, Edward, 4187, 4388, 4587; author, 4188; corres. with Paul A. W. Wallace, 4021, 4187; genealogy, 4188

Ahtena, 4031, *4103-4106a*; **archaeology**, 4032, 4106*a*, 4850; **contents of recordings**, 4105; **ethnology**, 4032, 4106*a*, 4850; **informants**: 4105; Andy Brown, Annie Ewan, Pete Ewan, Bacile George, Nancy George, Arthur Jackson, Martha Jackson, Billy Joe, Elizabeth Pete, Mentasta Pete, Jenny Peters, Kate Sanford, and Fanny Stanfield, 4057, 4104; **interviews**, 4032, 4057, 4104, 4106*a*, 4850; **language**, 4057, 4104; **recordings**, 4057, 4104; **songs**, 4057, 4104; **texts**, 4057, 4104

Aitken, Barbara, 4779

*Akwesasne* adoption, 4530; Mohawk Counsellor Organization, 4388; Mohawks, 4382

Alaapa, 4366

Alabama, Atmore, 4546*a**, 4732*a**, 4922*a**; Creek Indians, 4548; Supreme Court, Creek Indian land dispute, 4549

Alaska, 4107-4107*a*; **Angoon**, Tlingit ethnology, 4032, 4106*a*, 4850; **archaeology**, 4032, 4106*a*, 4274*a*, 4289*a*, 4589*b*, 4850; **artifacts**, 4107; **attire**, 4601*a**; **Chistochina**, Ahtena ethnology, 4032, 4106*a*, 4850; **Chitina**, Ahtena ethnology, 4032, 4106*a*, 4850; **Copper Center**, 4057, 4104; Ahtena ethnology, 4032, 4106*a*, 4850; **Copper River**, 4031, 4103, 4105-4106; **Eskimo**, 4249, 4251*a**; **ethnography**, 4601*a**; **informants**, 4105; **Native languages**: dictionaries, 4043, 4107*a*; hymns, 4043, 4107*a*; linguistics, 4043, 4107*a*; manuscripts regarding, 4043, 4107*a*; religious material, 4043, 4107*a*; sermons, 4043, 4107*a*; texts, 4043, 4107*a*; vocabularies, 4043, 4107*a*, **Prince of Wales Island**: Old Kasaan, 4333*a*; Sukkwan, 4107; **totem poles**, 4107; **totems**, 4601*a**; **Totlin**, 4031, 4106; **Upper Tanana**, 4031, 4057, 4104, 4106; **Yakutat**, Tlingit ethnology, 4032, 4106*a*, 4850

Alberta, Canada, 4065, 4204*a*; Fort Chipewyan, 4143*b**; Plains Cree, 4098, 4192-4193; Stoney Reserve, Morley, 4091, 4209-4210

Alderfer, E. Gordon, corres. with Paul A. W. Wallace, 4211

Alegre, Francisco Javier, 4436, 4455, 4781

Alexander, L. T., photographer, 4301*b*

Alfaro, Captain Colon Eloy, corres. with Harry B. Wright, 4740
Algic, 4540; **eastern**: ethnography, 4644; language, 4644
Algonquian, 4037, *4108-4109d*, 4289, 4304; artifacts, 4240; block-stamp decoration, 4240; languages, 4020*e*, 4109*b*; linguistics, 4020*e*, 4109*a*; manuscript, Labrador, 4108; northeastern, archaeological relations to southern Caddoans, 4793
Algonquin, 4602*b**; ethnography, 4602*b**; people, 4602*b**
Alliot, Hector, corres. with DeMoss Bowers, 4131
Altars, 4790; antelope, 4790; paintings of, 4797
American Anthropological Association, 4020*a*, 4152, 4155, 4158, 4180, 4295*a*, 4298, 4311, 4327*a*, 4339*a*, 4362*a*, 4452, 4593, 4842; *American Anthropologist*, 4017, 4295*a*, 4331*a*
American Association for the Advancement of Science, 4827, 4875, 4878
American Folklore Society, 4311, 4352, 4622
American Indian, **manuscript collections pertaining to**: 4415; American Philosophical Society Library, 4036, 4123, 4295; bibliography, 4036, 4123; linguistics: bibliography, 4039*a*, 4334*a*, 4592; origin, 4272; sign language, 4029, 4588
Americanists, International Congress of, Mexico, 4154, 4513
American Museum of Natural History, 4206, 4339*a*
American Philosophical Society, 4108, 4215, 4316, 4412, 4415, 4556, 4587, 4828; **bibliography**, 4036, 4123, 4125, 4151; **corres. with**: Frank Hamilton Cushing, 4367; Noah Fields Drake, 4276; A. J. Holman & Co., 4491; John Welsh, 4494; John Dyneley Prince, 4643-4644; **Flexner Collection**, 4575*a*; **Library**, 4295, 4718*a*; **Library Committee report**, 4488; **Parker Collection**, 4415; **Print Collection**, Native American, 4016*a**; ***Proceedings***, 4405*a*, 4646; **Shindler Collection**, 4592*a*; ***Transactions***, 4557
American Revolution, Delawares in, 4393; Iroquois in, 4027, 4372, 4392-4393; Oneidas in, 4393; Six Nations in, 4027, 4372; Tuscaroras in, 4393
*The Amerindian: American Indian Review*, 4393
Ames, J. Z., corres. with Spencer Fullerton Baird, 4260
Amoss, Pamela T., compiler, 4599; donor, 4599
Amshelwood, R., engraver, 4588*a*
Amuesha, 4758
Amuexia, 4143
Amuzgo, vocabulary, 4525
Anderson, J. E., corres. with Paul A. W. Wallace, 4650
Andes, 4756; archaeology, 4752; artifacts, 4749; bibliography, 4126; civilization, 4126, 4747; culture and history, preconquest, 4749; Indians, Ecuador, 4464; Peruvian, 4759*a**
Andrade, Manuel J., 4075, 4693; collector, 4037*a*, 4693*a*; corres. with John Alden Mason, 4498*c*
Andre, Father, S. J., 4603
Andrews, J., engraver, 4588*a*
Angel, W. P., corres. with Ely S. Parker, 4726
Angulo, Jaime de, **author**, 4100, 4160; **collector**, 4101, 4929; **and Lucy S. Freeland**, authors, 4117-4118, 4857; collectors, 4102, 4856, 4928; compilers, 4858
Animals, **associated with disease** (Keres), 4793; **Catawba**, 4020*c*, 4148*b*; **Sandia** (Tiwa), 4055, 4844; **domesticated**: Assiniboin, 4194*a**; Hopi, 4097*a**; 4363*a*; Lacandone, 4497; Montagnais-Naskapi, 4188*b**; Tewa, 4097*a*; 4363*a*; **Specimens** (Panama), 4310; **transportation**, of artifacts by migratory, 4331*a*. *See also* Fauna
Annon, ______, 4668
Antelope, altar, 4790; clan, Keres, 4449; sand painting, Mishongnovi, 4790; society, Hopi, 4787-4789
*Anthropologie der Feuerland-Indianer*, 4284
Anthropology, 4003*b*, 4268*c*, 4299, 4415; history of American, 4299; laboratory of, Santa Fe, N. Mex., 4312, 4779; *Pioneers in American Anthropology*, 4799
Antiquities, 4322-4323
Apache, 4010, 4165; anthropometric data, 4268*c*; dance, 4796*a**; Gila Apaches, 4768; Hopi-Apache masked dance songs, 4052, 4349; people, 4796*a**. *See also* Chiricahua; Jicarilla; Kiowa Lipan; Mescalero; San Carlos
Appleton, ______, 4300
Arapaho, ceremony, 4081, 4616; contents of recording, 4223, 4616*a*; dance, 4081, 4616; dictionary, 4044, 4592*b*; dwellings, 4682*f**; ethnography, 4081, 4616, 4683; language, 4044, 4592*b*; linguistics, 4044, 4592*b*; people, 4682*f**; recordings, 4081, 4616; songs, 4081, 4616; texts, 4044, 4592*b*. *See also* Gros Ventre
Araucanian, 4759*a**
Arawak, 4869; continental, men's and women's speech, 4476
Archaeology, 4004, 4017, *4110*, 4296, 4298; **Acoma**, 4796*a**; **Alaska**, 4032, 4106*a*, 4274*a*, 4289*a*, 4589*b*, 4850; **British Honduras**, 4159*b*; **California**, 4131-4134, 4136-4137, 4139-4142; **Canada**, 4289*a*; **Central America**, 4152*a*, 4157*a*, 4158*a*, 4159, 4159*a*, 4331*a*, 4339*a*, 4504*a**; **Central Andean**, 4752; **Chaco Canyon**, 4014, 4769; **Cherokee**, 4010, 4165, 4171; **Columbia**, 4331*a*; **Copper River Atna**, 4032, 4106*a*, 4850; **Greenland**, 4250, 4251*; **Guatemala**, 4152*a*, 4157*a*, 4158*a*, 4159*a*-4159*b*, 4331*a*, 4524*a*; Piedras Negras, 4153, 4157, 4159; **Honduras**, Caracol Ruins, 4159; **Indiana**, 4370; **Inugsuk**, 4250, 4251*; **Iroquois**, 4386; **Isleta**, 4796*a**; **Laguna**, 4796*a**; **Mesa Verde**, 4796*a**; **mescalbeans**, 4590;

**Mexico**, 4017, 4152*a*, 4157*a*, 4158*a*, 4159*a*-4159*b*, 4289*a*, 4293*a*, 4331*a*, 4504*a**, 4507, 4524*a*, 4525*a*; Chalchihuites, 4517; Chiapas, Palenque, 4521*a**; Coahuila, 4512; Durango, 4507, 4512; Sonora, 4017, 4506; Yaxchilan, 4159; Zape, 4515; **New Mexico**, 4796*a**; Clovis, 4020*a*, 4327*a*; Santa Fe, Laboratory of Anthropology, 4312, 4779; **Panama**, 4157*a*, 4331*a*; **Papago**, 4634; **Peru**, Aymara tomb, 4303*a**; **Pima Bajo**, 4669; **Pueblo Bonito**, 4014, 4769; **Puerto Rico**, 4331*a*; **Saskatchewan**, 4289*a*; **Schroeder Pyramid**, 4507; **Slayton Creek**, Delaware, 4518*; **Snake Creek**, 4110; **South America**, 4331*a*, 4339*a*; **Southwest**, 4014, 4454, 4769; **Tennessee**, 4805; **Tepecano**, 4806, 4809; **Texas**, 4159*a*; **Tlingit**, 4032, 4106*a*, 4850; **United States**, South, 4793; West, 4289*a*; **Venezuela**, 4331*a*; **West Coast**, 4134

Architecture, ancient American, 4307; Central America, 4504*a**; Hopi, 4351*a**; Mayan, 4020*a*, 4159*b*, 4327*a*; Mexico, 4504*a**; Piedras Negras, Guatemala, 4157

Archivo General de Indias, Seville, Spain, 4024, 4499

*Arctic Summer*, 4250

*Aren Akweks*. *See* Ray Fadden

Arikara, ethnography, 4683

Arivechi Opata, comparative vocabulary, 4887; lexicostatistics, 4887

Arizona, 4575*a**; **Colorado River Indian Reservation**, 4699, 4764; **Cucurbita moschata**, 4514; **dwellings**, 4575*a**; **ethnography**, 4575*a**; **Gila River**, Yumas of, 4331*a*; **Hopi villages**, 4052, 4349; **Navajo**, 4060, 4083, 4561, 4577; **Oraibi**, Flute Society, 4780; **Papago Reservation**, Ak Cin and Sikol Himadk, 4047*b*, 4622*b*; **Parker**, 4699, 4764; **people**, 4575*a**; **Phoenix**, 4047*b*, 4622*b*; **Santa Rosa**, 4047*b*, 4622*b*

Arkansa. *See* Dhegiha; Quapaw

Armytage, J. C., engraver, 4291*b*, 4598*a*, 4865*a*

Arrowheads, Lummi, 4057*a*, 4600*a*

Art, ancient American, 4307; Jesse J. Cornplanter (Iroquois), 4419; Eskimo, 4586*a*; John Fadden (Mohawk), 4534; Indian, 4336; Iroquois, 4377, 4381, 4384, 4389, 4419; Mohawk, 4533-4534; Museum of Primitive Art, 4208; Nootka, 4586; North Pacific Coast, 4586*a*; Penobscot, 4658; Pueblo, 4796; sand painting, 4790; Southwest, 4797

Artifacts, 4261, 4271, 4301*b**, 4305-4306, 4308, 4314, 4331, 4334; Alaska, 4107; Algonquian, 4240; Andean region, 4749; baskets, 4281; California, 4140-4142; Canada, 4145-4148; Catawba, 4148*a**, 4275, 4688*d**; Cayuga, 4714*a**; Central America, 4504*a**; Cherokee, 4162*a**; Chickahominy, 4275, 4687*a**; Choctaw, 4179*b**, 4301*b**; Comanche, 4682*a**; Creek, 4275; Delaware, 4213*a**, 4216, 4219, 4224, 4231; Durango, Mexico, 4507; Eastern North America, 4239-4241; East Indies, 4896; Eskimo, 4251*, 4251*a**; Iroquois, 4377*a**; Jemez, 4778; Lummi, 4057*a*, 4600*a*; Malecite, 4275; masks, 4301, 4332; Mattaponi, 4275, 4687*b**; Mayan, 4524*a*; Mexico, 4504*a**; Micmac, 4275, 4527*a**; Mohawk, 4536*a**; Mohegan, 4539*a**; Montagnais-Naskapi, 4188*b**; Nanticoke, 4275, 4558*a**; Naskapi, 4275; Northeast, 4595, 4598*a**; Northwest Coast, 4275; Ojibwa, 4012*a**, 4301*b**, 4603*a**; Ottawa, 4609*b**; Palenque, Chiapas, Mexico, 4521*a**; Pamunkey, 4275, 4688*b**; Penobscot, 4275, 4663*a**; Peru, 4301*a**; Pima Bajo, 4668, 4670*, 4671*; Plains, 4682*e**; Rappahannock, 4275, 4688*d**; San Carlos Apache, 4703*a**; Sandia (Tiwa), 4055, 4844; San Felipe, 4453, 4848; Santa Clara, 4778; Seneca, 4727*a**; Shield (Plains), 4682*e**; skulls, 4303; Snake Creek, 4110; South America, 4759*a**; Southwest, 4785; stone age, 4315, 4317-4318; Tennessee, 4805; Tepecano, 4809; Têtes de Boule, 4190*a**; transportation of by migratory animals, 4331*a*; Tunica, 4275, 4763*a**; Tuscarora, 4864*a**; West Indies, 4896; Yuchi, 4275. *See also* Crafts, and names of specific items

Ashluslay, linguistics, 4753

Ashmolean Museum, Oxford University, U.K. 4598*a*

Asia, languages, 4267

Assiniboin, 4194*a**, 4682*e**; camps, 4682*e**; cognates, 4204; dances, 4682*e**; dictionary, 4044, 4592*b*; engraving, 4682*e**; ethnography, 4194*a**, 4683; language, 4044, 4091, 4210, 4592*b*; linguistics, 4204; people, 4194*a**, 4682*e**; recordings, 4091, 4210; texts, 4044, 4091, 4210, 4592*b*; transportation, travois, 4194*a**

Atakapa, vocabulary, 4516

Athabasca River, Canada, 4143*b**

Athapascan, *4111-4116*; cognates, 4113; collection, manuscript, 4114; comparative dictionary, 4115, 4342, 4552, 4851; Coast, John Spencer, 4137*b**; comparative vocabularies, 4552, 4851; dialects, 4112, 4115, 4342; ethnography, 4114; ethnohistory, 4113*a*; historical linguistics, 4012, 4113, 4116, 4575; linguistics, 4112-4113, 4115-4116, 4342, 4552, 4851; prefixes, 4112; relations with Whites, 4111; social history, 4111

Atna. *See* Ahtena

Atsina. *See* Arapaho and Gros Ventre

Atsugewi, *4117-4118*; linquistics, 4117; texts, 4102, 4117-4118

Attire, 4273*a**; Alaska, 4601*a**; Eskimo, 4319*a**; Hopi, 4097*a*, 4351*a**, 4363*a*; Kachina, 4097*a*, 4363*a*; Kiowa Apache, 4682*c**; Mohegan, 4598*a**; Oglala, 4194*a**; Oto, 4178*a**; Penobscot, 4663*a**; Plains, 4682*e**; Tewa, 4097*a*, 4363*a*

Atwamdzini. *See* Achumawi

Autobiography, 4457-4458; Achumawi, Willard Carmony, 4101; Navajo, Mrs. Elsie Benally,

4083, 4577; Shawnee, Mary Williams, 4734*b*; Tfalati Kalapuya, Louis Kenoy, 4856. *See also* Biography
Ayer, Mary Farwell, 4489
Aymara, *4119-4121*, 4759; geographical distribution, historical linguistics, 4121; linguistics, 4120-4121; person markers, 4121; recording, 4066, 4119*a*; sociological factors affecting, 4121; texts, 4066, 4119, 4119*a*; tomb, 4303*a**; transcript of recording, 4119; typology, 4121
Azqueltan, acculturation, history, Indian-White relations, 4368, 4833
Aztec, 4301*a**, 4504*a**, 4534, 4553, 4912; comparative vocabulary, historical linquistics, 4885; masks, 4454; Montezuma, 4291*a**; orthography, 4880. *See also* Nahua
Aztec-Pueblo, comparisons, 4454
Aztec-Tanoan, 4889

Baer, Phillip, and William R. Merrifield, authors, 4497; donors, 4497
Baffin Island, N.W.T., Canada, 4003*b*, 4097, 4251*a**, 4255
Bahr, Donald M., author, 4622*a*; collector, 4047*b*, 4622*b*; corres. with Whitfield J. Bell, Jr., 4622*a*; donor, 4047*b*, 4622*a*-4622*b*
Bailey, A. G., corres. with Frank G. Speck, 4109
Bailey, Edna (Mrs. Nick), 4006, 4716
Baird, Spencer Fullerton, corres. with J. T. Ames, 4260; corres. with Stephen Bowers, 4132
Ball, Carl C., corres. with Frank G. Speck, 4261
Ballard, Arthur, 4599
Ball-player, Sioux, 4587*b**
Bandelier, Adolph F. A., 4523, 4757, 4795
Banks, Sir Joseph, corres., 4037, 4289
Barbeau, Charles Marius, 4586*a*; **author**, 4001-4002, 4712, 4853; **corres. with**: Ethel Gandy, 4658, John Alden Mason, 4017, 4524*a*, 4586*a*; Paul A. W. Wallace, 4021, 4587; **donor**, 4001-4002, 4712, 4853; **photographer**, 4598*a*
Barbour, James, Secretary of War, 4589
Barnsley, Edward R., donor, 4594, 4598
Barnsley, Thomas, corres. with Horatio Gates, 4594, 4598
*Barnstable County, History of* (Mass.), 4489
Bartholomew, Doris, author, 4495; collector, 4048, 4496; donor, 4048, 4495-4496
Bartlett, W. H., artist, 4598*a*
Barton, Benjamin Smith, 4322; **corres.**, 4003; **corres. with**: John G. E. Heckewelder, 4161, 4212-4213, 4262-4268, 4558, 4595, 4713-4714; Joseph Priestley, 4322; **manuscript collection**, 4003
Bartram, William, 4164
Bascom, Burton W., Jr., 4521*a**; author, 4814; compiler, 4813, 4830-4831; corres., 4641; corres. with John Alden Mason, 4814
Baskets, birchbark, 4147, 4271, 4301*b**; Canada, 4145; Cherokee, 4308; Chitimacha, 4308; Eastern North America, 4239-4240; Lummi, 4057*a*, 4600*a*; Malecite storage, 4281; Nipmuc, 4598*a**; Penobscot carrying, 4281; Pima Bajo, 4670*, 4671*; splint, 4301*b**; splitwood, 4240; Tunica (La.), 4281. *See also* Artifacts
Battles, of O-Ke-Cho-Bee, Col. [Zachary] Taylor at the, 4865*a**; of Wyoming, Pa., 4655
Beadwork, Iroquois, 4598*a**; Micmac, 4598*a**; Passamaquoddy, 4598*a**; Penobscot, 4598*a**; San Carlos Apache, 4703*a**
Beals, Jessie Tarbox, photographer, 4900*a*
Beals, Ralph L., 4787; author, 4436; corres. with John Alden Mason, 4295*a*
Bear, Clan, Iroquois, 4383; grizzly, 4320
Bear Creek, text, 4203
Beauchamp, William M., corres. with John W. Jordan, 4721
Beaver, social history, 4111
Bell, Robert, **corres. with**: Franz Boas, Elliot Coues, William Isbister, J. M. LeMoine, E.F.S.J. Petitot, and James C. Pilling, 4003*a*, 4268*a*; **manuscript collection**, 4003*a*, 4268*a*
Bell, Whitfield J., Jr., **corres. with**: Donald M. Bahr, 4622*a*; H. Russell Bernard, 4617-4619; Margaret B. Blackman, 4341*a**; Lyle Campbell, 4913; Richard T. Carter, Jr., 4196; Elizabeth A. Edwards, 4341*b*; Jimm G. Good Tracks, 4177*a*; Abraham M. Halpern, 4698*a*; Eric P. Hamp, 4695; Sam B. Hilliard, 4865; Carleton T. Hodge, 4351; Dell H. Hymes, 4891; Hazel V. Dean John, 4718*a*; Shepard Krech III, 4113*a*; Paul V. Kroskrity, 4838*b*; LaVerne Masayesva, 4357; Pamela Munro, 4699, 4764; Michele Nathan, 4548*a*; Bruce E. Nevin, 4128, 4917; Hugo G. Nutini, 4521; Marc Okrand, 4137*a*; Jesus Salinas Pedraza, 4618; Paul Proulx, 4528; Carol K. Rachlin, 4613; Noel W. Schutz, 4734; P. David Seaman, 4361; Michael Silverstein, 4892, 4907; George Simeon, 4482, 4684, 4914; Nancy P. Troike, 4529; Donald Watkins, 4611; **donor**, 4320, 4596
Bella Bella, anthropometric data, 4268*c*
Bella Coola, anthropometric data, 4268*c*; texts, 4599*a*; vocabulary, 4599*a*
Bellemont, Arizona, Navajo, 4083, 4577
Belts, Choctaw, 4179*b**, 4301*b**; Hopi, 4097*a*, 4363*a*; Huichol, 4097*a*, 4363*a*; Tarahumara, 4097*a*, 4363*a*
Benedict, Ruth Fulton, 4020*a*, 4327*a*, 4777; **corres. with**: John Alden Mason, 4017, 4295*a*, 4869*a*; Elsie Clews Parsons, 4311
Bennett, [Foster?], corres. with Frank G. Speck, 4148
Beothuk-Micmac, Santu and family, 4595*a**
Berkhofer, Robert F., author, 4025, 4268*b*
Bernard, H. Russell, author, 4617, 4622; collector, 4049-4050, 4620-4621; corres. with Whitfield J. Bell, Jr., 4617-4619; donor, 4049-4050, 4617-4618, 4620-4622
Bersimis, 4188*b**
Bertelson, Ernest, 4599

Bertz, Deitrich, 4472; translator, 4174, 4735, 4854
Bethlehem, Pa., Moravian Church Archives, 4039, 4591
Betty's Neck, Mass., 4491*a**
Bever, Marion G. (Mrs. Michael), corres. with Frank G. Speck, 4489
Bible, 4714; Eliot Indian, 4488, 4490-4492, 4494
Bibliography, *4122-4130*; American Philosophical Society, 4036, 4123, 4125, 4151; "Andean Civilization," 4126, 4747; Central America, 4125, 4151; languages, 4127, 4750, 4761; linguistics, 4125, 4151, 4334*a*; manuscripts, 4036, 4123; Mexico, 4125, 4151; Pima Bajo, 4682; South America, 4122, 4125-4127, 4151, 4738, 4750, 4761; Frank G. Speck, 4124, 4129, 4285, 4292; Uto-Aztecan, 4130, 4879; Yahi, 4128, 4917; Yana, 4128, 4917
Bibliothèque Nationale, Paris, 4027, 4372
Billings, John S., corres. with Stephen Bowers, 4767
Bill of Rights, United States, influence of Iroquois Confederacy on, 4375
Biography, *Biographical Encyclopedia of the World*, 4292; Franz Boas, 4602; Canadian Indians, 4144; Florence Edenshaw Davidson (Haida), 4341*a*; Deganawidah (Iroquois), 4417; *Dictionary of Canadian Biography*, 4417; George G. Heye, 4287; Chief Joseph Montour (Iroquois), 4227; Madam Montour (Iroquois), 4398; Navajo, 4570; Frank G. Speck, 4292. *See also* Autobiography
Birchbark, baskets, 4147, 4271; Canada, 4145; canoes, 4148; Huron canoe, 4397*a**; technique, 4274; wigwam, Pokagon (Potawatomi), 4598*a**
Birds, Delaware, 4213; Malecite, 4645. *See also* Fauna
Black, Robert A., author, 4345-4347; collector, 4051-4052, 4348-4349; donor, 4051-4052, 4345-4346, 4348-4349
Blackfoot, *4130a**, 4295; **chiefs**: 4130*a**, Luke Big Turnips and Turned-Up-Nose, 4130*a**; **ethnography**, 4130*a*, 4683; **people**: 4682*d**; Henry Between Lodge, 4130*a**; **Piegan**: dictionary, 4044, 4592*b*; language, 4044, 4592*b*; linguistics, 4044, 4592*b*; texts, 4044, 4592*b*. *See also* Blood; Piegan
Blackman, Margaret B., author, 4341*a*; corres. with Whitfield J. Bell, Jr., 4341*a*; donor, 4341*a*
Blom, Frans, corres. with John Alden Mason, 4297
Blood, 4130*a**; chiefs, 4130*a*; ethnography, 4130*a*; people, Black Plume, 4130*a**. *See also* Blackfoot; Piegan
Bloomfield, Leonard, 4109*b*; **corres. with**: John Alden Mason, 4297; Carl F. Voegelin, 4109*a*
Blowguns, Houma, 4364*a**; Tunica, 4763*a**
Blumenbach, J. F., corres., 4037, 4289
Boas, Franz, 4196, 4249, 4319*a**, 4331*a*, 4443, 4459, 4461-4463, 4520*a*, 4667, 4698, 4772, 4807, 4847, 4869*a*-4869*b*, 4877; **Arctic pictures**, 4319*a**; **Arctic sketches**, 4319*a**; **author**, 4003*b*, 4174, 4195, 4472, 4735, 4854; **biography**, 4602; **collector**, 4003*b*, 4268*c*, 4504*b*, 4599*a*; **corres.**, 4026, 4248, 4269, 4600; **corres. with**: Robert Bell, 4003*a*, 4268*a*; Waldo G. Leland, 4270; John Alden Mason, 4017, 4297; Edward Sapir, 4437; **family**, 4319*a**; **genealogical data**, 4003*b*; **Mexico**, 4003*b*, 4504*b*; **Northwest Coast**, 4003*b*, 4026, 4599*a*, 4602
Boas, Norman F., donor, 4195
Boats, Houma, 4364*a**
Bock, Philip K., author, 4527; donor, 4527
Bodmer, Karl, 4020*b*; artist, 4589*a*, 4682*e*
Body parts, Cayuga (Seneca), 4001, 4712; Hopi, 4088, 4362; Kagaba, 4745*a*; Navajo, 4582; Tuscarora, 4076, 4863
Boilly, L., artist, 4589*a*
Bolivia, 4759
Bond, Charles E., corres. with Frank G. Speck, 4478
Bonners Ferry, Idaho, 4682*d*
Bonvillain, Nancy, author, 4531; donor, 4531
Botany, 4003
Bowers, Alfred W., collector, 4053-4054, 4343-4344, 4484-4485; donor, 4053-4054, 4343-4344, 4484-4485
Bowers, DeMoss, **corres. with**: Hector Alliot, 4131; Ira M. Buell, 4805; Edwin Walters, 4336; Mrs. Arthur X. Wilmot, 4142
Bowers, Stephen, 4132-4133, 4138-4141; **corres.**, 4004; **corres. with**: Spencer F. Baird, 4132; John S. Billings, 4767; R. H. Forbes, 4133; Ferdinand V. Hayden, 4134; Henry W. Henshaw, 4135; Ales Hrdlicka, 4136; Otis T. Mason, 4138; James Pilling, 4138; Stephen Powers, 4139; Frederick W. Putnam, 4140; Charles Rau, 4141; George M. Wheeler, 4338; **manuscript collection**, 4004; **papers**, 4131
Boyce, Douglas W., author, 4371, 4860-4861; donor, 4371, 4860-4861
Brandard, E. P., engraver, 4132*b*
Brandt, Elizabeth A., author, 4842-4843; collector, 4844; donor, 4842-4844
Brant, family (Iroquois), 4404; Joseph, 4291*a**
Brazil, 4759*a**; Kaingang, 4020*a*, 4327*a*; Mato Grosso, 4759*a**
Brinton, Daniel G., 4225*e*, 4522, 4644, 4646; corres. with John W. Jordan, 4721
British Association for the Advancement of Science, Oxford, England, 4307
British Columbia, 4601*a*; ethnogeography, 4796*a*; Indian Language Project, donor, 4174, 4472, 4735, 4854; people, 4601*a**; Queen Charlotte Islands, 4341*a*; Vancouver Island, Nootka, 4584
British Honduras, archaeology, 4159*b*
British Museum, Codex Zouche-Nuttal, 4529
Britten, Marian Hale, corres. with Frank G. Speck, 4739
Brooke, C. L., corres. with Florence Insley, 4301*b*

Brostup, John, photographer, 4405*a*
Brown, George W., corres. with Paul A. W. Wallace, 4144
Brown, Harcourt, donor, 4194
Brown, Mrs. Thatcher M. III, 4020, 4325
Brown Brothers, Harriman and Co., donor, 4020, 4325
Brownell, Charles DeWolf, 4291*a*
Brugge, David M., 4679; **author**, 4505-4506, 4668-4669, 4673, 4675; **collector**, 4674; **corres. with**: John Alden Mason, 4668, 4670-4672, 4679, 4682; Wenner-Gren Foundation, 4668
Brule, 4592*a**
Bryn Mawr College, 4221*a*, 4615
Buell, Ira M., corres. with DeMoss Bowers, 4805
Buffalo, dance (Okla.), 4081, 4616; hunt (Plains), 4682*e**
Buildings. *See* Dwellings
*Bulletin of the Bureau of American Ethnology*, 4688*b*, 4845, 4849
Bullroarer, 4791
Bunzel, Ruth, 4777
Burd, James, 4424; corres. with Jeremiah Dixon, 4596
Burgesse, J. Allan, 4271; corres. with Frank G. Speck, 4271
Burials, Kentucky, Massachusetts, Mississippi, Ohio, Rhode Island, and Tennessee, 4303*a*
Burrows, Edwin, narrator, 4071, 4606
Burt, C. K., engraver, 4588*a*, 4865*a*
Bushotter texts, 4207
Bustamente, ____, 4781
Butler, Elizur, author, 4162
Buttre, J. C., engraver, 4291*b*, 4865*a*
Byers, Douglas S., corres. with John Alden Mason, 4295*a*

*Cacique*, 4773; Acoma, 4467, 4796
Caddo, anthropometric data, 4268*c*
Caddoans, southern, archaeological relations to Algonquians, 4793
Caduveo, comparative vocabulary, historical linguistics, vocabulary, 4509
Cagaba. *See* Kagaba
Cahita, comparative vocabulary, linguistics, 4881
Cahuillo Indians, 4138
Cakchiquel, contents of recordings, language, 4686
Calaveras, skull, 4137
Calcasien, vocabularies, 4333
Calcott, Frank, corres. with Elsie Clews Parsons, 4311
Caldwell, Charles, corres. with Benjamin Horner Coates, 4272
Calendar, ancient America, 4307; ceremonial, 4447; Mayan, 4159; stone (Mexico), 4520*a**
California, *4131-4142*, 4137*b**; archaeology, 4131-4134, 4136-4137, 4139-4142; artifacts, 4140-4142; Calaveras skull, 4137; ethnography, 4132, 4132*a**; genetic relationships, 4139; Indian camp, 4132*b**; Jesuit missionaries, 4865*a**; languages, 4004; linguistics, 4135; map, 4139; Mount Shasta, 4132*b**; people, 4132*a**; Salton Basin, 4133; San Martin Mountains, Los Angeles County, 4141; San Nicholas Island, 4338; Santa Barbara stock, 4139; Santa Cruz Indians, 4139; Santa Cruz Island, 4136; Santa Rosa, 4132; sweathouse pit (Shasta County), 4132*a**
Calusa, 4010, 4165
Campa, *4143*, 4758, 4869; language, 4143
"Campaign against the Moqui Pueblos," 4790
Campbell, Lyle, collector, 4553; compiler, 4912; corres. with Whitfield J. Bell, Jr., 4913; donor, 4553, 4912
Camps, Assiniboin, 4682*e**; California, 4132*b**; Gros Ventre, 4682*e**; Micmac, 4598*a**; Oklahoma village, 4612*a**; Osage, 4231*a**; Pawnee, 4648*a**; Plains, 4682*e**, 4683*b**. *See also* Dwellings; Habitat; Pueblos; Settlements; Villages
Canada, 4003*a*, 4020*b**, 4027*, 4143*a**, 4143*b**, *4143a-4148*, 4268*a*, 4301*b**, 4372*, 4527*a**, 4536*a**, 4558*a**, 4587*a**; **Abenaki**, 4047, 4143*b**, 4592*c*, 4644, 4663*a**; **Alberta:** 4065, 4091, 4204*a*, 4209-4210; Fort Chipewyan, 4143*b**; Stoney Reserve, 4091, 4209-4210; **artifacts**, 4145-4148, 4148*b*, 4190*a**, 4275, 4609*b**; **Athabasca River**, 4143*b**; **British Columbia**, 4796*a*; ethnogeography, 4796*a*; Indian Language Project, 4174, 4472, 4735, 4854; Queen Charlotte Islands, history, 4341*a*; Queen Johnnie, 4601*a**; Vancouver Island, Nootka, 4584; **ceremony**, 4609*b**; **Cree**, 4143; **Dakota**, 4065, 4204*a*, 4209; **dialects**: Dakota, 4065, 4204*a*, 4736; Eskimo, 4097, 4255-4256; **Eskimo**, 4097, 4251*a**, 4255-4256; **ethnography**, 4143*a**, 4143*b**, 4188*a**, 4188*b**, 4189, 4190*a**, 4194*a**, 4683; **ethnohistory**, 4113*a*; **folklore**, French, 4587; **geological survey of**, 4003*a*, 4268*a*; **Hare Indians**, 4046, 4236-4238; **Indian**: biography, 4144; crafts, 4146; **Iroquois**, 4027, 4372, 4728; **Manitoba**: 4188*a**; Griswold, 4065, 4204*a*; Norway House, 4194; Rossville Mission, Cree, 4194; **Moravian**, missions among Indians, 4039, 4591; **National Museum of Man**, 4585; **New Brunswick**, 4527*a**; **Newfoundland**: 4188*b**, 4254*a**, 4527*a**; Algonquian manuscript, 4108; Labrador, 4108*, 4251*a**, 4301*b**, 4590*; **Northwest Territories**: Baffin Island (Baffin Land), 4003*b*, 4097, 4251*a**, 4255; Baker Lake, Cambridge Bay, Coppermine, and Eskimo Point, 4097, 4255; Fort Good Hope, 4046, 4087, 4236-4238; Keewatin, 4251*a**; Rankin Inlet, 4097, 4255; Southampton Island, 4251*a**; **Nova Scotia**, 4143*a**, 4527*a**, 4598*a**; **Ojibwa**, Temagami, 4609*a**; **Ontario**: 4188*a**, 4188*b**, 4244*a**, 4397*a**, 4558*a**, 4609*a**, 4609*b**, 4727*a**; Chippewa, 4071, 4606; Grand River Reserve, 4864*a**; Ir-

oquois, 4413, 4728; Lake Temagami, 4609*a**; Longlac, 4145; Moravian missions among Indians, 4039, 4591; Nanticoke, 4558*a**; New Fairfield, 4244*a**; Scarboro, Iroquois monument, 4413; Six Nations Reserve, 4213*a**, 4225*c*, 4229, 4397*a**; Smoothtown, 4225*c*; **orthographic systems**, 4256; **Ottawa** (Ojibwa), 4609*b**; **people**: 4143*a**, 4143*b**, 4587*a**; Queen Johnnie, 4601*a**; **pictures**, 4020*b**, 4143*a**, 4143*b**, 4188*a**, 4251*a**, 4301*b**, 4527*a**, 4536*a**, 4558*a**, 4587*a**; **Plains Cree**, 4098, 4192-4193; **postal cards**, 4143*b**, 4188*a**; **Quebec**: 4143*b**, 4188*a**, 4188*b**, 4397*a**; Batiscan River, 4143*b**; Batiscan Summit, 4143*b**; Lake St. John, 4145; Montreal, 4145; archives of St. Mary's College, 4910; Oka, 4397*a**, 4536*a**; Pierreville, Abenaki, 4143*b**; Pointe Bleue, 4145; Restigouche, 4527; Rupert House, James Bay, 4188*b**; St. Francis Abenaki, 4663*a**; Seminaire de Quebec, 4587; **Saskatchewan**: archaeology, 4289*a*; Fort Q'uapple, 4736; Sintaluta, 4065, 4204*a*; **Seneca**, 4727*a**; **Six Nations**, 4027, 4372; **terrain**, 4587*a**; **Tuscarora**, 4559, 4864; **Yukon Territory**, Burwash Landing, 4031, 4106. *See also* specific tribes and languages

Canger, Una, author, 4481; donor, 4481

Canoes, birchbark, 4148, Canada, 4145, Huron, 4397*a**; Lummi, 4057*a*, 4600*a*; Ojibwa, 4012*a**, 4603*a**, 4609*a**; paddles, 4148

Caracol Ruins, Honduras, archaeology, 4159

Carey, Lea and Blanchard, corres. with Henry Rowe Schoolcraft, 4326

Cargo system, Mayan (Chiapas, Mexico), 4498*a*

Carlisle Barracks, Indian Training School, people, 4273*a**

Carlson, Barry F., author, 4801; donor, 4801

Carrier, language, 4012; linquistics, 4012

Carrington, Henry Beebee, author, 4005, 4373

Carson, Joseph, corres. with A. J. Holman and Co., 4491

Carter, Richard T., Jr., compiler, 4196; corres. with Whitfield J. Bell, Jr., 4196; donor, 4196

Cashibo, language, 4143

Catawba, *4148a-4149*, 4148*a**, 4688*d**; **animals**, 4020*c*, 4148*b*; **artifacts**, 4148*a**, 4275; **ceremonies**, 4020*c*, 4148*b*; **charms**, 4020*c*, 4148*b*; **curative practices**, 4149; **economics**, 4020*c*, 4148*b*; **ethnography**, 4148*a**, 4688*d**; **fauna**, 4020*c*, 4148*b*; **folk medicine**, 4020*c*, 4148*b*; **food**, 4020*c*, 4148*b*; **history**, 4020*c*, 4148*b*; **hunting and fishing equipment**, 4688*d**; **language**, 4020*c*, 4148*b*; **marriage**, 4020*c*, 4148*b*; **medicine**, 4020*c*, 4148*a**, 4148*b*, 4149; **myths**, 4020*c*, 4148*b*; **omens**, 4020*c*, 4148*b*; **people**: 4148*a**; Margaret Wiley Brown and Mrs. Sampson Owl, 4688*d**; **pottery**, 4308; **religion**, 4020*c*, 4148*b*; **subsistence**, 4020*c*, 4148*b*; **taboos**, 4020*c*, 4148*b*; **texts**, 4020*c*, 4148*b*

Catholicism, folk, Tlaxcalan, 4521

Catlin, George, 4020*b*, 4179*a*; artist, 4865*b*; photographs of his paintings, 4587*b*

Cattaraugus Reservation, 4723; Old Party Caucus, 4718; politics, 4718

Cayer, Andre, 4331

Cayuga, 4714*a**; **body parts**, 4001, 4712; **ceremony**, 4081, 4616; **contents of recording**, 4223, 4616*a*; **dance**, 4081, 4616; **ethnography**, 4081, 4616, 4728; **fauna**, 4001, 4712; **flora**, 4001, 4712; **foods**, 4001, 4712; **informants**, Mr. and Mrs. Cuthbert Davey, 4001, 4712; **kinship terms**, 4001, 4712; **language**, 4001, 4712; **longhouse**, 4714*a**; Upper Cayuga, 4397*a**; **masks**, 4332, 4714*a**; **names for Nanticokes**, 4559, 4864; **numerals**, 4001, 4712; **paradigms**, 4001, 4712; **people**, 4001, 4712, 4714*a**; **pronouns**, 4001, 4712; **recordings**, 4081, 4616; **song**, 4081, 4616; **Sour Springs Long House**, 4714*a**; **terms for people**, 4001, 4712; **vocabulary**, 4001, 4712. *See also* Seneca

*Cazique*, 4448; choice of by Antelope Clan, 4449

Census, Iroquois, 4005, 4373, 4396; Nootka, 4586; Seneca, 4723; Six Nations, 4005, 4373; United States, 4005, 4373

Centennial, 4132; Exposition, 4491

Central Alaskan Yupik, dictionary, 4043, 4107*a*; language, 4043, 4107*a*; linguistics, 4043, 4107*a*; texts, 4043, 4107*a*

Central America, *4149a-4159b*, 4149*a**, 4504*a**, 4739*a**; **archaeology**, 4152*a*, 4153, 4157*a*, 4158*a*, 4159-4159*b*, 4331*a*, 4339*a*, 4504*a**; **architecture**, 4504*a**; **artifacts**, 4504*a**; **bibliography**, 4125, 4151; **British Honduras**, 4159*b*; **dwellings**, 4149*a**, 4739*a**; **ethnography**, 4149*a**, 4739*a**; **ethnology**, 4152*a*; **genetic classification**, 4334*a*, 4525*a*; **genetic relationships** (linguistic), 4155-4156; **Guatemala**, 4035, 4150, 4152*a*, 4157*a*, 4158*a*, 4159*a*-4159*b*; **language families**, 4513; **languages**: 4154-4156; geographical distribution, 4156; **linguistics**, 4125, 4151-4152*a*, 4158, 4513; **Panama**, 4157*a*; **people**, 4149*a**, 4504*a**, 4739*a**. *See also* Middle America

Ceremonialism, Hopi, 4783, 4798; Iroquois, 4728; Oklahoma Seneca-Cayuga, 4728; Zuni, 4783, 4798

Ceremonies, **adoption**, of Paul A. W. Wallace by Mohawks, 4530; **Antelope**, sand painting (Mishongnovi), 4790; **Arapaho**, 4081, 4616; **basket dance** (Tewa), 4836; **calendar**, 4447; **Catawba**, 4020*c*, 4148*b*; **Cayuga**, 4081, 4616; **Cherokee**, 4081, 4616; **Cheyenne**, 4081, 4616; **clowns**: (Pueblo Mayo-Zoque), 4787; Southwest, 4782; **corn dance** (Michigan Indians, Ojibwa), 4038, 4609; **corn people's** (Keres), 4447; **Crow**, 4682*b**; **dance to the four winds** (Michigan Indians, Ojibwa), 4038*, 4609*; **Delaware**, 4080-4081, 4217-4218, 4222, 4616; **Feast of the Dead** (Dakota), 4207; **Fiesta for the Dead** (Tepehuan), 4816; **Flute** (Tusayan),

4790; **Flute society** (Oraibi), 4780; **functions**, 4447; **Great Feast for the Dead** (Iroquois), 4399; **great feather dance** (Iroquois), 4388*a**; Hopi, 4779; **Iroquois**, 4537; ***Kachina* cult** (Sahagun), 4454; **kinship** (Tlaxcalan), 4521; **kiva** (San Juan Pueblo), 4059, 4835; **Memorial Feast of the Dead** (Dakota), 4682*f**; **Menomini**, 4245*a**; **mescalbeans**, 4590; **Mohawk**, 4537; **Night Chant** (Navajo), 4566; **offerings to still-born and dead**, 4448; **Ojibwa**, 4071, 4606; **Oklahoma**, 4081, 4616; **Oto**, 4081, 4616; **Ottawa**, 4609*b**; ***Papago*** ceremonies, 4869*a*; **partridge dance** (Michigan Indians, Ojibwa), 4038*, 4609*; **Pawnee**, 4081, 4616; **Pima Bajo**, 4668; **Ponca**, 4081, 4616; **Quapaw**, 4081, 4616; **rain festival** (Tepecano), 4811; **religious** (southeastern Chiapas, Mexico), 4498*a*; **round dance** (Michigan Indians, Ojibwa), 4038*, 4609*; **Sandia** (Tiwa), 4055, 4844; **San Juan Pueblo**, cycle (Tewa), 4836; **scalp** (Zuni), 4771; **Seneca**, 4081, 4616; ***senshare*** (San Juan Pueblo, Tewa), 4015, 4059, 4834-4835, 4839; **Shawnee**, 4081, 4616; **Snake**, 4790; **snake dance**: Hopi, 4351*a**; Michigan Indians (Ojibwa), 4038*, 4609*; **snake swallowers** (Chamahiya), 4790; **stomp dance** (Michigan Indians, Ojibwa), 4038*, 4609*; **sun dance**: Crow, 4682*b**; Dakota, 4206; **sweathouse pit** (Shasta County, California), 4132*a**; **sweat lodge** (Dakota), 4207; **Thlewarle Indian Baptist Church**, Oklahoma, 4547; **Tutelo**, 4246*a**; adoption rite wampum beads, 4397*a**; **war dance**: Crow, 4682*b**; Michigan Indians (Ojibwa), 4038*, 4609*; **warrior's purification** (Mexico), 4927; **Yuchi harvest**, 4546*a**, 4732*a**, 4922*. *See also* Dances; Festivals; Fiestas

Cessions, Indian land, 4865

Chaco Canyon, N. Mex. archaeology, 4014, 4769

Chafe, Wallace L., author, 4715; donor, 4715

Chalmers, Harvey, II corres. with Paul A. W. Wallace, 4374

Chama, 4758; language, 4143

*Chamahia* stones, 4847

*Chamahiya* snake swallowers, 4790

Champlain, Samuel de, 4911

Chants, Hopi, 4345

Chapin, J. R., artist, 4291*b*, 4865*a*

Chappel, A., artist, 4291*b*

Chappel, Alonzo, artist, 4865*a*

Chappelle, Mary M., corres. with Frank G. Speck, 4539*a*

Charms, Catawba, 4020*c*, 4148*b*

Chase, Fannie S. (Mrs. Walter G.), corres. with Frank G. Speck, 4273

Chasta Costa, **people**: Jack Orton, Stanley Orton, Wolverton Orton, 4137*b**; **songs**, 4803

Chatino, *4160*; linguistics, 4160; texts, 4504*b*; vocabulary, 4504*b*, 4525

Chehalis, Lower, language, 4039*a*, 4592

Chelan (Columbian), texts, 4044, 4592*b*

Chemehuevi, linguistic interaction with Mohave, 4699, 4764

Cherokee, 4010*, 4039, 4148*, *4161-4171*, 4162*a**, 4165*, 4291*b**, 4591, 4592*a**; anthropometric data, 4268*c*; archaeology, 4010, 4165, 4171; artifacts, 4162*a**, 4261; baskets, 4308; ceremony, 4081, 4616; chief, *Eoneguski*, 4170; contents of recording, 4223, 4616*a*; dance, 4081, 4616; ethnography, 4010, 4081, 4148*a**, 4162*a**, 4165, 4616; folklore, 4010, 4165; history, 4010, 4165; language, 4079, 4086, 4168-4169, 4190, 4208, 4665; linguistics, 4010, 4079, 4165, 4168; masks, 4332; medicine, 4028, 4163; missions to, 4047, 4592*c*; morphology, 4079, 4168; music, 4010, 4165; (Cherokee) Nation, address to, 4162; North Carolina, 4332; paradigms, 4079, 4168; people, 4162*a**, 4865*b**; prefixes, 4079, 4168; recordings, 4079, 4081, 4086, 4168-4169, 4190, 4208, 4616, 4665, 4903; song, 4081, 4616; suffixes, 4079, 4168; syllabary, 4028, 4163; texts, 4079, 4168; vocabulary, 4164*a*, 4378*a*, 4532*a*

Cheyenne, *4171a-4173*, 4171*a**, 4592*a**; **battle with Sumner**, 4271; **ceremony**, 4081, 4616; **contents of recording**, 4223, 4616*a*; **dance**, 4081, 4616; **ethnography**, 4081, 4616, 4683; **informants**: Bearbow, Flying Out, Howling Crane, Yellow Eagle, 4172; **language**, 4077, 4172-4173; **orthography**, 4173; **people**: 4171*a**, 4273*a**; 4865*b**; Mad Wolf and Man on Cloud, 4273*a**; John Wicks Okestehei, 4171*a**; **recordings**, 4077, 4081, 4172, 4616; **song**, 4081, 4616; **texts**, 4077, 4172-4173; **transcripts of recordings**, 4173

Chiapanec, vocabulary, 4525

Chiapas, Mexico, Mayan cargo system, 4498*a*; Palenque, 4504*a**, 4521*a**; Sac Balam, 4498; southeastern religious practices, 4047*a*, 4498*a**, 4498*b*

Chibchan, genetic classification, 4762; linguistics, 4152

Chichen Itza, Yucatan, 4158*a*, 4500*a**, 4504*a**

Chichimeca, vocabulary, 4525

Chickahominy, 4687*a**, 4688; artifacts, 4275, 4687*a**; people, 4687*a**

Chickasaw, anthropometric data, 4268*c*; missions to, 4047, 4592*c*

Chicomuceltec, 4498*a*; informant, 4913

Chiefs, **Blackfoot**: 4130*a**; Luke Big Turnips, 4130*a**; Turned-Up-Nose, 4130*a**; **Blood**, 4130*a**; **Cuna**: Manitinali's wife and children, 4149*b**; **Delaware**: Joseph Montour, 4221; James C. Weber (War Eagle), 4213*a**, 4215, 4224-4225; **Iowa**, 4291*b**; **Iroquois**: 4005, 4373, Deskaheh (*see also* General, Alexander), 4378; genealogical studies, 4391; Hess, 4414; Joseph Logan, 4397*a**; David Thomas, 4397*a**; **Kaw**: Washunga, 4231*a**; **Kickapoo**: 4291*b**; **Maine**: Frances, 4478; **Mandan**: Shahaka, 4683*a**; **Mohawk**: 4390; Joseph Brant, 4291*a*; William Dewaseragech Loft, 4397;

William Loft, 4400, 4414, 4536; Split Cloud(?) (Cook), 4536*a**; **Musquakie**: Peah-Mus-Ka, 4589*a**; **Nanticoke**: Josiah Hill and brother, 4558*a**; **Northeast**: John Neptune, 4598*a**; (Temagami) **Ojibwa**: White Bear, 4609*a**; **Omaha**: Ong Pa Ton Ga, 4589*a**; **Pawnee**: Tom Morgan, 4648*a**; **Pennsylvania**: Running Wolf, 4652*a**; **Penobscot, 4658**; **Ponca**: White Eagle, 4682*e**; **Rappahannock**: Big Otter Nelson, 4688*d**; **Scatticook**: Frank Coggswell, 4598*a**; **Sioux**: Hollow Horn Bear, 4737*a**; Sitting Bull, 4291*b**, 4682*e**, 4683*a**; Spotted Tail, 4273*a**; **Six Nations**, 4005, 4373; **Southwest**, 4773; **Tlingit**: Louis Shotridge, 4601*a**; **town chief**, 4448; **Tuscarora**: Elton Greene, 4062, 4076, 4862-4863; **war**, 4447, 4773; **Winnebago**: Black Snake, 4904*a**
Chihuahua, Mexico, 4519*, 4669; Baborigame, 4820
Chilcotin, anthropometric data, 4268*c*
Children, deforming heads of, 4263; Native American in school, 4301*b**
Chimakum, ethnobotany, 4698
Chimariko, 4183
Chinantec, vocabulary, 4525
Chinook (Wasco-Wishram), 4891; ethnography, 4893, 4909; linguistics, 4892-4894, 4907-4909; paradigms, 4892, 4907; people, 4865*b**; semantics, 4894; syntax, 4894, 4908; vocabulary, 4892, 4907
Chinook Jargon, 4174; comparative text, 4857; language, 4857; legends, 4174, 4472, 4735, 4854; myths, 4174; songs, 4803
Chipewyan, 4143*b**; cognates, linguistics, 4113; social history, 4111
Chippewa, 4010, 4039, 4108, 4165, 4591, 4592*a**; anthropometric data, 4268*c*; people, 4865*b**; revival hymns, 4071, 4606. *See also* Ojibwa
Chiricahua, *4175-4177*; language, 4012, 4175-4177; linguistics, 4012; texts, 4175-4177, 4502
Chitimacha, 4364*a**; baskets, 4308; vocabulary, 4333, 4516
Chiwere, *4177a-4179*; cognates, 4178, 4232; dictionary, 4177*a*; historical and comparative linguistics, 4178, 4232; language, 4178-4179, 4232; linguistics, 4178, 4232; texts, 4178, 4232. *See also* Iowa, Oto
Choates, J. N., photographer, 4273*a*
Chocho (Tlapanec), vocabulary, 4525
Choco, 4019, 4755; genetic classification, 4762
Choctaw, 4010, 4037, 4165, *4179a-4182*, 4289, 4592*a**; anecdotes, 4067, 4182; artifacts, 4261; belts, 4179*b**, 4301*b**; Choctaw village, Louisiana, 4301*b**; engraving, 4179*a**; ethnography, 4067, 4179*a**, 4182; fauna, 4067, 4182; game of ball, 4179*a**; informants, 4179*b*; language, 4067, 4182; linguistics, 4180-4181; missions to, 4047, 4592*c*; Mississippi, 4067, 4181-4182; people, D. I. Bushnell, 4301*b*; person markers, 4180; recording, 4067, 4182; texts, 4067, 4182; vocabulary, 4516
Chol, ethnography, ethnohistory, 4498
Cholo, 4019, 4755
Cholon, *4183*
Cholti-Lacandon Maya, ethnography, 4498
Chontal, Highland. *See* Highland Chontal; Mountain Tequistlateco
Choreography, 4470; Creek and Yuchi, 4550, 4923
Choroti, linguistics, 4753
Christian Indian Monument, Gnadenhütten, Ohio, 4244*a**
Church, Herring Pond Indian (Nipmuc), 4598*a**; Isleta Pueblo, 4301*a**; Ontario, 4244*a*; *Thlewarle* Indian Baptist, Oklahoma, 4547
Citara, 4019, 4755
Civilization, ancient America, 4307; and the American Indian, 4041, 4327
Clans, 4447; Hopi, 4358-4359; Iroquois: Bear, 4383; symbols, 4377*a**; Keres: Antelope, 4449; Penobscot, 4658; Tsimshian, Raven, 4002, 4853
Clanship, Mexico and Peru, 4523, 4757
Clement, William L., Library, 4594, 4598
Cliff, dwellers, 4280; **dwellings**, Mesa Verde, Colo. 4796*a**; Mezquital, Durango, Mexico, 4507
Clothing, Iroquois, 4395
Clovis, N. Mex., archaeology, 4020*a*, 4327*a*
Clowns, Mayo-Zoque, 4787; songs (Hopi), 4052, 4349; Southwest, 4782
Coahuila, Mexico, archaeology, 4512
Coahuiltec, vocabulary, 4516
Coates, Benjamin Horner, 4272; **corres. with**: Charles Caldwell, 4272; Eli K. Price, 4492
Coates, D.S.B.H., 4488
Cobb, Rodney D., corres. with Frank G. Speck, 4274
Cocama. *See* Kokama
Cocamilla, 4758
Cochiti, 4359, 4771, 4773, 4799; language, 4439; songs, 4470; transcript of recording, 4470
Codex Zouche-Nuttal, 4529
Coeur d'Alene, language, 4044, 4592*b*
Cognates. *See* Comparative vocabularies; *see also* under specific language and language family
Collections, **artifacts**, 4767; **contents of**, 4042, 4328; **drawings**, Frank G. Speck, 4020*b*; **Eskimo**, 4252; **Indian related**: Haverford College Library, 4320, 4415; Historical Society of Pennsylvania, 4415; Quaker Historical Association, 4415; **manuscripts**: *4001-4023a*; Alaska Native languages, 4043, 4107*a*; American Indian, 4415; American Indian linguistics, 4039*a*, 4592; American Philosophical Society Library, 4036, 4123, 4295; Athapascan, 4114; Benjamin Smith Barton, 4003; Robert Bell, 4003*a*, 4268*a*; Stephen Bowers, 4004; Crawford manuscripts, 4524; Draper Collection, Princeton University, 4416; Eskimo, 4252,

4601; Flexner, 4575*a*; Harry Hoijer, 4012; Indian conferences, 4042, 4328; Iroquois, 4027, 4164*a*, 4372, 4378*a*, 4532*a*; Iroquois in American Revolution, 4392; John Alden Mason, 4017; Mayan, 4024, 4499; Mexico, 4521; Moravian Church Archives, 4039, 4591; Nootka, 4585; Northwest Coast, 4252, 4599, 4601; Pacific Northwest tribal languages, 4044, 4592*b*; Reina-Jimenez, 4024, 4499; Marian Smith, 4599; Stevenson, 4469; United Church Board for World Ministries, 4047, 4592*c*; University of Washington libraries, 4034, 4841; Carl F. Voegelin, 4020*e*; Paul A. W. Wallace, 4021; **microfilms**, *4024-4047*; **museum**: Eskimo, 4252, 4601; mescalbeans, 4590; Northwest Coast, 4252, 4601; photographs of Iroquois costumes, 4395; **photographs**: Durango, Mexico, 4515*; Iroquois costumes, 4395*; American Philosophical Society Library, 4016*a*; John Alden Mason, 4017; Shindler, North American Indians, 4592*a*; Frank G. Speck, 4020*b*; Paul A. W. Wallace, 4021; **prints**, American Philosophical Society Library, 4016*a*; **private**: Jean Rumsey, sign language, 4029, 4588; stone-age artifacts, 4315; **sketches**, Benjamin Smith Barton, 4003
College of Physicians, Philadelphia, 4283, 4476, 4558; Gilbert Collection, 4161, 4212-4213, 4262-4267, 4713-4714
Colombia, archaeology, 4331*a*; ethnology, 4755*a*; Indians of, 4019, 4755
Colorado, Denver Art Museum, 4275; Mesa Verde, cliff dwellings and Sun Temple, 4796*a**
Colorado River Indian Reservation, Arizona, 4699, 4764
Columbian, *4184-4185a*; Chelan, 4044, 4592*b*; language, 4044, 4070, 4185-4185*a*, 4592*b*; linguistics, 4044, 4184, 4592*b*; recordings, 4070, 4185*a*; transcripts of recordings, 4185; texts, 4044, 4592*b*
Colville (Okanogan), language, 4044, 4592*b*
Comalcalco, 4504*a**
Comanche, anthropometric data, 4268*c*; people, 4587*b**; war shield, 4682*a**
Comecrudo, vocabulary, 4516
Commissioner of Indian Affairs, 4020, 4325
Committee on Research in Native American Languages, 4269-4270
Communication, Arapaho, Arikara, Assiniboin, Blackfoot, Cheyenne, Crow, Gros Ventre, Hidatsa, Mandan, Ojibwa (Plains), Plains Cree, Sarsi, and Sioux, 4683
Comparative vocabularies. *See* Dictionaries, Vocabularies. *See also* under specific languages and language families
Comrie, Howard F., corres. with Paul A. W. Wallace, 4375
Conchilla Valley, 4138
Condolence to the Dead, Iroquois, 4399
Condoling Council, Mohawk, 4537
Conferences, Indian, 4042, 4328; Iroquoian studies, 4376; Lake Mohonk, 4042, 4328; second on Iroquois research, 4387
Congdon, Charles E., corres. with Paul A. W. Wallace, 4376
Conibo, *4186*; language, 4143; linguistics, 4186; myths, 4186
Conklin, E. G., corres. with H. J. Ostrander, 4572
Connecticut, Moravian missions among Indians, 4039, 4591; Kent, Scatticook Indian Reservation, 4598*a*; Wesleyan University, 4836
Conoy, 4651
Constitution, United States, influence of Iroquois Confederation on, 4375, 4379
Contrecoeur, Claude Pierre Pécaudy, Sieur de, papers, 4587
Cook, Chief Julius, corres. with Paul A. W. Wallace, 4532
Cooking. *See* Food preparation
Cooper, James Fenimore, 4374
Cooper, John W., corres. with Elsie Clews Parsons, 4311
Copper River, Alaska, 4031, 4103, 4105-4106; archaeology, ethnology, 4032, 4106*a*, 4850; informants, 4032, 4105, 4106*a*, 4850; interviews, 4032, 4106*a*, 4850
Copway, George (*Kah-ge-ga-gah-bowh*), corres. with F. W. Porter, 4604
Cora, linguistics, 4870, 4887; religion, compared with Tepecano, 4808; vocabulary, 4870. *See also* Pima Bajo
Corbould, E. H., artist, 4291*b*
Cornell, John R., collector, 4056, 4676; donor, 4056, 4676
Cornell University, 4025, 4268*b*
Corner, George W., corres. with Eric P. Hamp, 4694
Cornplanter, Edward, 4732; author, 4006, 4716
Cornplanter, Jesse J., 4006, 4716; artist, 4377-4377*a*; corres. with Paul A. W. Wallace, 4021, 4419
Cornplanter, talk, 4416
Coroado, linguistics, 4753
Coropo, linguistics, 4753
Cosmogony, 4416
Coues, Elliot, corres. with Robert Bell, 4003*a*, 4268*a*
Coxoh (Mayan), 4498*a*; colonial project, 4498*a*
Coyote, stories, Navajo, 4570; Papago, 4629; Quechan, Coyote and Quail, 4698*a*; Tewa (Arizona), Coyote and Bullsnake, 4838*b*
Craig, Isaac, corres. with John W. Jordan, 4721
Crawford, T. Hartly, manuscripts, 4524
Creation myth. *See* Myth
Cree, 4020*a*, 4111, *4187-4194*, 4188*a**, 4188*b**, 4190*a**, 4295, 4327*a*; **ethnography**, 4187-4189; **hunting territories**, 4189; **informants**, 4187-4188; **language**, 4086, 4190, 4194; **medicine man**, 4598*a**; **people**, 4188*a**; **Plains Cree**: Canada, 4193; classification of texts, 4191; contents of recording, 4193; ethnography, 4187-4188, 4683; geographic dis-

tribution, 4191; informants, 4191; language, 4193; linguistics, 4191; recording, 4098, 4192; status, 4191; texts, 4098, 4192-4193; transcript of recording, 4193; **recordings**, 4086, 4169, 4190, 4208, 4665, 4903; **Rossville Mission**, 4194; **vocabulary**, 4194. *See also* Montagnais-Naskapi

Creek, 4301*b**, 4546*a**, 4548, 4590*a**, 4732*a**, 4922*a**; artifacts, 4261, 4275; Creek Nation, Oklahoma, 4546*a**, 4732*a**, 4922*a**; dances, 4550, 4923; ethnography, 4546*a**, 4732*a**, 4922*a**; Florida Seminole, 4548*a*, 4549*a**; land dispute, 4549; language, 4039, 4591, 4923; legal brief, 4549; missions to, 4047, 4592*c*; people, 4273*a**, 4546*a**, 4732*a**, 4922*a**; religion, 4546*a**, 4732*a**, 4922*a**; songs, 4550-4551, 4923-4924; vocabulary, 4551, 4924. *See also* Muskogee; Seminole

Croghan, George, 4598

Crops, Six Nations, 4005, 4373

Crow, 4682*b**; anthropometric data, 4268*c*; dictionary, 4044, 4592*b*; ethnography, 4682*b**, 4683; language, 4044, 4592*b*; linguistics, 4044, 4592*b*; people, 4682*b**; sun dance, 4682*b**; texts, 4044, 4592*b*; war dance, 4682*b**

Crypt, Palenque, 4521*a**

*Cucurbita moschata*, Arizona and Sonora, Mexico, 4514

Cuicatec, vocabulary, 4525

Cuitlateco, vocabulary, 4525

Culin, Robert Stewart, corres. with: Isaac Minis Hays, 4554; Marshall Howard Saville, 4554, 4557

Culture, Andean region, 4749; change, Seneca, 4425; development, Iroquois, 4407; Hidatsa, 4053, 4343, 4484; Iroquois, 4371, 4413; Mandan, 4053, 4343, 4484; Ojibwa, 4610; Pocomam Central, and 4687; South America, 4759; relations, Pima and Pueblo, 4667. *See also* Ethnography; Ethnology

Cuna, 4019, 4149*b**, 4755; genetic classification, 4762; people, 4149*b**

Curative practices. *See* Ethnomedicine; Folk medicine

Curtis, Cyrus, 4273

Curtis, Edward W., photographer, 4251*a*

Cushing, Frank Hamilton, corres. with: American Philosophical Society, 4367; Isaac Minis Hays, 4164, 4367

Cusick, Albert, corres. with John W. Jordan, 4721

Customs. *See* Ethnography; Ethnology

Dakota, *4194a-4210*; **Assiniboin**, 4044, 4592*b*; **cognates**, 4178, 4204, 4232; **dialects**, 4065, 4204-4205; **dictionary**, 4044, 4592*b*; **dwellings**, 4682*f**; **engraving**, 4682*e**; **ethnography**, 4197-4198, 4200, 4202-4203, 4206-4207; **games**, 4197; **greeting**, 4198; **humor**, 4199, 4201-4202; **language**, 4044, 4091, 4198, 4203, 4208-4210, 4592*b*; **linguistics**, 4178, 4195-4197, 4199, 4201-4202, 4204-4205, 4232; **Memorial Feast of the Dead**, 4207, 4682*f**; **missions to**, 4047, 4592*c*; **music**, 4207; **mutual intelligibility between dialects**, 4065, 4204-4204*a*; **naming the dead**, 4198, 4203; **paradigms**, 4195; **people**: 4682*f**; Red Cloud, 4682*e**; **phonology**, 4205; **prayer**, 4198; **proverb**, 4200; **puns**, 4199, 4201; **recordings**, 4065, 4086, 4091, 4169, 4190, 4204*a*, 4208, 4210, 4665, 4903; **Santee**, 4206; **sun dance**, 4206; **sweat lodge**, 4682*f**; **taboos**, 4200; **Teton**, 4206; **texts**, 4044, 4065, 4091, 4197-4203, 4204*a*, 4207, 4209-4210, 4592*b*; **vocabulary**, 4195-4196, 4333; **yuwipi meeting**, 4682*f**. *See also* Assiniboin; Oglala; Santee; Sioux; Teton

Dalhousie Muniments, 4030, 4243

Dalrymple, E. A., collector, 4688*b*

Dance, 4358*, 4588*a**; **Apache**, 4796*a**; **Arapaho**, 4081, 4616, 4683; **Arikara**, 4683; **Assiniboin**, 4682*e**, 4683; **Blackfoot**, 4683; Calumet, 4071, 4606; **Cayuga**, 4081, 4616; **Cherokee**, 4081, 4616; **Cheyenne**, 4081, 4616, 4683; Corn, 4038*, 4609*; **Creek**, 4550, 4923; **cross-cultural comparison**, 4353; **Crow**, 4682*b**, 4683; **Delaware**, 4080-4081, 4218, 4222, 4616; **four winds**, dance to the, 4038*, 4609*; gourd, 4081, 4616; **Gros Ventre**, 4682*e**, 4683; **guide for data collection**, 4293; **Hidatsa**, 4683; **Hopi**, 4353; **Lac du Flambeau Chippewa**, 4071, 4606; **Mandan**, 4683; **Menomini**, 4071, 4606; **Michigan**, 4038*, 4071, 4605, 4606, 4609*; **Musquakie**, 4071, 4606; **Narraganset**, 4071, 4606; **Ojibwa**, 4038*, 4071-4072, 4606-4607, 4609*; Partridge, 4038*, 4609*; Plains, 4683; **Oklahoma**, 4081, 4616; **Osage**, 4231*a**; **Oto**, 4081, 4616; **Pamunkey**, 4688*b**; **Pawnee**, 4081, 4616, 4648*a**; **Plains**, 4682*e**; **Plains Cree**, 4683; **Polynesian**, 4353; **Ponca**, 4081, 4616; **Quapaw**, 4081, 4616; **San Juan Pueblo**, basket dance, 4836; **Sarsi**, 4683; **Seneca**, 4081, 4616; **Shawnee**, 4081, 4616; **Sioux**, 4207, 4683; Tewa, 4836; **Wisconsin**, 4071, 4606; **Yuchi**, 4550, 4923; songs, Acoma, 4439; Hopi-Apache, 4052, 4349. *See also* Music; Song; Stomps

Dancers, Iowa and Ponca, 4682*e**

Darley, F.O.C., artist, 4291*b*, 4650*a*

Davidson, D. S., corres. with Elsie Clews Parsons, 4311

Davidson, George, corres. with H. Newell Wardle, 4103

Davis, Dr., 4314

Davis, Irvine, author, 4438; donor, 4438

Davis, J. P., engraver, 4865*a*

*Dawendine*. *See* Winslow, Bernice Loft (Mrs. Arthur H.)

Day, Gordon M., corres. with Frank G. Speck, 4656

Dead, Condolence to the, Iroquois, 4399; Great

Feast for the, Iroquois, 4399; Memorial Feast of the, Dakota, 4207, 4682*f**; naming of the, Dakota, 4198, 4203; offerings to the, 4448; Penobscot mortuary customs, 4223*a*; person, laying out deer as if it were, 4460, 4792
Death Cry, 4865*a**
Decoration, 4334; block-stamp, 4240
Deer, laying out as if dead person, 4460, 4792
*Deganawidah*, biography, 4417; legend, 4386, 4402, 4411
de Laguna, Frederica, 4020*a*, 4327*a*, 4589*b*; author, 4250, 4849; collector, 4057, 4104; compiler, 4105; corres. with John Alden Mason, 4017, 4274*a*, 4295*a*; donor, 4105, 4249, 4251, 4849; and Marie Françoise Guédon, collectors, 4031, 4106; and Catherine McClellan, compilers, 4032, 4106*a*, 4850; photographer, 4251
Delaware, 4010, 4020*e*, 4033, 4165, *4211-4231*, 4213*a**, 4238*a*, 4246, 4301*b**, 4587, 4590*a**, 4651; **anthropometric data**, 4268*c*; **artifacts**, 4213*a**, 4216, 4219, 4224, 4231; **Big House**, 4080, 4219, 4222; **ceremonies**, 4081, 4217-4218, 4616; **chiefs**: Joseph Montour, 4221; James C. Weber (War Eagle) (*wi tapanóxwe* "Walks by Daylight"), 4213*a**, 4215, 4224-4225; **comparative vocabulary**, 4109*d*; **contents of recording**, 4223, 4616*a*; **dances**, 4080-4081, 4218, 4222, 4616; **Delawares-as-women problem**, 4226, 4228; **dialects**, 4223*a*, 4225*e*; **doll**, 4231; **educational materials**, 4225*d*; **entry into the League**, 4389; **ethnography**, 4080-4081, 4213*a**, 4217, 4219, 4222, 4225, 4225*b*, 4616; **false face**, 4080, 4222; **fauna**, 4080, 4222; **feasts**, 4218; **history**, 4220, 4227; **honor**, 4221*a*; **in American Revolution**, 4393; **Indian preacher**, 4229; **informant**: Chief James C. Weber, 4215, 4225, 4225*e*; **language**, 4039, 4080, 4222, 4225, 4225*b*, 4225*e*, 4591; **legitimacy**, 4221*a*; **linguistics**, 4225*d*, 4225*e*; **medicine**, 4080, 4222; **morphology**, 4225*d*; **myths**, 4225*b*; **Oklahoma**, 4221*a*; **oral literature**, 4211; **people**, 4213*a**, 4865*b**; **phonology**, 4225*d*; **phonotactics**, 4225*d*; **portrait of**, 4214; **prayers**, 4080, 4222; **recordings**, 4080-4081, 4222, 4616; **relations with Six Nations**, 4227, 4230, 4389; **religion**, 4225; **songs**, 4080-4081, 4215, 4222-4223, 4225*b*, 4616; **texts**, 4080, 4215, 4222–4223, 4225*b*; **transcript of recording**, 4215; **vocabulary**, 4080, 4109*d*, 4222, 4225*a*; **Walam Olum**, 4020*e*, 4218*a*, 4223*a*, 4225*c*, 4225*e*; **weather**, 4080, 4222. *See also* Munsee
Delaware (state), archaeology, Slayton Creek, 4518*; Nanticoke, 4558*
Delaware Valley, Indian trails, 4412
Delight makers, 4795
Deloria, Ella Cara, 4196, 4206; author, 4197-4203
De Marcus, Richard, 4549
Demers, Richard, collector, 4057*a*, 4600*a*; donor, 4057*a*, 4600*a*
Demography, sociohistorical, Tuscarora, 4861. *See* Geographic distribution
Densmore, Frances, 4795
*Deskaheh*, Chief. *See* General, Alexander
*Deskaheh*, *Hi-wyi-iss*. *See* General, Levi
Deuman, Mrs., corres. with Sir Richard Owen, 4310
Deyo, Simeon L., 4489
Dhegiha, *4231a-4232*; cognates, 4178, 4232; engraving (Punka), 4682*e**; language, 4178, 4232; linguistics, 4178, 4232. *See also* Kansa; Omaha; Osage; Ponca; Quapaw
Diachronic linguistics. *See* historical under specific languages and language families
Diagrams, Southwest, 4797
Dialects. *See* under specific languages, language families, countries, continents, regions, etc.
Diaries, Moravian missions among Indians, 4039, 4591; Eugene Roy's, 4271
Dictionaries, Acoma, 4438; Alaska native languages, 4043, 4107*a*; Assiniboin (Dakota), 4044, 4592*b*; Athapascan, 4115, 4342; Blackfoot (Piegan), 4044, 4592*b*; Canadian Indian Biography, 4144; Central Alaskan Yupik, 4043, 4107*a*; Coeur d'Alene, 4044, 4592*b*; Columbian, 4044, 4592*b*; Colville (Okanogan), 4044, 4592*b*; Crow, 4044, 4592*b*; Gros Ventre (Arapaho), 4044, 4592*b*; Haida, 4115, 4342; Hopi, 4350-4351, 4361; Ingalik (Ingalit), 4043, 4107*a*; Iñupiaq (Inuit), 4043, 4107*a*; Iowa-Oto, 4177*a*; Kalispel, 4044, 4592*b*; Koyukon, 4043, 4107*a*; Kutenai, 4044, 4592*b*; Mandan, 4486; Na-Dene, 4115, 4342; Nahuatl, 4520*a*; Navajo, 4565, 4580; Nez Perce, 4044, 4592*b*; Onondaga, 4033, 4238*a*; Pacific Northwest tribal languages, 4044, 4592*b*; Sino-Tibetan, 4115, 4342; Spokane, 4801; Tlingit, 4115, 4342; Wintu, 4905; Yakima (Sahaptin), 4044, 4592*b*, 4701; Yuchi, 4925. *See also* Vocabulary and vocabularies
*Dictionary of Canadian Biography*, 4417
Diegueño, *4233-4234*; dialects, 4233; language, 4073, 4234; linguistics, 4233; recording, 4073, 4234; texts, 4073, 4233-4234; vocabulary, 4233
Diehl, H. C., collector, 4057*b*, 4349*a*; compiler, 4006*a*, 4349*b*
Diorama, cave scene, 4301*b**; Sioux, 4737*a**
Directions (compass), Sandia (Tiwa), 4055, 4844
Discipline, of Iroquois children, 4383
Discourse analysis, Yana, 4128
Diseases, animals associated with (Keres), 4793; Keres, 4793; Navajo, 4022, 4579; Pocomam Central, 4687; Six Nations, 4005, 4373. *See also* Medicine; Pathology
Dismal Swamp, Virginia, 4688*a**
Distribution, geographical. *See* **Geographical distribution**
Ditch opening, 4794
Divination, devices, Montagnais-Naskapi, 4188*b**; divining rod, Pennsylvania, 4652*a**

Dixon, Jeremiah, corres. with James Burd, 4596
Dogrib, *4234a-4238*; contents of recordings, informants, 4238; language, 4046, 4235, 4237-4238; legends, 4087, 4236; linguistics, 4235; myths, 4238; paradigms, 4235; recordings, 4087, 4236; vocabulary, 4235, 4238. *See also* Hare
Dogs, meat, 4313; Montagnais-Naskapi, 4188*b**
Dolls, Corn husk, Iroquois, 4377*a**
Dolores, Juan, 4626, 4639-4640; author, 4623-4624, 4815; contents of notebook, 4638
Dorsey, James Owen, 4178, 4232
Douglas, Frederic H., 4281; and Frances Raynolds, corres. with Frank G. Speck, 4275
Dowsing, Pennsylvania, 4652*a**
Drake, Charley G., corres. with Frank G. Speck, 4763
Drake, Noah Fields, 4276-4277; **corres. with**: American Philosophical Society, 4276; Isaac Minis Hays, 4277
Drake, Robert J., corres. with John Alden Mason, 4681
Draper Collection, Princeton University, New Jersey, 4416
Drawings, Aztec, 4301*a**; Iroquois, 4377*, 4377*a**, 4388*a**; Montagnais-Naskapi, 4188*b**; Moravian, 4244*a*; Native American, 4020*b**; Nootka, 4586*; Palenque, 4521*a**; Penobscot, 4663*a**; Peru, 4303*a*; skeletons, 4303*a**; Tutelo, 4246*a**. *See also* Engravings; Paintings; Pictures; Postal cards; and Sketches
Dreams, Ojibwa, 4610
Druke, Mary A., author, 4164*a*, 4378*a*, 4532*a*; donor, 4164*a*, 4378*a*, 4532*a*
Drunkenness, Lacandon, 4497
du Jaunay, Father, Jesuit, 4603
Dunbar, William, vocabularies, 4323
Dunn, John A., author, 4855; donor, 4855
Dunnack, Henry E., corres. with: Fannie H. Eckstorm, 4657; Frank G. Speck, 4278
Dunnigan, Timothy, author, 4677; collector, 4058, 4678; donor, 4058, 4678
Du Ponceau, Peter S., 4108, 4282; **author**, 4321, 4646; **corres. with**: Albert Gallatin, 4589; John G. E. Heckewelder, 4033, 4238*a*; William Hickling Prescott, 4321; Theodore Schulz, 4476
Durand, A. B., engraver, 4291*b*
Durango, Mexico, 4515*, 4519*, 4525*a*; archaeology, 4507, 4512; artifacts, 4507; cliff dwellings, Mezquital, 4507; "Pygmy Race of Durango," 4289*a*; tribal strife, 4507; Xoconoxtle, 4816
Durston, Harry C., corres. with Paul A. W. Wallace, 4379
Dwellings, **Acoma**, 4796*a**; **Arapaho**, 4682*f**, 4683; **Arikara**, 4683; **Arizona**, 4575*a**; **Assiniboin**, 4683; **Blackfoot**, 4683; **Central America**, 4149*a**, 4739*a**; **Cheyenne**, 4683; **Crow**, 4683; **Dakota**, 4682*f**; **Eskimo**, 4251*a**; **Gros Ventre**, 4683; **Harbor Springs**, Michigan, 4603; **Hidatsa**, 4683; **Houma**, 4364*a**; **Iroquois**, 4005, 4373; **Isleta**, 4796*a**; **Kickapoo**, 4256*a**; **Laguna**, 4796*a**; **Mandan**, 4683; **Mesa Verde**, 4796*a**; **Mexico**: 4520*; Mezquital, Durango, 4507; **Micmac**, 4598*a**; **New Mexico**, 4575*a**; **Oglala**, 4682*f**; **Ojibwa**: 4012*a**, 4603*a**; Plains, 4683; **Oklahoma**, village, 4612*a**; **Osage**, 4231*a**; **Pamunkey**, 4688*b**; **Pima Bajo**, 4668, 4670*; **Plains Cree**, 4683; **Pokagon** (Potawatomi), 4598*a**; **Sandia** (Tiwa), 4055, 4844; **Sarsi**, 4683, 4708*a**; **Sauk**, 4256*a**; **Scatticook**, 4598*a**; **Seminole** (Florida), 4549*a**; **Seneca**, 4732*; **Sioux**, 4683; **Six Nations**, 4005, 4373; **South America**, 4149*a**, 4739*a**; **Southern Paiute**, 4766*a**; **Stockbridge-Munsee**, 4540*a**; **Têtes de Boule**, 4190*a**; **Ute**, 4766*a**; **Wichita**, 4900*a**. *See also* Camps; Habitat; Pueblos; Settlements; Villages
Dyk, Walter, 4020*a*, 4327*a*; compiler, 4892, 4907

Eagle Butte, S. Dak., 4065, 4204*a*
Eames, Wilburforce, corres. with Isaac Minis Hays, 4490
Earthquake, Indian references to, 4212
Eastern North America, artifacts, 4239-4241; baskets, 4239-4240. *See also* specific place-names and tribes
Eastern United States, 4301*b**; Indian trails, 4247. *See also* specific place-names and tribes
East Indies, artifacts, 4896; fauna, 4896
Eastman, Seth, 4020*b*; artist, 4588*a*, 4865*a*
Eastwood, Stewart A., 4251*a*
Eckstorm, Fannie H., **corres. with**: Henry E. Dunnack, 4657; Frank G. Speck, 4657
Economics, Catawba, 4020*c*, 4148*b*; group identification, 4614; Micmac, 4527; Penobscot, 4657; Pima Bajo, 4668; primitive (Incan), 4020*a*, 4327*a*; Stockbridge-Munsee community, 4539
Ecuador, 4740; Andean Indians, 4464, 4756; Indians of, 4019, 4755
Ecuadorian Oriente, ethnology, 4740; linguistics, 4740
Edel, May Mandelbaum, 4034, 4841
Edgerton, Franklin, corres. with Frank G. Speck, 4279
Edinburgh, Scotland, Scottish Record Office, 4030, 4243
Education, 4273*a**; Delaware, 4225*d**; methods, 4109*b*; Mexican Indians, 4511; Micmac, 4527; Nootka, 4584; Ojibwa, 4604; Onondaga, 4016, 4720; Tonawanda, 4727
Edwards, Elizabeth A., author, 4341*b*; corres. with Whitfield J. Bell, Jr., 4341*b*; donor, 4341*b*
Eggan, Fred, corres. with Elsie Clews Parsons, 4311

Einhorn, Arthur (*Skaroniate*), corres. with Paul A. W. Wallace, 4380
Eliot, Indian Bible, 4488, 4490-4492, 4494; John, 4490*a*, 4865*a**; Oak, Mass., 4490*a**
Embroidery, moose hair, 4334
Emigration, Seneca, 4723
England, **British Association for the Advancement of Science**, Oxford, 4307; **British Museum**, Codex Zouche-Nuttal, 4529; **Oxford University**: Ashmolean Museum, 4598*a*; Pitt Rivers Museum, 4334; **Public Record Office**, London, 4027, 4372; **Royal Anthropological Institute of Great Britain and Ireland**, 4599; **Shelton**, 4314
Engravings, after Karl Bodmer, 4020*b*, 4682*e*; after Seth Eastman, 4020*b*, 4588*a*; Assiniboin, 4682*e**; Choctaw, 4179*a**; Dakota, 4682*e**; Dhegiha, 4682*e**; Fort Mackenzie, 4682*e**; Fox, 4682*e**; Hidatsa, 4682*e**; Indian camp, Rocky Mountains, 4683*b**; Mandan, 4682*e**; Mannitarri, 4682*e**; Mount Shasta, California, 4132*b**; Native American, 4016*a**, 4020*b**, 4291*a**, 4291*b**, 4865*a**, 4865*b**; Pennsylvania, 4650*a**; Punka, 4682*e**; Rio Colorado, 4796*a**; Sauk, 4682*e**. *See also* Drawings; Paintings; Pictures; Postal cards; Sketches
Enos, Suzie, compiler, 4007, 4625
*Eoneguski, or the Cherokee Chief*, 4170
Erie, 4651
*Erythrina flabelliformis*, 4590
Eskew, James W., corres. with Frank G. Speck, 4280
Eskimo, 4010, 4026, 4165, *4248-4256*, 4251*a**, 4254*a**, 4274*a*; **Alaska**, 4251*a**; **archaeology** (Greenland), 4251*; **art**, 4586*a*; **artifacts** (Greenland), 4251*; **attire**, 4319*a**; **Canada**, 4097, 4251*a**, 4255-4256; **comparative vocabulary**, 4256; **dialects**, 4097, 4255-4256; **dwellings**, 4251*a**; **ethnography**, 4026, 4251*a**, 4253-4254, 4254*a**, 4600; **European exhibits**, 4252; **Greenland**, 4251*, 4694; **habitat**, 4254*a**; **informants**: Jimmy Gibbons, Thomas Kadlak, Doris Kipan, Naomi, Hugh Ungunga, and David Uvinaiyak, 4097, 4255; **language**, 4026, 4097, 4255-4256; **linguistics**, 4256; **manuscript collections**, 4252, 4601; **masks**, 4251*a**, 4301, 4332; **museum collections**, 4252, 4601; **orthography**, 4256; **people**, 4251*a**, 4254*a**, 4319*a**; **phonology**, 4256; **property marks**, 4249; **recordings**, 4097, 4255; **texts**, 4097, 4255; **vocabulary**, 4256. *See also* Iñupiaq
Espinosa, Aurelio M., Jr., corres. with Elsie Clews Parsons, 4311
*Estufa*, Keres comparison with Zuni, 4448
Ethics, Delaware, 4221*a*; Oklahoma Indians, 4615; sanctions (ethical), 4304
Ethnoanatomy, Hopi, 4088, 4360, 4362; Navajo, 4360, 4582
Ethnobotany, 4461; Chimakum, 4698; Quileute, 4695, 4698
Ethnogeography, British Columbia, 4796*a*
Ethnography, 4004, 4010, 4017, 4273*a**, 4455, 4588*a**, 4934; **Alaska**, 4601*a**; **Algonquin**, 4602*b**; **Amazon basin**, 4149*a**, 4739*a**; **Arapaho**, 4081, 4616, 4683; **Arikara**, 4683; **Arizona**, 4575*a**; **Assiniboin**, 4194*a**, 4683; **Athapascan**, 4114; **Blackfoot**, 4130*a*, 4683; **Blood**, 4130*a*; **California**, 4132*a*; **Canada**, 4143*a**, 4143*b**, 4188*a**; **Catawba**, 4020*c*, 4148*a**, 4688*d**; **Cayuga**, 4081, 4616; **Central America**, 4149*a**, 4739*a**; **Cherokee**, 4010, 4081, 4148*a**, 4162*a**, 4165, 4616; **Cheyenne**, 4081, 4616, 4683; **Chickahominy**, 4687*a**; **Chinook** (Wasco-Wishram), 4893, 4909; **Choctaw**, 4067, 4179*a**, 4182; **Cholti-Lacandon**, 4498; **Cree**, 4187-4189, 4188*a**, 4188*b**; **Creek**, 4546*a**, 4732*a**, 4922*; **Crow**, 4682*b**, 4683; **Dakota**, 4197-4198, 4200, 4202-4203, 4206-4207; **Delaware**, 4080-4081, 4213, 4213*a**, 4217, 4219, 4222, 4225*b*, 4616; **Eskimo**, 4026, 4248, 4251*a**, 4253-4254, 4254*a**, 4600; **Gros Ventre**, 4683; **Guatemala**, 4024, 4499; **Hare**, 4234*a**; **Hidatsa**, 4683; **Hopi**, 4097*a*, 4363*a*; **Houma**, 4364*a**; **Hupa**, 4132*a**; **Iroquois**, 4377*a**, 4397*a**; **Isleta**, 4845; **Jicarilla**, 4427, 4433; **Kansa**, 4231*a**; **Keres**, 4448-4449, 4460; **Kickapoo**, 4256*a**; **Lacandon**, 4497-4498; **Lipan**, 4473; **Little Lake Pomo**, 4132*a**; **Lummi**, 4057*a*, 4600*a*; **Mandan**, 4683; **Mattaponi**, 4687*b**; **Mayan**, 4024, 4498-4499; **mescalbeans**, 4590; **Mexico**, 4017, 4520*, 4521; **Michigan**, 4038*, 4605, 4609*; **Micmac**, 4143*a**, 4527*a**; **Mohawk**, 4531; **Mohegan**, 4539*a*; **Montagnais-Naskapi**, 4188*b**, 4189; **Musquakie**, 4256*a**; **Nanticoke**, 4558*a**; **Narraganset**, 4491*a**; **Native American**, 4016*a**, 4020*b**, 4301*b**, 4588*a**; **New England**, 4143*a**; **New Mexico**, 4575*a**; **Nootka**, 4586; **Northeast**, 4598*a**; **Northwest Coast**, 4026; **Oglala**, 4194*a**, 4207; **Ojibwa**: 4012*a**, 4038*, 4603*a**, 4605, 4609*, 4609*a**; Plains, 4683; **Oklahoma**, 4081, 4207, 4615-4616; **Omaha**, 4231*a**; **Onondaga**, 4721; **Osage**, 4231*a**; **Oto**, 4081, 4178*a**, 4616; **Pamunkey**, 4688*b**; **Panama**, 4149*a**, 4739*a**; **Papago**, 4634; **Pawnee**, 4081, 4616; **Penobscot**, 4223*a*, 4660, 4662, 4663*a**; **Peru**, 4149*a**, 4739*a**; **Piegan**, 4130*a*; **Pima Bajo**, 4668, 4673, 4682; **Plains**, 4682*e**; **Plains Cree**, 4683; **Ponca**, 4081, 4616; **Quapaw**, 4081, 4616; **Rappahannock**, 4688*d**; **Salinan**, 4702; **San Carlos Apache**, 4703*a**; **Sandia** (Tiwa), 4055, 4843-4844; **San Juan Pueblo**, 4836; **Santee**, 4194*a**; **Sarsi**, 4683; **Sauk**, 4256*a**; **Seminole** (Florida), 4549*a**; **Seneca**: 4081, 4616, 4727*a**; Cayuga (Oklahoma), 4728; **Shawnee**, 4081, 4546*a**, 4616, 4732*a**, 4734*b*, 4922*; **Sioux**, 4207, 4683; **South America**, 4017, 4149*a**, 4739*a**, 4759*a**; **Southern Paiute**, 4765, 4766*a**; **Southwest**, 4017, 4796*a**; **Taos**, 4453; **Tepecano**, 4825; **Tepehuan**, 4816-

4817, 4825, 4829; **Têtes de Boule**, 4190*a**; **Tewa**, 4097*a*, 4363*a*, 4836; **Tiwa**, 4843-4845; **Tlaxcalan**, 4521; **Tlingit**, 4849; **Tojolabal**, 4047*a*, 4498*b*; **Tunica**, 4763*a**; **Tutelo**, 4246*a**; **Tzeltal**, 4047*a*, 4498*b*; **Upland Yuman**, 4868; **Ute**, 4765, 4766*a**; **Wampanoag**, 4491*a**; **Wasco-Wishram** (Chinook), 4893, 4909; **Wintun**, 4132*a**; **Wishram**, 4906; **Yana**, 4132*a**; **Yavapai**, 4868; **Yuchi**, 4546*a**, 4732*a**, 4922*; **Yuki**, 4132*a**; **Yurok**, 4132*a**; **Zuni**, 4931*a*. *See also* Culture; Ethnology; and items such as Ceremonies, Music, Religion, and Specific language or tribe
Ethnohistory, Chol, 4498; Haida, 4341*a*; Hidatsa, 4053-4054, 4344, 4484-4485; Highland Chontal, 4093, 4545; Iroquois, 4415; Mandan, 4053-4054, 4344, 4484-4485; Mayan, 4498; Northern Athapascan, 4113*a*; Quejache, 4498; Seneca, 4709, 4711, 4732; Toquegua Maya, 4498; Verapaz Chol, 4498; Ytza, 4498
Ethnolinguistics, Sandia (Tiwa), 4842-4843
Ethnology, 4296; Alaska, 4032, 4106*a*, 4850; American, 4011, 4394; California, 4132; Columbia, 4755*a*; Copper River Atna, 4032, 4106*a*, 4850; Ecuadorian Oriente, 4740; Guatemala, 4152*a*; Kagaba, 4755*a*; Mexico, 4152*a*, 4525*a*; Six Nations, 4385; South America, 4755*a*; Tepecano, 4806-4807, 4809; Tlingit, 4032, 4106*a*, 4850. *See also* Culture; Ethnography; and items such as Music, Religion, etc.
Ethnomedicine, Navajo, 4022, 4579, 4582; Pocomam Central, 4687. *See also* Folk Medicine; Medicine
Ethnoscience, Navajo, 4582
Ettawageshik, Jane E. Willets, author, 4603; donor, 4603
Europe, museums, Eskimo, 4252; Northwest Coast, 4252
Ewers, John C., corres. with Paul A. W. Wallace, 4214
Exogamy, Hopi, 4359
Exposition of Indian Tribal Arts, Inc., 4308-4309

Fabroni, Giovanni, corres. with Filippo Mazzei, 4300
Fadden, John (*Ka-Hon-Hes*) (Mohawk) 4397*a**; artist, 4381, 4384, 4534; corres. with Paul A. W. Wallace, 4533
Fadden, Ray (*Aren Akweks*) (Mohawk), 4388-4389, 4397*a**, 4530; author, 4383-4384; corres. with Paul A. W. Wallace, 4021, 4382
False face, Delaware, 4080, 4222; Iroquois, 4301*b**, 4397*a**, 4590*a**
Farabee, William C., photographer, 4759*a*
Fauna, Acoma, 4468; birds, 4080, 4222, 4264, 4645; Catawba, 4020*c*, 4148*b*; Cayuga (Seneca), 4001, 4712; Choctaw, 4067, 4182; deer, 4460; Delaware, 4080, 4213, 4222; East Indies, 4896; fish, 4080, 4222; grizzly bear, 4320; hermit thrush, 4383; Hopi, 4097*a*, 4363*a*; Kagaba, 4745*a*; Malecite, 4645; opossum, 4265; Passamaquoddy, 4645; Sandia (Tiwa), 4055, 4844; Santa Ana, 4468; sea otters, 4310; Tewa, 4097*a*, 4363*a*; Tiwa, 4055, 4844; West Indies, 4896
Fejos, Paul, corres., 4668; corres. with John Alden Mason, 4299
Fellows, Joseph, corres. with Ely S. Parker, 4717
Fenton, William N., 4020*a*, 4244, 4327*a*, 4405*a*; author, 4385, 4387; corres. with Paul A. W. Wallace, 4021, 4386; donor, 4005, 4373
Festivals, Ojibwa, 4012*a*, 4603*a*. *See also* Ceremonies; Dances; Fiestas
Field, Clark, corres. with Frank G. Speck, 4281
Field, Henry, corres. with John Alden Mason, 4295*a*
Fiestas, Pima Bajo, 4668; Tepehuan, for the dead, 4816. *See also* Ceremonies; Dances; Festivals
Fife, Sharon A., author, 4547; donor, 4547
Fishing, equipment, Catawba and Rappahannock, 4688*d**; Lacandon, 4497; Pamunkey, 4688*b**; weirs, 4133
Five Nations, 4005, 4373; founding of, 4379, 4412; history of, 4405. *See also* Six Nations; Iroquois Confederacy
Flatheads, 4020*a*, 4327*a*; people, 4865*b**
Flora, Cayuga (Seneca), 4001, 4712; Chimakum, 4698; *cucurbita moschata* (Mexico), 4514; *erythrina flabelliformis*, 4590; gourds, 4763; Hopi, 4097*a*, 4363*a*; Kagaba, 4745*a*; medicinal plants (Pocomam Central), 4687; mescal-beans, 4590; peyote, 4590; Quileute, 4698; Sandia (Tiwa), 4055, 4844; squash, 4688*d**; Tewa, 4097*a*, 4363*a*; Tiwa, 4055, 4844
Florida, Seminole. *See* Creek; Muskogee; Seminole
Floyd, Troy S., collector, 4035, 4150; donor, 4035, 4150
Flute, ceremony, Tusayan, 4790; society, Oraibi, Arizona, 4780
Folklore, Cherokee, 4010, 4165; French Canadian, 4587; Hopi, 4352, 4362*a*; Negro-Indians, 4613-4614; northeastern United States, 4559, 4864
Folk medicine, Catawba, 4020*c*, 4148*b*, 4149; Cherokee, 4028, 4163; Delaware, 4080, 4222; Keres, 4793; Papago, 4047*b*, 4622*b*; Pima, 4047*b*, 4622*b*; Pocomam Central, 4687; Takelma, 4803. *See also* Ethnomedicine, Medicine
Folk tales, Mohawk, 4535; Otomi, 4050, 4621; Taos, 4848. *See also* Legends; Myths; Oral literature; Stories; Tales
Folsom horizon, 4512
Foods, 4306, 4313; Catawba, 4020*c*, 4148*b*; Cayuga (Seneca), 4001, 4712; Lacandon, 4497; preparation: Indians of New England, 4294; Lummi, 4057*a*, 4600*a*; Sandia (Tiwa), 4055, 4844; taxonomies, Navajo, 4582. *See also* Subsistence

Forbes, John, French and Indian War, 4030, 4243
Forbes, R. H., corres. with Stephen Bowers, 4133
Fort Mackenzie, 4682*e**
Fort Pitt, Pa., 4594, 4652
Fort William Henry, N.Y., Indian-White relations, 4008, 4597; journal, 4008, 4597
Fox, 4010, 4109*a*, 4165, 4256*a**, *4256a-4258*, 4301*b**, 4590*a**, 4592*a**, 4682*e**; language, 4095, 4258; linguistics, 4257; Musquakie calumet dance, 4071, 4606; orthography, 4904; people, Black Hawk, 4291*a**; recordings, 4095, 4258; texts, 4095, 4258
Fraenkel, Gerd, compiler, 4901; donor, 4901
France, Bibliothèque Nationale, Paris, 4027, 4372
Franklin, Sir John, 4114, 4253
Freeland, Lucy S., and Jaime de Angulo, authors, 4117-4118, 4857; collectors, 4102, 4856, 4928; compilers, 4858
Freeman, John F., compiler, 4036, 4123; corres. with Paul A. W. Wallace, 4388
French, and Indian War, John Forbes expedition, 4030, 4234; contact with Indians, 4008, 4597; Canadian, folklore, 4587
Furnishings, household, Lacandon, 4497; Pima Bajo, 4668

Gabor, Ray, and Robert Gabor, artists, 4388*a*; Robert (*Sagotaoala*), artist, 4389; corres. with Paul A. W. Wallace, 4389
Galice, *4259*; language, 4012, 4259
Gallatin, Albert, corres., 4282; corres. with Peter S. Du Ponceau, 4589
Games, Arapaho, 4683; Arikara, 4683; Assiniboin, 4683; Blackfoot, 4683; Cheyenne, 4683; Choctaw, 4179*a**; Crow, 4683; Dakota, 4197; Gros Ventre, 4683; Hidatsa, 4683; Laguna, 4448; Mandan, 4683; Ojibwa, 4012*a*, 4603*a*; Ojibwa (Plains), 4683; Oto, 4081, 4616; Plains Cree, 4683; Sarsi, 4683; Sioux, 4683; Tunica, 4763*a**
Gamiz, Everardo, 4515
Gandy, Ethel, corres. with Charles Marius Barbeau, 4658
Gapp, S. H., corres. with Paul A. W. Wallace, 4021, 4244
Garcia, Antonio (Tewa), author, 4834; recorder, 4059, 4835
Garcia, Miguel (Papago), author, 4626
Garner, Beatrice, Medicine, author, 4736
Garrison, Edward R., author, 4560; collector, 4060, 4561; donor, 4060, 4560-4561
Garro, J. Eugenio, author, 4741
Garvin, Paul L., author, 4009, 4897; donor, 4009, 4897
Gates, Horatio, corres. with Thomas Barnsley, 4594, 4598
Gauss, ———, corres., 4037, 4289
Gauthier, E. S., corres. with Frank G. Speck, 4331
Gay Head, Indians, 4493; Mass., 4491*a**
Ge, linguistics, 4753
Genealogy, Ahenakew, 4188; Franz Boas, 4003*b*; Navajo, descendants of Whiteman Viller and Salt Woman, 4562; Six Nations chiefs, 4391
General, *4260-4341*
General, Alexander (Chief *Deskaheh*) (Iroquois), corres. with Paul A. W. Wallace, 4378, 4390; interview with, 4414
General, Emily, corres. with Paul A. W. Wallace, 4391
General, Levi (*Hi-wyi-iss*) (Iroquois), 4391
Genetic, **classification**: Central American languages, 4334*a*, 4525*a*; Chibchan, 4762; Choco, 4762; Cuna, 4762; Mexico, 4525*a*; Edward Sapir's, 4516; South American languages, 4334*a*, 4760, 4762; **relationships**: California, 4139; Central America, 4155-4156; Hokan, 4333*a*; Mayan, 4889; North America, 4339; Quechua, 4333*a*; Santa Barbara stock, 4139; Santa Cruz Indians, 4139; South America, 4753-4754; Tanoan, 4889; Uto-Aztecan, 4333*a*, 4889; Yuman, 4927
Geographical distribution, Aymara, 4121; Central American languages, 4156; Chol, 4498; Jaqi, 4121; Mexico, 4682; Nambikuara, 4746; Ojibwa, 4012*a*, 4603*a*; Parintintin, 4746; Peru, dialects of, 4741; Pima Bajo, 4668; Plains Cree, 4191; Pocomam Central, 4687; Quejache, 4498; Rama-Rama, 4746; South American languages, 4751, 4761; southeastern tribes (map), 4301*b*; Talamanca, 4804; Toquegua Maya, 4498; Tsimshian, 4855; Tupi, 4746; Tuscarora, 4861; Uru, 4869; Verapaz, 4498; Wishram, 4906; Ytza, 4498
Geography, 4003*a*, 4268*a*
Georgia, Moravian missions among Indians, 4039, 4591
Gestures, codes, Hopi dance, 4353; Polynesian dance, 4353
Ghinassi, Father Juan, 4434
Gila, Apaches, 4768; River, Yumas of, 4331*a*
Gilbert Collection, College of Physicians, Philadelphia, Pa., 4161, 4212-4213, 4262-4267, 4713-4714
Gillespie, Beryl C., author, 4111; donor, 4111
Gillespie, John Douglas, author, 4010, 4165
Glen, James, governor of South Carolina, 4030, 4243
Glottochronology. *See* Lexicostatistics
Gnadenhütten, Ohio, Christian Indian monument, 4244*a**
Godcharles, F. A., corres. with Frank G. Speck, 4224
Goddard, Pliny Earle, 4429
Goddard, R. H. Ives III, author, 4215
Godman, John Davidson, corres. with Reuben Haines, 4283

Goff, O. S., photographer, 4683*a*
Goldfrank, Esther, 4771, 4778; donor, 4845
Goodman, Linda S., author, 4836; collector, 4061, 4837; donor, 4061, 4836-4837
Good Tracks, Jimm G., author, 4177*a*; corres. with Whitfield J. Bell, Jr., 4177*a*
Gordon, Eugene S., author, 4659; donor, 4659
Gordon, G. B., corres. with John Dyneley Prince, 4540
Göttingen, Niedersachische Staats und Universitätsbibliothek, 4037, 4289
Gould, B. A., corres. 4037, 4289
Government, Chol, 4498; Indian, 4266; Ojibwa, 4012*a*, 4603*a*; Quejache, 4498; Toquegua Maya, 4498; Verapaz, 4498; Ytza, 4498
*Gowawaima Kachina*, Mexico, 4455
*Gowatcanyi* (*topiles*), 4455
Graham, A. W., engraver, 4291*b*
Grammar. *See* Linguistics under specific language
Graymont, Barbara, author, 4392; donor, 4027, 4372, 4392
Grayton, Ann H., corres. with Elsie Clews Parsons, 4311
Greene, Chief Elton (Tuscarora), informant, 4062, 4076, 4862-4863
Greenland, 4251*, 4254*a**; archaeology, 4250; Greenlandic Eskimo, 4694; map, 4254*a*; Upernivik, 4250
Green, Otis H., corres. with John Alden Mason, 4742
Greetings, Sandia (Tiwa), 4055, 4844; Tuscarora, 4076, 4863
Greywacz, Kathryn B., corres. with Frank G. Speck, 4216, 4239
Gridley, Marion E., corres. with Paul A. W. Wallace, 4393
Grimes, Joe, corres., 4641
Grossman, Julian A., author, 4011, 4394; donor, 4011, 4394
Gros Ventre, 4682*e**; **Arapaho**: dictionary, 4044, 4592*b*, language, 4044, 4592*b*, linguistics, 4044, 4592*b*, texts, 4044, 4592*b*; **camps**, 4682*e**; **dances**, 4682*e**; **ethnography**, 4683; **people**, 4682*e**. *See also* Arapaho (Algonquian); Hidatsa (Siouan)
Guajajara, 4859
Guarani, historical linguistics, 4745
Guaranian, historical linguistics, linguistics, vocabulary, 4743
Guatemala, 4084, 4483, 4685, 4915; archaeology, 4152*a*, 4153, 4157-4157*a*, 4158*a*, 4159-4159*b*, 4331*a*, 4524*a*; architecture, 4157; ethnography, 4024, 4499; ethnology, 4152*a*; *Handbook of*, 4153; history, 4035, 4150; languages, 4686; linguistics, 4152*a*; masks, 4301; Piedras Negras, 4153, 4157, 4158*a*, 4159, 4159*b*, 4524*a*; post-conquest, 4024, 4499; Santa Maria Ixhuatan, 4553, 4912-4913; Sociedad de geografia e historia de Guatemala, Anales, 4157; Todos Santos, 4481
Guèdon, Marie Françoise, and Frederica de Laguna, collectors, 4031, 4106
Guernsey, ———, artist, 4301*b*
Guerra, Francisco, and R. Jerrel Williams, corres. with Paul A. W. Wallace, 4291
[Guillemin]-Tarayre, Edmont, 4515
Gunther, Erna, corres. with Richard H. Shryock, 4252, 4601
Gusinde, Martin, 4284; corres. with Frank G. Speck, 4189, 4284
Guthe, Alfred R., corres. with Paul A. W. Wallace, 4395

Habitat, 4301*b**; Eskimo, 4254*a**; Micmac, 4527*a**; Montagnais-Naskapi, 4188*b**; Nansemond, 4688*a**; Pamunkey, 4688*b**; Penobscot, 4336*a**; Pima Bajo, 4670*; Têtes de Boule, 4190*a**. *See also* Camps; Dwellings; Pueblos; Settlements; Villages
Haida, *4341a-4342*; anthropometric data, 4268*c*; biography, Florence Edenshaw Davidson, 4341*a*; comparative dictionary, 4115, 4342, 4552, 4851; ethnohistory, 4341*a*; linguistics, 4115, 4341*b*, 4342, 4552, 4851; myths, 4002, 4853; syntax, 4341*b*; texts, 4599*a*; totem poles, 4333*a*; vocabulary, 4599*a*
Haile, Father Berard, OFM, 4012; author, 4429; collector, 4426-4427; compiler, 4428
Haines, Reuben, corres. with John Davidson Godman, 4283
Hale, Horatio, corres. with John W. Jordan, 4721; "Iroquois Book of Rites," 4537
Hall, J., engraver, 4865*a*
Hallowell, A. Irving, 4020*a*, 4327*a*, 4603; **author**, 4286; **corres. with**: John Alden Mason, 4295*a*; Elsie Clews Parsons, 4311; John Witthoft, 4124, 4285
Halpenny, Francess G., corres. with Paul A. W. Wallace, 4144
Halpern, Abraham M., author, 4698*a*; corres. with Whitfield J. Bell, Jr., 4698*a*; donor, 4698*a*
Hammawi. *See* Achumawi
Hammond, Blodwen, and Mary Shepardson, authors, 4562
Hamp, Eric P., **author**, 4694-4695; **collector**, 4063-4064, 4696-4697; **corres. with**: Whitfield J. Bell, Jr., 4695; George W. Corner, 4694; **donor**, 4063-4064, 4694, 4696-4697
*Handbook of American Indians*, 4340
*Handbook of Guatemala*, 4153
*Handbook of North American Indians*, 4371
*Handbook of South American Indians*, 4122, 4127, 4738, 4741, 4744, 4751; bibliography, 4750; corres., 4748, 4750; language, 4750; John Alden Mason, 4750
Handsome Lake, 4388*a**, 4732; code of, 4006, 4716; religion, 4403; visions, 4384
Harbeck, Warren A., author, 4204; collector, 4065, 4204*a*; donor, 4065, 4204-4204*a*

Harbor Springs, Michigan, 4693
Hardman-de-Bautista, M. J., author, 4121; collector, 4066, 4119-4119*a*; corres. with Gertrude D. Hess, 4120; donor, 4066, 4119-4119*a*, 4121
Hare, 4234*a**; **contents of recordings**, 4238; **ethnography**, 4234*a**; **informants**: 4238; Berthy Boniface, Jane Boniface, Marie Rose Clement, Noel Kakfwi, Naura Masuzumi, Gregory Shae, and Paul Voudrach, 4087, 4236; **language**, 4046, 4087, 4236-4238; **legends**, 4087, 4236; **myths**, 4238; **people**, 4234*a**; **recordings**, 4087, 4236; **songs**, 4087, 4236; **texts**, 4087, 4236, 4238; **vocabulary**, 4087, 4236, 4238
Hare, David, 4796
Harrington, John P., 4293*a*; author, 4183, 4434, 4471, 4689, 4691, 4743, 4745, 4869; corres. with John Alden Mason, 4017, 4295*a*, 4690, 4744; and Luis Valcarcel, authors, 4692
Harrington, Mark R., 4213*a*
Harris, Ebenezor, 4282
Harris, John, corres. with James W. Henry and Samuel Hodgdon, 4166
Harris, Zellig S., 4109*b*; author, 4125, 4151; corres. with John Alden Mason, 4125, 4748
Harrison, Charles, 4341*a*
Harrison, William Henry, 4865*a**
Hart, Brete R., corres. with John Alden Mason, 4816
Harvard University, Mass., 4872; Houghton Library, 4047, 4592*c*
Harvest ceremony, Yuchi, 4546*a**, 4732*a**, 4922*
Hassler, F. R., corres., 4037, 4289
Hauser, W.H.M., photographer, 4520*a*
Haverford College, Pa., 4042, 4328; **Library**: Edward Wanton Smith Collection, 4320; materials related to Indians, 4415
Hayden, Ferdinand V., 4134; corres. with Stephen Bowers, 4134
Hays, Isaac Minis, **corres. with**: Robert Stewart Culin, 4554; Frank Hamilton Cushing, 4164, 4367; Noah Fields Drake, 4277; Wilburforce Eames, 4490; James Mooney, 4167; Joseph George Rosengarten, 4524
Heath, A., engraver, 4291*b*
Heath, Jeffrey G., author, 4180-4181; collector, 4067, 4182; donor, 4067, 4182
Heckewelder, John G. E., 4021*, 4033, 4238*a*, 4244-4245, 4295, 4374; **corres. with**: Benjamin Smith Barton, 4161, 4212-4213, 4262-4268, 4558, 4595, 4713-4714; Peter S. Du Ponceau, 4033, 4238*a*; illustrations, 4244a; **photographs regarding**, 4245
Heckewelder, Polly, 4231
Height, average Indian, 4650; Seneca, 4730
Heimnick, John E., corres. with John Alden Mason, 4681
Hellmuth, Nicholas M., author, 4498; donor, 4498
Hematite, 4800
Henry, James W., and Samuel Hodgdon, corres. with John Harris, 4166
Henry, Thomas Charlton, corres. with John L. Le Conte, 4768
Henshaw, Henry W., corres. with Stephen Bowers, 4135
Herskovits, Melville J., **corres. with**: John Alden Mason, 4295*a*, 4324; Elsie Clews Parsons, 4311; George L. Trager, 4324
Herzog, George, 4772, 4795; **corres.**, 4641; **corres. with**: John Alden Mason, 4627, 4639, 4869*b*; Elsie Clews Parsons, 4311
Hess, Gertrude D., **corres. with**: M. J. Hardman-de-Bautista, 4120; Gertrude P. Kurath, 4059, 4835
Heve, comparative vocabulary, 4886
Hewitt, J.N.B. (Iroquois), corres. with Seth Newhouse, 4405*a*; interview with, 4414; photographer, 4405*a*
Hey(?), H., photographer, 4490*a*
Heye, George G., 4251*a*, 4664, 4865*a**; **biography**, 4287; **corres. with**: John Alden Mason, 4017; Frank G. Speck, 4539*a*; **obituary**, 4287
Hiawatha, return of, 4420
Hidatsa, *4343-4344*; contents of recordings, 4053-4054, 4343-4344, 4484-4485; cultural change, 4053, 4484; culture, 4053, 4343; ethnography, 4683; ethnohistory, 4053-4054, 4344, 4484-4485; language, 4053, 4134, 4343, 4484; linguistics, 4053-4054, 4343-4344, 4484-4485; Mannitarri, 4682*e**; recordings, 4053-4054, 4343-4344, 4484-4485; texts, 4053-4054, 4343-4344, 4484-4485; vocabulary, 4053-4054, 4343-4344, 4484-4485. *See also* Gros Ventre
Hieroglyphs, 4266; Maya, 4159*b*, 4888
Higgins, F. R., author, 4555; donor, 4555
Highland Chontal, dialect survey, 4543; ethnohistory, 4093, 4545; linguistics, 4094, 4542-4544, 4546; maps, 4543; recordings, 4093-4094, 4545-4546; texts, 4094, 4546. *See also* Mountain Tequistlateco
Highways, Indian, 4247, 4412, 4653-4655
Hill, Archibald A., 4931
Hill, David, corres. with Ebenezer Meriam, 4016, 4720
Hill, Jennie-Keith, author, 4564; corres. with Richard H. Shryock, 4563; donor, 4564
Hill, L. A., corres. with Ebenezer Meriam, 4016, 4720
Hiller, Wesley R., corres. with Frank G. Speck, 4288
Hilliard, Sam B., corres. with Whitfield J. Bell, Jr., 4865
Hinshelwood, R., engraver, 4683*b*
Historical linguistics, Athapascan, 4112-4113, 4115-4116, 4575; Aymara, 4121; Aztec, 4885; Cholon, 4183; Diegueño, 4233; Guarani, 4745; Guaranian, 4743; Heve, 4886; Huichol, 4884; Jaqi, 4121; Mataco, 4509; Mayan,

4498*c*; Miranya, 4743, 4745; Na-Dene, 4115; Nahua, 4884; Opata, 4884; Papago, 4884; South American languages, 4751, 4754; Tarahumare, 4885-4886; Tepecano, 4825, 4884-4885; Tepehuan, 4825; Tubar, 4886; Tupi-Guarani, 4745; Uto-Aztecan, 4876, 4881-4886, 4888; Witoto, 4743, 4745; Yaqui, 4884-4886. *See also* Lexicostatistics; Genetic Classification; and specific languages and language families

Historical Society of Pennsylvania, materials related to Indians, 4415

History, 4010; American, role of Indian, 4330; Andean region, 4749; Azqueltan, 4368, 4833; Catawba, 4020*c*, 4148*b*; Cherokee, 4010, 4165; Delaware, 4220, 4227; demographic, Coast Tsimshian, 4855; Five Nations, 4405; Guatemala, 4024, 4035, 4150; Huichol, 4368; Iroquois, 4371-4372, 4415, 4418; Iroquois Confederacy, 4379; Ixmiquilpan, Hidalgo, Mexico (Otomi), 4050, 4621; Jeffersonian era, 4041, 4327; Lipan, 4473; Lummi, 4057*a*, 4600*a*; Northeast, 4598; Ojibwa, 4610; Otomi, 4050, 4621; Penobscot, 4660; Pennsylvania, 4246; Pima Bajo, 4056, 4669, 4676; Queen Charlotte Islands, 4341*a*; role of Indian, 4335; Sandia Pueblo, 4843; San Sebastian, 4368, 4833; Six Nations, 4372; Southern Lacandon, 4497; Tepehuan, 4833; Thlewarle Indian Baptist Church, Oklahoma, 4547; Tuscarora, sociohistorical demography, 4861. *See also* History, Texts, etc., under specific languages and tribes

*Hi-wyi-iss*. *See* General Levi

Hiyekit, vocabulary, 4333

Hobgood, John, author, 4817; corres. with John Alden Mason, 4817

Hodgdon, Samuel, and James W. Henry, corres. with John Harris, 4166

Hodge, Carleton T., author, 4350; corres. with Whitfield J. Bell, Jr., 4351

Hodge, Frederick W., 4170

Hoijer, Harry, 4502, 4569; **author**, 4112-4113, 4177, 4431-4432, 4473-4474, 4565; **collector**, 4067*a*, 4175-4176, 4430, 4433, 4477, 4502-4504, 4566-4567; **compiler**, 4705; **corres. with**: John Alden Mason, 4295*a*, 4748; Chic Sandoval, 4572; Edward Sapir, 4116; **donor**, 4707; **manuscript collection**, 4012; and Edward Sapir, authors, 4575

Hoijer, Mrs. Harry, donor, 4012

Hokan, 4690, 4880; comparative vocabulary, 4509; genetic relationships, 4333*a*; historical linguistics, 4509; languages, conference on, 4233; linguistics, 4753; vocabulary, 4509, 4526

Hokan-Siouan Phylum, 4152

Hollow, Robert C., Jr., author, 4486; donor, 4486

Holman, A. J. & Co., 4488, 4494; **corres. with**: American Philosophical Society, Joseph Carson, J. Peter Lesley, and Eli K. Price, 4491

Holmer, Nils M., 4149*b**

Holt, Hamilton, corres. with Elsie Clews Parsons, 4311

Honduras, Caracol Ruins, 4159

Honniasont, 4651

Honor, Delaware, 4221*a*; Oklahoma Indians, 4615

Hoover, Herbert C., 4020, 4325

Hopi, *4345-4364*, 4351*a**, 4355*, 4775, 4791; **animals** (domestic), 4097*a*, 4363*a*; **Antelope society**, 4787-4789; **architecture**, 4351*a**; **attire**, 4097*a*, 4351*a**, 4363*a*; **belts**, 4097*a*, 4363*a*; **ceremonialism**, 4783, 4798; **ceremonies**, 4779; **chants**, 4345; **clans**, 4358-4359; **clown songs**, 4052, 4349; **contents of recordings**, 4006*a*, 4023*a*, 4349*b*, 4363*b*; **dance**, 4353; **dictionary**, 4350, 4361; **dictionary project**, 4351; **ethnoanatomy**, 4088, 4360, 4362; **ethnography**, 4097*a*, 4363*a*; **fauna**, 4097*a*, 4363*a*; **flora**, 4097*a*, 4363*a*; **folklore**, 4352, 4362*a*; **formal hairdo**, 4351*a**; **gesture codes**, 4353; **hunting songs**, 4052, 4349; **informants**: Walter Albert, 4052, 4349; Frank Capella, 4097*a*, 4363*a*; Irving Charley, 4052, 4349; Lester Charley, 4052, 4349; Ralph Charlie, 4097*a*, 4363*a*; George Cochise, 4097*a*, 4363*a*; Willie Coin, 4057*b*, 4349*a*; Alfred Joshongiva, 4052, 4349; Glenn Joswaytewa, 4052, 4349; Jimmy Kay, 4052, 4349; Kelnimtewa, 4052, 4349; Jimmy Kewanwaytiwa, 4057*b*, 4349*a*; Jim Kewanwytewa, 4097*a*, 4363*a*; Elridge Masa, 4052, 4349; Nettie Masayumptewa, 4097*a*, 4363*a*; Mary Maypi, 4052, 4349; Sylvin Nash, 4052, 4349; Edmund Nequatewa, 4097*a*, 4363*a*; Bennie Nuvanisa, 4057*b*, 4349*a*; Garnet Pavatea, 4097*a*, 4363*a*; Poli Payestewa, 4052, 4349; Williard Sakiestewa, 4088, 4362; Frank Sehma, 4097*a*, 4363*a*; Helen Sekaquaptewa, 4052, 4349; Henry Sheldon, 4097*a*, 4363*a*; Annette Silas, 4097*a*, 4363*a*; Albert Sinquah, 4097*a*, 4363*a*; Dennis Sinquah, 4097*a*, 4363*a*; Charlie Talawepi, 4052, 4349; Paul Talawepi, 4052, 4349; David Talawietema, 4052, 4349; Mrs. David Talawietema, 4052, 4349; David Tawameiniwa, 4097*a*, 4363*a*; Joe Tevenyouma, 4097*a*, 4363*a*; Albert Yava, 4057*b*, 4349*a*; **interviews**, 4354, 4838; **kachina songs**, 4052, 4349; **kinship terms**, 4097*a*, 4363*a*; **language**, 4006*a*, 4057*b*, 4088, 4349*a*-4349*b*, 4351*b*, 4357, 4362, 4364; **linguistics**, 4057*b*, 4347, 4349*a*, 4351*b*, 4362*a*, 4364; **medicine man**, 4097*a*, 4363*a*; **migration legend**, 4097*a*, 4363*a*; **morphology**, 4351*b*; **music**, 4051-4052, 4347-4349, 4470; **numerals**, 4057*b*, 4097*a*, 4349*a*, 4363*a*; **people**, 4351*a**; **placenames**, 4097*a*, 4363*a*; **potters**, 4352, 4355; **pottery**, 4097*a*, 4363*a*; **recordings**, 4051-4052, 4057*b*, 4068, 4088, 4097*a*, 4348-4349*a*, 4356, 4362, 4363*a*, 4838*a*; **semantics**, 4347, 4362*a*; **snake dance**, 4351*a**; **Snake society**,

4788-4789; **song domains**, 4346; **songs**, 4051-4052, 4348-4349; **song-texts**, 4347; **syntax**, 4351*b*, 4362*a*; **Tewa of Hamo**, 4790; **texts**, 4057*b*, 4068, 4097*a*, 4349*a*, 4356, 4363*a*, 4838*a*; **transcript of recordings**, 4006*a*, 4023*a*, 4349*b*, 4354, 4363*b*, 4838; **villages**, 4052, 4349; **vocabulary**, 4057*b*, 4088, 4349*a*, 4351*b*, 4362; **weaving**, 4097*a*, 4363*a*

*Hopi and Zuni Ceremonialism*, 4798

Hopi-Apache, masked dance songs, 4052, 4349

Horn, George Henry, 4488, 4492; corres. with Henry Chapman Mercer, 4370

Horsford, Eben Norton, corres. with John W. Jordan, 4396

Houma, *4364a-4365*, 4364*a**, 4763*a**; blowguns, 4364*a**; boats, 4364*a**; daub and wattle houses, 4364*a**; dwellings, 4364*a**; ethnography, 4364*a**; people, 4364*a**; thatched roofs, 4364*a**

Houses. *See* Dwellings

Howard, Agnes McClain, 4817; corres. with John Alden Mason, 4507

Howard, Edgar B., 4020*a*, 4327*a*, 4589*b*; corres. with John Alden Mason, 4289*a*

Howren, Robert, collector, 4235; donor, 4235

Hrdlička, Aleš, archaeological work in Alaska, 4289*a*; corres. with Stephen Bowers, 4136

Huantan, informants, 4066, 4119*a*; linguistics, 4120; recording, texts, 4066, 4119*a*

Huastec. *See* Huaxtec

Huave, *4366*

Huaxtec, 4498*c*; vocabulary, 4516

Huaxteca, Mexico, 4781

Hudson's Bay Company, corres. with Frank G. Speck, 4145

Huepec Opata, 4887

Hufman, Peter, 4549

Huichol, *4367-4368*; belts, 4097*a*, 4363*a*; comparative vocabulary, 4870, 4882, 4884, 4887; comparisons with Cora, 4870; historical linguistics, 4884; lexicostatistics, 4887; linguistics, 4870; religious beliefs compared with Tepecano, 4808; vocabulary, 4870

Humboldt, Alexander von, corres., 4508; corres. with Rembrandt Peale, 4290

Humor, Dakota, 4199, 4201-4202; Otomi, 4622

Hunting, 4588*a**; **equipment**: Catawba and Rappahannock, 4688*d**; **Lacandon**, 4497; **songs**, Hopi, 4052, 4349; **territories**, Cree (Montagnais), 4189

Hupa, 4132*a**, *4369*, 4877; ethnography, 4132*a**; language, linguistics, 4369; people, 4132*a**; texts, vocabulary, 4369

Hüpsch-Lontzen, Johann Wilhelm, 4896

Huron, 4397*a**, 4587; allies of (1615), 4911; birchbark canoe, 4397*a**; linguistics, 4587; silkwork, 4397*a**; vocabulary, 4910

Hyler, D. Scribner, corres. with Mae (resident of Old Town, Maine), 4663*a*

Hymes, Dell H., 4339, 4366, 4902, 4905; compiler, 4892, 4907; corres. with Whitfield J. Bell, Jr., 4891

Hymns, Alaska native languages, 4043, 4107*a*; Chippewa, 4071, 4606; Nez Perce, 4029, 4588

Ichcateco, vocabulary, 4525

Idaho, Bonners Ferry, 4682*d*

Illinois, 4037, 4289; *Chicago*: Newberry Library, Ayer Collection, 4818; University of, 4544, 4572; World's Columbian Fair, 4544, 4818, 4900*a**

Inca, Empire, position of Uru, 4869; primitive economics, 4020*a*, 4327*a*

Indiana, *4370*; Historical Society, 4219; Moravian missions among Indians, 4039, 4591

Indian Affairs, Commissioner of, Charles James Rhoads, 4020, 4325

*Indian Legends of the North Pacific Coast of North America*, 4174

*The Indian Races of North and South America*, 4291*a*

Indian(s), **average height**, 4650; **biography**, Canadian, 4144; **busts of**, 4260; **conferences**, 4042, 4328; **crafts**, Canada, 4146; **descriptions of**, 4271; **deforming heads of children**, 4263; **educational materials pertaining to**, 4294; **factor in American history**, 4330; **food**, 4306; **government intentions toward**, 4724-4725; **houses**, Harbor Springs, Michigan, 4603; **masks**, 4301; **meaning of names**, 4386; **medical information on**, 4263; **medicine**, 4291; **Mexico**: 4508; education, 4511; innate capabilities, 4511; **Moravian missions to**, 4039, 4591; **Negro**, 4613-4614; **New England**, cooking, 4294; **oral literature**, 4211; **origin**, 4272; **Pennsylvania**, 4295; **pipe**, 4283; **preacher** (Delaware), 4229; **Protestant missionaries to**, 4025, 4047, 4268*b*, 4592*c*; **railroads** and, 4341; **Shakers**, 4599; **students**, brass band, 4273*a**; **trails**: 4653-4655; Delaware Valley, 4412; eastern United States, 4247; **village**: Oklahoma, 4612*a**; tourist attraction, 4380

"Indian Scene," 4598*a**

Indian Territory, 4276-4277

Indian Training School, Carlisle Barracks, Pennsylvania, people, 4273*a**

Indian-White, comparison, physical, 4262; relations, 4041, 4724; Athapascans, 4111; Azqueltan, 4833; Fort William Henry, 4008, 4597; Huichol, 4368; Huron, 4911; Iroquois, 4416; land cessions, 4865; Maicoba Pima (Pima Bajo), 4668, 4672; Mexico, tribute system, 4520*b*; missionaries to American Indians, 4025, 4268*b*; Mohawk, 4532; Moravian missions among Indians of North America, 4039, 4591; Northeast, 4594, 4596; Onondaga, 4016, 4720; Pima Bajo, 4668, 4672; railroads, 4341; San Sebastian, 4368, 4833; Santa Maria Ocotlan, 4817; Seneca, 4709, 4732; Tepehuan, 4833; Tonawandas, 4717; United Church Board for World Ministries, missions, 4047, 4592*c*

*Indice del Archivo del Juzgado de Teposcolula, Oaxaca: epoca colonial*, 4520*b*

Informants, **Achumawi**: Willard Carmony, 4101; **Ahtena**: 4032, 4105, 4106*a*, 4850; Andy Brown, Annie Ewan, Pete Ewan, Bacile George, Nancy George, Arthur Jackson, Martha Jackson, Billy Joe, Elizabeth Pete, Mentasta Pete, Jenny Peters, Kate Sanford, and Fanny Stanfield, 4057, 4104; **Alaska**: 4105; **Cayuga**: Mr. and Mrs. Cuthbert Davey, 4001, 4712; **Cheyenne**: Bearbow, Flying Out, Howling Crane, and Yellow Eagle, 4172; **Chicomuceltec**: 4913; **Choctaw**: 4179*b*; **Cree**: Edward Ahenakew, 4187-4188; **Delaware**: Chief James C. Weber, 4215, 4225, 4225*e*; **Dogrib**: 4238; **Eskimo**: Jimmy Gibbons, Thomas Kadlak, Doris Kipan, Naomi, Hugh Ungunga, and David Uvinaiyak, 4097, 4255; **Hare**: 4238, Berthy Boniface, Jane Boniface, Marie Rose Clement, Noel Kakfwi, Nauva Masuzumi, Gregory Shae, and Paul Voudrach, 4087, 4236; **Hopi**: Walter Albert, 4052, 4349; Frank Capella, 4097*a*, 4363*a*; Irving Charley and Lester Charley, 4052, 4349; Ralph Charlie and George Cochise, 4097*a*, 4363*a*; Willie Coin, 4057*b*, 4349*a*; Alfred Joshongiva, Glenn Joswaytewa, Jimmy Kay, and Kelnimtewa, 4052, 4349; Jimmy Kewanwaytiwa, 4057*b*, 4349*a*; Jim Kewanwytewa, 4097*a*, 4363*a*; Elridge Masa, 4052, 4349; Nettie Masayumptewa, 4097*a*, 4363*a*; Mary Maypi and Sylvin Nash, 4052, 4349; Edmund Nequatewa, 4097*a*, 4363*a*; Bennie Nuvanisa, 4057*b*, 4349*a*; Garnet Pavatea, 4097*a*, 4363*a*; Poli Payestewa, 4052, 4349; Williard Sakiestewa, 4088, 4362; Frank Sehma, 4097*a*, 4363*a*; Helen Sekaquaptewa, 4052, 4349; Henry Sheldon, Annette Silas, Albert Sinquah, and Dennis Sinquah, 4097*a*, 4363*a*; Charlie Talawepi, Paul Talawepi, David Talawietema, and Mrs. David Talawietema, 4052, 4349; David Tawameiniwa, 4097*a*, 4363*a*; Joe Tevenyouma, 4097*a*, 4363*a*; Albert Yava, 4057*b*, 4349*a*; **Huantan**: 4066, 4119*a*; **Isleta** (Tiwa): 4055, 4844; **Jaquaru**: 4066, 4119*a*; **Kawki**: 4066, 4119*a*; **Lipan**: Augustina Zuazua, 4473; **Lummi**: Al Charles, 4057*a*, 4600*a*; **Matlatzinca**: Ezequiel Hernández, 4048, 4496; **Mescalero**: Sam Chino, Arnold K., Leon Pariko, and John Shanta, 4503; Charles Smith(?), 4504; Horace Torres, 4503; **Micmac**: Peter Perro, 4528; **Mountain Tequistlateco**: Damian Flores, Porfirio Nicolas Flores, and Clemente Zarate, 4093, 4545; **Munsee**, Nickodemus Peters, 4225*c*; **Navajo**: 4563, Mrs. Elsie Benally, 4577; **Nevome** (Pima Bajo): 4674; **Northern Tepehuan**: Pedro Valencia, 4822; **Ojibwa**: George Brown, 4072, 4607; Willie Catfish, 4072, 4607-4608; Fred Lacasse and John Martin, 4072, 4607; Jim Pontiac, 4610; **Otomi**: Jesús Salinas Pedraza, 4049, 4620; **Papago**: Listo Antone and Lupe Antone, 4047*b*, 4622*b*; Miguel Garcia, 4626; Juan Gregorio, Maila Kelaila, Ligali (Mrs. Masi Loin), Baptisto Lopez and family, Mendes Lopez, Jose Manol, Arturo Mendez, Chico Moreno, Jose Pancho, and Frances Ventura, 4047*b*, 4622*b*; Jose Ventura, 4007, 4047*b*, 4622*b*, 4625; Rosana Ventura, 4047*b*, 4622*b*; **Pawnee**: Sam Allen, Harry Cummings, and Phillip Jim, 4078, 4648; **Pima**: Paul Manuel, 4047*b*, 4622*b*; **Pima Bajo**: 4674, 4679; María Córdova, 4056, 4676; Leonardo Duarte O., 4058, 4678; Pedro Estrella Tánori, 4056, 4676; **Plains Cree**: 4191; **Ponca**: James Howard, 4072, 4607; **Quiché Maya**: Remigio Cochojil-González, 4037*a*, 4693*a*; **Quileute**: Beatrice Black, 4696-4697; **Sahaptin** (Umatilla): 4040, 4701*a*; **Seneca**, Leroy Cooper, 4792*a*; **Shawnee**, Mary Williams, 4734*b*; **Takelma**: Francis Johnson, 4803; **Tewa**: Frank Capella, Grace Chapella, and George Cochase, 4097*a*, 4363*a*; Antonio Garcia and Peter Garcia, 4015, 4839; Donald Mahkewa and Dennis Sinquah, 4097*a*, 4363*a*; Juanito Trujillo, 4015, 4839; **Tfalati Kalapuya**: Louis Kenoy, 4856-4857; **Tiwa**: 4055, 4844; Mrs. Jojola, 4074, 4844*a*; Lorenzo Martinez, 4846; **Tlingit**: 4032, 4106*a*, 4849-4850; **Tojolabal**: Hermalindo Jimenez, 4047*a*, 4498*b*; **Tuscarora**: Nellie Cansworth, 4864*a**; Chief Elton Greene, 4062, 4076, 4862-4863; Daniel Smith, 4864*a**; **Tzeltal**: Francisco Aguilar, Ramiro Garcia, Jose Hernandez, and Francisco Calvo Perez-Romerias, 4047*a*, 4498*b*; **Wenatchee**: Agnes Miller and Jerome Miller, 4070, 4185*a*; **Winnebago**: 4901; **Yavapai**: Harold Sine, 4069, 4866*a*; **Yurok**: Robert Nat, 4928

Ingalik (Ingalit), dictionary, language, texts, 4043, 4107*a*

Innocent, Rev. Priestmonk. *See* Gordon H. Marsh

Insley, Florence. *See* Florence Speck

International Congress of Americanists, 4498*a*; Mexico, 4154, 4513

*International Journal of American Indian Languages*, 4297

Interviews with, **Ahtena**: 4032, 4057, 4104, 4106*a*, 4850; **Hopi**: 4354, 4838; **Iroquois**: Jerry Aaron, Alec General, Chief Hess, and J.N.B. Hewitt, 4414; Chief William Loft, 4397, 4414; Chief Joseph Montour, Nick Peters, and Isaiah Williams, 4414; **Ojibwa**: Michigan Indians, 4605; Jim Pontiac, 4610; **Tewa**: 4354, 4838; **Tlingit**: 4032, 4106*a*, 4850; **Zuni**: 4934

Inugsuk, archaeology, 4250-4251; photographs, 4251

Inuit. *See* Eskimo, Iñupiaq

Iñupiaq (Inuit), dictionary, linguistics, texts, 4043, 4107*a*

Iowa, 4178*, 4232*; chief, 4291*b**; cognates, 4178, 4232; dancers, 4682*e**; dictionary, 4177*a*; language, 4177*a*, 4178-4179, 4232;

people, *Shau-Hau-Napo-Tinia*, 4589*a**; texts, 4178, 4232. *See also* Chiwere, Oto

Iowa (state), Tama, 4257

Iroquois, 4010-4011, 4020*a*, 4165, 4304, 4327*a*, *4371-4425*, 4377*a**, 4397*a**; **Akwesasne Mohawk Counsellor Organization**, 4388; **archaeology**, 4386; **archival research**, 4728; **art**, 4377, 4381, 4384, 4389, 4419; **artifacts**, 4377*a**; **ascendancy**, 4420; **beadwork**, 4598*a**; **book of rites**, 4537; **Brant family**, 4404; **Canada**, 4027, 4372, 4413, 4728; **census**, 4396; **ceremonialism**, 4728; **chiefs**: 4005, 4373; genealogical studies of, 4391; Alexander General (Chief *Deskaheh*), 4378, 4390, 4414; Joseph Logan and David Thomas, 4397*a**; **clan symbols**, 4377*a**; **condolence to the dead**, 4399; **conferences**, 4228, 4376, 4387, 4407; **corn husk dolls**, 4377*a**; **costumes**, 4395; **crooked knife**, 4536*a**; **crops**, 4005, 4373; **cultural development**, 4407; **culture**, 4413; **Deganawidah**: biography, 4417; legend, 4386, 4402, 4411; **diseases**, 4005, 4373; **eastern**: compared with Oklahoma Seneca-Cayuga, 4728; contact with Oklahoma Seneca-Cayuga, 4728; **ethnography**, 4377*a**, 4397*a**; **ethnohistory**, 4415; **false faces**, 4301*b**, 4397*a**, 4590*a**; **founding of Five Nations Confederacy**, 4412; **great feast for the dead**, 4399; **great feather dance**, 4388*a**; **Handsome Lake religion**, 4403; **history**, 4027, 4372, 4405, 4415, 4418, 4422; **houses**, 4005, 4373; **in the American Revolution**, 4027, 4372, 4392-4393; **influence on U.S. Constitution**, 4379; **Institute of Iroquoian Studies**, 4587; **interviews with**, 4414; **journal**, 4414; **literature**, 4383; **longhouse**, 4397*a**; **"The Longhouse People,"** 4421; **manuscript collections**, 4027, 4164*a*, 4372, 4378*a*, 4392, 4532*a*; **masks**, 4332, 4425; **Montour, Madam**, 4398; **Montour family**, 4404; **Naked Bear**, 4377*a**; **New York**, 4005, 4373, 4728; **North Carolina**, 4371; **Ontario**, 4728; **people**: 4397*a**, John Alexander, Charles A. Cooke, John Fadden, and Ray Fadden (*Aren Akweks*), 4397*a**; Handsome Lake, 4388*a**; Mrs. Joseph Logan, 4397*a**; Seth Newhouse, 4405*a**; **poetry**, 4423; **political history**, 4385-4386; **political organization**, 4410; **population**, 4005, 4373; **property**, 4005, 4373; **property in Philadelphia**, 4401; **relations with Whites**, 4416; **religion**, 4296, 4377*a**, 4384, 4410; **role in New York history**, 4422; **Scarboro**, monument at, 4413; **seminar**, 4228, 4387; 4407, **Three Sisters**, 4377*a**; **trails in Delaware Valley**, 4412; **utensils**, 4377*a**; **Virginia**, 4371; **wampum beads**, 4397*a**; **wampum belt**, 4397*a**

Iroquois Confederacy, 4005, 4373, 4378, 4409, 4534; **adoption complex**, effects of, 4389; **Delawares**: entry of, 4389; relations with, 4227, 4230; **Delawares-as-women problem**, 4226, 4228; **influence on U.S. Constitution and Bill of Rights**, 4375; **names**, meaning of, 4390. *See also* Five Nations, Six Nations

Isbister, William, corres. with Robert Bell, 4003*a*, 4268*a*

Ishi (Yana), 4137*b**

Isleta, New Mexico, 4442, 4448, 4775, 4777-4778, 4794, 4796*a**; archaeology, 4796*a**; church, 4301*a**; dwellings, 4796*a**; ethnography, 4845; informants (Tiwa), 4055, 4074, 4844-4844*a*; *Isleta Paintings*, *Isleta Pictures with Notes*, 4845; people, 4796*a**; ritual tobacco, 4793; roundhouse, 4301*a**; Tiwa recordings, 4055, 4074, 4844-4844*a*

Ixmiquilpan, Hidalgo, Mexico, local history (Otomi), 4050, 4621

Ixtlan, 4366

Iztaccihuatl, 4504*a**

"Jacob," legend in Micmac, 4528

Jacobs, Melville, 4331*a*

Jade, Palenque, Chiapas, Mexico, 4521*a**

James, Edward T., corres. with Paul A. W. Wallace, 4398

James Bay, Rupert House, Quebec, Canada, 4188*b**

Jameson, J. Franklin, 4273

Jamieson, M. J., corres. with Paul A. W. Wallace, 4399

Jaqaru, informants, 4066, 4119*a*; linguistics, 4120; recording, 4066, 4119*a*; texts, 4066, 4119*a*

Jaqi, 4121

Jasper, 4370

Jeanne, LaVerne M., author, 4351*b*; donor, 4351*b*

Jefferson, Thomas, 4300; corres. with Zebulon Montgomery Pike, 4320; Jeffersonian Era, 4041, 4327

Jemez, masks, 4778

Jenness, Diamond, 4012; **collector**, 4706; **corres. with**: John Alden Mason, 4017, 4589*b*; Paul A. W. Wallace, 4021

Jesuits. *See* Society of Jesus

Jibaro. *See* Jivaro

Jicarilla, *4426-4433*, 4768; **ethnography**, 4427, 4433; **language**, 4012, 4426-4427, 4429-4433; **linguistics**, 4012; **texts**: 4426-4427, 4429-4433; in translation, 4428

Jimenez, Alfredo, and Ruben E. Reina, collections, 4024, 4499

Jimenez, Hermalindo (Tojolabal), informant, 4047*a*, 4498*b*

Jimeson, C. C., 4718

Jivaro, *4434*, 4742

John, Hazel V. Dean, corres. with Whitfield J. Bell, Jr., 4718*a*

Johnson, Frederick, author, 4152; corres. with John Alden Mason, 4525, 4804; photographer, 4188*b*

Johnson, F. Roy, Johnson Publishing Co., donor, 4062, 4862

Johnson, Henry W., corres. with William Parker, 4719
Johnson, Jacob Bridgens, corres. with John Alden Mason, 4143
Johnson, Sir William, 4596
Jokes, Dakota, 4202; Otomi, 4622
Jones, Louis C., corres. with Frank G. Speck, 4535
Jones, Volney C., 4461
Jones, William, author, 4012*a*, 4603*a*
Jordan, John W., **corres. with**: William M. Beauchamp, Daniel G. Brinton, Isaac Craig, Albert Cusick, Horatio Hale, and DaCost Smith, 4721; Eben Norton Horsford, 4396
Journal, Fort William Henry, New York, 4008, 4597; Six Nations, 4414
Judd, Neil, corres. with Alfred V. Kidder, 4014, 4769
Juzgado Archives of Teposcolula, Oaxaca, Mexico, Mixteca Alta, 4520*b*

*Kabina*, Keres, 4448
*Kabixiana*, 4746
*Kachina*, 4773, 4775, 4782; **attire**, 4097*a*, 4363*a*; **cult**: Keres, 4449; Sahagun, 4454; **Gowawaima**, 4455; **masks**, 4454; **organization**, 4447; **songs**: 4772; Hopi, 4052, 4349
Kaduveo, linguistics, 4753
Kagaba, ethnology, 4755*a*; language, 4745*a*
*Kah-ge-ga-gah-bowh*. *See* Copway, George
*Ka-Hon-Hes*. *See* Fadden, John
Kaibab Paiute, 4766
Kaingang, 4020*a*, 4327*a*; linguistics, 4753
Kalapuya, Tfalati, autobiography, 4856; comparative text, 4857; informant, Louis Kenoy, 4856-4857; language, 4856-4858; linguistics, 4857; morphology, 4857; phonology, 4857; texts, 4856, 4858
Kalispel, 4044, 4592*b*
Kamakan, linguistics, 4753
Kansa, cognates, 4178, 4232; ethnography, 4231*a**; linguistics, 4178, 4232; people, 4231*a**, Washunga, 4231*a**. *See also* Dhegiha
Kansas, Moravian missions among Indians, 4039, 4591; Ottawa, 4256*a**
*Kapina* society, 4787; Acoma, 4788; Zia, 4788
Karankawa, 4010, 4165; vocabulary, 4516
Kaufman, Ellen S., author, 4568; donor, 4568
Kaw. *See* Kansa
Kawki, informants, 4066, 4119*a*; linguistics, 4120; recording, 4066, 4119*a*; texts, 4066, 4119-4119*a*; transcript of recording, 4119
Kaye, S. A., corres. with Frank G. Speck, 4292
Kealiinohomoku, Joann W., author, 4293, 4352-4353, 4355; collector, 4068, 4354, 4356, 4838-4838*a*; donor, 4068, 4293, 4352-4356, 4838-4838*a*
Kekchi, 4686
Kelley, David H., author, 4872; corres. with John Alden Mason, 4871
Kelly, Elenor C. (Mrs. William M.), corres. with Carl F. Miller, 4020*d*, 4602*a*
Kendall, Daythal L., author, 4013, 4802; donor, 4013, 4802
Kendall, Martha B., author, 4866; collector, 4866*a*; donor, 4866-4866*a*
Kennard, Edward A., 4362*a*
Kentucky, burial sites, 4303*a*
*Kep-kiri-uat*, 4746
Keres, *4435-4470*, 4799; animals associated with disease, 4793; Antelope clan, 4449; art, 4448; ethnography, 4448-4449, 4460; fire and hunt societies, 4448; music, 4470; transcript of recording, 4470
Keresan, 4778, 4786, 4788-4789; mask, 4455; medicine societies, 4775; societies, influence on other pueblos, 4775; stories, 4439
Keur, Dorothy L., corres. with Elsie Clews Parsons, 4311
Kickapoo, 4109*a*, 4256*a**; chief, 4291*b**; dwelling, 4256*a**; ethnography, 4256*a**.
Kidder, Alfred V., 4020*a*, 4327*a*, 4340, 4453, 4478, 4759, 4847-4848; **Award**, 4014, 4769; **corres. with**: Neil Judd, 4014, 4769; John Alden Mason, 4017, 4152*a*
Kidder, Alfred II, 4752
Kilpatrick, J. F., 4028, 4163
King, Dale S., corres. with John Alden Mason, 4681
King Philip. *See* Metacomet
Kinkade, Marvin Dale, author, 4184; collector, 4070, 4185*a*; compiler, 4185; donor, 4070, 4184-4185*a*
Kinship, **and marriage**, Chol, Quejache, Toquegua Maya, Verapaz, and Ytza, 4498; **Catawba**, 4020*c*, 4148*b*; **charts**, Southern Lacandon, 4497; **Navajo**, 4562; **Ottawa**, 4603; **Papago**, 4630, 4633; **ritual** (Tlaxcalan), 4521; **terms**: Cayuga (Seneca), 4001, 4712; Hopi, 4097*a*, 4363*a*; Kagaba, 4745*a*; Kaibab Paiute, Kutenai, and Nootka, 4766; Northern and Southern Tepehuan, 4819; Sahaptin (Yakima), 4700-4701; Salish (Thompson River), 4766; Tepecano, 4819; Tewa, 4097*a*, 4363*a*; Tsimshian (Nass River), Uintah Ute, and Yurok, 4766
Kinzua Dam, 4732*; archaeology, 4386
Kiowa, 4020*a*, 4327*a*, 4605; anthropometric data, 4268*c*; people, 4865*b**; songs, 4071, 4606
Kiowa Apache, attire, 4682*c**; people, 4682*c**; travois, 4682*c**
Kirk, Paul L., author, 4501; donor, 4501
*Kiva*, 4014, 4769, 4773; ritual, San Juan Pueblo, 4059, 4835
Klamath River (lower), Yurok, 4928
Klokeid, Terry J., author, 4583-4585; donor, 4583-4585
Kluckhohn, Clyde, **corres. with**: John Alden Mason, 4295*a*; Elsie Clews Parsons, 4311
Knab, Tim, author, 4556-4556*a*; donor, 4556-4556*a*

Knecht, Laura, author, 4642; donor, 4642
Knives, crooked, 4271; Iroquois, 4536*a**
Knight, M. F., photographer, 4397*a*, 4642*c*
Knight, T., engraver, 4291*b*
Kohl, Dr., 4273
Kokama, *4471*, 4758; language, 4143; linguistics, 4471, 4692; phonetic inventory, 4471; vocabulary, 4743
*Koshare*, 4773; Santo Domingo, 4455
Koyukon, 4043, 4107*a*
Krech, Shepard III, corres. with Whitfield J. Bell, Jr., 4113*a*
Krieger, Alex, 4507
Kroeber, Alfred L., 4331*a*, 4456, 4702, 4759; corres. with John Alden Mason, 4107, 4293*a*, 4295*a*, 4509, 4628
Kroskrity, Paul V., author, 4838*b*; corres. with Whitfield J. Bell, Jr., 4838*b*; donor, 4838*b*
Kuchin, 4010, 4165. *See also* Loucheux
Kurath, Gertrude P., **author**, 4015, 4605, 4839; **collector**, 4038, 4071-4072, 4606-4607, 4609; **compiler**, 4470, 4608, 4839; **corres. with**: Gertrude D. Hess, 4059, 4835; John Alden Mason, 4017; **donor**, 4015, 4038, 4071-4072, 4605-4609, 4839
Kurath, William, 4637
Kutenai, dictionary, 4044, 4592*b*; kinship terms, 4766; language, 4044, 4592*b*; linguistics, 4044, 4592*b*; people, 4682*d**; texts, 4044, 4592*b*; vocabulary, 4599*a*
Kwakiutl, *4472*, 4599; legends, 4174, 4472, 4735, 4854; myths, 4174; people, George Hunt and family, 4319*a**; texts, 4599*a*; vocabulary, 4599*a*

La Barre, Weston, corres. with John Alden Mason, 4295*a*
Labrador, Newfoundland, Canada, 4108, 4251*a**, 4301*b**, 4590*a**; Algonquian manuscript, 4108
Lacandon, 4504*a**; ethnography, 4497-4498
Lac du Flambeau, Chippewa dances, 4071, 4606; Reservation, Wisconsin, 4072, 4607
La Fort, Thomas, corres. with Ebenezer Meriam, 4016, 4720
Laguna, N. Mex., (Keres), 4444, 4449, 4452, 4460, 4772, 4775, 4796*a**; archaeology, 4796*a**; dwellings, 4796*a**; ethnography, 4448; language, 4439; migration of 1880, 4773; people, 4273*a**, 4796*a**; Santo Domingo refugees, 4790
Lakota. *See* Dakota
LALY, engraving, 4796a
Land, cessions, 4865; dispute, Creek Indian, 4549; Onondaga, 4016, 4720; Seneca, 4732
Landes, Ruth, donor, 4012*a*, 4603*a*
Langdon, Margaret H., author, 4233; collector, 4073, 4234; donor, 4073, 4233-4234
Langer, Arthur, 4281
Language, families: Central America, 4513; Mexico, 4510, 4513; North America, 4593; South America, 4760; **phyla:** Hokan-Siouan, Macro-Chibchan, and Macro-Otomanguean, 4152; Macro-Penutian, 4152, 4339, 4666, 4880, 4889; speech, men's and women's: Arawak (Continental), 4476; locono 4476; **use:** Mohawk, 4531; Sandia (Tiwa), 4843
Languages, Alaska native languages, 4043, 4107*a*; American, 4323; Asiatic, 4267; California, 4004; Central America, 4154-4156; Mexico, 4003*b*, 4017, 4154, 4504*b*; Native American, 4017; North American, 4267; Northwest Coast, 4003*b*, 4026, 4248, 4599*a*, 4600; Pacific Northwest Tribal languages, 4044, 4592*b*; Peru, 4741; publications, 4270; Salishan, 4034, 4841; South American, 4017, 4122, 4127, 4738, 4744, 4750, 4751; studied, 4270; vanishing, 4270. *See also* specific language or language family
Larue, Mabel G. (Mrs. Daniel W.), corres. with Frank G. Speck, 4294
Laughlin, W., corres. with Paul A. W. Wallace, 4650
Launer, Philip, corres. with Frank G. Speck, 4240
Lauriault, Erwin H., author, 4186; corres. with John Alden Mason, 4186
Law, Six Nations, 4385; Shawnee, 4020*e*, 4734*b*
Lea and Blanchard, corres. with Henry R. Schoolcraft, 4326
League of the Iroquois. *See* Six Nations, Iroquois Confederacy
Le Conte, John L., **corres. with**: Thomas Charlton Henry, 4768; T. W. Yardley, 4341
Lee, Richard Henry, corres. with George Washington, 4337
Lee, Thomas A., Jr., author, 4498*a*
Legends, Chinook Jargon, 4174, 4472, 4735, 4854; *Deganawidah*, 4386, 4402, 4411; Delaware, 4211; Hare, 4087, 4236; Hopi, migration, 4097*a*, 4363*a*; Kwakiutl, 4174, 4472, 4735, 4854; Micmac, 4528; North Pacific Coast of North America, 4472, 4735, 4854; Shuswap, 4174, 4472, 4735, 4854; Taos, 4453; Tsimshian, 4174, 4472, 4735, 4854. *See also* Myths, Stories, Tales, Folk Tales, Oral Literature
Leland, Waldo, corres. with Franz Boas, 4270
Le Moine, J. M., corres. with Robert Bell, 4003*a*, 4268*a*
Lenape. *See* Delaware
Leon, Nicolas, author, 4510
Lesley, J. Peter, corres. with A. J. Holman & Co., 4491
Le Sourd, Philip S., collector, 4642*a*-4642*b*; donor, 4642*a*-4642*b*
Levi-Strauss, Claude, corres. with John Alden Mason, 4746
Lewis and Clark, vocabularies, 4323
Lexicostatistics, Cora, Huichol, Opata (Arivechi and Huepac), and Papago, 4887; Uto-Aztecan, 4880, 4887; Yaqui (Guaymas, Mocoriba, and Fuerte), 4887

Libby, Dorothy, corres. with Richard H. Shryock, 4114, 4253
Libraries:
Bibliothèque Nationale, Paris, 4027, 4372
Library, William L. Clements, 4594, 4598
Library of the American Philosophical Society. *See* American Philosophical Society
Library of Congress, 4114, 4253
Haverford College: Edward Wanton Smith Collection, 4320; materials related to Indians, 4415
Houghton Library, Harvard University, 4047, 4592*c*
Princeton University, Draper Collection, 4416
University of Washington Libraries, Seattle, Wash., 4039*a*, 4592; manuscript collection, 4034, 4841
Lillooet, anthropometric data, 4268*c*; vocabulary, 4599*a*
Lilly, Eli, corres. with: Frank G. Speck, 4219; Carl F. Voegelin, 4218*a*
Lincoln, E., 4282
Lingelbach, William E., corres. with Paul A. W. Wallace, 4295
Linguistic Institute, 4109*b*, 4225*d*
Linguistics, 4012, 4296, 4298, 4324, 4333, 4339; Alaska native languages, 4043, 4107*a*; American Indian, 4012, 4034, 4841; bibliography, 4125, 4151, 4334*a*; Central America, 4125, 4151-4152, 4158, 4513; Ecuadorian Oriente, 4740; Guatemala, 4152*a*; manuscript collection, 4039*a*, 4592; Mexico, 4125, 4151, 4152*a*, 4510, 4513, 4516, 4525*a*; North America, 4039*a*, 4592-4593; Pacific Northwest tribal languages, 4044, 4592*b*; South America, 4125, 4151. *See also* specific areas, topics, languages, and language families
Linton, Ralph, 4466; corres. with John Alden Mason, 4295*a*
Lipan, *4473-4475*; history and customs, 4473; informant, Augustina Zuazua, 4473; language, 4012, 4474-4475; people, 4273*a**; texts, 4474-4475
Lipkin, William, 4178, 4232
Lithographs, 4016*a*, 4589*a*, 4865*a*
Locono, *4476*
Loft, Bernice (*Dawendine*) (Iroquois). *See* Winslow Bernice Loft (Mrs. Arthur H.)
Loft, Chief William (*Dewaseragech*) (Iroquois), 4400, 4536; interviews with, 4397, 4414
Long, Ronald W., collector, 4074, 4844*a*; donor, 4074, 4844*a*
Long House, Cayuga, 4714*a**; Iroquois, 4388*a**; Seneca, 4397*a**; Upper Cayuga, 4397*a**
"The Longhouse People," film, 4421
Loosley, Elizabeth W., corres. with Paul A. W. Wallace, 4144
Loskiel, G. H., 4267
Louchens, 4010, 4165
Loucheux, *4477*; language, 4012, 4067*a*, 4477; recordings, 4067*a*, 4477
Louisiana, Bayou Blue and Bayou Grand Caillou, 4364*a**; Bayou La Combe, 4179*b*, 4301*b*, 4364*a**; Choctaw village, 4301*b**; Pointe du Chien, 4364*a**
Lower Chehalis, language, 4039*a*, 4592
Lower Pima. *See* Pima Bajo
Lowie, Robert H., corres. with John Alden Mason, 4017, 4295*a*
Lumholtz, Carl, 4367
Lummi, ethnography, language, 4057*a*, 4600*a*; informant, Al Charles, 4057*a*, 4600*a*

McCaskill, J. C., corres. with Frank G. Speck, 4365
McClellan, Catherine, and Frederica de Laguna, compilers, 4032, 4106*a*, 4850
McConnell, James, corres. with John Alden Mason, 4681
Machapunga, ethnography, 4148*a**; North Carolina, 4301*b**
Machiguenga, language, 4143
McKenny, Col. Thomas L., Office of Indian Affairs, 4589
Mackinaw, missions to, 4047, 4592*c*
MacKinlay, William E. W., corres. with John Alden Mason, 4487
Maclure, William, corres. with Samuel G. Morton, 4511
Macmillan, Mrs. Charles, artist, 4244*a*
McNickle, D'Arcy, corres. with Frank G. Speck, 4548
McQuown, Norman A., author, 4018, 4158, 4852; collector, 4075, 4693; compiler, 4037*a*, 4693*a*; donor, 4018, 4075, 4693, 4852
McRae, John C., engraver, 4588*a*
Macro-Chibchan, 4152
Macro-Otomanguean, 4152
Macro-Penutian, 4152, 4339, 4666, 4880, 4889
Macushi, 4759*a*
Mad Bear (Iroquois), corres. with Paul A. W. Wallace, 4401
Madison Historical Society, Madison, N.J., 4335
Mae (resident of Old Town, Me.), corres. with D. Scribner Hyler, 4663*a*
Magnetite, 4800
*Magyar Indomanyou Akademie*, 4319
Maicoba, Sonora, Mexico, 4505, 4669
Maine, *4478*, 4663*a**; Eastport, Pleasant Point Indian Village (Passamaquoddy), 4642*c**; Indians of, 4278, 4478; Old Town, 4663*a**; State Library, 4278
*Maiyanyi*, 4794; Santa Ana, 4793
Malali, linguistics, 4753
Malecite, *4479-4480*, 4663*a**; artifacts, 4275; bird names, 4645; recordings, 4089-4090, 4479-4480; storage basket, 4281; texts, 4089-4090, 4479-4480; vocabulary, 4645
Mam, *4481-4483*; contents of recordings, 4482, 4684, 4686, 4914; language, 4482, 4684, 4686,

4914; linguistics, 4084, 4483, 4685, 4915; recordings, 4084, 4483, 4685, 4915; Todos Santos dialect, 4481

Man ceremony. *See* Senshare ceremony

Mandan, *4484-4486*, 4682*e**; contents of recordings, 4053-4054, 4343-4344, 4484-4485; cultural change, 4053, 4343, 4484; dictionary, 4486; ethnography, 4683; ethnohistory, 4053-4054, 4343-4344, 4484-4485; language, linguistics, 4053-4054, 4343-4344, 4484-4486; morphology, phonology, 4486; recordings, 4053-4054, 4343-4344, 4484-4485; Shahaka (Chief), 4683*a**

Mandelbaum, David G., 4020*a*, 4327*a*; collector, 4703

Manebogo manuscript, 4587

Manitoba, Canada, 4188*a**; Griswold, 4065, 4204*a*; Norway House, 4194; Rossville Mission, Cree vocabulary, 4194

Manning, E. W. (Mrs. T. H.), corres. with Frank G. Speck, 4254

Manning, T. H., 4254

Manque, vocabulary, 4525

Manuscripts. *See* Collections, manuscripts

Maps, 4447; California, 4139; Coast Tsimshian, 4855; Greenland and Newfoundland, 4254*a*; Highland Chontal, 4543; Indian houses in Harbor Springs, Michigan, 4603; linguistic, northwestern Mexico, 4682; Mexico, 4829-4830; Newfoundland, 4143*a*, 4254*a*; Northern Tepehuan, 4830; Seneca, 4732; South American languages, 4746; southeastern tribes, 4301*b*; southwest, 4797; Tepehuan, 4829-4830

Mapuche, 4759*a**

Maratin, *4487*

Marbeson, Georgianna, artist, 4301*b*, 4590*a*

Maricopa, people, 4698*b**

Maring, Joel, collector, 4439; donor, 4439

Markman, Sidney D., author, 4498*a*

Marriage. *See* Kinship

Marriott, Alice L., and Carol K. Rachlin, authors, 4614; donors, 4614

Marsh, Gordon H., compiler, 4178, 4232; donor, 4178, 4232

Martha's Vineyard, Mass., Gay Head Indians, 4493; Herring Pond Indian Church (Nipmuc), 4598*a*

Martin, Paul S., corres. with Elsie Clews Parsons, 4311

Martindale, J. H., corres. with William Parker, 4722

Martinet, André, corres. with Morris Swadesh, 4880

Martinez, ———, 4790

Masayesva, LaVerne, corres. with Whitfield J. Bell, Jr., 4357

Mashakali, linguistics, 4753

Mashpee, 4489, 4605; people, 4598*a**

Masks, Aztec, 4454; Cayuga, 4332, 4714*a**; Cherokee, 4332; design, 4447; destruction of, 4455; Eskimo, 4251*a**, 4332; Indian, 4301; Iroquois, 4332, 4425; Jemez, 4778; *Kachina*, 4454; Keresan, 4455; paintings of, 4797; Santa Clara, 4778; Seneca, 4332; southwest, 4785; Tsimshian, 4332

Mason, John Alden, 4152, 4183, 4299, 4324, 4509, 4521*a**, 4623, 4627-4628, 4639-4641, 4673, 4675, 4689, 4691, 4743, 4762, 4877-4878, 4880; **author**, 4107, 4126-4127, 4153-4158, 4296, 4298-4299, 4512-4517, 4629-4634, 4636-4637, 4651, 4680-4681, 4702, 4747, 4749-4754, 4806-4809, 4818, 4820, 4823, 4825, 4827, 4829, 4874-4875, 4918; **collector**, 4635, 4822, 4919; **compiler**, 4819, 4821, 4824, 4826, 4828, 4873; **corres.**, 4017, 4127, 4295*a*, 4641, 4748, 4750; **corres. with**: Bernard W. Aginsky, 4295*a*; Ethel G. Aginsky, 4295*a*; Manuel J. Andrade, 4498*c*; Charles Marius Barbeau, 4017, 4524*a*, 4586*a*; Burton W. Bascom, Jr., 4814; Ralph L. Beals, 4295*a*; Ruth Benedict, 4017, 4295*a*, 4869*a*; Frans Blom, 4297; Leonard Bloomfield, 4297; Franz Boas, 4017, 4297; David M. Brugge, 4668, 4670-4672, 4679; Douglas S. Byers, 4295*a*; Frederica de Laguna, 4017, 4274*a*, 4295*a*; Robert J. Drake, 4681; Paul Fejos, 4299; Henry Field, 4295*a*; Otis H. Green, 4742; A. Irving Hallowell, 4295*a*; John P. Harrington, 4017, 4295*a*, 4690, 4744; Zellig S. Harris, 4125, 4151, 4748; Bret R. Hart, 4816; John E. Heimnick, 4681; Melville J. Herskovits, 4295*a*, 4324; George Herzog, 4627, 4639, 4869*b*; George G. Heye, 4017; John Hobgood, 4817; Harry Hoijer, 4295*a*, 4748; Agnes McClain Howard, 4507; Edgar B. Howard, 4289*a*; Diamond Jenness, 4017, 4589*b*; Frederick Johnson, 4525, 4804; Jacob B. Johnson, 4143; David H. Kelley, 4871; Alfred V. Kidder, 4017, 4152*a*; Dale S. King, 4681; Clyde Kluckhohn, 4295*a*; Alfred L. Kroeber, 4017, 4293*a*, 4295*a*, 4509, 4628; Gertrude P. Kurath, 4017; Weston La Barre, 4295*a*; Erwin H. Lauriault, 4186; Claude Levi-Strauss, 4746; Ralph Linton, 4295*a*; Robert H. Lowie, 4017, 4295*a*; James McConnell, 4681; William E. W. MacKinlay, 4487; Margaret Mead, 4295*a*; Robert H. Merrill, 4157*a*; David Lopez Molina, 4681; Sylvanus G. Morley, 4158*a*; George P. Murdock, 4295*a*; Eugene A. Nida, 4748; Willard Z. Park, 4755*a*; Elsie Clews Parsons, 4311; Fernando Pesqueira, 4681; Louis Rankin, 4758; Gladys A. Reichard, 4017; William A. Ritchie, 4017; Fr. Regis Rohder, O.F.M., 4333; John H. Rowe, 4759; Edward Sapir, 4017, 4297, 4876-4877, 4918; Linton Satterthwaite, Jr., 4159; Carl Sauer, 4293*a*; Dean F. Saxton, 4333; E. B. Sayles, 4159*a*; Frank G. Speck, 4143*b*, 4520*a*; Edward H. Spicer, 4681; Leslie Spier, 4295*a*, 4331*a*; Julian H. Steward, 4295*a*; David B. Stout, 4762; Morris Swadesh, 4017, 4333,

4880; John R. Swanton, 4333*a*; Sol Tax, 4295*a*; J. Eric S. Thompson, 4159*b*; Ruth M. Underhill, 4017, 4641*a*, 4927; George C. Vaillant, 4524*a*; Sue Vaillant (Mrs. George C.), 4524*a*; Carl F. Voegelin, 4295*a*, 4334*a*; Erminie W. Voegelin, 4295*a*; Charles Wagley, 4859; Phil C. Weigand, 4368, 4833; Robert J. Weitlaner, 4158, 4525*a*, 4681; Leslie A. White, 4295*a*; Benjamin L. Whorf, 4017, 4888; Gordon R. Willey, 4158; Clark Wissler, 4339*a*; John Witthoft, 4171; **donor**, 4017; **estate**, donor, 4017; **manuscript collection**, 4017; **photographs**, 4500, 4515, 4518-4520; and David M. Brugge, authors, 4682
Mason, Otis T., corres. with Stephen Bowers, 4138
Massachusett, *4488-4494*; **Eliot Indian Bible**, 4488, 4490-4492, 4494; **Eliot Oak**, 4490*a**; **Gay Head Indians**, 4493; **Mashpee**, Massachusetts, Indians around, 4489; **people**: Narraganset, 4491*a**; Wampanoag, 4491*a**
Massachusetts, Annawan's Rock (Taunton), 4598*a**; Betty's Neck, 4491*a**; burial sites, 4303*a*; Eliot Oak, 4490*a**; Gay Head, 4491*a**; Gay Head Indians, 4493; Harvard University, 4047, 4592*c*, 4872; Herring Pond Indian Church, Martha's Vineyard, 4598*a**; *History of Barnstable County*, 4489; Mashpee Indians, 4489; Matapoiset River, 4598*a**; Nipmuc, 4598*a**; *Richard Bourne, Missionary to the Mashpee Indians*, 4489
Masta, Henry, 4273
Mataco, 4509; linguistics, 4753
Material culture. *See* Artifacts
Mathews, Mrs. Henry, corres. with Frank G. Speck, 4539*a*
Matlatzinca, *4495-4496*; informant, Ezequiel Hernández, 4048, 4496; language, 4495; linguistics, 4048, 4495-4496; paradigms, 4048, 4496; phonology, 4495; recording, 4048, 4496; texts, 4048, 4495-4496; vocabulary, 4495, 4525
Mato Grosso, Brazil, 4759*a**
Mattaponi, 4010, 4165, 4687*b**; artifacts, 4275, 4687*b**; ethnography, 4687*b**; people, 4687*b**
Matthew, William D., corres., 4110
Matthews, G. Hubert, author, 4205
Maumee, missions to, 4047, 4592*c*
Maya, *4497-4498*, 4498*, 4498*c*, 4504*a**; Cholti-Lacandon, ethnography, 4498; hieroglyphs, 4159*b*, 4888
Mayan, 4020*a*, 4327*a*, 4339, 4498*a**, *4498a-4500*, 4500*; **architecture**, 4020*a*, 4159*b*, 4327*a*; **calendar**, 4159; **cargo system**, 4498*a*; **Coxoh**: 4498*a*; colonial project, 4498*a*; **ethnography**, 4024, 4498-4498*a*, 4499; **ethnohistory**, 4498; **genetic relationships**, 4889; **manuscript collection**, 4024, 4499; **pottery**, 4524*a*; **prayers**, 4498*a*; **recordings**, 4047*a*, 4075, 4084, 4483, 4498*b*, 4685, 4693, 4915; **religion**, 4047*a*, 4498*a*-4498*b*; **religious**: pilgrimages, 4498*a**; practices, 4498*a**; **subgrouping**, 4498*c*; **vocabulary**, 4526
Mayne, W. T., corres. with Stephen Powers, 4137
Mazahua, vocabulary, 4525
Mazatec, *4501*; Jalapa, linguistics, 4501; vocabulary, 4525
Mazzei, Filippo, corres. with Giovanni Fabroni, 4300
Mead, Margaret, corres. with John Alden Mason, 4295*a*
Meanings, of Indian names, 4386; of Iroquois names, 4390
Means, Philip Ainsworth, 4523, 4757
Measurements, anthropometric, 4003*b*, 4268*c*
Meat, horse and dog, 4313
Medicine, 4003; **Catawba**, 4020*c*, 4148*a**, 4148*b*, 4149; **Cherokee**, 4028, 4163; **Delaware**, 4080, 4222; **Indian**, 4291; **Iroquois**, 4383; **medical information**, Indian, 4263; **medicine man**: Cree, 4598*a**; Hopi, 4097*a*, 4363*a*; curing a patient, 4865*a**; **Pocomam Central**, medicinal plants, 4687; **societies**: 4447-4448; Keresan, 4775; Southwest, 4770; Zuni, 4932. *See also* Diseases, Ethnomedicine, Folk medicine, Pathology
Meier, Emil F., corres. with Frank G. Speck, 4301
Mekeel, H. Scudder, corres. with Elsie Clews Parsons, 4311
Melodrama, Indian, 4598*a**
Melody, Michael E., corres. with Murphy D. Smith, 4206
"Memoir on the Indian Languages," 4321
Menomini, 4245*a**; **dances**, 4071, 4606; **people**: 4245*a**, 4865*b**; Dewey Necomish, Howard Rain, Louis Thunder, and Mitchell Weso, 4245*a**
*Mental Elevator* (Seneca), 4723
Mercer, Henry Chapman, corres. with George Henry Horn, 4370
Meriam, Ebenezer, **corres. with**: David Hill, L. A. Hill, Thomas LaFort, and Jameson L. Thomas, 4016, 4720
Merrifield, William R., and Phillip Baer, authors, 4497; donors, 4497
Merrill, Robert H., 4512; corres. with John Alden Mason, 4157*a*
Merrill, William L., author, 4590; donor, 4590
Mesa Verde, Colo., cliff dwellings, Sun Temple, 4796*a**
Mescalbeans, 4590
Mescalero, *4502-4504;* **informants**: Sam Chino, Arnold K., Leon Pariko, and John Shanta, 4503; Charles Smith(?), 4504; Horace Torres, 4503; **language**, 4012, 4175; **texts**, 4175, 4502-4504
Metacomet (King Philip) (Wampanoag), 4291*a**, 4291*b**; death of, 4865*a**
Meteorology, data, Pacific, 4019, 4755. *See* Natural phenomena

Mexico, 4017*, 4020*b**, 4274*a*, 4312, 4358-4359, 4498*, 4500*, 4504*a*, *4504a-4526*, 4515*, 4518*, 4519*, 4520*, 4520*a**, 4670*, 4671*; **agriculture**, 4514; **archaeology**, 4017, 4152*a*, 4157*a*, 4158*a*, 4159-4159*b*, 4289*a*, 4293*a*, 4331*a*, 4504*a**, 4506-4507, 4512, 4515, 4517, 4521*a**, 4524*a*, 4525*a*, 4634, 4669, 4806, 4809; **architecture**, 4020*a*, 4327*a*, 4504*a**; **artifacts**, 4504*a**; 4507, 4521*a*, 4668, 4670*, 4671*, 4809; **Azqueltan**, 4368, 4833; **bibliography**, 4125, 4151, 4682; **calendar stone**, 4520*a**; **cargo system**, 4498*a*; **ceremony**, 4498*a*, 4521, 4668, 4811, 4816, 4927; **Chiapas**: cargo system, 4498*a*; Palenque, 4504*a**, 4521*a**; religion, 4047*a*, 4498*a**, 4498*b*; Sac Balam, 4498; **Chihauhua**: 4519*, 4669; Baborigame, 4820; **clanship**, 4523, 4757; **Coahuila**, 4512; **comparative vocabularies**, 4516, 4525; **cucurbita moschata**, 4514; **dialects**, 4510; **Durango**: 4512, 4515*, 4519*, 4525*a*; Mezquital, cliff dwellings, 4507; tribal strife, 4507; Xoconoxtle, 4816; **dwellings**, 4507, 4520*, 4668; **education of Indians**, 4511; ***Escuela Internacional de Ethnologia y Arqueologia Americanas***, 4806; **ethnography**, 4017, 4047*a*, 4497-4498, 4498*b*, 4520*, 4521, 4668, 4670, 4673, 4682, 4816-4817, 4825, 4829; **ethnohistory**, 4498; **ethnology**, 4152*a*, 4525*a*, 4806-4807, 4809; **ethnomedicine**, 4047*b*, 4622*b*, 4687; **genetic classification**, 4333*a*, 4525*a*, 4889; **government**, 4498; **Gowawaima Kachina**, 4455; **Hidalgo**, Ixmiquilpan, 4050, 4621; **Huaxteca**, 4781; **Huichol Indians**, 4367; **innate capabilities of Indians**, 4511; **Indian-White relations**, 4368, 4520*b*, 4668, 4672, 4817, 4833; **International Congress of Americanists**, 4154, 4513; **language families**, 4510, 4513; **languages**, 4003*b*, 4017, 4154, 4504*b*; **linguistic map**, 4682; **linguistics**, 4125, 4151, 4152*a*, 4510, 4513, 4516, 4525*a*, 4825, 4876, 4881-4886, 4888; **litigation**, 4520*b*; **manuscript collection**, 4521; **maps**, 4682, 4829-4830; **masks**, 4301; **Mexican Historical Congress**, Zacatecas, 4517, 4825; **migration routes**, 4515; **Museum of Mexico**, 4504*a**; **Oaxaca**: 4504*a**; San Matias Petacaltepec, 4093, 4545; Teposcolula, Juzgado Archives, 4520*b*; **people**, 4504*a**, 4520*; **Picture Chronical**, 4524; **pictures**, 4020*b**, 4498*, 4500*, 4504*a**, 4515*, 4518*, 4519*, 4520*, 4520*a**, 4670*, 4671*; **postal cards**, 4520*a**; **Puebla**, 4556*a** **"Pygmy Race of Durango,"** 4289*a*; **Pyramid of the Sun**, 4520*a**; **Rancho los Tepalcates**, 4670; **religion**, 4047*a*, 4498-4498*b*, 4521, 4668, 4687, 4806-4808, 4826-4827; **sacrificial stone**, 4520*a**; **San Juan de Teotihuacan**, 4520*a**; **San Sebastian**, 4368; **Santa Maria Ocotlan**, 4817; **Schroeder pyramid**, 4507; **la Sierra de la Candela**, 4515; **Sonora**: 4058, 4505-4506, 4519*, 4668-4669, 4674, 4677-4678; cucurbita moschata, 4514; expedition, 4681; Hermosillo, 4919; Maicoba, 4505, 4669; Ónabas, 4056, 4674, 4676; Santa Ana Rancheria, 4674; Yecora, 4058, 4678; **Tabasco**, 4504*a**; **temples**, Palenque, Chiapas, 4521*a**; **Teotihuacan**, 4504*a**, 4520*a**; **terrain**, 4520*; **Toltec**, 4504*a**; **tribal strife**, Durango, 4507; **tribute system**, 4520*b*; **vocabularies**, 4526; **warrior's purification**, 4927; **Yaxchilan**, 4159; **Yucatan**: Chichen Itza, 4158*a*, 4500*, 4504*a**; Uxmal, 4500*; **Zape**, 4515 (*see also* specific tribes and languages)

Miahuatec (Zapotec), text, 4929

Mica, 4595

Michael, Glynn, corres. with Paul A. W. Wallace, 4536

Michigan, 4609*b**; **calumet dance**, 4071, 4606; **ceremonies**, 4038*, 4609*; **Chippewa**: 4071, 4606; hymns, 4071, 4606; **dances**, 4038*, 4071, 4606, 4609*; **ethnography**, 4038*, 4071, 4605*, 4606, 4609*; **Harbor Springs**, 4603; **Lansing**, powwow, 4071, 4606; **Moravian missions among Indians**, 4039, 4591; **Pokagon** (Hartford), 4598*a**; **Red Man in**, 4071, 4606; **University of**, 4782

Micmac, 4143*a**, *4527-4528*, 4527*a**, 4663*a**; artifacts, 4275, 4527*a**; beadwork, 4598*a**; camp, 4598*a**; economics, 4527; education, 4527; encampment, 4143*a**; ethnography, 4143*a**, 4527*a**; habitat, 4527*a**; Nova Scotia, 4143*a**, 4598*a**; people, 4527*a**, 4595*a**; politics, 4527; text, 4528

Microfilms. *See* Collections, microfilms

Middle America, **genetic relationships**, 4155-4156; **languages**: 4155-4156; geographic distribution, 4156; **linguistics**, 4152, 4158. *See also* Central America

Migration, **Laguna**, 4773; **legend**, Hopi, 4097*a*, 4363*a*; **routes**: Asia to North America, 4293*a*, 4589*b*; Mexico, 4515

Millcayac, 4759

Miller, ———, 4846

Miller, Carl F., corres. with Elenor C. Kelly (Mrs. William M.) 4020*d*, 4602*a*

Miller, P. Schuyler, corres. with Paul A. W. Wallace, 4402

Miller, Wick, 4438

Mining, 4370

Minitari. *See* Gros Ventre, Hidatsa

Minnehaha, 4301*b**, 4590*a**

Minnesota, Prairie Island, 4194*a**; Redwing, 4194*a**

Mirabal family, Taos, 4846

Miranya, 4743, 4745

Miscegenation, 4614

Mishongnovi, Antelope sand painting, 4790; dialect, 4364; pueblo, 4364

Missions, 4865*a*; Jesuit, 4044, 4592*b*; Moravian among Indians of North America, 4039, 4591; to Indians, 4267; Protestant, 4025, 4286*b*; United Church Board for World Ministries, 4047, 4592*c*

Mississagua, anthropometric data, 4268*c*
Mississippi, burial sites, 4303*a*; Choctaw, 4067, 4181-4182; Valley, mounds, 4280
Mitchell, Mary-Elizabeth B., author, 4520*b*; donor, 4520*b*
Mithun, Marianne, collector, 4076, 4863; donor, 4076, 4863
Miwok, Bodega, language, 4137*a*; people, 4137*b**
Mixtec, 4504*a**, *4529*; vocabulary, 4525
Mixteca Alta, Juzgado Archives of Teposcolula, 4520*b*
Moccasins, 4334
Mochon, Marion J., author, 4539; corres. with Richard H. Shryock, 4539; donor, 4539; photographer, 4540*a*
Mohave, linguistic interaction with Chemehuevi, 4699, 4764
Mohawk, 4397*a**, *4530-4538*, 4536*a**; **adoption**, 4530; **Akwesasne**, 4382; **Akwesasne Counsellor Organization**, 4388; anthropometric data, 4268*c*; **art**, 4533-4534; **chiefs**: 4390; Chief Split Cloud(?) [Cook], 4536*a**; Chief William Loft, 4536, 4400; Privy and General Councils of, 4405; **ethnography**, 4531; **folk tale**, 4535; **Indian-White relations**, 4532; *language*, 4039, 4591; *language use*, 4531; *linguistics*, 4538; *names for Nanticokes*, 4559, 4864; *people*: 4536*a**; Tommy Cook, 4536*a**; *rites*, 4537; *St. Regis*, 4411; *St. Regis Indian Reserve*, 4531; *syntax*, 4538; *texts*, 4537; *village*, Oka, Quebec, 4536*a**; *vocabulary*, 4164*a*, 4378*a*, 4532*a*; *words in Onondaga dictionary*, 4721
Mohawk-Onondaga, Seth Newhouse, 4405*a**
Mohegan, *4539-4541*, 4539*a**, 4540*a**, 4651; artifacts, 4539*a**; attire, 4598*a**; ethnography, 4539*a**; people, 4539*a**, 4865*b**
Mohegan-Nehantic, Charles Mathews, 4539*a**
Mohegan-Pequot, 4540
Mojo, 4869
Moki man, 4531*a**
Molale, language, 4040, 4701*a*
Molina, David Lopez, corres. with John Alden Mason, 4681
Montagnais-Naskapi, 4143*a**, 4188*b**, 4304; artifacts, 4188*b**; divination devices, 4188*b**; dogs, 4188*b**; ethnography, 4188*b**; habitat, 4188*b**; Lake St. John, 4189; language, 4086, 4190; people, 4188*b**; recordings, 4086, 4169, 4190; scapulimancy, 4188*b**. *See also* Cree
Montana, Browning, 4682*d*; Fort Belknap Reservation, 4194*a**; Polson, 4682*d*
Montezuma (Aztec), 4291*a**; Tribute Roll, 4554, 4557
Montgomery, Charles B., corres. with Paul A. W. Wallace, 4021, 4246
Montgomery Creek, Milford Ralph Hill, 4137*b**
Months, Tuscarora, 4076, 4863. *See also* Time expressions
Montour, Andrew, author, 4220
Montour, Chief Joseph (Delaware), 4221, 4227, 4229; corres. with Paul A. W. Wallace, 4221; interview with, 4414
Montour, E. T., corres. with Paul A. W. Wallace, 4403
Montour, Ethel Brant, corres. with Paul A. W. Wallace, 4404
Montour, Madam, biographical sketch, 4398
Montour family, 4404
Montreal, Quebec, Canada, 4145; Archives of St. Mary's College, 4910
Mooney, James, 4170; **corres. with**: Isaac Minis Hays, 4167; Frank G. Speck, 4302
Moravian, Church Archives, Bethlehem, Pa., manuscript collection, 4039, 4591; missions, North American Indians, 4039, 4591; village, Schönbrunn, Ohio, 4244*a**
Morgan, Lewis Henry, 4011, 4394, 4603
Morgan, William, 4580
Moris, Chihuahua, Mexico, 4669
Morley, Sylvanus G., corres. with John Alden Mason, 4158*a*
Morphology, Abipon, 4099; Cherokee, 4079, 4168; Delaware, 4225*d*; Hopi, 4351*b*; Mandan, 4486; Nahua, 4555; Northern Tepehuan, 4831; Pawnee, 4649; Papago, 4629, 4640; Quechua, 4689, 4691; Sarsi, 4705; Shawnee, 4734*a*; Takelma, 4013, 4802-4803; Tepecano, 4812; Tepehuan, 4814, 4831; Tiwa, 4843; Tfalati Kalapuya, 4857; Walapai (Upland Yuman), 4867; Yana, 4916-4917; Yuki, 4926; Zacapoaxtla (Nahua), 4555
Morphophonemics, Yana, 4128
Morris, I. C., 4520*a*
Mortar, Pequot, 4539*b**
Morton, George, author, 4652
Morton, Samuel G., 4164; **artist**, 4303*a*; **corres. with**: William Maclure, 4511; Joseph N. Nicollet, 4303
Mosan, 4880
Moshkos, 4267
Mother (*yaya*), 4447
Motilon, linguistics, 4753
Mounds, Mississippi Valley, 4280; Ohio Valley, 4280; Tennessee, 4805
Mountain Tequistlateco, *4542-4546*; informants, Damian Flores, Porfirio Nicolas Flores, and Clemente Zarate, 4093, 4545. *See also* Highland Chontal
Mueller, Werner, corres. with University of Pennsylvania, 4688
Muhlenberg, family, 4021*, 4295
Muniments, Dalhousie, 4030, 4243
Munro, Pamela, corres. with Whitfield J. Bell, Jr., 4699, 4764
Munsee, 4213*a**, 4540*a**, 4651; acculturation, 4539; anthropometric data, 4268*c*; dwellings, 4545*a**, economics, 4539; ethnography, 4225*c*; informant, Nickodemus Peters, 4225*c*; language, 4225*c*; names for various tribes, 4225*c*; people, 4540*a**. *See also* Delaware
Murdock, George P., 4020*a*, 4327*a*, 4663; corres. with John Alden Mason, 4295*a*

Murphy, Grace E. B., donor, 4019, 4755
Murphy, Robert Cushman, author, 4019, 4755
Museum collections. *See* Collections, museum
Museum of Arts and Sciences, Rochester, 4395; Mexico, 4504*a**; Primitive Art, New York, 4086, 4169, 4190, 4208, 4665, 4903
Music, Arapaho, Arikara, Assiniboin, and Blackfoot, 4683; Cherokee, 4010, 4165; Cheyenne and Crow, 4683; Dakota, 4207; Gros Ventre and Hidatsa, 4683; Hopi, 4051-4052, 4347-4349, 4470; *achina* songs, 4772; Keresan, 4470; Mandan, 4683; Michigan Indians, 4605; Oglala, 4207; Ojibwa (Plains) and Plains Cree, 4683; San Juan Pueblo, 4061, 4837; Santa Fe, 4772; Sarsi, 4683; *senshare* ceremony, 4015, 4839; similarities between Hopi and Keresan, 4470; Sioux, 4207, 4683; Tepehuan, 4869*b*; Tewa, 4061, 4772, 4836-4837, 4839; Tutelo, 4246*a*; Zuni, 4772. *See also* Songs, Dances
Muskogee, 4010, 4165, *4546a-4551*; vocabulary, 4589. *See also* Creek, Seminole
Musquakie, 4256*a**, 4663*a**; chief, *Peah-Mus-Ka*, 4589*a**; dances, 4071, 4606; ethnography, 4256*a**; language, 4095, 4258; linguistics, 4257; people, 4256*a**; recordings, 4095, 4258; texts, 4095, 4258. *See also* Fox
Muysca, vocabularies, 4333
Myers(?), John L., corres. with Frank G. Speck, 4304
Mythology, Ojibwa, 4012*a*, 4603*a*; Shawnee, 4734; Tepecano, 4806
Myths, Catawba, 4020*c*, 4148*b*; Conibo, 4186; Delaware, 4225*b*; Dogrib, 4238; Haida, 4002, 4853; Hare, 4238; Keres, 4466; Northern Tepehuan, 4815, 4832; Ojibwa, 4610; Papago, 4047*b*, 4622*b*, 4638; Pima, 4047*b*, 4622*b*; Shawnee, 4734*b*; Shipibo, 4186; Takelma, 4803; Tiwa, 4074, 4844*a*; Tsimshian, 4002, 4853; Twin Myth, 4610; The Two Boys, 4610; *Wawenock Myth Texts*, 4278; Yakima (Sahaptin), 4701; Yavapai, creation, 4868. *See also* Legends, Stories, Tales, Folk tales, Oral literature

Na-Dene, *4552*; comparative dictionary, 4115, 4342, 4552, 4851
Nagualism, 4522
*Nahia* (Cochiti), 4359
Nahua, *4553-4557*, 4876; **comparative vocabulary**, 4884; **dialects**, 4556*a*; **morphology**, 4555; **Nahuatl**: 4781, 4847, 4888, 4913; dictionary, 4520*a*; language, 4556*a*; Spanish elements, 4504*b*; vocabulary, 4504*b*, 4556*a*, 4873; **phonology**: 4555; San Miguel, 4556; **text**, 4553; **vocabulary**, 4516. *See also* Aztec
*Naiya* (Santo Domingo), 4359
Najlis de Kreyness, Elena, author, 4099; corres. with Carl F. Voegelin, 4099
Naked Bear, 4377*a**
Nakota. *See* Dakota
Nambikuara, 4746
Names, **for Nanticoke**, 4559, 4864; **for various tribes in**: Munsee, 4225*c*; Shawnee, 4734*a*; **Nootka**, personal and place, 4586; **Talamanca**, 4804; **translation of**, 4218*a*
Naming, Arapaho, Arikara, Assiniboin, Blackfoot, Cheyenne, and Crow, 4683; the dead, Dakota, 4198, 4203; Gros Ventre, Hidatsa, Mandan, Ojibwa (Plains), Plains Cree, Sarsi, and Sioux, 4683
Nansemond, 4688, 4688*a**; habitat, 4688*a**; people, 4688*a**
Nanticoke, 4039, 4267, 4541, *4558-4559*, 4558*a**, 4591, 4651; **artifacts**, 4275, 4558*a**; **chief**, Josiah Hill and brother, 4558*a**; **council house**, 4558*a**; **ethnography**, 4558*a**; **names for**, 4559, 4864; **people**: 4558*a**; Sam Patterson and daughter, 4558*a**; **vocabulary**, 4559, 4864
Narraganset, 4037, 4289, 4491*a**, 4605; **dances**, 4071, 4606; **ethnography**, 4491*a**; **people**: Henry Harris, Jim Harris, Abigail Maumee(?), and Rachel Maumee(?), 4491*a**; Miantonomo, Death of, 4865*a**
Naskapi, 4143*a**, 4188*b**, 4278; artifacts, 4188*b**, 4275; divination devices, 4188*b**; dogs, 4188*b**; ethnography, 4188*b**; habitat, 4188*b**; language, 4086, 4169, 4190, 4208, 4665, 4903; masks, 4301; people, 4188*b**; recordings, 4086, 4169, 4190, 4208, 4665, 4903; scapulimancy, 4188*b**. *See also* Cree, Montagnais-Naskapi
Nassau, R. H., corres. with Frank G. Speck, 4662
*Natasquam*, 4188*b**
Natchez, 4020*a*, 4327*a*; vocabulary, 4589
Nathan, Michele, author, 4548*a*; corres. with Whitfield J. Bell, Jr., 4548*a*
Native American, culture, attempts to preserve, 4413; Languages, Committee on Research in, 4269-4270
Natural phenomena, earthquake, Indian reference to, 4212; Kagaba, 4745*a*; Sandia (Tiwa), 4055, 4844. *See also* Months, Seasons, Time expressions
Natural sciences, 4768
Navajo, 4010, 4020*a*, 4165, 4177, 4327*a*, *4560-4582;* **anatomical atlas**, 4582; **biography**: 4570; Elsie Benally, 4083, 4577; **body parts**, 4582; **cognates**, 4113; **conversations**, 4569, 4573; **dictionary**, 4565, 4580; **diseases**, 4022, 4579; **ethnoanatomy**, 4360; **ethnomedicine**, 4022, 4579, 4582; **food taxonomies**, 4582; **informants**: 4563; Elsie Benally, 4577; **kinship**, 4562; **language**, 4012, 4057*b*, 4175-4176, 4349*a*, 4560, 4569-4570, 4572-4574; **linguistics**, 4012, 4022-4023, 4113, 4563-4564, 4568, 4571, 4574-4575, 4578-4579, 4581; **Night Chant**, 4566; **paradigms**, 4574; **people**: Elsa Liza Greymountain and Jackson Greymountain, 4562*; **perception and labeling**, 4560; **phonology**, 4575; **prefixes**, 4574; **recordings**, 4057*b*, 4060, 4083, 4349*a*, 4561, 4577; **semantics**, 4022, 4579; **songs**, 4567; **syntax**,

4563-4564, 4568, 4578; **texts**, 4060, 4561, 4566, 4570, 4572, 4574; **trader Navajo**, 4023, 4581; **vocabulary**, 4022, 4057*b*, 4113, 4349*a*, 4574, 4579
Navajo Mountain, 4562
Negro-Indians, 4613-4614
Nehantic, Charles Mathews, 4539*a**
Neitzel, Stuart, corres. with Frank G. Speck, 4364*a*
Nelson, Dorothy M., corres. with Frank G. Speck, 4305
Neptune, Mrs., corres. with Florence Speck, 4663*a*
Neptune, Sachem John, 4598*a**
Nevin, Bruce E., author, 4128, 4916-4917; corres. with Whitfield J. Bell, Jr., 4128, 4917; donor, 4128, 4916-4917
Nevin, J. M., artist, 4291*b*
Nevome. *See* Pima Bajo
New Brunswick, Canada, 4527*a**
New England, 4143*a**, 4587*a**; cooking, 4294; ethnography, 4143*a**; people, 4587*a**; terrain, 4587*a**
New Fairfield, Ontario, Canada, 4244*a**
Newfoundland, Canada, 4188*b**, 4254*a**, 4527*a**; Labrador, 4108, 4251*a**, 4301*b**, 4590*; map, 4143*a*, 4254*a*
Newhouse, Seth (Mohawk-Onondaga), 4386, 4388, 4405*a**, 4411; **corres. with**: J.N.B. Hewitt, 4405*a*; Arthur C. Parker, 4405, 4408
New Mexico, 4451, 4575*a**, 4798; Anthropology, Laboratory of, Santa Fe, 4312, 4779; archaeology, 4014, 4020*a*, 4327*a*, 4769, 4796*a**; dwellings, 4575*a**; ethnography, 4575*a**; people, 4575*a**. *See also* Pueblos, Taos
New Spain, 4783
New York, 4397*a**, 4727*a**; Allegany State Park, Iroquois seminar, 4407; Cattaraugus Reservation, 4718, 4723; Cornell University, 4025, 4268*b*; Fort William Henry, 4008, 4597; Historical Society, 4214, 4422; history, influence by Iroquois, 4422; Iroquois, 4728; Kinzua Dam, 4386, 4732*; Lake George Indian Village (Iroquois), 4397*a**; Moravian missions among Indians, 4039, 4591; Museum of Primitive Art, 4086, 4169, 4190, 4208; Red House, Iroquois conference, 4228; Rochester Museum of Arts and Sciences, 4395; Six Nations, 4005, 4373; state government and the Seneca, 4732; State Museum and Science Service, Archives, 4408; Tonawanda Reservation, 4006, 4716, 4726-4727
Nez Perce, anthropometric data, 4268*c*; dictionary, 4044, 4592*b*; hymnal, 4029, 4588; linguistics, texts, 4044, 4592*b*
*Nichikun*, 4188*b**
Nicollet, Joseph N., corres. with Samuel G. Morton, 4303
Nida, Eugene A., corres. with John Alden Mason, 4748
Nidever, Mr., 4338
Niedersächische Staats und Universitätsbibliothek, Göttingen, 4037, 4289
Night Chant (Navajo), 4566
Nipmuc, baskets, 4598*a**; Herring Pond Indian Church, Martha's Vineyard, 4598*a**; people, 4598*a**
Nitinat, vocabulary, 4599*a*
Noanama, 4019, 4755
Nootka, *4583-4586*; art, 4586; census, 4586; drawings, 4586; educational materials, 4584; ethnography, 4586; kinship terms, 4766; language, 4584, 4586; linguistics, 4583–4584; manuscript collections, 4585; orthography, 4584; personal and place names, 4586; phonetics, 4584; phonology, 4584; texts, 4585; vocabulary, 4599*a*
North America, 4020*b**, *4587-4593*; early man in, 4589*b*; genetic relationships, 4339; languages, 4267; language families, 4593; linguistics, 4039*a*, 4592-4593; migration routes from Asia to, 4293*a*, 4589*b*; Moravian missions, 4039, 4591; sign language, 4029, 4588; United Church Board for World Ministries, 4047, 4592*c*; vocabularies, 4045, 4516, 4592. See also specific countries and regions
*North American Indians*, 4179*a*, 4865*b*
North Carolina, Cherokee, 4010, 4165, 4332; Iroquois, 4371; *Machapunga*, 4301*b**; Pasquotank River, 4688*a**; University of, 4860-4861
North Dakota, Fort Berthold Reservation, 4054, 4344, 4485; Fort Totten, 4065, 4204*a*
Northeast, *4594-4598a*; artifacts, 4595, 4598*a**; ethnography, 4598*a**; history, 4598; Indian-White relations, 4594, 4596; *Weetamoo*, 4598*a**
Northern Arizona University, Department of Anthropology, donor, 4006*a*, 4023*a*, 4057*b*, 4097*a*, 4349*a*-4349*b*, 4363*a*-4363*b*
Northern Tepehuan. *See* **Tepehuan, Northern**
North Pacific Coast, art, 4586*a*; legends, 4174, 4472, 4854; myths, 4174; Raven-Clan Outlaws, 4002, 4853. See also *Northwest Coast*
*Northumberland County Historical Society Proceedings*, 4654
Northwest Coast, 4274*a*, *4599-4602a*, 4599*, 4601*a**; artifacts, 4275; Franz Boas' activities, 4026, 4600, 4602; ethnography, 4026, 4600; European exhibits, 4252; languages, 4003*b*, 4026, 4248, 4599*a*, 4600; manuscript collections, 4599, 4601; manuscripts, 4252; museum collections, 4601; museums, 4252; people, 4601*a**. *See also* North Pacific Coast
Northwestern University Library, donor, 4003*b*, 4268*c*, 4504*b*, 4599*a*.
Northwest (Pacific) Tribal Languages, dictionaries, grammars, texts, and vocabularies, 4044, 4592*b*
North West Territories, Canada, Baffin Island (Baffin Land), 4003*b*, 4097, 4251*a**, 4255; Baker Lake, Cambridge Bay, Coppermine, and Eskimo Point, 4097, 4255; Fort Good

Hope, 4046, 4087, 4236-4238; Keewatin, 4251*a**; Rankin Inlet, 4097, 4255; Southampton Island, 4251*a**
Norton, Jeanette Young, correspondence with Frank G. Speck, 4306
*Notable American Women, 1609-1950*, 4398
Nova Scotia, Canada, 4143*a**, 4527*a**; Micmac, 4143*a**, 4598*a**
Numerals, Cayuga (Seneca), 4001, 4712; Hopi, 4057*b*, 4097*a*, 4349*a*, 4363*a*; Tuscarora, 4076, 4863; Uto-Aztecan, 4874; Yakima Sahaptin, 4701; Yaqui, 4920
Nutini, Hugo G., author, 4521; corres. with Whitfield J. Bell, Jr., 4521; donor, 4521
Nuttall, Zelia Maria Magdalena, author, 4307
*Nyenyek'a*, Keresan mask, 4455

Oak, Liston M., corres. with Frank G. Speck, 4308-4309
Oakupovi, 4759*a**
Oaxaca, Mexico, 4504*a**; Highland Chontal, 4542; Juzgado Archives of Teposcolula, 4520*b*; San Matias Petacaltepec, 4093, 4545
Ocuiltec, vocabulary, 4525
Oertel, J. A., artist, 4291*b*, 4865*a*
Office of Anthropology, Smithsonian Institution, 4026, 4248, 4600
Office of Indian Affairs, 4589
Ogden Company, treaty with Tonawandas, 4717
Ogden, Thomas, 4732
Oglala, 4194*a**, 4206; anthropometric data, 4268*c*; *attire*, 4194*a**; *dance*, 4207; *dwellings*, 4682*f**; *ethnography*, 4194*a**, 4207; *music*, 4207; *people*: 4194*a**, 4682*f**; Philip Iron Elk, Lays Hard, Nellie Lays Hard, Leading Charger, and Spotted Tail, 4194*a**. *See also* Dakota
Ohio, burial sites, 4303*a*; Gnadenhütten, Christian Indian Monument, 4244*a**; Moravian missions among Indians, 4039, 4591; Schönbrunn, Moravian village, 4244*a**; Shawnees, 4337; Valley, mounds, 4280
*Ohnedagowah*, annual pageant, 4391, seventh annual pageant, 4390
Ojibwa, 4012*a**, 4020*a*, 4038*, 4071-4072, 4327*a*, 4602*b**, *4602b-4610*, 4603*a**, 4605*, 4609*, 4609*a**-4609*b**; anthropometric data, 4268*c*; *artifacts*, 4012*a**, 4603*a**; *bands*, list of, 4012*a*, 4603*a*; comparative vocabulary, 4109*d*; *canoes*, 4012*a**, 4603*a**, 4609*a**; *ceremonies*, 4038*, 4609*; *chief*, White Bear (Temagami), 4609*a**; *contents of recordings*, 4605; *corn dance*, 4038*, 4609*; *cradle board*, 4301*b**; *crafts*, 4038*, 4609*; *culture*, 4610; *customs*, 4012*a*, 4603*a*; *dances*, 4038*, 4071-4072, 4605*, 4606-4607, 4609*; *dance to the four winds*, 4038*, 4609*; *dreams*, 4610; *dwellings*, 4012*a**, 4603*a**; *education*, 4604; *ethnography*, 4012*a**, 4038*, 4603*a**, 4605*, 4609*, 4609*a**, 4863; *festivals*, 4012*a*, 4603*a*; *games*, 4012*a*, 4603*a*; *geographical distribution*, 4012*a*, 4603*a*; *government*, 4012*a*, 4603*a*; *history*, 4610; *informants*: George Brown, 4071, 4607; Willie Catfish, 4072, 4607-4608; Fred Lacasse and John Martin, 4072, 4607; Jim Pontiac, 4610; *interviews*, 4605, 4610; *kinship*, 4603; *language*, 4012*a*, 4603*a*; *linguistics*, 4012*a*, 4603*a*; *missions to*, 4047, 4592*c*; *music*, 4605; *mythology*, 4012*a*, 4603*a*; *myths*, 4610; *parade*, 4038*, 4609*; *partridge dance*, 4038*, 4609*; *people*, 4012*a**, 4603*a**, 4609*a**; *recordings*, 4071-4072, 4606-4607; *religion*, 4071, 4606; *round dance*, 4038*, 4609*; *snake dance*, 4038*, 4609*; *social organization*, 4603; *songs*, 4072, 4607-4608; *speeches*, 4071, 4606; *stomp dance*, 4038*, 4609*; *transcripts of recordings*, 4608; *villages*, Upper Peninsula, 4610; *vocabulary*, 4012*a*, 4603*a*; *war dance*, 4038*, 4609*. *See also* Algonquin, Chippewa, Ottawa, Saulteaux
Oka, anthropometric data, 4268*c*
Okanagan, 4096, *4611-4612*; *dictionary*, 4044; 4592*b*; *Colville*: language, 4044, 4592*b*; linguistics, 4044, 4592*b*; texts, 4044, 4592*b*; *contents of recordings*, 4611; *recordings*, 4096, 4612; *songs*, 4096, 4611-4612; *stories*, 4096, 4611-4612; *vocabulary*, 4599*a*, 4611
Oklahoma, 4605, *4612a-4616a*, 4727*a**; *buffalo dance*, 4081, 4616; *ceremonies*, 4081, 4616; *Cherokee*, 4010, 4079, 4165, 4168; *Chiwere*, 4179; *contents of recordings*, 4223, 4616*a*; *Craterville Park*, 4682*c**; *Creek Nation*, 4546*a*, 4743*a*, 4922*a*; *dances*, 4081, 4616; *Delaware Indians*, 4080, 4218, 4221*a*, 4222-4223, 4225; *ethnography*, 4081, 4615-4616; *gourd dances*, 4081, 4616; *Indian*: ethics, 4615; honor, 4615; village, 4612*a**; *McCloud*, 4256*a**; *Moravian missions among Indians*, 4039, 4591; *Negro-Indians*, 4613-4614; *Pan-Indianism*, 4207; *Ponca wedding dance*, 4081, 4616; *recordings*, 4081, 4222, 4616; *Seneca-Cayuga*: ceremonialism, 4728; compared with eastern Iroquois, 4728; contact with eastern Iroquois, 4728; ethnography, 4728; green corn stomp, 4081, 4616; *snake dance*, 4081, 4616; *songs*, 4081, 4223, 4616; *stomps*, 4081, 4616; *Thlewarle Indian Baptist Church*, 4547; *war dances*, 4081, 4616. *See also* Indian Territory
Oklahoma Territory, Black Bear Creek, Pawnee Camp, 4648*a**
Okrand, Marc, author, 4137*a*; corres. with Whitfield J. Bell, Jr., 4137*a*.
Olson, Donald, collector, 4077, 4172; compiler, 4173; donor, 4077, 4172-4173
Olson, Ronald L., compiler, 4039*a*, 4592
Omaha, anthropometric data, 4268*c*; *chief*, *Ong Pa Ton Ga*, 4589*a**; *ethnography*, 4231*a**; *people*: 4231*a**; *Exákaská* 'White Horn (Elk)', 4231*a**. *See also* Dhegiha
Omens, Catawba, 4020*c*, 4148*b*

Onate expedition, 4782
Ónabas, Sonora, Mexico, 4056, 4674, 4676
Oneida, 4397*a**, 4651; in American Revolution, 4393; anthropometric data, 4268*c*; names for Nanticokes, 4559, 4864, people, 4865*b**
Onondaga, 4010, 4165, 4397*a**; education, 4016, 4720; ethnography, 4721; ethnohistory, 4016, 4720; grammar and dictionary, 4033, 4238*a*; Indians, correspondence, 4016, 4720; land, 4016, 4720; language, 4039, 4396, 4591; linguistics, 4033, 4238*a*, 4715, 4721; names for Nanticokes, 4559, 4864; phonology, 4715; politics, 4016, 4720; religion, 4713; sacrifice of tortoise, 4713; semantics, 4715; travel, 4016, 4720; vocabulary, 4714. *See also* Seneca
Ontario, Canada, 4188*a**, 4188*b**, 4397*a**, 4609*b**, 4727*a**; *Chippewa*, 4071, 4606; *Grand River Reserve* (Tuscarora), 4864*a**; *Iroquois*, 4413, 4728; *Lake Temagami*, 4609 *a**; *Longlac*, 4145; *Moravian missions among Indians*, 4039, 4591; *Nanticoke*, 4558*a**; *New Fairfield*, 4244*a**; *Scarboro*, Iroquois monument, 4413; *Six Nations Reserve*: 4213*a**, 4229, 4397*a**; Smoothtown, 4225*c*
Opata, Arivechi, lexicostatistics, 4887; cognates, 4884; comparative vocabulary, 4884; Huepec, lexicostatistics, 4887
Opi, 4447
Oral literature, Delaware, 4211; Indian, 4211; Papago, 4047*b*, 4622*b*; Pima, 4047*b*, 4622*b*
Oregon, 4137*b**; Celilo, 4892, 4907; Umatilla Indian Reservation, 4040, 4701*a*; Warm Springs, 4892, 4907; Warm Springs Reservation, 4894, 4908
Oregon Province Archives, Indian Language Collection, 4043-4044, 4107*a*, 4592*b*
Origin, American Indian, 4272
Orinoco, 4759*a**
Orthography, Aztec, 4880; Canada, 4256; Cherokee syllabary, 4028, 4163; Cheyenne, 4173; Eskimo, 4256; Fox, 4904; Jivaro, 4434; Nootka, 4584; Otomi, 4617-4618; Papago, 4637; Pima Bajo, 4675; Quiché-Maya, 4037*a*, 4693*a*; Southern Tepehuan, 4816; Winnebago, 4904
Osage, 4231*a**, 4592*a**; *camps*, 4231*a**; *cognates*, 4178, 4232; *dances*, 4231*a**; *dwellings*, 4231*a**; *ethnography*, 4231*a**; *linguistics*, 4178, 4232; *missions to*, 4047, 4592*c*; *people*: 4231*a**, 4865*b**; Grétomih, Kishagashugah, Marchanthitahtoongah, Minckchatahooh, Myhangah, and Washingasbha, 4589*a**; warrior, 4291*b**. *See also* Dhegiha
Osborne, Lilly de Jongh, 4153
Osceola (Seminole), 4291*a**
Osgood, Cornelius, *corres. with*: Elsie Clews Parsons, 4311; Frank G. Speck, 4663
Ostrander, H. J., *corres. with*: E. G. Conklin, University of Chicago, and Frederick Woodward, 4572
Oto, 4178*a**; attire, 4178*a**; ceremony, 4081, 4616; contents of recording, 4223, 4616*a*; dance, 4081, 4616; ethnography, 4081, 4178*a**, 4616; game, 4081, 4616; language, 4177*a*, 4179; people, 4178*a**; recordings, 4081, 4616; song, 4081, 4616. *See also* Chiwere, Iowa
Oto-Manguean, linguistics, 4152; vocabulary, 4526
Otomi, 4048, 4496, *4617-4622*; anecdotes, 4050, 4621; contents of recording, 4617; folk tales, 4050, 4621; informant, Jesús Salinas Pedraza, 4049, 4620; Ixmiquilpan, Hidalgo, Mexico, local history, 4050, 4621; jokes, 4622; language, 4049, 4617, 4620; linguistics, 4617; orthography, 4617-4618; recordings, 4049-4050, 4620-4621; sexual humor, 4622; songs, 4050, 4621; stories, 4049-4050, 4620-4621; taxonomy of sexual humor, 4622; texts, 4049-4050, 4617, 4620-4621; vocabulary, 4525
Ottawa, 4609*b**, 4651; *artifacts*, 4609*b**; *ceremonies*, 4609*b**; *people*: 4609*b**; Pontiac, 4291*b**. *See also* Ojibwa
Ottawa, Kansas, 4256*a**
Otto, *see* Oto, Chiwere, Iowa
Owen, Sir Richard, corres. with Mrs. Deuman, 4310
Oxford University, England, Ashmolean Museum, 4598*a*; Pitt Rivers Museum, 4334

Pacific Northwest. Indian Center, Spokane, Wash., 4043-4044, 4107*a*, 4592*b*; Tribal Languages, manuscript collection, 4044, 4592*b*
Paintings, George Catlin, 4587*b**; Cayuga, 4714*a**; Delaware, 4213*a**; John Fadden (Mohawk), 4533-4534; Iroquois, 4397*a**; Native Americans, 4016*a**; Oklahoma village, 4612*a**; Pawnee, 4648*a**; Plains, 4682*e*. *See also* drawings, engravings, pictures, postal cards, sketches
Paiute, 4877; songs, 4052, 4349. *See also* Southern Paiute, Ute
Palenque, Chiapas, Mexico, 4504*a**, 4521*a**; archaeology, 4521*a**; artifacts, 4521*a**; crypt, 4521*a**
Paleontology, 4003*a*, 4004, 4268*a*
Palmer, Ralph S., corres. with Frank G. Speck, 4188*a*
Pame, vocabulary, 4525
Pampticangs, 4558
Pamunkey, 4688*b**; artifacts, 4275, 4688*b**; dances, 4688*b**; dwellings, 4688*b**; fishing, 4688*b**; habitat, 4688*b**; people, 4688*b**; vocabulary, 4688*b*
Panama, 4149*a**, 4739*a**; animal specimens, 4310; archaeology, 4157*a*, 4331*a*; ethnography, 4149*a**, 4739*a**
Pan-Indianism, Pan-Tetonism, 4207
Papago, 4017, 4293*a*, 4331*a*, 4334*a*, 4518*, *4622a-4641a*, 4690, 4814, 4869*a*, 4876-4877,

4888; *abstract of recording*, 4622*a*; *archaeology*, 4634; *cognates*, 4640, 4821, 4884; *comparative vocabulary*, 4821, 4884, 4887; *comparisons with Tepecano*, 4630, 4634; *contents of notebook* (Juan Dolores), 4638; *coyote story*, 4629; *ethnography*, 4634; *folkmedicine*, 4047*b*, 4622*b*; *historical linguistics*, 4884; *informants*: Listo Antone and Lupe Antone, 4047*b*, 4622*b*; Miguel Garcia, 4626; Juan Gregorio, Maila Kelaila, Ligali (Mrs. Masi Loin), Baptisto Lopez and family, Mendes Lopez, Jose Manol, Arturo Mendez, Chico Moreno, Jose Pancho, and Frances Ventura, 4047*b*, 4622*b*; Jose Ventura, 4007, 4047*b*, 4622*b*, 4625; Rosana Ventura, 4047*a*, 4622*b*; *kinship terms*, 4630, 4633; *language*, 4007, 4624-4625, 4629-4631, 4633-4635, 4637, 4639, 4641*a*, 4869*a*-4869*b*; *lexicostatistics*, 4887; *linguistics*, 4007, 4623, 4625, 4627-4629, 4631-4633, 4636, 4639-4641, 4880; *morphology*, 4629, 4640; *myths*, 4047*b*, 4622*b*, 4638; *Northern Tepehuan cognates*, 4821; *oral literature*, 4047*b*, 4622*b*; *orthography*, 4637; *paradigms*, 4633, 4639; *phonology*, 4333, 4641, 4880; *placenames*, 4333*a*; *pronouns*, 4639; *recordings*, 4047*b*, 4622*b*; *sand paintings*, 4047*b*, 4622*b*; *songs*, 4047*b*, 4622*b*, 4634, 4638; *speeches*, 4047*b*, 4622*b*; *stories*, 4007, 4625; *Tepecano cognates*, 4821; *texts*, 4007, 4047*b*, 4622*b*, 4624-4626, 4629-4630, 4635; *vocabulary*, 4516, 4630, 4632, 4636; *war orations*, 4047*b*, 4622*b*

Papago Reservation, 4575*a**; *Ak Cin* and *Sikol Himadk*, Arizona, 4047*b*, 4622*b*

Paparo, 4019, 4755

Paradigms, *see* specific languages and language families

Parapsychology, 4333*a*

Parintintin, 4746; people, 4759*a**

Park, Willard Z., corres. with John Alden Mason, 4755*a*

Parker, Arthur C., 4020*a*, 4327*a*, 4537; *corres. with*: Seth Newhouse, 4405, 4408; Frank G. Speck, 4407; Paul A. W. Wallace, 4021, 4406; *photographer*, 4405*a*

Parker, Ely S., 4422, 4727; *author*, 4409-4410, 4537; *corres. with*: W. P. Angel, 4726; Joseph Fellows, 4717; Henry W. Johnson, 4719; Henry R. Schoolcraft, 4724-4725

Parker, William, *corres. with*: J. H. Martindale, 4722; Henry S. Randall, 4727

Parker Collection, American Philosophical Society, 4415

Parks, Douglas, author, 4647; collector, 4078, 4648; donor, 4078, 4648

Parry, Francis, corres. with Henry Phillips, 4522

Parsons, Elsie Clews, 4020*a*, 4311-4312, 4327*a*, 4331*a*, 4358-4359, 4453, 4771, 4775-4778, 4783-4784, 4786-4787, 4797-4798, 4800, 4848, 4930; *author*, 4845; *corres. with*: Bernard W. Aginsky, Ruth Benedict, Frank Calcott, John W. Cooper, D. S. Davidson, Fred Eggan, Aurelio M. Espinosa, Jr., Ann H. Grayton, A. Irving Hallowell, Melville J. Herskovits, George Herzog, Hamilton Holt, Dorothy L. Keur, Clyde Kluckhohn, Paul S. Martin, John Alden Mason, H. Scudder Mekeel, Cornelius Osgood, Juan B. Rael, and Robert Redfield, 4311; Edward Sapir, 4441, 4667; F. M. Setzler, Marian Smith, Leslie Spier, Bernhard J. Stern, William Duncan Strong, and Stith Thompson, 4311; Mischa Titiev, 4440; George C. Vaillant, Bella Weitzner, and Edward M. Weyer, 4311; Leslie A. White, 4311-4312, 4358-4359, 4363, 4442-4469, 4523, 4756-4757, 4770-4800, 4846-4848, 4930; Clark Wissler, 4311

Passamaquoddy, *4642-4645*, 4642*c**, 4663*a**; beadwork, 4598*a**; bird names (Malecite), 4645; language, paradigms, 4642-4642*b*: people. Lola Mohawk and Mary Selmore, 4642*c**; Pleasant Point Indian Village, Eastport, Maine, 4642*c**; vocabulary, 4642-4642*a*, 4645; wampum records, 4643-4644; witchcraft tales, 4644

Patagonian, *4646*; people, 4759*a**; vocabulary, 4646

Pathology, eastern U.S. Indians, 4161. *See also* diseases, medicine

Paul, C. F., corres. with Frank G. Speck, 4663*a*

Paul Wilhelm, Duke of Wurtemburg, corres., 4313

Pawnee, 4020*a*, 4327*a*, 4592*a**, *4647-4649*, 4648*a**; *camp*, 4648*a**; *ceremony*, 4081, 4616; *chief*, Tom Morgan, 4648*a**; *contents of recording*, 4223, 4616*a*; *dance*, 4081, 4616, 4648*a**; *ethnography*, 4081, 4616; *informants*: Sam Allen, Harry Cummings, and Phillip Jim, 4078, 4648; *linguistics*, 4649; *missions to*, 4047, 4592*c*; *morphology*, 4649; *people*: 4648*a**; Pet-A-Le-Shar-Ro, 4589*a**; *recordings*, 4078, 4081, 4616, 4648; *Skiri texts*, 4078, 4648; *songs*, 4081, 4616; *South Band*: dialect, 4649; texts, 4078, 4648; *texts*, 4078, 4648

Pawtuxet, *Tisquantum* (*Squanto*), 4291*a**

Payne, John Howard, 4164; author, 4167

Peabody Museum, 4140

Peale, ———, 4320

Peale, Benjamin Franklin, corres. with Titian Ramsay Peale, 4314-4318

Peale, Charles Willson, 4290

Peale, Rembrandt, corres. with Alexander von Humboldt, 4290

Peale, Titian Ramsay, corres. with Benjamin Franklin Peale, 4314-4318

Pedraza, Jesús Salinas, corres. with Whitfield J. Bell, Jr., 4618

Pemaquid Indians, 4273

Penn, John, 4424

Penn, William, Treaty with the Indians, 4865*a**

Pennsylvania, *4650-4655*; *Bryn Mawr College*, 4221*a*, 4615; *chief*, Running Wolf, 4652*a**; *dowsing*, 4652*a**; *Fort Pitt*, 4594, 4652; *Hav-*

*erford College*, 4042, 4320, 4328, 4415; Historical Society of Pennsylvania, 4415; *history*, 4246; *Indians of*, 4295; *Indian trails*, 4653-4654; *Indian Training School*, Carlisle Barracks, people, 4273*a**; *literary history*, 4211; *Moravian Church*, archives, 4039, 4591; Northumberland County Historical Society, 4654; *petroglyphs*, 4589*a**, 4652*a**; *Philadelphia*: College of Physicians, 4161, 4212-4213, 4262-4267, 4283, 4476, 4558, 4713-4714; property owned by Six Nations, 4401; State of, corres. with Frank G. Speck, 4225; *Susquehanna River*, 4220, 4652*a*; University of, 4013, 4296, 4603, 4802; correspondence with Werner Mueller, 4688; Department of Anthropology, donor, 4017; University Museum, 4339*a*, 4524*a*, 4664, 4749; *Wilkes-barre*, Massacre at, 4650*a**; *Wyoming*: 4220; Battle of, 4655; Massacre of, 4865*a**; *York*, 4335

Pennsylvania Historical Commission, 4651

Penobscot, 4223*a*, 4273, 4644, *4656-4665*, 4663*a**; art, 4658; artifacts, 4275, 4663*a**; attire, 4663*a**; beadwork, 4598*a**; carrying basket, 4281; chiefs, 4658; clans, 4658; culture, 4660; economic life, 4657; ethnography, 4660, 4662, 4663*a**; habitat, 4663*a**; history, 4660; language, 4086, 4169, 4190, 4208, 4659, 4665, 4903; linguistics, 4659; manuscript, 4657, 4662, 4664; missions to, 4047, 4592*c*; mortuary customs, 4223*a*; paradigms, 4659; *Penobscot, Man*, 4661, 4663, 4663*a*, *Transformer Texts*, 4656; people, Clara Paul, 4663*a**; recordings, 4086, 4169, 4190, 4208, 4665, 4903; social life, 4657; stories, 4662; texts, 4659; vocabulary, 4659

Penutian, 4339, *4666*, 4880; linguistics, 4152

People, 4020*b**, 4291*a**, 4291*b**, 4301*b**, 4589*a**; *Achumawi*, 4137*b**; *Acoma*, 4796*a**; *Algonquin*, 4602*b**; *Apache*, 4796*a**; *Arapaho*, 4682*f**; *Arizona*, 4575*a**; *Assiniboin*, 4194*a**, 4682*e**; *Aztec*, 4291*a**; *Beothuk-Micmac*, 4595*a**; *Blackfoot*, 4130*a**, 4682*d**; *Blood*, 4130*a**; *British Columbia*, 4601*a**; *California*, 4132*a**, 4137*b**; *Canada*, 4143*a**, 4143*b**, 4587*a**; *Catawba*, 4148*a**, 4688*d**; *Cayuga*: 4714*a**; terms for, 4001, 4712; *Central America*, 4149*a**, 4504*a**, 4739*a**; *Chasta Costa*, 4137*b**; *Cherokee*, 4162*a**, 4865*b**; *Cheyenne*, 4171*a**, 4273*a**, 4865*b**; *Chickahominy*, 4273*a**, 4301*b**, 4687*a**; *Chinook*, 4865*b**; *Chippewa*, 4865*b**; *Coast Athapascan*, 4137*b**; *Comanche*, 4587*b**; *Cree*, 4188*a**, 4188*b**, 4190*a**; *Creek*, 4273*a**, 4546*a**, 4732*a**, 4922*; *Crow*, 4682*b**; *Cuna*, 4149*b**; *Dakota*, 4194*a**, 4587*b**, 4682*e**, 4682*f**, 4737*a**; *Delaware*, 4213*a**, 4865*b**; *Eskimo*, 4251*, 4251*a**, 4254*a**; *Flat Head*, 4865*b**; *Fox*, 4291*a**; *Gros Ventre*, 4682*e**; *Hare*, 4234*a**; *Hopi*, 4351*a**; *Houma*, 4364*a**; *Hupa*, 4132*a**; *Indian Training School*, Carlisle Barracks, Pennsylvania, 4273*a**; *Iowa*, 4589*a**; *Iroquois*, 4388*a**, 4397*a**, 4405*a**; *Isleta*, 4796*a**; *Kansa*, 4231*a**; *Kiowa*, 4865*b**; *Kiowa Apache*, 4682*c**; *Kutenai*, 4682*d**; *Kwakiutl*, 4319*a**; *Laguna*, 4273*a**, 4796*a**; *Lipan*, 4273*a**; *Little Lake Pomo*, 4132*a**; *Machapunga*, 4148*a**, 4301*b**; *Maricopa*, 4698*b**; *Mashpee*, 4598*a**; *Mattaponi*, 4687*b**; *Menomini*, 4245*a**, 4865*b**; *Mexico*, 4504*a**, 4520*; *Micmac*, 4527*a**; *Miwok*, 4137*b**; *Mohawk*, 4397*a**, 4536*a**; *Mohegan*, 4539*a**, 4539*b**, 4865*b**; *Moki*, 4351*a**; *Montagnais-Naskapi*, 4188*b**; *Montgomery Creed*, 4137*b**; *Musquakie*, 4256*a**; *Nansemond*, 4688*a**; *Nanticoke*, 4558*a**; *Narraganset*, 4491*a**, 4865*a**; *Native American*, 4016*a**, 4020*b**, 4291*a**, 4291*b**, 4301*b**, 4393*, 4589*a**; *Navajo*, 4562*; *New England*, 4143*a**, 4587*a**, 4598*a**; *New Mexico*, 4575*a**; *Nipmuc*, 4598*a**; *Northeast*, 4291*a**, 4301*b**, 4590*a**; *Northwest Coast*, 4601*a**; *Oglala*, 4194*a**, 4682*f**; *Ojibwa*, 4012*a**, 4602*b**, 4603*a**, 4609*a**, 4609*b**, 4865*b**; *Omaha*, 4231*a**; *Oneida*, 4865*b**; *Ontario*, 4244*a**; *Oregon*, 4137*b**; *Osage*, 4231*a**, 4291*b**, 4589*a**, 4865*b**; *Oto*, 4178*a**; *Ottawa*, 4291*b**, 4609*b**; *Pamunkey*, 4688*b**; *Parintintin*, 4759*a**; *Passamaquoddy*, 4642*c**; *Patagonian*, 4759*a**; *Pawnee*, 4589*a**, 4648*a**; *Pawtuxet*, 4291*a**; *Penobscot*, 4663*a**; *Peoria*, 4273*a**; *Piegan*, 4130*a**, 4682*d**; *Plains*, 4682*e**, 4682*f**; *Pokagon* (Potawatomi), 4598*a**; *Potomac*, 4688*c**; *Powhatan*, 4291*a**, 4291*b**, 4301*b**, 4590*a**, 4865*a**; *Pueblo*, 4273*a**; *Rappahannock*, 4688*d**; *Rio Colorado*, 4796*a**; *Salivan*, 4759*a**; *San Carlos Apache*, 4703*a**; *San Felipe*, 4273*a**; *Santee*, 4194*a**; *Sarsi*, 4708*a**; *Sauk*, 4256*a**; *Scatticook*, 4598*a**; *Seminole*, 4291*a**, 4549*a**, 4865*b**; *Seneca*: 4727*a**, 4865*b**; terms for, 4001, 4712; *Shawnee*, 4291*a**, 4291*b**, 4546*a**, 4732*a**, 4865*a**, 4865*b**, 4922*; *Shoshoni*, 4301*b**, 4590*a**, 4682*d**; *Sioux*, 4273*a**, 4587*b**, 4737*a**; *South America*, 4149*a**, 4739*a**, 4759*a**; *Stockbridge-Munsee*, 4540*a**; *Takelma*, 4137*b**; *Têtes de Boule*, 4190*a**; *Tunica*, 4763*a**; *Tuscarora*, 4558*a**, 4864*a**, 4865*b**; *Tutelo*, 4246*a**; *Ute*, 4273*a**, 4766*a**; *Wampanoag*, 4291*a**, 4291*b**, 4491*a**, 4865*a**; *Wichita*, 4900*a**; *Winnebago*, 4865*b**, 4904*a**; *Wintun*, 4132*a**; *Yana*, 4132*a**, 4137*b**; *Yuchi*, 4546*a**, 4732*a**, 4922*; *Yuki*, 4132*a**; *Yurok*, 4132*a**; *Zuni*, 4273*a**. See also *chiefs*, *pictures*, as well as specific tribes and names of individuals.

Peoria, people, 4273*a**

Pequot, 4291*b**, 4540; mortar, 4539*b**; people, 4539*b**

Perkins, Ellavina, author, 4571; donor, 4571

Person markers, Aymara, 4121; Cayuga (Sen-

eca), 4001, 4712; Choctaw, 4180; Galice, 4259; Jaqi, 4121; Papago, 4639; Wichita, 4009, 4897; Yakima Sahaptin. See also specific languages

Peru, 4149*a**, 4519*, 4739*a**, 4759; ancient civilizations, 4752; Andes, 4759*a**; artifacts, 4749; Aymara tomb, 4303*a**; clanship, 4523, 4757; dialects of, 4741; ethnography, 4149*a**, 4739*a**; languages of, 4741; preconquest culture and history, 4749; silver statuette, 4301*a**

Pesqueira, Fernando, corres. with John Alden Mason, 4687

*Pet-A-Le-Shar-Ro* (Pawnee), 4589*a**

Petitot, E. F. S. J., corres. with Robert Bell, 4003a, 4268*a*

Petroglyphs, 4301*b**, 4590*a**; Pennsylvania, 4589*a**, 4652*a**; West Virginia, 4589*a**

Petrullo, V. M., photographer, 4759*a*

Peyote, 4590; songs (Ponca), 4072, 4607

Peyotism, Menomini, 4245*a*

Philadelphia, Pa., College of Physicians, 4161, 4212-4213, 4262-4267, 4283, 4476, 4558, 4713-4714; property owned by Six Nations, 4401

Phillips, Henry, Jr., corres. with: Francis Parry, 4522; Hugo von Meltzel, 4319

Phonetics, Kokama, 4471; Nootka, 4584; Tiwa, 4842; Shawnee, 4734*a*

Phonology, Abipon, 4099; Columbian, 4184; Dakota, 4205; Delaware, 4225*d*; Eskimo, 4256; Jalapa Mazatec, 4501; Mandan, 4486; Matlatzinca, 4495; Nahua, 4555-4556; Navajo, 4575; Nootka, 4584; Onondaga, 4715; Papago, 4333, 4641, 4880; Pima Bajo, 4677; Sandia, 4843; San Miguel Nahua, 4556; Shawnee, 4734*a*; Tiwa, 4843; Tfalati Kalapuya, 4857; Uto-Aztecan, 4875-4876, 4878, 4883; 4888; Wenatchee, 4184; Wichita, 4898; Winnebago, 4904; Yavapai, 4069, 4866*a*; Yuki, 4926; Zacapoaxtla (Nahua), 4555

Phonotactics, Delaware, 4225*d*; Uto-Aztecan, 4875, 4878

Photographs, *see* pictures

Pia, J. Joseph, corres. with Richard H. Shryock, 4765

Pickering, John, 4282, 4321

Pictures, 4010, 4016*a*, 4017, 4020*b*, 4021, 4311; *Abenaki*: 4663*a**; village, Pierreville, Quebec, 4143*b**; *Acoma*, 4796*a**; *Alaska*, Eskimo, 4251*a**; *Algonquin*, 4602*b**; *Allegheny River*, Seneca, 4732*; *Amazon basin*, 4149*a**, 4739*a**; *Annawan's Rock*, Taunton, Massachusetts, 4598*a**; *Annual Harvest Ceremony*, Yuchi, 4546*a**, 4732*a**, 4922*; *Araucanian*, 4759*a**; *archaeology*: Acoma, 4796*a**; Central America, 4504*a**; Isleta, 4796*a**; Laguna, 4796*a**; Mesa Verde, 4796*a**; Mexico, 4504*a**; Palenque, 4521*a**; Slayton Creek, Delaware, 4518*; *architecture*: Central America, 4504*a**; Hopi, 4351*a**; Mexico, 4504*a**; *Arctic*, Boas, 4319*a**; *Arizona*, 4575*a**; *artifacts*: 4301*b**; Central America, 4504*a*; Cherokee, 4162*a**; Chickahominy, 4687*a**; Delaware, 4213*a**; Greenland, 4251*; Iroquois, 4536*a**; Mattaponi, 4687*b**; Mexico, 4504*a**; Micmac, 4527*a**; Mohegan, 4539*a**; Montagnais-Naskapi, 4188*b**; Nanticoke, 4558*a**; Northeast, 4598*a**; Ojibwa, 4012*a**, 4603*a**; Ottawa, 4609*b**; Palenque, 4521*a**; Pamunkey, 4688*b**; Penobscot, 4663*a**; Plains, 4682*e**; Seneca, 4727*a**; South America, 4759*a**; Tunica, 4763*a**; Tuscarora, 4864*a**; *Assiniboin*, 4194*a**, 4682*e**; *Athabasca River*, Canada, 4143*b**; *Atmore*, Alabama, 4546*a**, 4732*a**, 4922*; *attire*: 4273*a**; Alaska, 4601*a**; Eskimo, 4319*a**; Hopi, 4351*a**; Kiowa Apache, 4682*c**; Mohegan, 4598*a**; Oglala, 4194*a**; Oto, 4178*; Penobscot, 4663*a**; Plains, 4682*e**; *Aztec*, 4301*a**, 4504*a**

Pictures, *ball player*, Sioux, 4587*b**; *bark containers*, Têtes de Boule, 4190*a*; *Barren Ground*, 4188*b**; *Burton W. Bascom*, 4521*a**; *baskets*, Nipmuc, 4598*a**; *Batiscan River*, Quebec, 4143*b**; *Batiscan Summit*, Quebec, 4143*b**; *beadwork*: Iroquois, 4598*a**; Micmac, 4598*a**; Passamaquoddy, 4598*a**; Penobscot, 4598*a**; San Carlos Apache, 4703*a*; *belts*, Choctaw, 4179*b**, 4301*b**; *Beothuk-Micmac*, 4595*a**; *Bersimis*, 4188*b**; *The Big Soldier*, 4589*a**; *birch-bark*: basket, 4301*b**; canoe, Huron, 4397*a**; wigwam, Pokagon, 4598*a**; *Black Bear Creek*, Oklahoma Territory, Pawnee camp, 4648*a**; *Blackfoot*, 4130*a**; *Blood*, 4130*a**; *blowguns*: Houma, 4364*a**; Tunica, 4763*a**; *Franz Boas*: 4319*a**; family, 4319*a**; *boats*, Houma, 4364*a**; *Brazil*, 4759*a*; *Brule*, 4592*a**; *Buffalo Hunt*, Plains, 4682*e**; *calendar stone*, Mexico, 4520*a**; *California*: 4131*, 4137*b**; Indians, 4132*a**; *camps*: Assiniboin, 4682*e**; California, 4132*b**; Gros Ventre, 4682*e**; Micmac, 4598*a**; Oklahoma, 4612*a**; Osage, 4231*a**; Pawnee, 4648*a**; Plains, 4682*e**, 4683*b**; *Canada*: 4020*b**, 4143*a**, 4143*b**, 4301*b**, 4527*a**, 4536*a**, 4558*a**, 4587*a**; Eskimo, 4251*a**; *canoes*, Ojibwa, 4012*a**, 4603*a**, 4609*a**; *Catawba*, 4148*a**, 4688*d**; *George Catlin*, paintings, 4587*b**; *cave scene*, diorama, 4301*b**; *Cayuga*, 4714*a**; *Central America*, 4149*a**, 4504*a**, 4739*a**; *ceremonies*, Ottawa, 4609*b**; *Cherokee*, 4010*, 4148*a**, 4162*a**, 4165*, 4291*b**, 4592*a**; *Cheyenne*, 4171*a**, 4592*a**; *Chichen Itza*, 4500*, 4504*a**; *Chickahominy*, 4687*a**

Pictures, chiefs, *Blackfoot*, Luke Big Turnips and Turned-Up-Nose, 4130*a**; *Blood*, 4130*a**; *Delaware*, James C. Weber (War Eagle), 4213*a**; *Iowa*, 4291*b**; *Iroquois*, Joseph Logan and David Thomas, 4397*a**; *Kaw*, Washunga, 4231*a**; *Kickapoo*, 4291*b**; *Mandan*, Shahaka, 4683*a**; *Mohawk*: Joseph Brant, 4291*a**; Split Cloud(?) Cook, 4536*a**;

*Musquakie*, Peah-Mus-Ka, 4589*a**; *Nanticoke*, Josiah Hill, 4558*a**; *North America*, Sachem John Neptune, 4598*a**; *Ojibwa*, White Bear, 4609*a**; *Omaha*, Ong Pa Ton Ga, 4589*a**; *Pawnee*, Tom Morgan, 4648*a**; *Pennsylvania*, Running Wolf, 4652*a**; *Ponca*, White Eagle, 4682*e**; *Rappahannock*, Big Otter Nelson, 4688*d**; *Scatticook*, Frank Coggswell, 4598*a**; *Sioux*: Hollow Horn Bear, 4737*a**; Sitting Bull, 4291*b**, 4682*e**, 4683*a**; Spotted Tail, 4273*a**; *Tlingit*, Louis Shotridge, 4601*a**; *Winnebago*, Black Snake, 4904*a**

Pictures, *Chihuahua*, Mexico, 4519*; *Chipewyan*, 4143*b**; *Chippewa*, 4592*a**; *Chitimacha*, 4364*a**; *Choctaw*: 4179*a**, 4592*a**; village, Louisiana, 4301*b**; *Christian Indian Monument*, Ohio, 4244*a**; *churches*: Isleta, 4301*a**; Nipmuc, 4598*a**; Ontario, 4244*a**; *clan symbols*, Iroquois, 4377*a**; *cliff dwellings*, Mesa Verde, 4796*a**; *Codex Zoache-Nuttal*, 4529*; *Comalcalco*, 4505*a**; *corn dance*, Michigan, 4038*, 4609*; *corn husk dolls*, Iroquois, 4377*a**; *Council House*, Nanticoke, 4558*a**; *cradle board*, Ojibwa, 4301*b**; *crafts*, Michigan, 4038*, 4609*; *Craterville Park*, Oklahoma, 4682*c**; *Cree*, 4188*a**, 4188*ba**; *Creek*, 4301*b**, 4546*a**, 4590*a**, 4732*a**, 4922*; *Crow*, 4682*b**; *crypt*, Palenque, 4521*a**; *Cuna*, 4149*b**; *dancers*: Iowa, 4682*e**; Ponca, 4682*e**; *dances*: 4358*, 4588*a**; Apache, 4796*a**; Assiniboin, 4682*e**; Gros Ventre, 4682*e**; Hopi, 4351*a**; Ojibwa, 4038*, 4609*; Osage, 4231*a**; Pamunkey, 4688*b**; Pawnee, 4648*a**; Plains, 4682*e**; to the four winds, Michigan, 4038*, 4609*; *daub and wattle houses*, Houma, 4364*a**; *The Death Cry*, 4865*a**; *Death of*: Philip Metacomet, 4865*a**; Miantonomo, 4865*a**; *Delaware*, 4213*a**, 4301*b**, 4590*a**; *Delaware* (state), 4518*, 4558*a**; *divination devices*, 4188*b**; *Dismal Swamp*, Virginia, 4688*a**; *dogs*, Montagnais-Naskapi, 4188*b*; *dowsing*, Pennsylvania, 4652*a**; *Durango*, Mexico, 4515*, 4519*

Pictures, dwellings, *Acoma*, 4796*a**; *Arapaho*, 4682*f**; *Arizona*, 4575*a**; *Central America*, 4149*a**; 4739*a**; *Dakota*, 4682*f**; *Eskimo*, 4251*a**; *Florida Seminole*, 4549*a**; *Houma*, 4364*a**; *Isleta*, 4796*a**; *Kickapoo*, 4256*a**; *Laguna*, 4796*a**; *Mesa Verde*, 4796*a**; *Mexico*, 4520*; *Micmac*, 4598*a**; *New Mexico*, 4575*a**; *Oglala*, 4682*f**; *Ojibwa*, 4012*a**, 4603*a**; *Osage*, 4231*a**; *Pamunkey*, 4688*b**; *Pokagon*, 4598*a**; *Sarsi*, 4708*a**; *Sauk*, 4256*a**; *Scatticook*, 4598*a**; *Seneca*, 4732*; *South America*, 4149*a**, 4739*a**; *Stockbridge-Munsee*, 4540*a**; *Têtes de Boule*, 4190*a**; *Ute*, 4766*a**; *Wichita*, 4900*a**

Pictures, *Eastern United States*, 4301*b**; *Elkton* (northern Plains), 4231*a**; *John Eliot*, 4865*a**; *Eliot Oak*, 4490*a**; *Eskimo*: 4251*a**, 4254*a**; family, 4319*a**; Greenland, 4251*

Pictures, ethnography, 4016*, 4020*b**, 4273*a**, 4301*b**, 4588*a**; *Alaska*, 4601*a**; *Algonquin*, 4602*b**; *Amazon Basin*, 4149*a**, 4739*a**; *Arizona*, 4575*a**; *Assiniboin*, 4194*a**; *Canada*, 4143*a**, 4143*b**, 4188*a**; *Catawba*, 4688*d**; *Central America*, 4149*a**, 4739*a**; *Cherokee*, 4148*a**, 4162*a**; *Chickahominy*, 4687*a**; *Choctaw*, 4179*a**; *Cree*, 4188*a**, 4188*b**, 4190*a**; *Creek*, 4546*a**, 4549*a**, 4732*a**, 4922*; *Crow*, 4682*b**; *Delaware*, 4213*a**; *Eskimo*, 4251*a**, 4254*a**; *Florida*, Seminole, 4549*a**; *Hare*, 4234*a**; *Houma*, 4364*a**; *Hupa*, 4132*a**; *Iroquois*, 4377*a**, 4397*a**; *Kansa*, 4231*a**; *Kickapoo*, 4256*a**; *Little Lake Pomo*, 4132*a**; *Mattaponi*, 4687*b**; *Mexico*; 4520*; *Michigan*, 4038*, 4609*; *Micmac*, 4143*a**, 4527*a**; *Montagnais-Naskapi*, 4188*b**; *Musquakie*, 4256*a**; *Nanticoke*, 4558*a**; *Narraganset*, 4491*a**; *New England*, 4143*a**; *New Mexico*, 4575*a**; *North America*, 4588*a**; *Northeast*, 4598*a**; *Oglala*, 4194*a**; *Ojibwa*, 4012*a**, 4038*, 4603*a**, 4609*, 4609*a**; *Omaha*, 4231*a**; *Osage*, 4231*a**; *Oto*, 4178*a**; *Pamunkey*, 4688*b**; *Panama*, 4149*a**, 4739*a**; *Penobscot*, 4663*a**; *Peru*, 4149*a**, 4739*a**; *Plains*; 4862*e**; *Rappahannock*, 4688*d**; *San Carlos Apache*, 4703*a**; *Santee*, 4194*a**; *Sauk*, 4256*a**; *Seminole*, 4549*a**; *Seneca*, 4727*a**; *Shawnee*, 4546*a**, 4732*a**, 4922*; *South America*, 4149*a**, 4739*a**, 4759*a**; *Southwest*, 4796*a**; *Têtes de Boule*, 4190*a**; *Tunica*, 4763*a**; *Tutelo*, 4246*a**; *Ute*, 4766*a**; *Wampanoag*, 4491*a**; *Wintun*, 4132*a**; *Yana*, 4132*a**; *Yuchi*, 4546*a**, 4732*a**, 4922*; *Yuki*, 4132*a**; *Yurok*, 4132*a**

Pictures, *false face*, Iroquois, 4301*b**, 4397*a**, 4590*a**; *fishing*, Pamunkey, 4688*b**; *Florida*, Seminole, 4549*a**; *formal hair-do*, Hopi, 4351*a**; *Fox*, 4256*a**, 4301*b**, 4590*a**, 4592*a**; *games*: Choctaw, 4179*a**; Tunica, 4763*a**; *Grand River Reserve*, Tuscarora, 4864*a**; *great feather dance*, Iroquois, 4388*a**; *Greenland*: 4254*a**; terrain, 4251*; *Grétomih*, Osage, 4589*a**; *Gros Ventre*, 4682*e**; *habitat*: 4301*b**; Eskimo, 4254*a**; Micmac, 4527*a**; Montagnais-Naskapi, 4188*b**; Nansemond, 4688*a**; Pamunkey, 4688*b**; Penobscot, 4663*a**; Pima Bajo, 4670*; Têtes de Boule, 4190*a**; *Hare*, 4234*a**; *General William Henry Harrison*, 4865*a**; *John G. E. Heckewelder*, 4021, 4244*a**, 4245*; *Herring Pond Indian Church*, Nipmuc, 4598*a**; *George G. Heye*, 4865*a**; *hide tanning*, Tunica, 4763*a**; *Hopi*: 4351*a**; pottery makers, 4355*; *Houma*, 4364*a**, 4763*a**; *hunting*, 4588*a**; *hunting and fishing equipment*: Catawba, 4688*d**; Rappahannock, 4688*d**; *Hupa*, 4132*a**; *Huron*, 4397*a**; *Indian*: Massacre at Wilkesbarre, 4650*a**; Scene, 4598*a**; students' brass band, 4273*a**;

village, Oklahoma, 4612*a**; *Inugsuk*, 4251*; *Iowa*, 4178*, 4232*; *Iroquois*, 4377*a**, 4397*a**; *Isleta*, 4796*a**; *Iztaccihuatl*, 4505*a**; *Jesuit missionaries*, California, 4865*a**

Pictures, *Kansa* (Kaw), 4231*a**; *Kickapoo*, 4256*a**; *Kinzua Dam*, 4732*; *Kiowa Apache*, 4682*c**; *Labrador*, Canada, 4251*a**, 4301*b**, 4590*a**; *Lacandon*, 4505*a**; *Laguna*, 4796*a**; *Lake Drummond*, Virginia, 4688*a**; *Lake George Abenaki*, 4663*a**; *Lake George Indian Village*, New York (Iroquois), 4397*a**; *Lake St. John*, 4188*b**; *Lake Temagami*, Ontario, Canada, 4609*a**; *Landing of Roger Williams*, 4865*a**; *Little Lake Pomo*, 4132*a**; *Long House*: Cayuga, 4714*a**; Iroquois, 4388*a**; Seneca, 4397*a**; Upper Cayuga, 4397*a**; *Louisiana*, 4364*a**; *Macushi*, 4759*a**; *Maine*, 4663*a**; *Malecite*, 4663*a**; *Manitoba*, Canada, 4188*a**; *Mapuche*, 4759*a**; *masks*: Cayuga, 4714*a**; Eskimo, 4251*a**; *John Alden Mason*, 4521*a**; *Massacre of Wyoming*, 4865*a**; *Mato Grosso*, Brazil, 4759*a**; *Mattaponi*, 4687*b**; *Maya*, 4498*, 4504*a**; *Mayan*, 4498*a**, 4500*; *McCloud*, Oklahoma, 4256*a**; *medicine man*: Cree, 4598*a**; curing a patient, 4865*a**; *memorial feast of the dead*, Dakota, 4682*f**; *Menomini*, 4245*a**; *Mexican Picture Chronicle*, 4524*; *Mexico*, 4020*b**, 4498*, 4500*, 4504*a**, 4515*, 4518*, 4519*, 4520*, 4520*a**, 4670*, 4671*; *Michigan*: 4609*b**; Indians, 4605*; *Michikamau*, 4188*b**; *Micmac*: 4143*a**, 4527*a**, 4598*a**; 4663*a**; encampment, 4143*a**; *missionaries*, 4865*a**; *Mixtec*, 4504*a**; *Mohawk*: 4397*a**, 4536*a**; village, Oka, Quebec, 4536*a**; *Mohegan*, 4539*a**, 4540*a**; *Moisie*, 4188*b**; *Montagnais-Naskapi*, 4143*a**, 4188*b**; *Moravian village*, Schönbrunn, Ohio, 4244*a**; *Mount Shasta*, California, 4132*b**; *Muhlenberg family*, 4021*; *Munsee*, 4213*a**; *The Murder of Major Waldron*, 4865*a**; *Musquakie*, 4256*a**, 4663*a**; *Museum of Mexico*, 4504*a**

Pictures, *Naked Bear*, 4377*a**; *Nansemond*, 4688*a**; *Nanticoke*, 4558*a**; *Narraganset*, 4491*a**; *Native American*, 4016*a**, 4017*, 4020*b**, 4301*b**; *Natasquam*, 4188*b**; *New Brunswick*, Canada, 4527*a*; *New England*, 4143*a*, 4587*a*; *Newfoundland*, Canada, 4188*b*, 4254*a*, 4527*a*; *New Mexico*, 4575*a*; *New York*, 4397*a*, 4727*a*; *Nichikun*, 4188*b**; *Northwest Coast*, 4599, 4601*a*; *Nova Scotia*, Canada, 4143*a*, 4527*a*; *Oakupovi*, 4759*a**; *Oaxaca*, Mexico, 4504*a*; *Oglala*, 4194*a**; *Ojibwa*, 4012*a**, 4038*, 4071*, 4602*b**, 4603*a**, 4605*, 4606*, 4609*, 4609*a**, 4609*b**; *Oka*, Quebec, Canada, 4397*a**; *Oklahoma*: 4727*a*, village, 4612*a**; *Omaha*, 4231*a**; *Oneida*, 4397*a**; *Onondaga*, 4397*a**; *Ontario*, Canada, 4188*a*, 4188*b*, 4213*a**, 4244*a*, 4397*a*, 4558*a*, 4609*a**, 4609*b*, 4727*a*; *Oregon*, 4137*b*; *Orinoco*, 4759*a**; *Osage*, 4231*a**, 4592*a**; *Osceola*, 4291*a**; *Oto*, 4178*a**; *Ottawa*, 4609*b**; *Ottawa*, Kansas, 4256*a*; *Palenque*, 4505*a**, 4521*a**; *Pamunkey*, 4688*b**; *Panama*, 4149*a*, 4739*a*; *Papago*: 4518*; reservation, 4575*a*; *parade*, Michigan Indians, 4038*, 4609*; *partridge dance*, Michigan, 4038*, 4609*; *Pasquotank River*, North Carolina, 4688*a**; *Passamaquoddy*, 4642*c**, 4663*a**; *Pawnee*, 4592*a**, 4648*a**; *William Penn's Treaty with the Indians*, 4865*a**; *Penobscot*, 4663*a**

Pictures, people, 4016*a**, 4020*b**, 4291*a**, 4291*b**, 4301*b**, 4589*a**; *Achumawi*: Bessie Mike and Lena Patterson, 4137*b**; *Acoma*, 4796*a**; *Algonquin*, 4602*b**; *Apache*, 4796*a**; *Arapaho*, 4682*f**; *Arizona*, 4575*a**; *Assiniboin*, 4194*a**, 4682*e**; *Aztec*: Montezuma, 4291*a**; *Beothuk-Micmac*: Santu and family, 4594*a**; *Blackfoot*: 4130*a**, 4682*d**; Henry Between Lodge, 4130*a**; *Blood*: 4130*a**; Black Plume, 4130*a**; *British Columbia*: Queen Johnnie, 4601*a**; *California*, 4132*a**, 4137*b**; *Canada*, 4143*a**, 4143*b**, 4587*a**; *Catawba*: 4148*a**, 4688*d**; Margaret Wiley Brown and Mrs. Sampson Owl, 4688*d**; *Cayuga*, 4714*a**; *Central America*, 4149*a**, 4504*a**, 4739*a**; *Chasta Costa*: Jack Orton, Stanley Orton, and Wolverton Orton, 4137*b**; *Cherokee*, 4162*a**, 4865*b**; *Cheyenne*: 4171*a**, 4273*a**, 4865*b**; Mad Wolf and Man on Cloud, 4273*a**; John Wicks Okestehei, 4171*a**; *Chickahominy*, 4687*a**; *children in school*, 4273*a**, 4301*b**; *Chinook*, 4865*; *Chippewa*, 4865*b**; *Coast Athapascan*: 4137*b**; John Spencer and sons, 4137*b**; *Comanche*, 4587*b**; *Cree*, 4188*a**, 4188*b**, 4190*a**; *Creek*, 4273*a**, 4546*a**, 4732*a**, 4922*; *Crow*, 4682*b**; *Cuna*, 4149*b**; *Dakota*: 4194*a**, 4587*b**, 4682*f**, 4737*a**; Red Cloud, 4682*e**; *Delaware*: 4213*a**, 4865*b**; James C. Weber (War Eagle), 4213*a**, 4251*; *Eskimo*, 4251*a**, 4254*a**; *Flat Head*, 4865*b**; *Florida Seminole*, 4549*a**; *Fox*: Black Hawk, 4291*a**; *Gros Ventre*, 4682*e**; *Hare*, 4234*a**; *Hopi*, 4351*a**; *Houma*, 4364*a**; *Hupa*, 4132*a**; *Indian Training School*, Carlisle Barracks, Pennsylvania, 4273*a**; *Iowa*: *Shau-Hau-Napo-Tinia*, 4589*a**; *Iroquois*: 4397*a**; John Alexander and Charles A. Cooke, 4397*a**; Handsome Lake, 4388*a**; Mrs. Joseph Logan, 4397*a**; Seth Newhouse, 4405*a**; *Isleta*, 4796*a**; *Kansa*, 4231*a**; *Kiowa*, 4865*b**; *Kiowa Apache*, 4682*c**; *Kutenai*, 4682*d**; *Kwakiutl*: George Hunt and family, 4319*a**; *Laguna*, 4273*a**, 4796*a**; *Lipan*, 4273*a**; *Little Lake Pomo*, 4132*a**; *Machapunga* (North Carolina), 4148*a**, 4301*b**; *Maricopa*, 4698*b**; *Mashpee*, 4598*a**; *Mattaponi*, 4687*b**; *Menomini*: 4245*a**, 4865*b**; Dewey Necomish, Howard Rain, Louis Thunder, and Mitchell Weso, 4245*a**; *Mexico*,

4504*a**, 4520*; *Micmac*, 4527*a**; *Miwok* (Lake County), 4137*b**; *Mohawk*: 4536*a**; Tommy Cook, 4536*a**; John Fadden and Ray Fadden, 4397*a**; *Mohegan*, 4539*a**, 4539*b**, 4865*b**; *Mohegan-Nehantic*, Charles Mathews, 4539*a**; *Moki*, 4351*a**; *Montagnais-Naskapi*, 4188*b**; *Montgomery Creek*: Milford Hill and Ralph Hill, 4137*b**; *Musquakie*, 4256*a**; *Nansemond*, 4688*a**; *Nanticoke*: 4558*a**; Sam Patterson and daughter, 4558*a**; *Narraganset*: 4491*a**; Henry Harris, Jim Harris, Abigail Maumee(?), and Rachel Maumee(?), 4491*a**; Miantonomo, death of, 4865*a**; *Navajo*: Elsa Lisa Greymountain and Jackson Greymountain, 4562*; *New England*: 4143*a**, 4587*a**; Weetamoo, 4598*a**; *New Mexico*, 4575*a**; *Nipmuc*, 4598*a**; *North America*: Samoset, 4291*a**; Maria Tallchief, 4393*a**; Weasel Tail, 4301*b**; Lottie Welsh and daughter, 4301*b**; *Northeast*: Minnehaha, 4301*b**, 4509*a**; *Northwest Coast*, 4601*a**; *Oglala*: 4194*a**, 4692*f**; Philip Iron Elk, Lays Hard, Nellie Lays Hard, Leading Charger, and Spotted Tail, 4194*a**; *Ojibwa*, 4012*a**, 4602*b**, 4603*a**, 4609*a**, 4609*b**, 4865*b**; *Omaha*: 4231*a**; Exákaská 'White Horn (Elk)', 4231*a**; *Oneida*, 4865*b**; *Ontario*, 4244*a**; *Oregon*, 4137*b**; *Osage*: 4231*a**, 4865*b**; Kishagashugah, Marchanthitahtoongah, Minckchatahooh, and Myhangah, 4589*a**; warrior, 4291*b**; Washingasbha, 4589*a**; *Oto*, 4178*a**; *Ottawa*: 4609*b**; Pontiac, 4291*b**; *Pamunkey*, 4688*b**; *Parintintin*, 4759*a**; *Passamaquoddy*: 4642*c**; Lola Mohawk and Mary Selmore, 4642*c**; *Patagonian*, 4759*a**; *Pawnee*: 4648*a**; Pet-A-Le-Shar-Ro, 4589*a**; *Pawtuxet*: Tisquantum (Squanto), 4291*a**; *Penobscot*: 4663*a**; Clara Paul, 4663*a**; *Peoria*, 4273*a**; *Piegan*, 4130*a**, 4682*d**; *Plains*: 4682*e**; Mr. and Mrs. William Horn Cloud, Mr. and Mrs. George Plenty Wolf and family, Mr. and Mrs. Charles Red Cloud, and Mrs. Melvin Red Cloud, 4682*f**; Wades-in-the-Water, 4682*e**; *Pokagon* (Potawatomi), 4598*a**; *Potomac*: 4688*c**; Luther Newton, 4688*c**; *Powhatan*: 4291*b**; Pocahontas, 4291*a**, 4291*b**, 4301*b**, 4590*a**; Pocahontas Saving the Life of Captain John Smith, 4865*a**; *Pueblo*, 4273*a**; *Rappahannock*: 4688*d**; Mrs. Little Otter Nelson and Mrs. Sam Nelson, 4688*d**; *Rio Colorado*, 4796*a**; *Salivan*: Pedro Encinales and Flujensio Santaṇa, 4759*a**; *San Carlos Apache*, 4703*a**; *San Felipe*, 4273*a**; *Santee*: 4194*a**; William Hoffman, James Wabasha, Jacob Walker, Joe Williams, Thomas Williams, and Joseph Winegro, 4194*a**; *Sarsi*, 4708*a**; *Sauk*, 4256*a**; *Scatticook*, 4598*a**; *Seminole*: 4549*a**, 4865*b**; Osceola, 4291*a**; *Seneca*: 4727*a**, 4865*b**; Red Jacket, 4291*a**; *Shawnee*: 4546*a**, 4732*a**, 4865*b**, 4922*; Tecumseh, 4291*a**, 4291*b**, 4865*a**; Tecumseh Saving Prisoners, 4865*a**; *Shoshoni*: 4682*d**; Sacajawea, 4301*b**, 4590*a**; *Sioux*: 4273*a**, 4587*b**, 4737*a**; Broken Arm, Flying Hawk, and Wander Horse, 4737*; *South America*, 4149*a**, 4739*a**, 4759*a**; *Stockbridge-Munsee*, 4540*a**; *Takelma*: 4137*b**; Francis Johnson and John Punzie, 4137*b**; *Têtes de Boule*, 4190*a**; *Tunica*, 4763*a**; *Tuscarora*: 4588*a**, 4864*a**, 4865*b**; Nellie Cansworth, Cassie Bennett Ninham, Daniel Smith, Running Deer, and Beullah Williams, 4864*a**; *Tutelo*: Nikonha, 4246*a**; *Ute*, 4273*a**, 4766*a**; *Wampanoag*: 4491*a**; King Philip (Metacomet), 4291*a**, 4291*b**; King Philip (Metacomet), death of, 4865*a**; Simon Thompson and Ti·wi·lí·ma 'Child of Woods', 4491*a**; *Wichita*, 4900*a**; *Winnebago*, 4865*b**, 4904*a**; *Yana*: 4132*a**, 4137*b**; Sam Batwi, Betty Brown, Dick Gere, Tom Grapevine, Ishi, Stonewall Jackson, and Frank Wilkes and children, 4137*b**; *Yuchi*, 4546*a**, 4732*a**, 4922*; *Yuki*, 4132*a**; *Yurok*, 4132*a**; *Zuni*, 4273*a**. See *people* and *pictures*, *chiefs* as well as names of individuals and specific languages or tribes

Pictures, *Pequot*, 4291*b**; 4539*b*; *Peru*: 4149*a**, 4519*, 4739*a**; Andes, 4759*a**; *petroglyphs*: 4301*b**, 4590*a**; Pennsylvania, 4589*a**, 4652*a**; West Virginia, 4589*a**; *Piegan*, 4130*a**, 4301*b**, 4590*a**; *Pima Bajo*, 4670*, 4671*; *Pine Ridge Indian Reservation*, South Dakota, 4682*f**; *Plains*, 4178, 4232, 4682*e*; *Pleasant Point Indian Village*, Eastport, Maine (Passamaquoddy), 4642*c**; *Ponca*, 4592*a**; *Potomac*, 4688*c**; *Prairie Island*, Minnesota (Santee), 4194*a**; *Pyramid of the Sun* (Mexico), 4520*a**; *Quebec*, 4143*b*, 4188*a*-4188*b*, 4397*a*; *Rappahannock*, 4688*d**; *Rappahannock River*, 4688*c**; *rattles* (Seneca), 4727*a**; *Redwing*, Minnesota (Santee), 4194*a**; *religion*: Creek, 4546*a**, 4732*a**, 4922*; Iroquois, 4377*a**, 4388*a**; Shawnee, 4546*a**, 4732*a**, 4922*; Southeastern Chiapas, Mexico, 4498*a**; Yuchi, 4546*a**, 4732*a**, 4922*; *Rio Negro*, 4759*a**; *round dance*, Michigan Indians (Ojibwa), 4038*, 4609*; *roundhouse* (Isleta Pueblo), 4301*a**; *Rupert House*, James Bay, Quebec, Canada, 4188*b**; *sacrificial stone* (Mexico), 4520*a**; *St. Augustine*, 4188*b**; *St. Francis Abenaki* (Quebec), 4663*a**; *Ste. Marguerite*, 4188*b**; *San Carlos Apache*, 4703*a**; *San Juan de Teotihuacan* (Mexico), 4520*a**; *Santee*, 4194*a**; *Sarsi*, 4708*a**; *Sauk*, 4256*a**, 4301*b**, 4590*a**, 4592*a**; *scapulimancy*, Montagnais-Naskapi, 4188*b**; *Seminole*: 4301*b**, 4590*a**, 4592*a**; Florida, 4548*a**; *Seneca*, 4397*a**, 4727*a**, 4732*; *shamans*, 4588*a**

Pictures, *Shawnee*, 4546*a**, 4732*a**, 4922*; *shields*, Plains, 4682*e**; *sign language*, 4029*, 4588*; *silkwork*, Huron, 4397*a**; *silver statuette* (Peru), 4301*a**; *Siouan*: 4178*,

4232*; diorama, 4737*a**; *Sioux*, 4737*a**; *Six Nations*, 4021*; *Six Nations Reserve*, Ontario, Canada: 4397*a*; Delaware, 4213*a**; *skeletons*, 4303*a**; skulls, 4303*a**; *Slayton Creek*, Delaware, 4518; *The Smoke Signal*, 4589*a**; *snake dance*: Hopi, 4351*a**; Michigan Indians (Ojibwa), 4038*, 4609*; *Sonora*, Mexico, 4519; *Sour Springs Long House* (Cayuga), 4714*a**; *South America*, 4020*b*, 4149*a*, 4739*a*, 4759*a**; *Southwest*, 4796*a**; *spirit adoption ceremony* (Tutelo), 4246*a**; *splint basket*, 4301*b**; *squash* (Rappahannock), 4688*d**; *Stockbridge-Munsee*, 4540*a**; *stomp dance*, Michigan Indians (Ojibwa), 4038*, 4609*; *stone pipe*, Seneca, 4727*a**; *sun dance*, Crow, 4682*b**; *sun disc staff*, 4727*a**; *Sun Temple*, Mesa Verde, Colorado, 4769*a**; *sweethouse pit*, Shasta County, California, 4132*a**; *sweat lodge*: Dakota, 4682*f**; San Carlos Apache, 4703*a**; *Tabasco*, Mexico, 4504*a**; *Col.* [Zachary] *Taylor at the Battle of O-Ke-Cho-Bee*, 4865*a**; *temples*, Palenque, Chiapas, Mexico, 4521*a**; *Teotihuacan*, 4504*a**; *terrain*: Canada, 4587*a**; New England, 4587*a**; South America, 4759*a**; *Têtes de Boule*, 4188*b**, 4190*a**; *thatched roofs*, Houma, 4364*a**; *Three Sisters* (Iroquois), 4377*a**; *Tojolabal*, 4498*a**; *Toltec*, 4504*a**; *tomb*, Aymara, 4303*a**; *totems*, Alaska, 4601*a**; *transportation*, Assiniboin, 4194*a**; *traps*, Rappahannock, 4688*d**; *travois*: Assiniboin, 4194*a**; Kiowa Apache, 4682*c**; *Tula*, 4504*a**; *Tunica*, 4364*a**, 4763*a**; *Tuscarora*: 4864*a**; school, 4864*a**; *Tutelo*, 4264*a**; *Tzeltal*, 4498*a**

Pictures, *Uinta*, 4766*a**; *Uncompahgre*, 4766*a**; *Ungava*, 4188*b**; *United States*, 4020*b*; *Ute*, 4592*a**, 4766*a**; *utensils*, Iroquois, 4377*a**; *Uxmal*, 4500*; *Venezuela*, 4759*a*; *Anthony F. C. Wallace*, 4864*a**; *Paul A. W. Wallace*, adoption by Mohawks, 4530*; *Wampanoag*, 4491*a**; *wampun*: beads, Tutelo adoption rite, 4397*a**; belts, Iroquois, 4397*a**; *war dance*: Crow, 4682*b*; Michigan Indians (Ojibwa), 4038*, 4609*; *war shield*, Comanche, 4682*a**; *Wilhelm Weike* and wife, 4319*a**; *Conrad Weiser*, 4021*, 4242*; *Wichita*, 4301*b**, 4590*a**; *Wintun*, 4132*a**; *Witoto*, 4759*a**; *Yana*, 4132*a**; *Yankton*, 4592*a**; *Yucatan*, 4504*a**; *Yucatec*, 4504*a**; *Yuchi*, 4546*a**, 4732*a**, 4922*a**; *Yuki*, 4132*a**; *Yupik*, 4251*a**; *Yurok*, 4132*a**; *yuwipi meeting*, Dakota, 4682*f**. *See also* drawings, engravings, paintings, postal cards, sketches

Piedras Negras, Guatemala, 4153, 4158*a*, 4159*b*, 4524*a*; archaeology, 4157, 4159; architecture, 4157

Piegan, 4130*a**, 4301*b**, 4590*a**; ethnography, 4130*a*; people, 4682*d**. *See also* Blackfoot, Blood

Pigafetta, Antonio, 4646

Pike, Zebulon Montgomery, correspondence with Thomas Jefferson, 4320; vocabularies, 4323

Pilant, Richard, 4587

Pilgrimages, religious, southeastern Chiapas, Mexico, 4498*a**; Tojolabal and Tzeltal, 4498*a**

Pilling, James C., *corres. with*: Robert Bell, 4003*a*, 4268*a*; Stephen Bowers, 4138

Pima, 4159*b*, 4331*a*, 4443, *4667*, 4690, 4814; cognates, 4640; comparisons with Tepecano, 4807; cultural relations with Pueblo, 4667; folkmedicine, 4047*b*, 4622*b*; informant, Paul Manuel 4047*b*, 4622*b*; language, 4624, 4869*a*-4869*b*; linguistics, 4623; myths, 4047*b*, 4622*b*; oral literature, 4047*b*, 4622*b*; recording, 4047*b*, 4622*b*; sand paintings, 4047*b*, 4622*b*; songs, 4047*b*, 4622*b*; speeches, 4047*b*, 4622*b*; texts, 4047*b*, 4622*b*, 4624; war orations, 4047*b*, 4622*b*. *See also* Papago

Pima Bajo, 4017, *4668-4782*, 4670*, 4671*; *archaeology*, 4669; *artifacts*, 4668, 4670-4671; *bibliography*, 4682; *comparative vocabulary*, 4882; *contents of recordings*, 4675; *economy*, 4668; *ethnography*, 4673, 4682; *fiestas*, 4668; *furnishings*, 4668; *geographic distribution*, 4668; *habitat*, 4670*; *handicrafts*, 4668; *highland dialect*, 4677; *history*, 4056, 4669, 4676; *houses*, 4668; *informants*: 4674, 4679; María Córdova, 4056, 4676; Leonardo Duarte O., 4058, 4678; Pedro Estrella Tánori, 4056, 4676; *language*, 4056, 4058, 4675-4676, 4678-4679; *linguistics*, 4677, 4679; *Nevome*: 4681; informants, 4674; linguistics, 4680; vocabulary, 4674; *phonetic key*, 4675; *phonology*, 4677; *recording*, 4056, 4058, 4676, 4678; *relations with Whites*: 4672; Maicoba, 4668; *religion*, 4668; *social structure*, 4668; *syntax*, 4677; *texts*, 4056, 4675-4676; *vocabulary*, 4056, 4676, 4679. *See also* Cora

Pinart, Alphonse, 4135

Pine Ridge, South Dakota, 4207; Indian Reservation, 4682*f**

Pipe, Indian, and stem, 4283; stone (Seneca), 4727*a**

Piro, language, 4143

Pitman, ———, artist, 4301*b*

Pittman, Dean, 4324

Placenames, Hopi, 4097*a*, 4363*a*; Papago, 4333*a*; Tewa, 4097*a*, 4363*a*; Wishram, 4906

Plains, 4178*, 4232*, *4682a-4683b*, 4682*e**, 4682*f**, 4683*a**, 4737*a**; *artifacts*, 4682*e**; *attire*, 4682*e**; *buffalo hunt*, 4682*e**; *camps*, 4682*e**; *dances*, 4682*e**; *ethnography*, 4682*e**, 4683; *memorial feast of the dead*, 4682*f**; *people*: 4682*f**; Mr. and Mrs. William Horn Cloud, Mr. and Mrs. Charles Red Cloud, and Mrs. Melvin Red Cloud, 4682*f**; Wades-in-the-Water, 4682*e**; Mr. and Mrs. George Plenty Wolf and family, 4682*f**;

*shields*, 4682*a**, 4682*e**; *sweat lodge*, 4682*f**; *yuwipi meeting*, 4682*f**
Plains Cree, see *Cree*
Plains Ojibwa, see *Ojibwa*.
Pocahontas (Powhatan), 4291*a**, 4291*b**, 4301*b**, 4590*a**; Saving the Life of Capt. John Smith, 4865*a**
Pocomam, Central, *4684-4687*; contents of recording, 4482, 4684, 4686, 4914; culture, 4687; ethnomedicine, 4687; geographical distribution, 4687; language, 4084, 4482-4483, 4684-4685, 4687, 4915; linguistics, 4084, 4483, 4685-4686, 4915; medicinal plants, 4687; medicine, 4687; recordings, 4084, 4483, 4685, 4915; sorcery, 4687
Poetry, Iroquois, 4423
Pokagon (Potawatomi), birch-bark wigwam, 4598*a**; people, 4598*a**. *See also* Potawatomi
Politics, 4614; Cattaraugus Reservation, New York, 4718; effect on language use (Mohawk), 4531; Iroquois, 4386, 4410; Micmac, 4527; Onondaga, 4016, 4720; Seneca, 4709-4711, 4722; Seneca Nation, 4729; Six Nations, 4244, 4385; Tuscarora, 4860-4861
Pollard, Jno. Garland, 4688*b*
Polynesian, comparisons with Uto-Aztecan, 4871-4872; dance, 4353; gesture codes, 4353; linguistics, 4871-4872
Pomo, 4183; *Little Lake*: ethnography, 4132*a**; people, 4132*a**
Ponca, 4592*a**; ceremony, 4081, 4616; chief, White Eagle, 4682*e**; cognates, 4178, 4232; contents of recordings, 4223, 4616*a*; dance, 4081, 4616; dancers, 4682*e**; ethnography, 4081, 4616; informant, James Howard, 4072, 4607; linguistics, 4178, 4232; peyote songs, 4072, 4607; recordings, 4072, 4081, 4607, 4616; songs, 4072, 4081, 4607, 4616; wedding dance, 4081, 4616. *See also* Dhegiha
Pontiac (Ottawa), 4291*b**
Popoloca, vocabulary, 4525
Population, Chol and Quejache, 4498; Six Nations, 4373; Toquegua Maya, Verapaz, and Ytza, 4498
Porter, F. W., correspondence with George Copway (*Kah-ge-ga-gah-bowh*), 4604
Portraits, Pueblo, 4796
Postal, Paul M., author, 4538; donor, 4538
Postal cards, 4020*b*; Blackfoot, 4130*a**; Brazil and Venezuela, 4759*a**; California and Oregon, 4137*b**; Canada, 4143*b**, 4188*a**; Cree, 4188*a**; Crow, 4682*b**; Eskimo, 4251*a**; Hopi, 4351*a**; Iroquois, 4405*a**; Kiowa Apache, 4682*c**; Kutenai, 4682*d**; Mexico, 4520*a**; Montagnais-Naskapi, 4188*b**; Musquakie, 4256*a**; Northwest Coast, 4601*a**; Oregon, 4137*b*; Pawnee, 4648*a**; Penobscot, 4663*a**; Pueblo, 4796*a**; Sarsi, 4798*a**; Sioux, 4737*a**; Venezuela, 4759*a**
Potawatomi, 4020*e*; comparative vocabulary, 4109*d*; language, linguistics, paradigms, texts, 4109*c*. *See also* Pokagon
Potier, Pierre, compiler, 4910
Potomac, 4688*c**; *people*: 4688*c**; Luther Newton, 4688*c**
Pottery, Catawba, 4308; Hopi, 4097*a*, 4363*a*; makers, Hopi, 4352, 4355; Mayan, 4524*a*; Pima Bajo, 4670*. *See also* artifacts
Poulte, William, collector, 4079, 4168
Powell, J. V., donor, 4698; and Fred Woodruff, authors, 4698
Powers, Stephen, *corres. with*: Stephen Bowers, 4139; W. T. Mayne, 4137
Powers, William K., author, 4207, 4683; donor, 4207, 4682*f*, 4683; photographer, 4682*f*
Powhatan, 4291*b**, 4688; *Pocahontas*: 4291*a**, 4291*b**, 4301*b**, 4590*a**; Saving the Life of Capt. John Smith, 4865*a**
Powhatan Tribes, *4687a-4688d*
Powwows, Lansing, Michigan, 4071, 4606; Michigan Indians, 4605
Pragmatics, 4582
Prayer, Delaware, 4080, 4222; Mayan, 4498*a*; *Rezo Tzeltal*, 4498*a*; Tepecano, 4807; Tepehuan, 4826; sticks: 4447; San Felipe, 4453, 4848
Prediction, 4447
Prefixes, Athapascan, 4112; Cherokee, 4079, 4168; Navajo, 4574
Prescott, William Hickling, corres. with Peter S. Du Ponceau, 4321
Price, Eli K., 4488; *corres. with*: Benjamin Hornor Coates, 4492; A. J. Holman and Co., 4491
Priest, Catholic, words for, 4847
Priestley, Joseph, corres. with Benjamin Smith Barton, 4322
Priestmonk Innocent, Rev., *see* Gordon H. Marsh
Prince, John Dyneley, *corres. with*: American Philosophical Society, 4643-4644; G. B. Gordon, 4540
Prince of Wales Island, Alaska, 4107, 4333*a*
Print, Collection, Library of the American Philosophical Society, Philadelphia, Pennsylvania, 4016*a*
Pronouns, *see* person markers and specific languages
Property, nature and function of, 4286; Six Nations, 4005, 4373; marks, Eskimo, 4249
Prosody, Zuni, 4931a
Proto-Athapascan, 4575
Proulx, Paul, collector, 4528; corres. with Whitfield J. Bell, Jr., 4528; donor, 4528
Proverb, Dakota, 4200
Pueblos, 4010, 4020*a*, 4165, 4280, 4327*a*, 4772, 4775; *Acoma*, 4796*a**; *Bonito*, archaeology, 4014, 4769; *cultural relations*, with Pima, 4667; *ethnography*, 4448; *Indians*, 4444; *Isleta*: 4796*a**; church, 4301*a**; roundhouse, 4301*a**; *Laguna*, 4796*a**; *Mayo-Zoque clowns*, 4787; *Mishongnovi*, 4364; *Moqui*, 4790; *people*, 4273*a**; *portraits*, 4796; *reli-*

*gion*, 4787, 4791-4793; *war captains*, 4784. *See also* San Felipe, Sandia, San Juan Pueblo, Santa Ana, Santa Clara, Santo Domingo, Zia. and names of other pueblos
Pueblo-Aztec comparisons, 4454
Puerto Rico, archaeology, 4331*a*
Puns, Dakota, 4199, 4201
Putnam, Frederick W., corres. with Stephen Bowers, 4140
Pyramid of the Sun, Mexico, 4520*a**

Quaker, 4732; Historical Association, materials related to Indians, 4415
Quapaw, ceremony, 4081, 4616; contents of recording, 4223, 4616*a*; dance, 4081, 4616, ethnography, 4081, 4616; recordings, 4081, 4616; song, 4081, 4616. *See also* Dhegiha
Quartritch, 4524
Quebec, Canada, 4143*b**, 4188*a**, 4188*b**, 4397*a**; *Batiscan River* and *Batiscan Summit*, 4143*b**; *Montreal*, St. Mary's College, Archives, 4910; *Oka*: 4397*a**; Mohawk village, 4536*a**; *Pierreville*, Abenaki village, 4143*b**; *Pointe Bleue*, 4145; *Restigouche*, 4527; *Rupert House*, James Bay, 4188*b**; *St. Francis Abenaki*, 4663*a**; *Seminaire de*, 4587
Quechan, "Coyote and Quail," 4698*a*; language, 4698*a*; linguistics, 4698*a*; text, 4698*a*
Quechua, 4183, *4689-4692*, 4759; genetic relationships, 4333*a*; linguistics, 4689, 4691-4692; morphology, 4689, 4691; relation with Hokan, 4690
Queen Charlotte Islands, British Columbia, history, 4341*a*
Quejache, 4498
Quiché (Maya), *4693-4693a*; informant, Remigio Cochojil-González, 4037*a*, 4693*a*; language, 4037*a*, 4075, 4693-4693*a*; orthography, 4037*a*, 4693*a*; recording, 4075, 4693; texts, 4037*a*, 4075, 4693-4693*a*; vocabulary, 4037*a*, 4693*a*
Quileute, *4694-4698*; *ethnobotany*, 4695, 4698; *language*, 4039*a*, 4063-4064, 4592, 4694-4697; *recordings*: informant, Beatrice Black, 4696-4697; 4063-4064, 4696-4697; discussion of, 4694-4695; *texts*, 4064, 4697
Quillwork, 4283, 4334
Quinault (Lower Chehalis), language, 4039*a*, 4592

Rachlin, Carol K., corres. with Whitfield J. Bell, Jr., 4613
Rachlin, Carol K., and Alice L. Marriott, authors, 4614; donors, 4614
Radin, Paul, 4901; author, 4366, 4610; compiler, 4902, 4905
Radin, Mrs. Paul, donor, 4339, 4366, 4902, 4905
Rael, Juan B., corres. with Elsie Clews Parsons, 4311
Rafinesque-Schmaltz, Constantine S., 4225*e*; corres. with John Quincy Adams, 4323
Railroads, and Indians, 4341
Rain, festival song: Tepecano, 4811; makers: scalps, 4792
Rama-Rama, 4746.
Randall, Henry S., corres. with William Parker, 4727
Rankin, Louis, corres. with John Alden Mason, 4758
Rappahannock, 4688, 4688*d**; *artifacts*, 4275; *chief*, Big Otter Nelson, 4688*d**; *ethnography*, 4688*d**; *hunting and fishing equipment*, 4688*d**; *people*: 4688*d**; Mrs. Little Otter Nelson and Mrs. Sam Nelson, 4688*d**; River, Virginia, 4688*c**; *squash*, 4688*d**; *traps*, 4688*d**
Rathbone, Perry T., corres. with Frank G. Speck, 4241
Rattles, Seneca, 4727*a**
Rau, Charles, corres. with Stephen Bowers, 4141
Raven-Clan Outlaws on the North Pacific Coast, 4002, 4853
Raynolds, Frances, and Frederic H. Douglas, corres. with Frank G. Speck, 4275
Recordings, *4047a-4098*; *abstract of*, Papago, 4622*a*; *contents of*: Ahtena, 4105; Arapaho, 4223, 4616*a*; Atna, 4105; Cakchiquel, 4686; Cayuga, Cherokee, Cheyenne, and Delaware, 4223, 4616*a*: Dogrib, 4238; Hare, 4238; Hidatsa, 4053-4054, 4343-4344, 4484-4485; Hopi, 4006*a*, 4023*a*, 4346, 4349*b*, 4363*b*; Kekchi, 4686; Mam, 4482, 4684, 4686, 4914; Mandan, 4053-4054, 4343-4344, 4484-4485; Ojibwa, 4605; Okanagan, 4611; Oklahoma, 4223, 4616*a*; Oto, 4223, 4616*a*; Otomi, 4617; Pawnee, 4223, 4616*a*; Pima Bajo, 4675; Plains Cree, 4193; Pocomam Central, 4482, 4684, 4686, 4914; Ponca, Quapaw, and Seneca, 4223, 4616*a*; Shawnee, 4223, 4616*a*, 4734; Spokane, 4801; Tepehuan (Southern), 4675; Winnebago, 4901; Xinca, 4482, 4684, 4686, 4914; Yaqui, 4675; *transcripts of*: Aymara, 4119; Cheyenne, 4173; Columbian, 4185; Delaware, 4215; Hopi, 4006*a*, 4023*a*, 4349*b*, 4354, 4363*b*, 4838; Kawki, 4119; Keresan, Cochiti Pueblo, 4470; Ojibwa, 4608; Plains Cree, 4193; *Senshare* ceremony, 4834; Tepehuan (Northern), 4823; Tepehuan (Southern), 4828; Tewa, 4354, 4834; Tlingit, 4849; Wenatchee, 4185; Wichita, 4899. *See also* specific languages
Redden, James E., author, 4867; donor, 4867
Redfield, Robert, 4784; corres. with Elsie Clews Parsons, 4311
Red House, New York, Iroquois conference, 4228
Rehnstrand, Jane, corres. with Frank G. Speck, 4146
Reichard, Gladys A., 4020*a*, 4327*a*; corres. with John Alden Mason, 4107

Reina-Jimenez Collection, 4024, 4499
Reina, Ruben E., donor, 4024, 4499; and Alfredo Jimenez, collectors, 4024, 4499
Reinhart, C. S., artist, 4598*a*, 4865*a*
Religion, 4004; *Alaska*, 4043, 4107*a*; *ancient American*, 4307; *Arapaho*, *Arikara*, *Assiniboin*, and *Blackfoot*, 4683; *Catawba*, 4020*c*, 4148*b*; *Cheyenne*, 4683; *Chippewa*, 4071, 4606; *Chol*, 4498; *Creek*, 4546*a**, 4732*a**, 4922*; *Crow*, 4683; *Delaware*, 4225; *effect on language use* (Mohawk), 4531; *Gros Ventre*, 4683; *Handsome Lake*, 4006, 4384, 4388*a**, 4403, 4716, 4732; *Hidatsa*, 4683; *Indian Shakers*, 4599; *Iroquois*, 4296, 4377*a**, 4384, 4410; *Jesuits*, among the Pacific Northwest tribes, 4044, 4592*c*; *Mandan*, 4683; *Mayan*, 4047*a*, 4498*a**, 4498*b*; *Mexico*, 4047*a*, 4498-4498*b*, 4521, 4668, 4687, 4806-4808, 4826-4827; *missionaries*: 4025, 4268*b*, 4865*a**; Jesuit, 4043-4044, 4107*a*, 4592*b*; Moravian, 4039, 4591; United Church Board for World Ministries, 4047, 4592*c*; *Nipmuc*, 4598*a**; *Ohio*, 4244*a**; *Ojibwa* (Plains), 4683; *Onondaga*, 4713; *Ontario*, 4244*a**; *Pacific Northwest tribes*, 4044, 4592*b*; *Passamaquoddy*, witchcraft tales, 4644; *Pima Bajo*, 4668; *Plains Cree*, 4683; *Pocomam Central*, sorcery, 4687; *Pueblo*, 4787, 4791-4793; *Quejache*, 4498; *Santa Ana*, supernaturals, 4793; *Sarsi*, 4683; *shamans*, 4588*a**; *Shawnee*, 4546*a**, 4732*a**, 4922*; *Sioux*, 4683; *Southwest*, 4790; *Tepecano*, 4806-4808, 4827; *Tepehuan*, 4826; *Tewa*, 4059, 4834-4835; *Thlewarle Indian Baptist Church*, Oklahoma, 4547; *Tlaxcalan*, 4521; *Tojolabal*, 4047*a*, 4498*a**, 4498*b*; *Toquegua Maya*, 4498; *Tzeltal*, 4047*a*, 4498*a**, 4498*b*; *United Church Board for World Ministries*, 4047, 4592*c*; *Verapaz* and *Ytza*, 4498; *Yuchi*, 4546*a**, 4732*a**, 4922*. *See also* prayers
Remington, Frederick, artist, 4589*a*
Revolutionary War, *see* American Revolution
Rhoads, Charles James, Commissioner of Indian Affairs, papers, 4020, 4325
Rhode Island, burial sites, 4303*a*
Rhombus, 4791
Richmond, Donald, corres. with Paul A. W. Wallace, 4411
Ridgway, W., engraver, 4291*b*, 4865*a*
Riggs, Robert, artist, 4682*e*
Rigsby, Bruce J., author, 4700-4701; compiler, 4040, 4701*a*; donor, 4700-4701
Riley, Carroll, 4817
Rinaldini, Benito, 4818
Rindisbacher, Peter, artist, 4682*e*
Ritchie, William A., 4020*a*, 4327*a*; *corres. with*: John Alden Mason, 4017; Paul A. W. Wallace, 4021, 4412, 4650
Rites, *see* ceremonies
River Yuman, *4698a-4699*; language, 4698*a*; linguistics, 4698*a*; linguistic interaction between Mohave and Chemehuevi, 4699; people, 4698*b**; text, 4698*a*
Rivet, Paul, 4877
Roark-Calnek, Sue N., author, 4221*a*, 4615; collector, 4080-4081, 4222, 4616; compiler, 4223, 4616*a*; donor, 4080-4081, 4221*a*, 4222-4223, 4615-4616*a*
Rochelle, James, 4282
Rochester Museum of Arts and Sciences, Rochester, New York, 4395
Rogers, John, engraver, 4291*b*, 4650*a*
Rohder, Fr. Regis, O.F.M., corres. 4641; corres. with John Alden Mason, 4333
Rohner, Ronald P., author, 4602; donor, 4602.
Romig, Joseph, photographer, 4256*a*
Rood, David S., author, 4899; collector, 4082, 4900; corres. with Richard H. Shryock, 4898; donor, 4082, 4899-4900
Rosenbaum, Harvey, author, 4931
Rosengarten, Joseph George, corres. with Isaac Minis Hays, 4524
Rossville Mission, Manitoba, Canada, vocabulary (Cree), 4194
Rowe, John H., corres. with John Alden Mason, 4759
Roy, Eugene, diary, 4271
Royal Anthropological Institute of Great Britain and Ireland, 4599
Ruins, *see* archaeology
Rumsey, Jean, 4029, 4588
Russell, ____, 4667
Russell, Fred F., photographer, 4575*a*
Rutter, Charles A., donor, 4520*a*
Ryan, Mrs. Charles, corres. with Frank G. Speck, 4493
Ryan, W. Carson, 4890

*Sacajawea* (Shoshoni), 4301*b**, 4590*a**
Sacrifice, Onondaga, 4713
*Sagotaoala*, *see* Robert Gabor
Sahaptin, 4020*a*, 4044, 4327*a*, 4592*b*, *4700-4701a*; *dictionary*, 4701; *informants*, Umatilla, 4040, 4701*a*; *kinship terms*, 4700-4701; *language*, 4040, 4701-4701*a*; *linguistics*, 4700; *myths*, 4701; *numerals*, 4701; *paradigms*, 4040, 4700-4701*a*; *pronouns*, 4701; *texts*, 4040, 4701*a*; *vocabulary*, 4040, 4701*a*; *Yakima*: dictionary, 4044, 4592*b*; language, 4044, 4592*b*; linguistics, 4044, 4592*b*; texts, 4044, 4592*b*.
St. Clair, H. H., 4803
St. Mary's College, Archives, Montreal, Quebec, Canada, 4910
St. Mémin, Charles B. J. Févret de, 4214; artist, 4683*a*
Salinan, *4702*; ethnography, 4702; linguistics, 4702; texts, 4702
Salish, 4599; Conference, Fifth International, 4698; dialects, 4034, 4841; languages, 4034, 4841; linguistics, 4034, 4841; Thompson River, kinship terms, 4766

Salivan, Pedro Encinales (San Antonio) and Flujensio Santana (San Miguel), 4759*a**

Salton Basin, California, 4133

San Antonio, vocabulary, 4135

San Carlos, *4703-4704*, 4703*a**; beadwork, 4703*a**; language, 4012, 4703, 4704; linguistics, 4012; people, 4703*a**; sweat lodge, 4703*a**; texts, 4703, 4704

Sandia (Tiwa), ceremonies, directions, and dwellings, 4055, 4844; ethnography, 4055, 4843-4844; ethnolinguistics, 4842-4843; fauna, flora, foods, and greetings, 4055, 4844; history, 4843; household items, 4055, 4844; language use, 4843; linguistics, 4055, 4843-4844; linguistic stratification, 4842; morphology, 4843; natural phenomena, 4055, 4844; phonology, 4843; pronouns, 4055, 4844; recordings, texts, time expressions, and vocabulary, 4055, 4844

Sandoval, Chic, author, 4572; corres. with Harry Hoijer, 4572

Sand paintings, Mishongnovi Antelope, 4790; Papago and Pima, 4047*b*, 4622*b*

San Felipe, New Mexico, 4443, 4453, 4465, 4770, 4772-4775, 4848; language, 4439; people, 4273*a*; prayer sticks, 4848

San Juan de Teotihuacan, Mexico, 4520*a**

San Juan Pueblo, N. Mex., basket dance, ceremonial cycle, and ethnography, 4836; music, 4061, 4837; recordings, 4059, 4061, 4835, 4837; *Senshare* ceremony, 4015, 4059, 4834-4835, 4839; song-texts, 4836

San Sebastian, acculturation, history, and Indian-White relations, 4368, 4833

Santa Ana, N. Mex., 4458, 4463-4466, 4469, 4756, 4787, 4798-4800; fauna, 4468; language, 4439; supernaturals, 4793

Santa Barbara, 4338; genetic relationships, 4139; vocabulary, 4135

Santa Clara, N. Mex., 4779; masks, 4778

Santa Cruz, genetic relationships, 4139

Santa Fe, music, 4772

Santa Fe, New Mexico, Laboratory of Anthropology, 4312, 4779

Santa Maria, Fr., 4487

Santa Maria Ixhuatan, Guatemala, 4553, 4912-4913

Santa Maria Ocotlan, Indian-White relations, 4817

Santee (Dakota), 4194*a**, 4206; anthropometric data, 4268*c*; *cognates*, 4178, 4232; *ethnography*, 4194*a**; *language*, 4086, 4169, 4190, 4208, 4665, 4903; *linguistics*, 4178, 4232; *people*: 4194*a**; William Hoffman, James Wabasha, Jacob Walker, Joe Williams, Thomas Williams, and Joseph Winegro, 4194*a**; *recordings*, 4086, 4169, 4190, 4208, 4665, 4903

Santo Domingo, N. Mex., 4359, 4443, 4454-4455, 4465, 4770, 4773, 4782-4784, 4794-4795, 4798-4799; *Koshare*, 4455, 4784; language, 4439; refugees at Laguna, 4790

Sapir, Edward, 4012, 4109*b*, 4296, 4331*a*, 4340, 4443, 4516, 4705, 4869*b*, 4877; *author*, 4115, 4369, 4552, 4574, 4586, 4766, 4851, 4906; *collector*, 4569, 4573, 4707, 4803; *compiler*, 4342, 4708, 4892, 4907; *corres. with*: Franz Boas, 4437; Harry Hoijer, 4116; John Alden Mason, 4017, 4297, 4876-4877, 4918; Elsie Clews Parsons, 4441, 4667; Frank G. Speck, 4188*a*, 4251*a*, 4351*a*, 4601*a*, 4796*a*; *photographer*, 4137*b*; and Harry Hoijer, authors, 4575; family, donors, 4586, 4766

Saponi, 4651

Sarcee, *see* Sarsi

Sargent, R. S., Ltd., 4147

Sargent, R. W., corres. with Frank G. Speck, 4147

Sarsi, *4705-4708a*, 4708*a**; cognates, 4113; dwellings, 4708*a**; ethnography, 4683; language, 4012, 4706-4708; linguistics, 4012, 4113, 4705-4707; morphology, 4705; paradigms, 4705-4707; people, 4708*a**; texts, 4706-4708; vocabulary, 4113, 4705-4707

Sartain, J., engraver, 4291*b*

Saskatchewan, Canada, archaeology, 4289*a*; Ft. Q'uapple, 4736; Sintaluta, 4065, 4204*a*

Satterthwaite, Linton, Jr., 4020*a*, 4327*a*; corres. with John Alden Mason, 4159

Sauer, Carl, corres. with John Alden Mason, 4293*a*

Sauk, 4010, 4109*a*, 4165, 4256*a**, 4301*b**, 4590*a**, 4592*a**, 4682*e**; dwelling, 4256*a**; ethnography, 4256*a**; people, 4256*a**. *See also* Fox

Saulteaux, 4020*a*, 4327*a*. *See also* Ojibwa

Saville, Marshall Howard, corres. with Robert Stewart Culin, 4554, 4557

Saxton, Dean, *corres.*, 4641; *corres. with*: John Alden Mason, 4333; Morris Swadesh, 4880; *donor*, 4007, 4625

Sayles, E. B., corres. with John Alden Mason, 4159*a*

Scalp, 4773; as rain-makers, 4792; takers, 4447

Scapulimancy, Montagnais-Naskapi, 4188*b**

Scarboro, Ontario, Canada, Iroquois monument, 4413

Scatticook, chief, Frank Coggswell, dwelling, people, Indian Reservation, Kent, Connecticut, 4598*a*

Schaeffer, Claude E., corres. with Frank G. Speck, 4301*b*, 4682*b*, 4682*d*

Schepers, E. M., author, 4360; donor, 4360

Schoff, S. A., engraver, 4598*a*

Schönbrunn, Ohio, Moravian village, 4244*a**

Schoolcraft, Henry R., *corres. with*: Messrs. Carey, Lea, and Blanchard, 4326; Ely S. Parker, 4724-4725

Schuesele, C., engraver, 4865*a*

Schulz, Theodore, corres. with Peter S. Du Ponceau, 4476

Schutz, Noel W., Jr., *author*, 4733; *corres. with*: Richard H. Shryock, 4733; Whitfield J. Bell, Jr., 4734

Seaman, P. David, 4006*a*, 4023*a*, 4057*b*,

4097*a*, 4349*a*-4349*b*, 4363*a*-4363*b*; corres. with Whitfield J. Bell, Jr., 4361; donor, 4361
Sea otters, skinning of, 4310
Seasons, Tuscarora, 4076, 4863. *See also* time expressions
Seler, Eduard, 4557
Semantics, 4582; Chinook (Wasco-Wishram), 4894; Hopi, 4347, 4362*a*; Navajo, 4022, 4579; Onondaga, 4715; Wichita, 4899
Seminaire de Quebec, Canada, 4587
Seminole, 4010, 4165, 4301*b**, 4590*a**, 4592*a**; *Florida*: 4548*a*, 4549*a**; dwellings, ethnography, and people, 4549*a**; *people*: 4865*b**; Osceola, 4291*a**. *See also* Creek, Muskogee
Seneca, 4010, 4020*a*, 4020*e*, 4165, 4327*a*, 4397*a**, 4651, *4709-4732*, 4727*a**, 4732*; Allegheny River, 4732*; and the New York state government, 4732; and the U.S. government, 4732; artifacts, 4727*a**; attitudes toward land, 4732; census, 4723; ceremony, 4081, 4616; changes in life-style, 4732; contents of recording, 4223, 4616*a*; cultural change, 4425; dance, 4081, 4616; dwellings, 4732*; emigration to West, 4723; ethnography, 4081, 4616, 4727*a**, 4728; ethnohistory, 4709, 4711, 4732; government intentions toward, 4724-4725; height of, 4730; Indian-White relations, 4709, 4732; informant, Leroy Cooper, 4729*a*; land, 4732; language, 4001, 4712, 4718*a*, 4729*a*, 4731; linguistics, 4729*a*; Long House, 4397*a**; maps, 4732; masks, 4332; names for Nanticokes, 4559, 4864; paradigms, 4729*a*, 4731; people, 4727*a**, 4865*b**; political history, 4710; political system, 4709, 4711; politics, 4722, 4729; rattles, 4727*a**; recordings, 4081, 4616; song, 4081, 4616; stone pipe, 4727*a**; sun disc staff, 4727*a**; terms for people, 4001, 4712; texts, 4723, 4729; vocabulary, 4001, 4712. *See also* Cayuga, Onondaga, Tonawanda
*Senshare* ceremony (Tewa), San Juan Pueblo, New Mexico, 4015, 4059, 4834-4835, 4839; music, 4015, 4839; recordings, 4059, 4835
Sermons, Alaska Native languages, 4043, 4107*a*
*Serpent Symbol*, 4167
Serres, John, corres. with Paul A. W. Wallace, 4413
Settlements, Chol, Quejache, Toquegua Maya, Verapaz, and Ytza, 4498. *See also* camps, dwellings, habitat, pueblos, villages
Setzler, F. M., corres. with Elsie Clews Parsons, 4311
Seville, Spain, 4498; *Archivo General de Indias*, 4024, 4499
Shahaka (Mandan), chief, 4683*a**
Shakers, Indian, 4599
Shalako strings, Zuni, 4787
Shamans, 4588*a**
Shasta, songs, 4803
Shasta County, California, sweathouse pit, 4132*a**
*Shau-Hau-Napo-Tinia* (Iowa), 4589*a**
Shawnee, 4010, 4020*e*, 4039, 4165, 4546*a**, 4591, 4651, 4732*a**, *4732a-4734b*, 4922*; *autobiography*, Mary Williams, 4734*b*; *ceremony*, 4081, 4616; *contents of recording*, 4223, 4616*a*, 4734; *dance*, 4081, 4616; *ethnography*, 4081, 4546*a**, 4616, 4732*a**, 4734*b*, 4922*; *informant*, Mary Williams, 4734*b*; *language*, 4734, 4734*b*; *law*, 4020*e*, 4734*b*; linguistics, 4734*a*; morphology, 4734*a*; *mythology*, 4734; *myths*, 4734*b*; *Ohio*, 4337; *people*: 4546*a**, 4732*a**, 4865*b**, 4922*; Tecumseh, 4291*a**, 4291*b**, 4865*a**; Tecumseh Saving Prisoners, 4865*a**; *phonetics*, 4734*a*; *phonology*, 4734*a*; *recordings*, 4081, 4616; *religion*, 4546*a**, 4732*a**, 4922*; *song*, 4081, 4616; *syntax*, 4733; *texts*, 4734*b*; *tribes*, names for, 4734*a*
Sheehan, Bernard W., author, 4041, 4327
Shelton, England, 4314
Shepardson, Mary, and Blodwen Hammond, authors, 4562
Shetter, William Z., author, 4576, collector, 4083, 4577; donor, 4083, 4576-4577
Shields, Plains, 4682*e**
Shindler Collection, American Philosophical Society, North American Indians, 4592*a**
Shipibo, language, 4143; myths, 4186; linguistics, 4186
Shoshoni, *people*: 4682*d**; Sacajawea, 4301*b**, 4590*a**
Shotridge, Louis (Tlingit), chief, 4601*a**
Shryock, Richard H., *corres. with*: Erna Gunther, 4252, 4601; Jennie-Keith Hill, 4563; Dorothy Libby, 4114, 4253; Marion Mochon, 4539; J. Joseph Pia, 4765; David S. Rood, 4898; Noel W. Schutz, Jr., 4733; George Simeon, 4686; Rondal B. Smith, 4179; Paul R. Turner, 4542; Oswald Werner, 4580; Barbara Wyler, 4425
Shuswap, anthropometric data, 4268*c*; legends, 4174, 4472, *4735*, 4854; texts, 4599*a*; vocabulary, 4599*a*
Siebert, Frank, corres. with Carl F. and Erminie Wheeler Voegelin, 4223*a*; donor, 4645
Sign language, 4336; illustrations and symbols, 4029, 4588
Silkwork, Huron, 4397*a**
Silverstein, Michael, 4891; author, 4893-4894, 4908-4909; corres. with Whitfield J. Bell, Jr., 4892, 4907; donor, 4893-4894
Silver work, 4306
Simeon, George, *author*, 4686-4687; *collector*, 4084, 4483, 4685, 4915; *corres. with*: Whitfield J. Bell, Jr., 4482, 4684, 4914; Richard H. Shryock, 4686; *donor*, 4084, 4483, 4685-4687, 4915
Simoncics, Peter, collector, 4867*a*; donor, 4867*a*
Singer, Ernestine H. Wieder, compiler, 4020*a*, 4327*a*
Sino-Tibetan, comparative dictionary, 4115,

4342, 4552, 4851; linguistics, 4115, 4342, 4552, 4851
Siouan, 4020*a*, 4152, 4178*, 4232*, 4327*a*, *4736-4737*
Sioux, 4010, 4165, 4737*a**; anthropometric data, 4268*c*; *chiefs*: Hollow Horn Bear, 4737*a**; Sitting Bull, 4291*b*, 4682*e**, 4683*a**; Spotted Tail, 4273*a**; *dialects*, Canada, 4736; *diorama*, 4737*a**; *ethnography*, 4207, 4683; *language*, 4086, 4169, 4190, 4208, 4665, 4903; *linguistics*, 4589; *people*: 4273*a**, 4737*a**; ball player, 4587*b**; Broken Arm, Flying Hawk, and Wander Horse, 4737*a**; *recordings*, 4086, 4169, 4190, 4208, 4665, 4903. *See also* Dakota
Sitting Bull (Sioux), chief, 4291*b**, 4682*e**, 4683*a**
Six Nations, 4021*, 4246, 4295, 4374, 4382, 4386, 4397, 4400, 4404, 4406, 4409, 4423-4424; Canada, 4027, 4372; Delaware, relations with the, 4227, 4230, 4389; Delawares-as-women problem, 4226, 4228; genealogical studies of chiefs, 4391; history, 4027, 4372; in American Revolution, 4027, 4372; influence on U.S. Constitution, 4379; Journal, 4414; law, 4385; New York, 4005, 4373; political history, 4244, 4385; property in Philadelphia, 4401; Reserve, Ontario, Canada, 4213*a**, 4225*e*, 4229, 4397*a**; *White Roots of Peace*, 4378. *See also* Five Nations, Iroquois Confederacy
*Skaroniate*, *see* Arthur Einhorn
Skeletons, 4303*a**; prehistoric, 4767
Sketches, 4003, 4016*a*, 4020*b*; Arctic, 4319*a*; Labrador, 4301*b*, 4590*a*; skeletons, 4303*a**. *See also* drawings, engravings, paintings, pictures, postal cards
Skinner, Alanson, corres. with Frank G. Speck, 4188*a*
Skiri (Pawnee), texts, 4078, 4648
Skulls, 4303*a**, 4314; Calavaras, California, 4137; human, California, 4136; Indian, 4303; prehistoric, 4767
Slave, 4010, 4165; social history, 4111
Slayton Creek, Delaware, archaeology, 4518*
Sloane, Emily-Sue, author, 4868; donor, 4868
Slotkin, J. S., "Menomini Peyotism," 4245*a*
Smiley, family, 4042, 4328
Smillie, J. D., artist, 4132*b*
Smith, C. H., engraver, 4865*a*
Smith, De Cost, corres. with John W. Jordan, 4721
Smith, Edgar F., corres. with Frank G. Speck, 4329
Smith, Edward Wanton, Collection, Haverford College Library, Pennsylvania, 4320
Smith, Capt. John, Pocahontas Saving the Life of, 4865*a**
Smith, Marian, corres. with Elsie Clews Parsons, 4311; manuscript collection, 4599
Smith, Murphy D., corres. with Michael E. Melody, 4206
Smith, Rondal B., author, 4179; corres. with Richard H. Shryock, 4179
Smith, S. S., engraver, 4865*a*
Smithsonian Institution, Washington, D.C., 4318; donor, 4026, 4248, 4600; Office of Anthropology, 4026, 4248, 4600; ***Bulletin of the Bureau of American Ethnology***, 4688*b*, 4845, 4849; Bureau of American Ethnology, 4790
Snake Creek, archaeology, 4110; artifacts, 4110.
Snake, *ceremony* (Tusayan), 4790; *dance*: 4081, 4616; Hopi, 4351*a**; Michigan Indians (Ojibwa), 4038, 4609; *society*: Acoma, 4787-4788; Hopi, 4788-4789; Zia, 4788; *swallowers*, Chamahiya, 4790
Snyderman, George S., author, 4415
Societies, *Antelope*, Hopi, 4787-4789; *Fire*, Keres, 4448; *Flute*, Oraibi, 4780; *Hunt*, Keres, 4448; *Kachina*: Keres, 4449; Sahagun, 4454; *Kapina*: 4787; Acoma, 4788; Zia, 4788; *Keresan*, 4775; *medicine*, *see* medicine societies; *Snake*: Acoma, 4787-4788; Hopi, 4788-4789; Zia, 4788; *Squash group*, 4775; *Turquoise group*, 4775; *Water People*, Isleta, 4448; *Zuni*, ritual, 4932
Society, for American Indian Linguistics, 4297; for Historic Archaeology, 4498*a*; of American Indians, 4405; of Canadian Indians, 4408; of Jesus, *California*, missionaries, 4865*a**; *Indian Language Collections*: The Oregon Province Archives, 4043, 4107*a*; Pacific Northwest Tribal Languages, 4044, 4592*b*; *materials collected by*, 4043-4044, 4107*a*, 4592*b*, 4603
Songs, 4319; *Acoma*, 4462; *Ahtena*, 4057, 4104; *Arapaho*, 4081, 4616; *Cayuga*, 4081, 4616; *Chasta Costa*, 4803; *Cherokee*, 4081, 4616; *Cheyenne*, 4081, 4616; *Chinook Jargon*, 4803; *Chippewa*, 4071, 4606; *clown* (Hopi), 4052, 4349; *Creek*, 4550-4551, 4923-4924; *Delaware*, 4080-4081, 4215, 4222-4223, 4225*b*, 4616; *Hare*, 4087, 4236; *Hopi*, 4051-4052, 4347-4349; *Kachina*, 4052, 4349, 4772; *Keresan*, 4470; *Kiowa*, 4071, 4606; *Maratin*, 4487; *masked dance*, Hopi-Apache, 4052, 4349; *Navajo*, 4567; *Ojibwa*, 4071-4072, 4606-4608; *Okanagan*, 4096, 4611-4612; *Oklahoma*, 4081, 4223, 4616; *Oto*, 4081, 4616; *Otomi*, 4050, 4621; *Paiute*, 4052, 4349; *Papago*, 4047*b*, 4622*b*, 4634, 4638; *Pawnee*, 4081, 4616; *Pima*, 4047*b*, 4622*b*; *Ponca*: 4072, 4081, 4607, 4616; peyote, 4072, 4607; *Quapaw*, 4081, 4616; *Seneca*, 4081, 4616; *Shasta*, 4803; *Shawnee*, 4081, 4616; *Takelma*, 4803; *Tepecano*, 4811; Tewa, 4836; *Tlingit*, 4849; *Walapai*, 4052, 4349; *Yaqui*, 4919; *Yuchi*, 4550-4551, 4923-4924. *See also* music, dance
Sonora, Mexico, 4505, 4519*, 4668-4669, 4674, 4677; archaeology, 4506; *cucurbita moschata*, 4514; expedition, 4681; Hermosillo, 4919; Ónabas, 4056, 4676; Yecora, 4058, 4678
Sonoran languages, 4877

*Sophora secundiflora, see* mescalbeans
Sorcery, Pocomam Central, 4687
South America, 4017*, 4020*b**, 4122, 4127, 4149*a**, 4293*a*, *4738-4762*, 4739*a**, 4759*a**; *Amazon Basin*, 4149*a**, 4739*a**; *Andean*: civilization, 4126, 4747; region, 4464, 4749, 4752, 4756; *Andes*, 4759*a**; *archaeology*, 4017, 4331*a*, 4339*a*; *artifacts*, 4759*a**; *bibliography*, 4122, 4125-4127, 4151, 4738, 4750, 4761; *cultures*, 4759; *dialects of*, 4761; *dwellings*, 4149*a**, 4739*a**; *ethnography*, 4017*a**, 4149*a**, 4739*a**, 4759*a**; *ethnology*, 4755*a**; *historical and comparative linguistics*, 4754; *language*: families, 4760; map, 4746; *languages*: 4017, 4122, 4127, 4331*a*, 4646, 4738, 4741, 4744, 4750-4751, 4759-4761; genetic classification, 4334*a*, 4760, 4762; genetic relationships, 4753-4754; geographical distribution, 4746, 4751, 4761; *linguistics*, 4125, 4151, 4745, 4753; *people*, 4149*a**, 4739*a**, 4759*a**; *Peru*, 4752, 4759*a**; *terrain*, 4759*a**. *See also* specific languages, tribes, countries, and areas
South Band (Pawnee), texts, 4078, 4648
South Carolina, government, 4030, 4243; Indian policy, 4030, 4243; politics, 4030, 4243
Southeast, *4763-4763a*
South Dakota, Eagle Butte, 4065, 4204*a*; Pine Ridge, 4207; Pine Ridge Indian Reservation, 4682*f**
Southern Paiute, *4764-4766a*, dwellings, 4766*a**; ethnography, 4765, 4766*a**, linguistics, 4765-4766; people, 4766*a**. *See also* Paiute, Ute
Southern Tepehuan, *see* Tepehuan, Southern
Southern Tuchone, 4031, 4106
Southwest, 4017, 4274*a*, 4280, *4767-4800*, 4796*a*; archaeology, 4014, 4017, 4769; clown ceremonies, 4782; diagrams, 4797; ethnography, 4017, 4796*a**; languages, 4017; maps, 4797; masks, 4785; medicine societies, 4770; paintings, 4797. *See also* specific tribes and places
Soviet Union, manuscript collections, 4252
Spain, Seville, 4024, 4498-4499
Spearfish, Washington, Chinook, 4892, 4907
Speck, Florence (Mrs. Frank G.), *corres. with*: C. L. Brooke, 4301*b*; 4663*a*; Frank G. Speck, 4231*a*, 4301*b*, 4663*a*
Speck, Frank G., 4146, 4148*a*, 4149, 4219, 4223*a*, 4225*e*, 4246*a*, 4270, 4278-4279, 4284, 4288, 4296, 4304, 4331*a*, 4407, 4540-4541, 4657, 4663*a*, 4688, 4739, 4869*b*, 4877; *artist*, 4397*a*, 4612*a*, 4648*a*, 4714*a*; *author*, 4129, 4330, 4559, 4645, 4664, 4864; *bibliography*, 4124, 4129, 4285, 4292; *biography*, 4292; collection, 4215; *collector*, 4020*b*, 4086, 4169, 4190, 4208, 4550-4551, 4665, 4903, 4923-4924; *compiler*, 4020*c*, 4149*b*; *corres.*, 4130*a*, 4660-4661, 4663*a*, 4682*b*, 4708*a*; *corres., re*: Delaware Indian Big House Ceremony, 4217; Oklahoma Delaware Ceremonies, Dances, and Feasts, 4218; *corres. with*: A. G. Bailey, 4109; Carl C. Ball, 4261; [Foster?] Bennett, 4148; Marion G. Bever (Mrs. Michael), 4489; Charles E. Bond, 4478; Marian Hale Britten, 4739; Allan J. Burgesse, 4271; Mary M. Chappelle, 4539*a*; Fannie S. Chase (Mrs. Walter G.), 4273; Rodney D. Cobb, 4274; Gordon M. Day, 4656; Frederic H. Douglas and Frances Raynolds, 4275; Charley G. Drake, 4763; Duke, 4251*a*; Henry E. Dunnack, 4278; Fannie H. Eckstorm, 4657; Franklin Edgerton, 4279; James W. Eskew, 4280; Clark Field, 4281; E. S. Gauthier, 4331; F. A. Godcharles, 4224; Kathryn B. Greywacz, 4216, 4239; Martin Gusinde, 4189, 4284; George G. Heye, 4539*a*; Wesley R. Hiller, 4288; Hudson's Bay Company, 4145; Louis C. Jones, 4535; S. A. Kaye, 4292; Mabel G. Larue (Mrs. Daniel W.), 4294; Philip Launer, 4240; Eli Lilly, 4219; E. W. Manning, (Mrs. T. H.), 4254; John Alden Mason, 4143*b*, 4520*a*; Mrs. Henry Mathews, 4539*a*; J. C. McCaskill, 4365; D'Arcy McNickle, 4548; Emil F. Meier, 4301; James Mooney, 4302; John L. Myers(?), 4304; R. H. Nassau, 4662; Stuart Neitzel, 4364*a*; Dorothy M. Nelson, 4305; Jeanette Young Norton, 4306; Liston M. Oak, 4308-4309; Cornelius Osgood, 4663; Ralph S. Palmer, 4188*a*; Arthur C. Parker, 4407; C. F. Paul, 4663*a*; Perry T. Rathbone, 4241; Jane Rehnstrand, 4146; Roop, 4351*a*; Mrs. Charles Ryan, 4493; Sam, 4251*a*; Edward Sapir, 4188*a*, 4251*a*, 4351*a*, 4601*a*, 4796*a*; R. W. Sargent, 4147; Claude E. Schaeffer, 4301*b*, 4682*b*, 4682*d*; Alanson Skinner, 4188*a*; Edgar F. Smith, 4329; Florence Speck, 4231*a*, 4301*b*, 4663*a*; State of Pennsylvania, 4225; Peter Staub, 4332; John R. Swanton, 4149; G. E. S. Turner, 4334; Abraham M. Walker, 4890; Paul A. W. Wallace, 4021; Richard Walser, 4170; Christopher L. Ward, 4541; Clark Wissler, 4340
Speck, Frank Stanford, artist, 4301*b*, 4590*a*
Speech, men's and women's, Arawak (Continental), 4476
Speeches, Ojibwa, 4071, 4606; Papago and Pima, 4047*b*, 4622*b*
Spicer, Edward H., corres. with John Alden Mason, 4681
Spier, Leslie, 4463, 4783-4784, 4877; *corres. with*: John Alden Mason, 4295*a*, 4331*a*; Elsie Clews Parsons, 4311
Spokane, 4801; dictionary, 4801; language, 4020*d*, 4602*a*, 4801; linguistics, 4801; vocabulary, 4020*d*, 4602*a*, 4801
Spokane, Washington, Pacific Northwest Indian Center, 4043-4044, 4107*a*, 4592*b*
Sports, Arapaho, Arikara, Assiniboin, Blackfoot, Cheyenne, Crow, Gros Ventre, Hidatsa, Mandan, Ojibwa (Plains), Plains Cree, Sarsi, and Sioux, 4683
Squanto (Tisquantum) (Pawtuxet), 4291*a**
Squash, group, 4775; Rappahannock, 4688*d**

Squier, Ephraim G., 4164, 4167
Staff, sun disc (Seneca), 4727*a**
Stalagmite, 4370.
Starr, F. 4781
Staub, Peter, corres. with Frank G. Speck, 4332
*Stcamun*, 4800.
Steele, Susan, author, 4130, 4879; donor, 4130, 4879
Stephen, Alexander M., Journal of, 4358, 4363
Stephenson, J., engraver, 4291*b*.
Stern, Bernhard J., corres. with Elsie Clews Parsons, 4311
Stern, Theodore, photographer, 4687*a*, 4688*a*, 4703*a*
Stevenson, [Matilda C. (?)], 4847
Stevenson Collection, 4469
Steward, Julian H., 4782; corres. with John Alden Mason, 4295*a*
Stewart. T. D., corres. with Paul A. W. Wallace, 4650
Still-born, offerings to, 4448
Stirling, Matthew W., 4340, 4440, 4459, 4461-4463, 4467, 4777, 4790, 4795; corres. with Paul A. W. Wallace, 4021
Stockbridge, missions to, 4047, 4592*c*; vocabulary, 4225*a*
Stockbridge-Munsee (Wisconsin), 4540*a**; acculturation, 4539; dwellings, 4540*a**, economics, 4539; people, 4540*a**
Stomps, Michigan Indians (Ojibwa), 4038, 4609; green corn (Seneca-Cayuga), 4081, 4616; Oklahoma, 4081, 4616. *See also* dances
Stone, artifacts, 4315, 4317; tools, 4316-4318
Stoney, 4209, 4210; cognates, 4204; language, 4209; linguistics, 4204; texts, 4209
Stories, *Choctaw*, 4067, 4182; *coyote*: Navajo, 4570; Papago, 4629; Quechan, 4698*a*; Tewa, 4838*b*; *Iroquois*, 4383; *Keresan*, 4439; *Malecite*, 4089-4090, 4479-4480; *Okanagan*, 4096, 4611-4612; *Otomi*, 4049-4050, 4620-4621; *Papago*, 4007, 4625; *Penobscot*, 4662; *Tiwa*, 4074, 4844*a*; *Tlingit*, 4849; *Zuni*, 4092, 4933, 4935. *See also* legends, myths, tales, folktales, oral literature
Stout, David B., corres. with John Alden Mason, 4762
Strange, Robert, author, 4170
Stratification, linguistic, 4842
Strong, William D., corres. with Elsie Clews Parsons, 4311
Sturtevant, William C., author, 4728; donor, 4728
Subgrouping, 4888. *See also* specific languages
Subsistence, Arapaho, Arikara, Assiniboin, and Blackfoot, 4683; Catawba, 4020*c*, 4148*b*; Cheyenne, 4683; Chol, 4498; Crow, Gros Ventre, and Hidatsa, 4683; Lacandone, 4497; Mandan, Ojibwa (Plains), and Plains Cree, 4683; Quejache, 4498; Sarsi and Sioux, 4683; Toquegua Maya, Verapaz, and Ytza, 4498
Subtiaba, comparative vocabulary, 4509; linguistics, 4753
Sue, Hiroko, 4234*a*; collector, 4087, 4236; compiler, 4046, 4237-4238; donor, 4046, 4087, 4234*a*, 4236-4238
Suffixes, Cherokee, 4079, 4168
Sullivan, General, 4655
Summer Institute of Linguistics, 4813
Sumner, ———, battle with Cheyennes, 4271
Sun dance, Crow, 4682*b**; Dakota, 4206
Sundaro, 4781
Sun Temple, Mesa Verde, Colorado, 4796*a**
Supernaturals, Santa Ana, 4793
Susquehannocks, 4651; allies of Hurons, 4911
Swadesh, Morris, 4334*a*, 4641, 4880; *corres. with*: André Martinet, 4880; John Alden Mason, 4017, 4333, 4880; Dean Saxton, 4880; Carl F. Voegelin, 4225*a*
Swanson, Richard A., collector, 4088, 4362; donor, 4088, 4362
Swanton, John R., *corres. with*: John Alden Mason, 4333*a*; Frank G. Speck, 4149
Sweathouse pit, Shasta County, California, 4132*a**
Sweat lodge, Dakota, 4207, 4682*f**; San Carlos Apache, 4703*a**
Syllabary, Cherokee, 4028, 4163
Syntax, Abipon, 4099; Haida, 4341*b*; Hopi, 4351*b*, 4362*a*; Lummi, 4057*a*, 4600*a*; Mohawk, 4538; Navajo, 4563-4564, 4568, 4578; Pima Bajo, 4677; Shawnee, 4733; Takelma, 4013, 4802; Wasco (Chinook), 4908; Wichita, 4899; Wishram (Chinook), 4908; Yana, 4128, 4916-4917; Yavapai, 4069, 4866*a*; Yuki, 4926; Zapotec, 4931
Szabo, Laszlo, collector, 4089-4090, 4479-4480; donor, 4089-4090, 4479-4480

Tabasco, Mexico, 4504*a**
Taboos, Catawba, 4020*c*, 4148*b*; Dakota, 4200.
Takelma, 4296, *4802-4803*; informant, Francis Johnson, 4803; language, 4803; linguistics, 4013, 4802-4803; medicine formulas, 4803; morphology, 4013, 4802-4803; myths, 4803; paradigms, 4803; people, Francis Johnson and John Punzie, 4137*b**; songs, 4803; syntax, 4013, 4802; texts, 4803; vocabulary, 4803
Talamanca, *4804*; dialects, 4804; geographical distribution, 4804; names, 4804; tribes, 4804
Tales, Santa Ana, 4466; witchcraft, Passamaquoddy, 4644. *See also* legends, folktales, myths, oral literature, stories, texts
Tallchief, Maria, 4393*
Tama, Iowa, 4257
Tanana, Upper, *see* Upper Tanana
Tanoan, genetic relationships, 4889
Tanning, hides, Tunica, 4763*a**
Taos, New Mexico, 4778, 4786, 4846-4847, 4930; feud involving Mirabal family, 4846; folk tales, 4453, 4848; informant, Lorenzo Martinez, 4846; social organization, 4453, 4848
Tapirape, 4859

Taptto, Mary H., author, 4578; donor, 4578
Tarahumara, belts, 4097*a*, 4363*a*; comparative vocabulary, 4881, 4885-4886; historical and comparative linguistics, 4885-4886; linguistics, 4881
Tarascan, 4020*a*, 4327*a*; linguistics, 4152
Tarasco, vocabulary, 4525
Tarayre, *see* Guillemin-Tarayre Edmont
Tax, Sol, corres. with John Alden Mason, 4295*a*
Taxonomy, and paradigm, 4582; of Otomi sexual humor, 4622
Taylor, Allan R., author, 4209; collector, 4091, 4210; donor, 4091, 4209-4210
Taylor, Archer, 4466
Taylor, Col. [Zachary], at the Battle of O-Ke-Cho-Bee, 4865*a**
Tecumseh (Shawnee), 4291*a**, 4291*b**, 4865*a**; Saving Prisoners, 4865*a**
Tedlock, Dennis, author, 4931*a*-4934; collector, 4092, 4935; donor, 4092, 4931*a*-4935
Tembe, 4859
Temples, Palenque, Chiapas, Mexico, 4521*a**
Tennessee, *4805*; archaeology and artifacts, 4805; burial sites, 4303*a*; Indian mounds, 4805
Teotihuacan, Mexico, 4504*a**, 4520*a**
Tepecano, 4017, 4520*a*, *4806-4812*, 4814, 4876, 4888; *archaeology*, 4806, 4809; *artifacts*, 4809; *cognates*, 4640, 4821, 4882, 4884-4885; *comparisons with*: Northern Tepehuan, 4814; Papago, 4630, 4634; Piman, 4807; *cultural affiliations*, with Tepehuan, 4825; *ethnology*, 4806-4807, 4809; *historical linguistics*, 4884-4885; *kinship terms*, 4819; *language*, 4807, 4809-4810; *linguistic affiliations with Tepehuan*, 4825; *linguistics*, 4806-4807, 4810, 4812; *morphology*, 4812; *mythology*, 4806; *prayers*, 4807; *religion*, 4806-4808, 4827; *religious beliefs*, compared with Coras and Huichols, 4808; *song*, 4811; *texts*, 4809; *vocabulary*, 4516, 4810, 4812, 4873. *See also* Tepehuan
Tepehuan, *4813-4833*, 4876-4877, 4888; acculturation, 4833; ceremony, fiesta for the dead, 4816; comparative vocabulary, 4882; contents of recordings, 4675; cultural affiliations, with Tepecano, 4825; dialects, 4813; ethnography, 4816-4817, 4829; history, 4833; Indian-White relations, 4933; language, 4675, 4817, 4869*b*; linguistic affiliations with Tepecano, 4825; linguistics, 4813; maps, 4829; morphology, 4814; music, 4869*b*; prayers, 4826; vocabulary, 4814, 4873. *See also* Tepecano, Tepehuan, Northern, and Tepehuan, Southern
Tepehuan, Northern, 4017, 4814; cognates, 4640; comparative vocabulary, 4813, 4821; comparison with Tepecano, 4814; informant, Pedro Valenca, 4822; kinship terms, 4819; language, 4814-4815, 4821-4824, 4832; linguistic expedition, 4820; linguistics, 4814, 4822-4823, 4830-4831; map, 4830; morphology, 4831; paradigms, 4830; settling marital difficulties, 4832; texts, 4815, 4822-4824, 4832; vocabulary, 4821-4822
Tepehuan, Southern, 4017, 4814; comparative vocabulary, 4813; kinship terms, 4819; language, 4828; linguistics, 4828; orthography, 4816; texts, 4828; transcript of recordings, 4828
Tequistlateco, Mountain, *see* Mountain Tequistlateco
Terrain, Canada, 4587*a**; Greenland, 4251*; Mexico, 4520*; New England, 4587*a**; South America, 4759*a**
Têtes de Boule, 4188*b**, 4190*a**, bark containers, dwellings, ethnography, habitat, and people, 4180*a**
Teton, 4205-4206; anthropometric data, 4268*c*; cognates, 4178, 4232; linguistics, 4178, 4195, 4232; paradigms, 4195; vocabulary, 4195. *See also* Dakota
Tewa, 4773, 4775, 4800, *4834-4839*; *animals* (domestic), 4097*a*, 4363*a*; *attire*, 4097*a*, 4363*a*; *basket dance*, 4836; *ceremonial cycle*, 4836; *ethnography*, 4097*a*, 4363*a*, 4836; *fauna*, 4097*a*, 4363*a*; *flora*, 4097*a*, 4363*a*, *Hamo*, 4790; *informants*: Frank Capella, Grace Chapella, and George Cochase, 4097*a*, 4363*a*; Antonio Garcia and Peter Garcia, 4015, 4839; Donald Mahkewa and Dennis Sinquah, 4097*a*, 4363*a*; Juanito Trujillo, 4015, 4839; *interviews*, 4354, 4838; *kinship terms*, 4097*a*, 4363*a*; *language*, 4836, 4838, 4838*b*; *linguistics*, 4838*b*; *music*, 4061, 4772, 4836-4837, 4839; *placenames*, 4097*a*, 4363*a*; *recordings*, 4059, 4061, 4068, 4097*a*, 4363*a*, 4835, 4837, 4838*a*; *Senshare ceremony*, 4059, 4834-4835, 4839; *social organization*, 4776, 4797; *song texts*, 4836; *texts*, 4097*a*, 4363*a*, 4838*b*; *transcript of recording*, 4354, 4834
Texas, 4682*a**, archaeology, 4159*a*
Texts, *Achumawi*, 4100-4102, 4118; *Acoma*, 4439; *Ahtena*, 4057, 4104; *Alaska Native languages*, 4043, 4107*a*; *Arapaho*, 4044, 4592*b*; *Assiniboin*, 4044, 4091, 4210, 4592*b*; *Atsugewi*, 4102, 4117-4118; *Aymara*, 4066, 4119-4119*a*; *Bella Coola*, 4599*a*; *Blackfoot* (Piegan), 4044, 4592*b*; *Catawba*, 4020*c*, 4148*b*; *Central Alaskan Yupik*, 4043, 4107*a*; *Chatino*, 4504*b*; *Chelan* (Columbian), 4044, 4592*b*; *Cherokee*, 4079, 4168; *Cheyenne*, 4077, 4173; *Chiwere*, 4178, 4232; *Chiricahua*, 4175-4177, 4502; *Choctaw*, 4067, 4182; *Coeur d'Alene*, 4044, 4592*b*; *Columbian*, 4044, 4592*b*; *Colville* (Okanagan), 4044, 4592*b*; *Conibo*, 4186; *Cree*: classification of, 4191; Plains, 4098, 4192-4193; *Crow*, 4044, 4592*b*; *Dakota*, 4044, 4065, 4091, 4197-4203, 4204*a*, 4207, 4209-4210, 4592*b*; *Delaware*, 4080, 4215, 4222-4225*b*; *Diegueño*, 4073, 4233-4234; *Eskimo*, 4043, 4097, 4107*a*, 4255; *Fox*, 4095, 4258; *Gros Ventre* (Arapaho), 4044, 4592*b*; *Haida*, 4599*a*; *Hare*, 4087, 4236; *Hidatsa*, 4053-4054, 4343-4344, 4484-

4485; *Highland Chontal*, 4094, 4546; *Hopi*, 4057*b*, 4068, 4097*a*, 4349*a*, 4356, 4363*a*, 4838*a*; *Huantan*, 4066, 4119*a*; *Hupa*, 4369; *Ingalik* (Ingalit), 4043, 4107*a*; *Iñupiaq*, 4043, 4107*a*; *Iowa*, 4178, 4232; *Jaqaru*, 4066, 4119*a*; *Jicarilla*, 4426-4433; *Kagaba*, 4745*a*; *Kaibab Paiute*, 4766; *Kalispel*, 4044, 4592*b*; *Kawki*, 4066, 4119-4119*a*; *Koyukon*, 4043, 4107*a*; *Kutenai*, 4044, 4592*b*; *Kwakiutl*, 4599*a*; *Lipan*, 4474-4475; *Lummi*, 4057*a*, 4600*a*; *Malecite*, 4089-4090, 4479-4480; *Mandan*, 4053-4054, 4343-4344, 4484-4485; *Matlatzinca*, 4048, 4495-4496; *Maya*, 4037*a*, 4075, 4693-4693*a*; *Mescalero*, 4175, 4502-4504; *Micmac*, 4528; *Mohawk*, 4537; *Musquakie*, 4095, 4258; *Nahua*, 4553; *Navajo*, 4060, 4561, 4566, 4570, 4572, 4574; *Nez Perce*, 4044, 4592*b*; *Nootka*, 4585; *Okanagan*, 4612; *Otomi*, 4049-4050, 4617, 4620-4621; *Pacific Northwest tribal languages*, 4044, 4592*b*; *Papago*, 4007, 4047*b*, 4622*b*, 4624-4626, 4629-4630, 4635; *Pawnee*, 4078, 4648; *Penobscot*, 4656, 4659; *Pima*, 4047*b*, 4622*b*; *Pima Bajo*, 4056, 4675-4676; *Plains Cree*, 4098, 4192-4193; *Potawatomi*, 4109*c*; *Quechan*, 4698*a*; *Quiché Maya*, 4037*a*, 4075, 4693-4693*a*; *Quileute*, 4064, 4697; *River Yuman*, 4698*a*; *Sahaptin*, 4040, 4044, 4592*b*, 4701-4701*a*; *Salinan*, 4702; *San Carlos*, 4703-4704; *Sarsi*, 4706-4708; *Seneca*, 4723, 4729; *Shawnee*, 4734*b*; *Shipibo*, 4186, *Shuswap*, 4599*a*; *Skiri* (Pawnee), 4078, 4648; *South Band* (Pawnee), 4078, 4648; *Stoney*, 4209; *Takelma*, 4803; *Tepecano*, 4809; *Tepehuan*: Northern, 4815, 4822-4824, 4832; Southern, 4828; *Tewa*, 4097*a*, 4363*a*, 4836, 4838*b*; *Tfalati Kalapuya*, 4856, 4858; *Tiwa*, 4055, 4074, 4844-4844*a*; *Tlingit*, 4599*a*; *Totonac*, 4018, 4852; *Tsimshian*, 4599*a*; *Uintah Ute*, 4766; *Uncompahgre*, 4766; *Upland Yuman*, 4868; *Wawenock Myth Texts*, 4278; *Wichita*, 4082, 4899-4900; *Yakima* (Sahaptin), 4044, 4592*b*, 4701; *Yaqui*, 4919-4920; *Yavapai*, 4868; *Zapotec*, 4929; *Zuni*, 4092, 4934-4935

Thomas, Jameson L., corres. with Ebenezer Meriam, 4016, 4720

Thompson, Harold, 4240

Thompson, J. Eric S., corres. with John Alden Mason, 4159*b*

Thompson, Simon (Wampanoag), 4491*a**

Thompson, Stith, corres. with Elsie Clews Parsons, 4311

Thompson-River (Salish), kinship terms, 4766

Three Sisters, The, 4377*a**

Tillamook, *4841*; language, 4043, 4841; linguistics, 4034, 4841

Time, Sandia, 4055, 4844; Tuscarora, 4076, 4863. *See also* months, seasons, etc.

Timucua, 4010, 4165

Tisquantum (Squanto) (Pawtuxet), 4291*a**

Titiev, Mischa, 4784; corres. with Elsie Clews Parsons, 4440

Tiwa, *4842-4848*; ethnography, 4055, 4844-4845; ethnolinguistics, 4842-4843; informant, Mrs. Jojola, 4074, 4844*a*; Isleta, 4074, 4844*a*, 4845; language, 4055, 4074, 4844-4844*a*; language use, 4843; linguistics, 4055, 4843-4844; linguistic stratification, 4842; morphology, 4843; phonetics, 4842; phonology, 4843; recordings, 4055, 4074, 4844-4844*a*; texts, 4055, 4074, 4844-4844*a*; vocabulary, 4055, 4844. *See also* Sandia

Tlapanec, vocabulary, 4525

Tlaxcalan, ethnography, 4521; ritual kinship, 4521; pre-Hispanic era, 4521; religion, 4521

Tlingit, *4849-4851*; Angoon, 4032, 4850; anthropometric data, 4268*c*; archaeology, 4032, 4106*a*, 4850; chief, Louis Shotridge, 4601*a**; comparative dictionary, 4115, 4342, 4552, 4851; ethnography, 4849; ethnology, 4032, 4106*a*, 4850; informants, 4032, 4106*a*, 4849-4850; interviews, 4032, 4106*a*, 4850; linguistics, 4115, 4342, 4552, 4851; songs, 4849; stories, 4849; texts, 4599*a*; transcript of recording, 4849; vocabulary, 4599*a*; Yakutat, 4032, 4106*a*, 4850

Tobacco, 4448, 4793

Tojolabal, ethnography, 4047*a*, 4498*b*; informant, Hermalindo Jimenez, 4047*a*, 4498*b*; pilgrimages, 4498*a**; recording, 4047*a*, 4498*b*; religion, 4047*a*, 4498*a*-4498*b*

Toltec, 4504*a**

Tomb, Aymara, 4303*a**

Tonawanda (Seneca), 4020*a*, 4327*a*, education, 4727; government intentions toward, 4724-4725; treaty rights, 4726; treaty with Ogden Company, 4717; Reservation, New York, 4006, 4716, 4726-4727

Tonkawa, vocabulary, 4487

Tooker, Elizabeth, donor, 4006, 4716

Tools, Lacandon, 4497; stone, 4316-4318

*Topiles* (*Gowatcanyi*), 4455

Torkana, vocabulary, 4516

Tortoise, sacrifice of, 4713

Totems, 4107; Alaska, 4601*a**; Haida, 4333*a*

Totonac, *4852*; language, 4018, 4852; texts, 4018, 4852

Towothli, linguistics, 4753

Trager, George L., 4055, 4334*a*, 4844; corres. with Melville J. Herskovits, 4324

Trails, **Delaware Valley**, 4412; **Indian**: 4247, 4412, 4653-4655; military use of, 4655

Transcript of recordings, *see* recordings, transcript of

Transportation, Arapaho and Arikara, 4683; Assiniboin, 4194*a**, 4683; Blackfoot, Cheyenne, Crow, Gros Ventre, Hidatsa, and Mandan, 4683; Ojibwa, 4012*a**, 4603*a**, 4609*a**; Ojibwa (Plains), Plains Cree, Sarsi, and Sioux, 4683

Traps, Rappahannock, 4688*d**

Travel, Onondaga, 4016, 4720

Travois, Assiniboin, 4194*a**; Kiowa Apache, 4682*c**
Treaty, western Indians, 4337; rights, Tonawanda, 4726; with the Indians, William Penn's, 4865*a**
Trique, vocabulary, 4525
Troike, Nancy P., author, 4529; corres. with Whitfield J. Bell, Jr., 4529; donor, 4529
Tsimshian, *4853-4855*; demographic history, 4855; kinship terms (Nass River), 4766; language, 4855; legends, 4174, 4472, 4735, 4854; linguistic history, 4855; map, 4855, masks, 4332; myths, 4002, 4174, 4853; texts, 4599*a*; vocabulary, 4599*a*
Tualatin, *4856-4858*. *See also* Kalapuya.
Tubar, cognates, 4886
Tuchone, Southern, 4031, 4106.
Tucura, 4019, 4755
Tula, 4504*a**
Tunica, 4364*a**, 4763*a*; artifacts, 4275, 4763*a**; basket, 4281; blowguns, 4763*a**; ethnography, 4763*a**; games, 4763*a**; hide tanning, 4763*a**; people, 4763*a**; vocabularies, 4333, 4516
Tupi, 4746, *4859*
Tupi-Guarani, historical linguistics, 4745
Tupi-Kawahib, 4746
Turner, G. E. S., corres. with Frank G. Speck, 4334
Turner, Paul R., author, 4542-4544; collector, 4093-4094, 4545-4546; corres. with Richard H. Shryock, 4524; donor, 4093-4094, 4542-4546
Turquoise, group, 4775
Tusayan, Flute and Snake ceremonies, 4790
Tuscarora, 4010, 4062, 4165, 4651, *4860-4864a*, 4864*a**; *artifact*, 4864*a**; *body parts*, 4076, 4863; *Canada*, 4559, 4864; *ethnic identity*, 4861; *geographic distribution*, 4861; *Grand River Reserve*, Ontario, Canada, 4864*a**; *greetings*, 4076, 4863; *in American Revolution*, 4393; *informants*: Nellie Cansworth, 4864*a**; Chief Elton Greene, 4062, 4076, 4862-4863; Daniel Smith, 4864*a**; *language*, 4062, 4076, 4862-4863; *linguistics*, 4076, 4863; *months*, 4076, 4863; *names for Nanticokes*, 4559, 4864; *numerals*, 4076, 4863; *people*: 4558*a**, 4864*a**, 4865*b**; Cassie Bennett Ninham, Running Deer, and Beullah Williams, 4864*a**; *political organization*, 4860-4861; *recordings*, 4062, 4076, 4862-4863; *school*, 4864*a**; seasons, 4076, 4863; *sociohistorical demography*, 4861; *vocabulary*, 4076, 4863; *weather*, 4076, 4863
Tutelo, 4010, 4165, 4246*a**, 4651; adoption rite, wampum beads, 4397*a**; ethnography, 4246*a**; music, 4246*a*; Nikonha, 4246*a**; spirit adoption ceremony, 4246*a**
Tygh Valley (Sahaptin), language, 4700
Typology, Aymara, 4121; Jaqi, 4121
Tzeltal, *ethnography*, 4047*a*, 4498*b*; *informants*: Francisco Aguilar, Ramiro Garcia, Jose Hernandez, and Francisco Calvo Perez-Romerias, 4047*a*, 4498*b*; *pilgrimages*, 4498*a**; *recordings*, 4047*a*, 4498*b*; *religion*, 4047*a*, 4498*a**, 4498*b*

Uhle, Max, 4759
Uintah Ute, 4766*a**; kinship terms, 4766; linguistics, 4766; paradigms, 4766; texts, 4766
Uldall, Hans J., author, 4926
Umatilla Indian Reservation, Oregon, 4040, 4701*a*
Uncompahgre, 4766, 4766*a**
Underhill, Ruth, 4869*a*-4869*b*; corres. with John Alden Mason, 4017, 4641*a*, 4927
Ungava, 4188*b**
Union of Soviet Socialist Republics, manuscript collections, 4252
*Unitas Fratrum*, *see* Moravian
United Church Board for World Ministries, North American Indian Papers, 4047, 4592*c*
United States, 4020*b**, *4865-4865b*; Bill of Rights, influence of Iroquois Confederacy on, 4375, 4379; government and the Seneca, 4732; Senate, 4532; State Department, vocabularies, 4323; War Department, vocabularies, 4323; western archaeology, 4289*a* *See also* specific items, places, and tribes
University Museum, University of Pennsylvania, Philadelphia, Pennsylvania, 4339*a*, 4524*a*, 4664, 4749
University of Chicago, Chicago, Ill., 4544; corres. with H. J. Ostrander, 4572
University of Michigan, Ann Arbor, Mich., 4782
University of North Carolina, Chapel Hill, N.C., 4860-4861
University of Pennsylvania, Philadelphia, Pa.; 4013, 4296, 4603, 4802; corres. with Werner Mueller, 4688; Department of Anthropology, donor, 4017; University Museum, 4339*a*, 4524*a*, 4664, 4749
University of Virginia, Charlottesville, Va., 4041, 4327
University of Washington Libraries, Seattle, Wash., 4039*a*, 4592; manuscript collection, 4034, 4841
Upernivik, Greenland, 4250
Upland Yuman, *4866-4868*; ethnography, 4868; language, 4866*a*, 4868; linguistics, 4866-4868; morphology, 4867; recording, 4866*a*; text, 4868
Upper Tanana, 4031, 4057, 4104, 4106
Uru, *4869*; geographic distribution, 4869; place in Inca Empire, 4869
Uru-Puquina, 4869
Urubu, 4859
Utaztecan, *see* Uto-Aztecan
Ute, 4592*a**, 4766*a**; dwellings, 4766*a**; ethnography, 4765, 4766*a**; linguistics, 4765-4766; people, 4273*a**, 4766*a**; vocabulary, 4873. *See also*, Paiute, Southern Paiute
Utensils, Iroquois, 4377*a**

Uto-Aztecan, 4293*a*, 4334*a*, 4339, 4520*a*, 4666, 4816, *4869a-4889*; bibliography, 4130, 4879; cognates, 4884-4886; comparative phonology, 4888; comparative vocabularies, 4873, 4882, 4884-4887; comparisons with Polynesian, 4871-4872; genetic relationships, 4333*a*, 4889; glottochronology, 4880; historical linguistics, 4876, 4881-4886; lexicostatistics, 4880, 4887; linguistics, 4871-4872, 4875, 4878, 4918; numeral systems, 4874; phonotactics, 4875, 4878; vocabulary, 4526

Uxmal, Yucatan, Mexico, 4500*

Vachon, André, *corres. with* Paul A. W. Wallace, 4144

Vaillant, George C., *corres. with*: John Alden Mason, 4524*a*; Elsie Clews Parsons, 4311; *obituary*, 4524*a*

Vaillant, Sue (Mrs. George C.), corres. with John Alden Mason, 4524*a*

Valcarcel, Luis, and John P. Harrington, authors, 4692

Vancouver Island, British Columbia, Canada, Nootka, 4584

Vaughan, John, 4321

Vejoz, linguistics, 4753

Venezuela, 4759*a**; archaeology, 4331*a*

Verapaz, geographic distribution, 4498; ethnohistory, 4498; government, 4498; kinship and marriage, 4498; population, 4498; religion, 4498; settlements, 4498; subsistence, 4498

Vermilion, for Six Nations, 4424

Villages, Choctaw (Louisiana), 4301*b**; Hopi (Arizona), 4052, 4349; Iroquois (Lake George Indian Village, New York), 4397*a**; Mohawk (Oka, Quebec, Canada), 4536*a**; Moravian (Schönbrunn, Ohio), 4244*a**; Ojibwa (Upper Peninsula), 4610; Oklahoma, 4612*a**; Passamaquoddy (Pleasant Point Indian Village, Eastport, Maine), 4642*c**. *See also* camps, dwellings, habitat, pueblos, settlements

Virginia, *4890*; Dismal Swamp, 4688*a**; Indian Neck (Rappahannock), 4688*d*; Indians of, 4688, 4890; Iroquois, 4371; Lake Drummond, 4688*a**; Pamunkey Indians of, 4688*b*; Rappahannock River, 4688*c*; University of, 4041, 4327

Visions of Handsome Lake, 4384

Vocabulary and vocabularies, *Acoma*, 4438; *Alaska Native languages*, 4043, 4107*a*; *Amerindian non-cultural*, 4333; *Amuzgo*, 4525; *Arivechi Opata*, 4887; *Assiniboin*, 4204; *Atakapa*, 4516; *Athapascan*, 4115, 4342, 4552, 4851; *Bella Coola*, 4599*a*; *Caduveo*, 4509; *Calcasien*, 4333; *Cayuga* (Seneca), 4001, 4712; *Chatino*, 4504*b*, 4525; *Cherokee*, 4164*a*, 4378*a*, 4532*a*; *Chiapanec*, *Chichimeca*, and *Chinantec*, 4525; *Chipewyan*, 4113; *Chitimacha*, 4333, 4516; *Chiwere*, 4178, 4232; *Chocho* (Tlapanec), 4525; *Choctaw* and *Coahuiltec*, 4516; *Cocama* (Guaranian), 4743; *collection of*, 4282; *Comecrudo*, 4516; *Cora*, 4870, 4887; *Cree*, 4194; *Creek*, 4551, 4924; *Cuicatec and Cuitlateco*, 4525; *Dakota*, 4178, 4195-4196, 4204, 4232, 4333; *Delaware*, 4080, 4109*d*, 4222, 4225*a*; *Dhegiha*, 4178, 4232; *Diegueño*, 4233; *Dogrib*, 4087, 4235-4236, 4238; *William Dunbar*, 4323; *Eskimo dialects*, 4256; *Fuerte Yaqui* and *Guaymas Yaqui*, 4887; *Haida*, 4115, 4342, 4552, 4599*a*, 4851; *Hare*, 4087, 4235-4236, 4238; *Heve*, 4886; *Hidatsa*, 4053-4054, 4343-4344, 4484-4485; *Hiyekit*, 4333; *Hokan*, 4509, 4526; *Hopi*, 4057*b*, 4088, 4347*a*, 4351*b*, 4362; *Huave*, 4366; *Huaxtec*, 4516; *Huepac Opata*, 4887; *Huichol*, 4870, 4884, 4887; *Hupa*, 4369; *Huron*, 4910; *Ichcateco*, 4525; *Iowa*, 4178, 4232; *Kansa*, 4178, 4232; *Karankawa*, 4516; *Kutenai*, 4599*a*; *Kwakiutl*, 4599*a*; *Lakota*, 4204; *Lewis and Clark*, 4323; *Lillooet*, 4599*a*; *Malecite*, 4645; *Mandan*, 4053-4054, 4343-4344, 4484-4486; *Manque*, 4525; *Mataco*, 4509; *Matlatzinca*, 4495, 4525; *Mayan*, 4526; *Mazahua*, 4525; *Mazatec*, 4525; *Mexico*, 4516, 4525-4526; *Miranya*, 4743; *Mixtec*, 4525; *Mocoriba Yaqui*, 4887; *Mohawk*, 4164*a*, 4378*a*, 4532*a*; *Muskogee*, 4589; *Muysca*, 4333; *Na-Dene*, 4115, 4342, 4552, 4851; *Nahua*, 4504*b*, 4516, 4556*a*, 4873, 4884-4885; *Nakota*, 4204; *Nanticoke*, 4559, 4864; *Natchez*, 4589; *Navajo*, 4022, 4057*b*, 4113, 4349*a*, 4574, 4579, 4582; *Nevome* (Pima Bajo), 4674; *Nitinat*, 4599*a*; *Nootka*, 4586, 4599*a*; *North America*, 4039*a*, 4592; *Ocuiltec*, 4525; *Ojibwa*, 4012*a*, 4109*d*, 4603*a*; *Okanagan*, 4599*a*, 4611; *Onondaga*, 4714; *Opata*, 4884, 4887; *Osage*, 4178, 4232; *Oto-Manguean*, 4526; *Otomi*, 4525; *Pacific Northwest Tribal Languages*, 4404, 4592*b*; *Pame*, 4525; *Pamunkey*, 4688*b*; *Papago*, 4516, 4630, 4632, 4636, 4821, 4884, 4887; *Passamaquoddy*, 4642-4642*a*, 4645; *Patagonian*, 4646; *Penobscot*, 4659; *Zebulon Montgomery Pike*, 4323; *Pima Bajo*, 4056, 4674, 4676, 4679; *Ponca*, 4178, 4232; *Popoloca*, 4525; *Potawatomi*, 4109*d*; *Quiché Maya*, 4037*a*, 4693*a*; *Rossville Mission* (Cree), 4194; *Sahaptin*, 4040, 4701*a*; *San Antonio language*, 4135; *Sandia* (Tiwa), 4055, 4844; *Santa Barbara Indians*, 4135; *Santee*, 4178, 4232; *Sarsi*, 4113, 4705-4707; *Seneca*, 4001, 4712; *Shuswap*, 4599*a*; *Sino-Tibetan*, 4115, 4342, 4552, 4851; *Spokane*, 4020*d*, 4602*a*, 4801; *Stoney*, 4204; *Subtiaba*, 4509; *Takelma*, 4803; *Tarahumare*, 4881, 4885-4886; *Tarasco*, 4525; *Tepecano*, 4516, 4810, 4812, 4821, 4873, 4882, 4884-4885; *Tepehuan*, 4814, 4873, 4882; Northern, 4813, 4821-4822; Southern, 4813; *Teton*, 4178, 4195, 4232; *Tiwa*, 4055, 4844; *Tlapanec*, 4525; *Tlingit*, 4115, 4342, 4552, 4599*a*, 4851; *Tonkawa*, 4487; *Torkana*, 4516; *Trique*, 4525; *Tsimshian*, 4599*a*; *Tubar*, 4886; *Tunica*, 4333,

4516; *Tuscarora*, 4076, 4863; *United States*, State Department and War Department, 4323; *Ute*, 4873; *Uto-Aztecan*, 4526, 4873, 4882, 4884-4887; *Wasco*, 4892, 4907; *Wenatchee*, 4070, 4185*a*; *Wichita*, 4899; *Winnebago*, 4178, 4232, 4902; *Wintu*, 4905; *Wishram*, 4892, 4906-4907; *Witoto*, 4743; *Xinca*, 4553, 4912; *Yaqui*, 4884-4887; *Yuchi*, 4551, 4589, 4924-4925; *Yurok*, 4928; *Zapotec*, 4525. *See also* dictionaries

Voegelin, Carl F., 4057*b*, 4349*a*; *author*, 4109*b*, 4734*a*; *collector*, 4109*c*, 4225*b*-4225*c*, 4729*a*, 4734*b*; *compiler*, 4109*d*, 4225*d*-4225*e*; *corres.*, 4020*e*; *corres. with*: Leonard Bloomfield, 4109*a*; Eli Lilly, 4218*a*; John Alden Mason, 4295*a*, 4334*a*; Elena Najlis de Kreyness, 4099; Morris Swadesh, 4225*a*; Paul A. W. Wallace, 4021; *donor*, 4020*e*, 4099, 4109*a*-4109*d*, 4218*a*, 4225*a*-4225*e*, 4729*a*, 4734*a*-4734*b*; *manuscript collection*, 4020*e*; and Erminie Wheeler, corres. with Frank Siebert, 4223*a*; and Florence M., authors, 4362*a*; donors, 4362*a*

Voegelin, Ermine Wheeler, corres. with John Alden Mason, 4295*a*; and Carl F., corres. with Frank Siebert, 4223*a*

Voegelin, Florence M., and Carl F., authors, 4362*a*; donors, 4362*a*

von Meltzel, Hugo, corres. with Henry Phillips, Jr., 4319

Voorhis, Paul, author, 4257; collector, 4095, 4258; donor, 4095, 4257-4258

Wagley, Charles, corres. with John Alden Mason, 4859

Wagner, Gunter, compiler, 4925

Wagstaff, C. E., engraver, 4588*a*

Wainwright, Nicholas B., corres. with Paul A. W. Wallace, 4226

Walam Olum, 4020*e*, 4211, 4218*a*, 4223*a*, 4225*c*, 4225*e*

Walapai, linguistics, 4867; morphology, 4867; songs, 4052, 4349

Waldron, Major, The Murder of, 4865*a**

Walker, Abraham M., corres. with Frank G. Speck, 4890

Walker, J. R., M.D., 4206

Walker, Rev. Luke, 4206

Walker, Willard, author, 4904

Wallace, Anthony F. C., 4017, 4864*a**; author, 4416

Wallace, Paul A. W., 4144, 4242, 4244*a*, 4295, 4378, 4399, 4407; *adoption by Mohawks*, 4530; *author*, 4227-4230, 4245, 4335, 4417-4418, 4420, 4653-4655, 4911; *corres.*, 4021, 4242, 4245, 4417; *corres. with*: Edward Ahenakew, 4021, 4187; E. Gordon Alderfer, 4211; J. E. Anderson, 4650; Charles Marius Barbeau, 4021, 4587; George W. Brown, 4144; Harvey Chalmers, 2nd, 4374; Howard F. Comrie, 4375; Charles E. Congdon, 4376; Chief Julius Cook, 4532; Jesse J. Cornplanter, 4021, 4419; Harry C. Durston, 4379; Arthur Einhorn (Skaroniate), 4380; John C. Ewers, 4214; John Fadden (*Ka-Hon-Hes*), 4533; Ray Fadden (*Aren Akweks*), 4021, 4382; William N. Fenton, 4021, 4386; John F. Freeman, 4388; Robert Gabor (*Sagotaoala*), 4389; S. H. Gapp, 4021, 4244; Alexander General (Chief *Deskaheh*), 4378, 4390; Emily General, 4391; Marion E. Gridley, 4393; Francisco Guerra and R. Jarrel Williams, 4291; Alfred R. Guthe, 4395; Francess G. Halpenny, 4144; Edward T. James, 4398; M. J. Jamieson, 4399; Diamond Jenness, 4021; W. Laughlin, 4650; William E. Lingelbach, 4295; Elizabeth W. Loosley, 4144; Mad Bear, 4401; Glynn Michael, 4536; P. Schuyler Miller, 4402; Charles B. Montgomery, 4021, 4246; E. T. Montour, 4403; Ethel Brant Montour, 4404; Chief Joseph Montour, 4221; Arthur C. Parker, 4021, 4406; Donald Richmond, 4411; William A. Ritchie, 4021, 4412, 4650; John Serres, 4413; Frank G. Speck, 4021; T. D. Stewart, 4650; Matthew W. Stirling, 4021; André Vachon, 4144; Carl F. Voegelin, 4021; Nicholas B. Wainwright, 4226; Allan Wargon, 4421; George Wheeler, 4247; Bernice Loft Winslow (Mrs. Arthur H.) (*Dawendine*), 4400, 4423; Charles F. Wray, 4650, 4730; *interview with*: Alexander General, 4414; *manuscript collection*, 4021; *photographs collection*, 4021; family, donors, 4021

Walla Walla (Sahaptin), language, 4700

Walser, Richard, corres. with Frank G. Speck, 4170

Walters, Edwin, corres. with De Moss Bowers, 4336

Wampanoag, 4491*a**; *ethnography*, 4491*a**; *people*: 4491*a**; Metacomet (King Philip), 4291*a**, 4291*b**, death of, 4865*a**; Simpson Thompson and *Ti · wi · lí · ma* 'Child of Woods', 4491*a**

Wampum, 4306, 4559, 4643-4644, 4864; beads, Tutelo adoption rite, 4397*a**; belts, 4384, 4397*a**

War, *captains*, Pueblo, 4784; *chiefs*, 4447; *chieftain*, 4773; *dance*: Crow, 4682*b**; Michigan Indians (Ojibwa), 4038*, 4609*; Oklahoma, 4081, 4616; *orations*: Papago, 4047*b*, 4622*b*; Pima, 4047*b*, 4622*b*; shield, Comanche, 4682*a**. *See also* warfare, warrior

Ward, Christopher L., corres. with Frank G. Speck, 4541

War Department, United States, 4166, 4323

Wardle, H. Newell, corres. with George Davidson, 4103

War Eagle (Delaware chief), *see* James C. Weber

Wares, Alan Campbell, 4233

Warfare, Arapaho, Arikara, Assiniboin, Blackfoot, Cheyenne, Crow, Gros Ventre, Hidatsa,

Mandan, Ojibwa (Plains), Plains Cree, Sarsi, and Sioux, 4683
Wargon, Allan, corres. with Paul A. W. Wallace, 4421
Warm Springs, Oregon, Chinook, 4892, 4907; Reservation, Oregon, 4894, 4908
Warren, H., artist, 4291*b*
Warrior, Osage, 4291*b**; purification, Mexico, 4927
Wasco (Upper Chinook), *4891-4894*; ethnography, 4893, 4909; linguistics, 4892-4894, 4907-4909; paradigms, 4892, 4907; semantics, 4894, 4908; syntax, 4894, 4908; vocabulary, 4892, 4907
Washington (state), *ethnobotany* (western), 4698; *Spearfish*, 4892, 4907; *Spokane*, Pacific Northwest Indian Center, 4043-4044, 4107*a*, 4592*b*; *University of*: 4341*b*; Libraries, 4034, 4039*a*, 4592, 4841; *White Swan*, 4892, 4907; *Yakima Reservation*, 4893-4894, 4908-4909
Washington, George, correspondence with Richard Henry Lee, 4337
Wassen, Dr. ____, 4149*b**
Water people, Isleta, 4448
Watkins, Donald, collector, 4096, 4612; correspondence with Whitfield J. Bell, Jr., 4611; donor, 4096, 4611-4612
Waugh, F. W., 4405*a*
Wawenock, 4273, 4278
Weather, Delaware, 4080, 4222; Tuscarora, 4076, 4863. *See also* natural phenomena
Weaving, Hopi, 4097*a*, 4363*a*
Weber, Chief James C. (Delaware), 4213*a**, 4224; informant, 4215, 4225, 4225*e*
Webster, Donald H., and Wilfried Zibell, collectors, 4097, 4255; compilers, 4256; donors, 4097, 4255-4256
*Weetamoo* (Northeast), 4598*a**
Weigand, Phil C., corres. with John Alden Mason, 4368, 4833
Weirs, fish, 4133
Weiser, Conrad, 4021*, 4242*, 4246-4247, 4406-4407, 4587
Weitlaner, Robert J., 4512; author, 4525-4526; corres. with John Alden Mason, 4158, 4525*a*, 4681
Weitzner, Bella, corres. with Elsie Clews Parsons, 4311
Welsh, John, corres. with the American Philosophical Society, 4494
Weltfish, Gene, 4020*a*, 4327*a*, 4869*b*; author, 4649
Wenatchee, informants, Agnes Miller and Jerome Miller, 4070, 4185*a*; language, 4070, 4185-4185*a*; linguistics, 4184; recordings, 4070, 4185*a*; transcript of recordings, 4185; vocabulary, 4070, 4185*a*
Wenner-Gren Foundation, 4299; correspondence with David M. Brugge, 4668
Werner, Oswald, 4360; author, 4022-4023, 4579-4581; corres. with Richard H. Shryock, 4580; donor, 4022, 4579, 4582; et al., authors, 4582
Wesleyan University, Middletown, Connecticut, 4836
West, Benjamin, artist, 4865*a*
West Indies, *4896*; artifacts, 4896; fauna, 4896
West Virginia, petroglyphs, 4589*a**
Weyer, Edward M., corres. with Elsie Clews Parsons, 4311
Wheeler, George, corres. with Paul A. W. Wallace, 4247
Wheeler, George M., corres. with Stephen Bowers, 4338
White, Leslie A., 4437, 4440-4442, 4453-4456, 4461, 4463, 4667, 4770, 4774-4779, 4781-4786, 4794, 4797-4798, 4800, 4848, 4930; *corres. with*: John Alden Mason, 4295*a*; Elsie Clews Parsons, 4311-4312, 4358-4359, 4363, 4442-4469, 4523, 4756-4757, 4770-4800, 4846-4848, 4930
Whites, contact with, *see* Indian-White relations; use of Indian trails, 4653-4655
White Swan, Washington, 4892, 4907
Whiting, Alfred F., collector, 4097*a*, 4363*a*; compiler, 4023*a*, 4363*b*
Whitteredge, W., artist, 4683*b*
Whizzer, 4791
Whorf, Benjamin L., 4877; author, 4339, 4364, 4593, 4666, 4889; corres. with John Alden Mason, 4017, 4888
Wichita, 4301*b**, 4590*a**, *4897-4900a*; anthropometric data, 4268*c*; grass house, 4900*a**; language, 4899; linguistics, 4009, 4897-4899; paradigms, 4009, 4897; people, 4900*a**; person markers, 4009, 4897; phonology, 4898; recordings, 4082, 4900; semantics, 4899; syntax, 4899; texts, 4082, 4899-4900; transcript of recordings, 4899; vocabulary, 4082, 4899-4900
Willey, Gordon R., 4364*a*; correspondence with John Alden Mason, 4158
Williams, R. Jerrel, and Francisco Guerra, corres. with Paul A. W. Wallace, 4291
Williams, Roger, Landing of, 4865*a**
Wilmot, Mrs. Arthur X., corres. with De Moss Bowers, 4142
Wilson, Peter, author, 4422
Winnebago, 4605, *4901-4904a*; anthropometric data, 4268*c*; chief, Black Snake, 4904*a**; cognates, 4178, 4232; contents of recordings, 4901; informants, 4901; language, 4086, 4169, 4190, 4208, 4665, 4903; linguistics, 4178, 4232; orthography, 4904; people, 4865*b**, 4904*a**; phonology, 4904; recordings, 4086, 4169, 4190, 4208, 4665, 4903; vocabulary, 4902
Winock, rag ball, Laguna, 4448
Winslow, Bernice Loft (Mrs. Arthur H.) (*Dawendine*) (Iroquois), 4388; author, 4423; corres. with Paul A. W. Wallace, 4400, 4423
Wintun, 4132*a**, *4905*; dictionary, 4905; eth-

nography, 4132*a**; people, 4132*a**; vocabulary, 4905
Wisconsin, dances, 4071-4072, 4606-4607; Lac du Flambeau Reservation, 4072, 4607, Ojibwa songs, 4072, 4607-4608; State Historical Society, 4033, 4238*a*; Stockbridge-Munsee, 4539, 4540*a**
Wishram (Upper Chinook), *4906-4909*; ethnography, 4893, 4906, 4909; linguistics, 4892-4894, 4907-4909; paradigms, 4892, 4907; place names, 4906; semantics, 4894, 4908; syntax, 4894, 4908; vocabulary, 4892, 4906-4907
Wissler, Clark, 4658; *corres. with*: John Alden Mason, 4339*a*; Elsie Clews Parsons, 4311; Frank G. Speck, 4340
*Wi · tapanóxwe* 'Walks by Daylight' (War Eagle) (Delaware), *see* James C. Weber
Witchcraft tales, 4644
Witoto, 4759*a**; historical linguistics, 4743, 4745; linguistics, 4743; vocabulary, 4743
Witthoft, John, *author*, 4231; *corres. with*: A. Irving Hallowell, 4124, 4285; John Alden Mason, 4171
Wolf, J., 4906
Wolfart, H. Christoph, author, 4191; collector, 4098, 4192-4193; donor, 4098, 4191-4193
Women's and Men's speech, Arawak (Continental), 4476
Wood, S., 4282
Woodruff, Fred, and J. V. Powell, 4698
Woodward, Frederic, corres. with H. J. Ostrander, 4572
Wooley, Peter, 4424
Word lists, *see* vocabulary
Wray, A. H., artist, 4291*b*
Wray, Charles F., corres. with Paul A. W. Wallace, 4650, 4730
Wright, Asher(?), author, 4731
Wright, Barton, 4097*a*, 4363*a*
Wright, Harry B., corres. with Captain Colon Eloy Alfaro, 4740
Wright, Margaret, 4097*a*, 4363*a*
Wyandot, 4010, 4165, 4587, 4651, *4910-4911*
Wyandotte Cave, 4370
Wyler, Barbara, author, 4425, 4732; corres. with Richard H. Shryock, 4425

Xinca, *4912-4915*; Chignimulilla, 4913; contents of recordings, 4482, 4684, 4686, 4914; Guazacapan and Jumaytepeque, 4913; language, 4084, 4482-4483, 4684-4686, 4912, 4914-4915; linguistics, 4084, 4483, 4553, 4685, 4912, 4915; recordings, 4084, 4483, 4685, 4915; vocabulary, 4553, 4912

Yahi, bibliography, 4128, 4917
Yakima (Sahaptin), dictionary, 4044, 4592*b*, 4701; kinship terms, 4700; language, 4044, 4592*b*, 4701; linguistics, 4044, 4592*b*, 4700-4701; myths, 4701; paradigms, 4700-4701; texts, 4044, 4592b, 4701
Yakima Reservation, Washington, 4893-4894, 4908-4909
Yakutat, Alaska, 4032, 4106*a*, 4850
Yalalag, 4366
Yana, 4132*a**, 4137*b**, *4916-4917*; *bibliography*, 4128, 4917; *ethnography*, 4132*a**; *internal reconstruction*, 4128; *linguistics*, 4128, 4916-4917; *morphology*, 4916-4917; *morphophonemics*, 4128; *people*: 4132*a**, 4137*b**; Sam Batwi, Betty Brown, Dick Gere, Tom Grapevine, Ishi, Stonewall Jackson, and Frank Wilkes and children, 4137*b**; *syntax*, 4128, 4916-4917
Yankton, 4205, 4592*a**; anthropometric data, 4268*c*
Yaqui, 4331*a*, 4869*a*, 4877-4888, *4918-4920*; comparative vocabulary, 4884-4887; contents of recordings, 4675; Fuerte and Guaymas, 4887; historical linguistics, 4884-4886; language, 4869a, 4918-4920; linguistics, 4918; Mocoriba, 4887; numerals, 4920; song, 4919; texts, 4919-4920
Yardley, T. W., corres. with John L. Le Conte, 4341
Yavapai, creation myth, 4868; ethnography, 4868; *ičkiyuka* text, 4868; informant, Harold Sine, 4069, 4866*a*; language, 4069, 4085, 4866-4868; linguistics, 4866-4867, 4868; morphology, 4867; phonology, 4069, 4866*a*; recordings, 4069, 4085, 4866*a*, 4867*a*; syntax, 4069, 4866*a*
Yaxchilan, Mexico, archaeology, 4159
*Yaya*, Mother, 4447
Year, length of, 4307
Yecora, Sonora, Mexico, 4058, 4505, 4669, 4678
Yonaguska, 4170.
Young, Egerton R., collector, 4194
Young, Robert W., 4580
Ytza, 4498
Yucatan, Mexico, 4500*, 4504*a**
Yucatec, 4504*a**
Yuchee, 4540
Yuchi, 4261, 4546*a**, 4732*a**, 4922*, *4922-4925*; annual harvest ceremony, 4546*a**, 4732*a**, 4922*; artifacts, 4275; dances, 4550, 4923; dictionary, 4925; ethnography, 4546*a**, 4732*a**, 4922*; language, 4923; people, 4546*a**, 4732*a**, 4922*; songs, 4550-4551, 4923-4924; vocabulary, 4551, 4589, 4924-4925
Yuki, *4926*; ethnography, 4132*a**; linguistics, 4926; morphology, 4926; paradigms, 4926; people, 4132*a**; syllable structure, 4926; syntax, 4926; tones, 4926
Yukon, 4031, 4106
Yuma, Gila River, 4331*a*
Yuman, 4233, *4927*; genetic relationships, 4927; Upland, *see* Upland Yuman
Yupik, 4251*a**; Central Alaskan, *see* Central Alaskan Yupik

Yurok, 4132*a**, *4928*; ethnography, 4132*a**; informant, Robert Nat, 4928; kinship terms, 4766; people, 4132*a**; vocabulary, 4928
Yutonahuan, *see* Uto-Aztecan
Yuwipi, 4207; meeting, Dakota, 4682*f**

Zacapoaxtla (Nahua), morphology, 4555; phonology, 4555
Zacatecas, Mexican Historical Congress, 4517, 4825
Zape, Mexico, archaeology, 4515
Zapotec, *4929-4931*; language, 4929; linguistics, 4931; Miahuatec dialect, 4929; syntax, 4931; text, 4929; vocabulary, 4525
Zeisberger, David, 4033, 4238*a*, 4558; Onondaga grammar, 4721
Zepozthan, 4784
Zia, New Mexico, 4456, 4463, 4779, 4783, 4787, 4799; *Kapina* society, 4788; language, 4439; Snake society, 4788
Zibell, Wilfried, and Donald H. Webster, collectors, 4097, 4255; compilers, 4256; donors, 4097, 4255-4256
Zouche-Nuttal, Codex, 4529
Zuni, 4020*a*, 4327*a*, 4444, 4448, 4773, 4775, 4777, 4791, *4931a-4935*; ceremonialism, 4783, 4798; ethnography, 4931*a*, 4934; interviews, 4934; language, 4931*a*, 4934; linguistics, 4931*a*; medicine societies, 4932; music, 4772; people, 4273*a**; prosody, 4931*a*; "raised up" speech, 4931*a*; recordings, 4092, 4935; scalp ceremony, 4771; *shalako* strings, 4787; *telapnaawe*, 4933; texts, 4092, 4933-4935

www.ingramcontent.com/pod-product-compliance
Lightning Source LLC
Chambersburg PA
CBHW080926100426
42812CB00007B/2383

*9780871696502*